C000095336

StepbyStep

Cliff Keeys

www.Bible.org.uk

Visit the Walk Through the Bible Website

Having started as an interactive "Big Picture" Bible teaching ministry
we remain focussed on bringing people back to the Bible,
in fun and relevant ways.

www.Bible.org.uk

First published in the U.K. in 2010 by
Walk Through the Bible Ministries
Oak Business Park
Beaumont
Essex
CO16 0AT
This second edition published in 2013

mail@Bible.org.uk

Charity Registration Number 299 722

THE REVISED ACROSTIC BIBLE (ISBN 0615361897)
used by kind permission of
BARRY HUDDLESTON Copyright registered 2010

ISBN 978-0-9566872-0-3
Printed and bound by CPI Group (UK) Ltd, Croydon, CR0 4YY
Graphic Design by steve-oakley.com

Dedication

Margaret Keeys

From the very beginning in 1984 Margaret has been the visionary, enabler and ideal partner for me. Without her encouragement and considerable ability Walk Through the Bible would never have been established in such a sound and Biblical way.

In the early years of the ministry in the United Kingdom her administrative gifts were used to the full to form a well-organised platform for the influence of Walk Through to spread throughout the UK and many other parts of the world.

Whenever new technology became available it was Margaret who used it first. She is still always on the lookout for new and better ways to grow the ministry even more.

She faithfully read and checked the whole manuscript before it was handed on to be prepared for printing and her contribution of correction and suggestions have been such a positive part of the production of this book.

This book would never have been produced without her and I regularly thank God for giving me such a loving and able wife.

Cliff Keeys

Acknowledgements

The Late John W Hoover

Without the initial spark from John Hoover who established Walk Thru the Bible International and trained our first event Instructors the dream of this book would never have been fulfilled. Thanks to John's vision Walk Through the Bible was planted in the United Kingdom in 1984 under the leadership of Cliff Keeys who was then a pastor in Essex and went on to lead the ministry in the UK until 2008.

The Late Ted Hubbard

Ted was a founder member of our original Board of Trustees and a constant encourager and enthusiast who promoted Bible reading as a way of life. It is thanks to the generosity of Ted's estate that the first print of this book could be undertaken at this time and we give thanks to God for Ted and his faithfulness to the Word and his Saviour.

Barry Huddleston

We appreciate Barry Huddleston making the whole of his 'Acrostic Bible' freely available to us. We think this is an innovative addition to our book and a real help in memorising the outlines of whole books of the Bible.

Kai and Denise Svvennsen

We'd like to express our thanks to Kai and Denise for their dedication to this book in so many different areas, especially designing many charts and tables. We pray they'll continue to enjoy Walking Through the Bible with us for many years to come.

Steve Oakley

Steve's artistic flair in Graphic Design has helped us produce such a beautiful looking book. His hard work has also been instrumental in proof-reading the finished manuscipt. We look forward to working with Steve on our future projects.

Contents Old Testament

Contents New Testament

How To Use This Book

Big Picture of Each Book

At the beginning of each book we provide a simple overview with some background to aide understanding.

Charts and Tables

Throughout the book we have inserted various charts, tables and pictures to further facilitate your understanding of the whole Bible.

Big Picture of Daily Reading

Each day begin by asking God to show you what you need for the day and then read the Big Picture of the passage. This is designed to give you a very brief overview and so provide a platform to take the details you are about to read.

Bible Reading

Choose which version of the Bible you prefer and then read the chapters for the day. If you prefer these may be split over the day rather than all at one sitting. We have chosen to use the New Living Translation wherever we have quoted the Scriptures. This was all with a view to making the Bible as readily understandable as possible.

Thinking Step

Every day there will be an insight that comes from the passage you have read. We trust it will be a shaft of light on a particular point and a source of useful information about the Bible and its ethos.

Action Step

Bible knowledge without action is very limiting. So every day we have supplied a short devotional and challenge for that day. Most of these are from Cliff's personal experience and are best understood in a northern accent!

A Brief History Of
Walk Through The Bible

After its early days in the U.S.A. where it had its birth, this innovative ministry soon spread throughout the other English speaking nations and was eventually translated into many other languages. Bruce H Wilkinson was its originator with John Hoover as his International Vice President and it was John who made contact with Cliff Keeys to introduce this ministry into the United Kingdom in 1984. Actually Cliff discarded the letter but Margaret rescued it and ironed it smooth otherwise history could have been much different!

From the beginning it was obvious that this was a ministry like no other and it continues to be eagerly welcomed by Churches across the denominations. Our OT and NT live events have opened up the Bible for tens of thousands of adults from theological college students to enquirers for whom it is the method God uses to bring salvation. Our team of trained Instructors teach scores of events every year and are available for your Church if you would like to contact us!

Since its introduction into the UK we have regularly made quality publications, DVDs and other helpful resources to continue to meet people's thirst for God's life changing word and to develop it in many lives too. A full list is on our website www.Bible.org.uk

In the mid 1990s we developed a childrens' version of our OT and NT events that we called Bible Explorer. We have a team of many hundreds of trained volunteers who share the exciting storyline of the Bible as well as some of its culture and geography with primary school pupils in schools throughout the UK. It is a well established part of the RE programme for thousands of schools who have discovered that pupils can be enthused with the Bible when it is taught enthusiastically by our well trained presenters.

Our team of staff and volunteers all believe that the Bible is God's life changing message for the 21st century and beyond. We thank you for buying this book and trust it will open up the Bible like never before.

OLD TESTAMENT

Old Testament Structure

	HISTORY	POETRY	PROPHECY	
PENTATEUCH	Genesis	Job	Isaiah	**MAJOR**
	Exodus	Psalms	Jeremiah	
	Leviticus	Proverbs	Lamentations	
	Numbers	Ecclesiastes	Ezekiel	
	Deuteronomy	Song of Songs	Daniel	
OTHER HISTORICAL	Joshua		Hosea	**MINOR**
	Judges		Joel	
	Ruth		Amos	
	1 Samuel		Obadiah	
	2 Samuel		Jonah	
	1 Kings		Micah	
	2 Kings		Nahum	
	1 Chronicles		Habakkuk	
	2 Chronicles		Zephaniah	
	Ezra		Haggai	
	Nehemiah		Zechariah	
	Esther		Malachi	

Genesis

Genesis

Our great adventure to read the whole Bible from beginning to end begins with reading the book of Genesis which means origins or beginnings. Genesis has been described as the seed bed of the Bible as it contains the beginnings of almost everything and covers the longest period of time of any Bible book - from Creation to when Jacob and his family settle in Egypt. Genesis splits into two unequal sections - the first 11 chapters describing the four major events of creation, fall, flood and the breaking into nations at the tower of Babel. This is followed by 39 chapters detailing the lives of the four patriarchs - Abraham, Isaac, Jacob and Joseph. Genesis closes just as the family of Jacob settles into Egypt under the protection of Joseph. This is the beginning of the nation of Israel from which would come the Messiah - Jesus Christ Himself.

Below is an acrostic which summarises each chapter of the book.

1. Inception of the world
2. Newly-weds placed in Eden

3. Temptation and man's fall
4. Hatred and first murder
5. Entire genealogy of Adam

6. Building of the ark
7. Eruption of the flood
8. Going from the ark
9. Initiation of rainbow promise
10. Noah's sons and grandsons
11. Nations scattered from Babel
12. Immigration of Abrams family
13. Nephew Lot leaves Abram
14. Gifts for Priest Melchizedek

15. God counts Abram righteous
16. Offspring Ishmael from Hagar
17. Designation changed to Abraham

18. Compassion for Sodom's righteous
19. Removal of Sodom, Gomorrah
20. Escapade of deceitful Abraham
21. Arrival of promised Isaac
22. Test of Abraham's faith
23. End of Sarah's life
24. Denoting Rebekah as bride

25. Twins Esau, Jacob born
26. Hostility between Isaac, Philistines
27. Esau robbed of birthright

28. Heavenly ladder at Bethel
29. Earning Leah and Rachel
30. Additions to Jacob's family
31. Venture away from Laban
32. Endeavouring to wrestle God
33. New friendship with Esau

34. Avenge for Dinah's defilement
35. Name changed to Israel
36. Descendants of Esau listed

37. Treachery of Joseph's brothers
38. Harlot Tamar deceives Judah
39. Enraged Potiphar jails Joseph

40. Explanation of two dreams
41. Appointing Joseph as ruler
42. Reuben held in Egypt
43. Trek to Egypt again
44. Holding Benjamin for cup

45. Announce Joseph's identity
46. New home in Egypt
47. Design to save Egypt

48. Manasseh and Ephraim adopted
49. Announcement of Jacob's blessing
50. New relationship among brothers

Out Of Nothing Comes Everything
In Six Days!

The Big Picture

The six days of creation are covered with broad strokes in chapter 1 and by the end of the chapter we have the finished project; a world full of wonder and life. Chapter 2 focuses on the creation of man and woman and their beautiful home, the Garden of Eden. Complete provision is made by God for all their needs as well as one prohibition not to eat from the tree of the knowledge of good and evil. All the animals are named by Adam but no helpmate is found. God then steps in and creates one for him in a very unusual way, from his rib. Her name is Eve.

Thinking Step

Two great lights are created by God; one to rule over the day and one to rule over the night. The words sun and moon are not used as they represented things to worship and pagan gods to fear at that time. By omitting their specific names any negativity attached to their worship could be avoided.

Action Step

Today you have started the most exciting reading project of your life. There's only one way to start and that's at the beginning – as the song says, "It's a very good place to start!" Today's reading shows the role for a designer if the creation is to be all that it was intended to be. The systematic way in which the creation unfolds is truly breathtaking and at the same time really beautiful. All of it "No Hands!" God simply spoke and it was so! Have you heard the story of a scientist who challenged God by saying that he could create life in the laboratory? "Tell me more" said God. "Well," the scientist began, "Firstly I collect some dust and then..." God interrupted! "That's not fair is it, surely you want this to be an even competition; when I created the world I had to make my own dust - so you have to begin by making your own dust, don't you?" No matter how clever we become and how inventive we are we always start at step two as God has already taken step one by putting us here in the first place! Follow the maker's instructions and you can't go far wrong. When you are tempted to go solo today with your own plan, try asking your designer what He thinks first!

3 - Adam Rebels And Falls
4 - Sin Takes Hold And Grows
5 - Faith Produces Good Fruit

Day 2
Genesis 3-5
2nd January

After Creation Comes Fall
And The First Covenant With God

The Big Picture

Right at the beginning of our reading today man and woman think they know better than God and are easily tricked by Satan in his guise as a serpent. This costs them their home and more importantly, an intimate relationship with God. This event is called the fall of mankind and marks the first time God's instructions are ignored by His creation. There is also an explanation of God's covenant with Adam. Then the first children of Adam and Eve are born – they're called Cain and Abel. Sadly, Cain became the first murderer in history. Finally we read the first genealogy which takes us as far as Noah; that obedient ark building servant of God.

Thinking Step

Temptation doesn't change! It's always based on lies! In our reading today the lie came as a question – "Did God really say?" In the New Testament Jesus was tempted with another erroneous question – "If you are the Son of God." Be prepared! Know your facts and know what you believe before temptation comes calling!

Action Step

In chapter four we learn of the first offerings made to God by Cain and Abel. At first it seems very unfair that God differentiates between them – until we read a little more carefully. 4:3-4 "In the course of time Cain brought some of the fruits of the soil as an offering to the LORD – but Abel brought fat portions from some of the first-born of his flock. The LORD looked with favour on Abel and his offering."It appears Cain does his duty but Abel does his best. We should always do our best! If, or should I say when we have failures, we need to be able to say, "I always gave it my best shot!" When asked by a newspaper reporter what he would do if his team weren't winning, this was the answer from the best football manager England never had – Brian Clough. "I would carefully check that we were doing the right things and doing them the best we could and then just keep doing them. Why not check today that all you are doing is your best. Paul urges in Col. 3:23 – "Whatever you do work at it with all your heart, as working for the Lord, not for men." Abel did, sadly Cain didn't! Actually, actions do speak louder than words. Try acting like a Christian today when you are shopping or driving!

Day 3
Genesis 6-9
3rd January

6 - An Ark Is Built By Noah
7 - God Provides Security in the Ark
8 - God Delivers Everyone Safely
9 - Noah's Covenant with God

A Fresh Start And A New Covenant With God

The Big Picture

We begin with an outline of the growth of ungodly people on the earth and how God resolves to wash His creation clean using his servant Noah, the only man on earth He can trust to do such an important job. The ark, built according to God's plans, is then filled with animals as God directs. Then as promised by God, the flood begins. After 150 days the rain stops and the water level gradually drops leaving the ark perched on Mount Ararat in Turkey. Birds are sent out to look for dry land and then Noah and his family disembark; then God makes a covenant with Noah.

Thinking Step

5:32 Noah is 500 years old and God tells him to build an ark. 7:11 Noah is now 600 years old and the ark is ready. So what happened to the 100 years that have passed by? Of course Noah's job was big but more importantly, God wanted to give the rest of mankind time to repent and come aboard!

Action Step

The sign of the rainbow is a very powerful symbolic reminder that God is trustworthy and always keeps His word; He has on numerous occasions throughout the Bible and continues to do so in daily lives today. Can you remember an instance today or this week of God blessing you? If you can't then maybe we all need to look more carefully or pray for a better memory! Lam 3:23 reminds us that His blessings are very dependable and regular – it says – "They are new every morning; great is your faithfulness". Remember these words were originally uttered at a very dark time for Israel as Babylonian forces were taking the Jews into exile as the whole of their world seemed to be crumbling around them. A friend of mine always has great illustrations from life when he preaches and I couldn't help but wonder why all these things happen to him on a regular basis – and not to me! He told me that he was always on the lookout and kept a notepad handy to record how good God is and also anything he could use to improve his preaching! In other words you have to look otherwise you won't see! Try looking today and you will be amazed at what God does around you and in you. Let yesterday be the last day you have to say to God, "Oh sorry I didn't notice!"

Population Grows And Languages Multiply

The Big Picture

We begin with another genealogy – of Japheth, Ham, Shem and Canaan, the three sons and one grandson of Noah. As the world's population grows – and there is still only one language spoken – the Tower of Babel is built. A beacon of mankind's vanity. 11:3-4 tells us the people said – "...Come, let us build ourselves a city with a tower that reaches to the heavens, so that we may make a name for ourselves." Lastly, we see Abram's family line back to Shem. This precedes the departure of Terah with his family including Abram and Sarai – bound for Canaan. They leave Ur of the Chaldeans in Iraq, and travel to Haran in eastern Turkey.

Thinking Step

4000 years after the Tower of Babel and instead of one language we have thousands. A fortune is spent annually in the European Community making everything available in scores of languages. We have thousands of translations of the Bible and need thousands more if everyone is to be able to read God's Word. All because of the Tower of Babel!

Action Step

Just imagine the challenge that faced Abram. Explaining it to Sarai his wife... "We need to move Sarai" "Why?" "Because God says so" replies Abram "The moon god we worship here in Ur?" "No, the living God who has revealed Himself to me!" "Why you?" "I don't know." "And His name?" "I don't know." "To travel where?" "I don't know." "Who else worships this God?" "No one that I know of!" "But will you come with me Sarai?" "Of course Abram!" What about if He asks you today to do something potentially life changing – would you do it? What about a small thing – would you do that? Sometimes God leads us down a road and then the door closes because He just wanted to know if we were willing to go! That happened to us many years ago when my wife and I sensed a call to an overseas mission field. It was not our first choice but we wanted what God wanted. The door was closed at the first interview. We would have gone – and I know it would have been great! During a quiet moment today why not get alone with God and be candid with Him. Tell Him you're available to Him. Then relax and let Him take the next step.

The Names of God

NAME	MEANING	1ST REF.	EXPLANATION
Elohim	God	Gen. 1:1	Generally understood to denote the single God of Israel
Yahweh	The LORD	Gen. 2:4	The personal name of God in the Hebrew Bible, where it is written as four consonants (YHWH), called the tetragrammaton
El Elyon	God Most High	Gen. 14: 17-20	He is higher and more sacred than all gods and all things
El Roi	God Who Sees	Gen. 16:13	God revealed Himself to Hagar as "The God Who sees"
El Shaddai	God Almighty	Gen. 17:1	The root word "shadad" means "to overpower" or "to destroy"
Yahweh Yireh	The Lord will Provide	Gen. 22:14	God knows what our real needs are
Adonai	Lord	Deut. 6:4	Since Pronouncing YHWH is avoided out of reverence for the holiness of the name, Jews use Adonai instead in prayers
Qedosh Yisrael	Holy One of Israel	Isa. 1:4	God is Holy and perfect without sin
Yahweh Sabaoth	LORD of Hosts	1 Sam. 1:3	God the commander of Heavens armies has the resources to rescue us
El Olam	The Everlasting God	Isa. 40: 28-31	Olam literally means "forever", "eternity", or "everlasting", so God is eternal
Yahweh Tsidkenu	The LORD Is Our Righteousness	Jer. 23:6	It is God alone who provides righteousness to man, ultimately in the person of His Son, Jesus Christ
Yahweh Shammah	The LORD Is There	Ezek. 48:35	The promise of God completing the work He began in us at creation, to bring us to our final rest and glory
Attiq Yomin	Ancient of Days	Dan. 7: 9-13	"you are God, without beginning or end" (Ps 90:2)

12 - Abram's Covenant With God
13 - Abram Divides Land With Lot
14 - Abram Rescues Lot

Day 5
Genesis 12-14
5th January

Abram Is Called
And The Land Is Divided With Lot

The Big Picture

Here we have the amazing call to Abram to continue his journey and leave Haran to enter the Promised Land. He travels from north to south and settles at the Oak of Moreh near Shechem. In no time at all we discover that Abram is far from perfect as he lies about his wife to an unnamed Egyptian Pharaoh on a visit to Egypt for food. Abram soon discovers that the land isn't big enough for both him and Lot and they divide it between them. Finally Lot is captured in Sodom and Abram rescues him with a select army of 318. Afterwards Abram meets Melchizedek and shares bread and wine with him.

Thinking Step

When God told Abram to leave Haran in 12:1 the word He used was very specific. In most translations it is rendered leave which has negative connotations but it means so much more than that. It includes the idea of going for your own benefit, moving on to something better that God has for you.

Action Step

It's hard to imagine the enormous step of faith that was needed to take Abram into Canaan. Back in Ur the god everyone worshipped was the moon god. When Terah took his family, including Abram and Sarai, north through the entire land of Mesopotamia they settled in Haran – where the people worshipped the moon god too! A big move geographically but culturally only a small step. The bigger journey was south into Canaan. The sadness of these two journeys is that Terah led for the longer one but then he settled down without reaching his destination. He never entered the Promised Land which was his original intention in 11:32. There are few things more disappointing than someone who sets off on a quest only to be distracted and never make it to the end. Isn't it uplifting when you meet someone from years ago who you had the privilege to help on their spiritual journey, to discover how much they have matured in the Lord over the intervening period! Why not pray for someone who you haven't seen for ages in the hope that they will continue to grow in the Lord. On the other hand remember if you meet someone who had an impact in your life many years ago – will they be encouraged by you? You could bump into them today – so what 'one thing' do you need to change in your life without delay?

Day 6　　　　　　　　　　　15 - Descendants are Promised to Abram and Sarai
Genesis 15-17　　　　　　　16 - Abram Produces a Son with Hagar
6th January　　　　　　　　17 - A New Covenant With Circumcision

Names Change,
But God's Promises Remain Unchanging

The Big Picture

God makes a specific promise of an heir for Abram and he believes Him. The Apostle Paul refers to what happened when he wrote to the Galatians – "Consider Abraham: He believed God and it was credited to him as righteousness." The 400 years stay in Egypt is foretold. After ten years waiting and still no baby Sarai gives Hagar to Abram and she produces a son – his name is Ishmael. Thirteen years later Abram and Sarai have their names changed and the promise of an heir is confirmed, despite some laughter! The covenant of circumcision is introduced. Abram and Ishmael are both circumcised on the same day. Abram is ninety nine years old and Ishmael is thirteen.

Thinking Step

17:20 tells us that Ishmael will have twelve sons or rulers and become a great nation. Jacob will have twelve sons too! Uncle Ishmael produces the Arab nations and nephew Jacob creates the Jewish people. Just like most close relatives the Jews and Arabs always seem to have something to disagree about!

Action Step

How many times have you thought, I don't understand why God doesn't act now! The remedy is obvious, why can't He see it, perhaps if I could exert a little pressure... Stop right there! Sometimes we forget what is written in Isaiah 55:8-9 "For my thoughts are not your thoughts, neither are your ways my ways, declares the LORD. As the heavens are higher than the earth, so are my ways higher than your ways and my thoughts than your thoughts." In other words even if it seems a long wait – it's always worth waiting for the best rather than rushing on with your own plan. In the case of Sarai and Hagar it made so much sense to them to do it "the Canaanite way!" For a younger woman to bare a child for an older wife who would then adopt it. After all they had waited 23 years for a child and nothing seemed to be happening – and they were getting older all the time. Perhaps God had forgotten or changed His plans without telling them! Every time you see traffic lights today and have to wait for the green light let it be a reminder to always wait for God's green light – even when it seems to be taking a lot longer than you had expected at the beginning.

18 - Faith Of Sarah And Abraham Is Tested   Day 7
19 - Sodom And Gomorrah Are Destroyed   Genesis 18-20
20 - Abraham Lies About Sarah   7th January

Angelic Visit To Sodom And Gomorrah

The Big Picture

An heir for Abraham and Sarah is once again confirmed but Sarah laughs, just like her husband did in the previous chapter. Abraham debates with the Lord over whether Sodom could be saved if a number of righteous men are found there. They start at 50 and stop when they get to 10 but sadly, destruction is inevitable because of the sin ridden population. Two angels enter Sodom and Gomorrah before the cities are destroyed. Lot and his family escape only for his wife to look back with fatal consequences! Lot then fathers two sons in dubious circumstances beginning the Ammonite and Moabite nations. Then Abraham again lies about Sarah being his sister. This time to King Abimelech of Gerar.

Thinking Step

The birth of the Ammonite and Moabite nations create two groups of people who often cause problems for the Israelites. Watch out for them popping up several times in the coming weeks. Even at the chronological end of the Old Testament, Ezra, in 9:1-3, tells the Jews not to marry Moabites or Ammonites.

Action Step

18:17 says – 'Then the LORD said, Shall I hide from Abraham what I am about to do?' How often we think that God doesn't tell us enough and leaves us in the dark about what His plans are! It really is on a "needs to know" basis and as we read on we will see that God decided Abraham did need to know. There are times when knowing why isn't essential to the overall plan of God and the response we get then is like that of Jesus at the end of John's Gospel when He repeated the phrase – "What is it to you?" when challenged about John's death. Sometimes what we are doing for God makes sense to us as we can understand the logic of His guidance. However there are times when we are walking blind – but it's only us who don't know where we are heading! – God knows but has decided we don't need to know! O that we could be as obedient to God as we are to our satnavs – without questioning! When it says to turn right we do, when it says to take first exit at the next roundabout, that's the way we go. Bearing in mind God never makes mistakes but satnavs regularly do – who is worthy of our unquestioning obedience? Think of this next time you use your satnav!

Day 8
Genesis 21-24
8th January

21 - Isaac Born And Ishmael Rejected
22 - Isaac Almost Sacrificed
23 - Sarah Dies And Abraham Buys Cave At Machpelah
24 - Isaac Marries Rebekah

Isaac Arrives And Ishmael Departs!

The Big Picture

An heir is born at last and he is called Isaac. Sadly this results in Hagar and her son Ishmael being banished to the wilderness of Beersheba where God rescues them and they find water at a nearby well. God confirms that Ishmael will prosper. Following problems with Abimelech's men about the local well Abraham agrees a deal with Abimelech for the well at Beersheba and they take an oath. Isaac is almost sacrificed by Abraham until God provides a ram as his substitute. Sarah dies at 127 and Abraham buys a field and a cave from Ephron for her burial place. Isaac marries Rebekah – daughter of Bethuel, son of Abraham's brother Nahor.

Thinking Step

The son of Abraham and Sarah is called Isaac, which means laughter. It's God's way of reminding them every time they call him that they didn't believe God and laughed at the very thought of an old lady like Sarah ever giving birth to a child. Sarah may have been old but she still attracted other men!

Action Step

In the days of the Patriarchs offering your children as sacrifices to your gods was all too common an act. So on the face of it to sacrifice your only son was not that unusual. When you have waited so long for him and are very unlikely to have another it's a particularly poignant gesture. However that is what Abraham is convinced God wants him to do. So he heads off for the land of Moriah to obey! It could be that Abraham believed that God would raise Isaac from the dead if and when he did offer him as a sacrifice. In any event it was a real step of faith. God provided a substitute for Isaac this time. It can be really difficult to be flexible as we try to discern the will of God in our lives – and this is a good example of having the broad vision but getting some of the details wrong. Abraham was right that God wanted a sacrifice but he was wrong about Isaac being that sacrifice. Are you wrestling with a particular problem in your life unsure of all the details? Just take the first step and God will confirm things to you by showing the next step in due time. Don't try to finish the picture when God has only shown you the outline so far. Just take things a step at a time – like Abraham.

Abraham Dies
And Isaac Has Very Different Twins

The Big Picture

Abraham gets married for a second time following the death of his beloved Sarah. His new wife is called Keturah and she bears him 6 sons, one called Midian but none of them inherit Abraham's wealth and are sent away leaving only Isaac! He leaves all he has to Isaac and then dies aged 175 and is buried with his wife Sarah in the cave of Machpelah. Isaac has twin sons by Rebekah, Esau and Jacob. Jacob steals the birthright of Esau for a pot of red soup and then flees the country. Meanwhile Isaac repeats the lies of his father Abraham by saying his wife is his sister!

Thinking Step

Esau was born covered with red hair and had to grow up being called "Hairy," the literal meaning of Esau. After the big mistake of selling his birthright for a bowl of red stew, he then became known as "Red" or Edom and became the father of the Edomites. That's why there is no tribe of the 'Esau-ites!'

Action Step

I think that if I had the opportunity to meet either Esau or Jacob, I would choose Esau. The Bible tells us he was a skilful hunter who loved the outdoors – and his Father loved him best. He was a forgiving man whereas his brother Jacob was an opportunist and a devious schemer. The Bible tells us that God preferred Jacob! The reason was that Jacob had time for God whereas Esau never gave God a thought! Some of the nicest people I know are like Esau! A friend of my wife has a husband who she insisted never did anything wrong and therefore being a Christian was not a problem, he has always been one! It took ages before we finally got through that everyone needs forgiveness – even nice people! I remember hearing Johnny Cash give his testimony at Wembley Stadium. It was very clear that he had done lots of wrong things in his life and rejoiced that God had forgiven him. On our way out I heard a man say, "Well, he really needed saving didn't he!" Yes he did – but we all do! Do you know anyone who is a real Esau? A nice man or woman who is spiritually dead and heading for a Godless eternity? Mention their name now as God has brought them to your mind and ask God for an opportunity to share your faith with them.

Jacob Schemes His Way To The Top

The Big Picture

Isaac is getting towards the end of his life and Jacob, ever the opportunist, takes advantage of his Father's frailty and blindness. With the help of his Mother he tricks his Father into blessing him instead of his older brother Esau. Jacob flees from his angry brother and journeys to Haran which today is in eastern Turkey. On his way he sleeps with a stone as a pillow and dreams of a ladder with angels ascending and descending to and from Heaven. On waking Jacob renames the place Bethel, the house of God, and marks it with the stone pillow which he uses as an altar. He then promises God a tithe (10%) of his future income.

Thinking Step

Jacob is sent to Haran for a wife. The same place as his Grandfather Abraham's servant went to look for a wife for Isaac and found Rebekah. Both times because they didn't want their sons to be married to Canaanites. Already they were becoming a separate people, not intermarrying with other nations.

Action Step

Keeping your word is the mark of a true English gentleman! It seems this is true of an ancient Patriarch too. When Isaac didn't see through Jacob's disguise and blessed him instead of Esau, there was no going back. His spoken blessing could not be rescinded. Isaac had set his mind on a certain course of action and would not, indeed could not, be deflected. As it happens he was right because we read that when things went wrong for Esau – having already married two pagan wives which he knew would displease his parents he proceeds to marry Mahalath, a daughter of Ishmael, in 28:9. Not quite a Canaanite but not a true member of the inner family either as his Grandfather had rejected Ishmael and sent him away years before. Marks of real immaturity from Esau and confirmation of his unsuitability to lead the family under God. There are often times when we must stick to our principles even if it makes us unpopular. Do you have a particularly sticky problem to resolve because if you obey God you won't be very popular? It could be in your office or it could be in your church fellowship. Whichever it is – grasp the nettle and do the right thing. We are not in a popularity competition. We are disciples of the living God and when He approves you have the only majority approval you need!

Jacob Gets Some Of His Own Medicine, But Still Wins!

The Big Picture

Jacob settles in Haran and marries Rachel but only after being tricked into marrying Leah her sister! Taking on two maid servants as well Jacob then produces sons who will ultimately become the tribes of Israel after Jacob's name is changed! Jacob, outwitting his Father-in-Law Laban, acquires much wealth with vast flocks of speckled and spotted sheep as well as donkeys and camels. At the prompting of God Jacob leaves for Canaan with his family and animals. Laban pursues Jacob but relents when he finally catches up with him. The families are reconciled and Jacob continues his journey as Laban returns home.

Thinking Step

We often think of Jacob as being very impatient and acting as though he had no vowels! His name would then be J_C_B which is a bulldozer that pushes and shoves to get its own way! If only he had been patient and trusted God J_C_B could have saved himself a whole lot of pushing and shoving!

Action Step

A major problem in the Jacob household was favouritism and its inevitable consequence – jealousy. Despite getting the wife he so desperately wanted, namely Rachel, Jacob cannot love his sons as he should because none of them came from his beloved Rachel. When Rachel did finally give birth and produced Joseph – Jacob then ignored his other ten sons and appointed his youngest son as his heir thus building up a barrier between his sons that would not be removed for many years. In fact it took some unnecessary suffering and heartache in Egypt. Having favourites in a family is ultimately destructive and brings nothing but problems. I remember hearing of a woman who had rejected her least favourite daughter to such a degree that she couldn't think of anything positive to say about her. Her Mother remarked that she didn't dress well, her hair was a mess, she chose the wrong friends and showed no respect for her elders! (Sounds like every teenager I have ever met!!) It was only when she was challenged to write down all the positive things she could about her daughter that she realised she could see none! Thankfully she persevered and after a few days she finally thought of one! We know that God has no favourites so we shouldn't either. If you have a favourite child or grandchild then resolve today that you will promote all the others to co-favourites!

Brothers Re-United

The Big Picture

Jacob is met by the angels of God on his way to meet his brother Esau. As his journey progresses Jacob sends messengers on ahead to meet Esau and is disturbed to learn from them, upon their return, that Esau is on his way to meet Jacob – with 400 men! Jacob cautiously splits his group into two in the hope that at least half will survive any attack from Esau. He prepares gifts for Esau and sends his wives and children on ahead, remaining alone. He meets a man (angel of God) and wrestles with him all night. This results in a name change to Israel. Esau and Jacob are reconciled and then go their separate ways in peace.

Thinking Step

32:32 – Even today the people of Israel don't eat the tendon near the hip socket. Jews love word play so could this have been in Elijah's mind when he asked the Israelites in 1 Kings 18:21 "How long are you going to waiver between two opinions?" (lit. limp from one foot to another – like our father Jacob).

Action Step

In Jacob we have the first significant total name change of the Old Testament. Abram had previously been changed to Abraham but essentially they were still variations on a 'Father Theme' – from 'exalted father' to 'father of nations'. However when 'Jacob' was changed to 'Israel' the name change is complete. From being called supplanter or one who dispossesses he becomes wrestler or one who strives with God. Significantly he spends the rest of his life doing just that – arguing with God! Of course God, who knows the beginning from the end, knew what He was doing when He chose Jacob's new name but sometimes we don't when we choose. On a human level whilst we don't change names very often in our society we do like using pet names and nicknames. Please be aware there is a sense in which we can influence future behaviour by a careless or thoughtless choice of nickname. Many believe if you call a child lazy it's almost inevitable that you will produce a lazy child! I have to say I have seen concepts like this in action! Of course calling a child something positive rather than negative will probably have the positive effect! Next time you use someone's name whether it's their proper name or a nickname – be sure you use a positive emphasis rather than a negative one. It could shape their lives for ever!

34 - Dinah Is Abused By Shechem

35 - Benjamin Born As Rachel Dies

36 - Esau's Family Tree

Day 13

Genesis 34-36

13th January

Rachel And Isaac Die
Then There Were Twelve!

The Big Picture

Chapter 34 is a cameo on the life of the only named daughter of Jacob – Dinah, daughter of Leah. It covers her abuse by Shechem and the fury of her brothers. Then there's a mass circumcision of the whole family of Shechem before the massacre of a complete city in revenge for the raping of Dinah. Then the account of Jacob continues as he travels to Bethel at God's command – but only after purifying his whole household. The reason for Jacob's name being changed is then explained. Rachel dies giving birth to Benjamin and is buried by the road to Bethlehem. Isaac dies and is buried by his two sons. The genealogy of Esau concludes this section.

Thinking Step

Doesn't it seem strange that the favourite wife of Jacob is buried where she dies and yet most of his close relatives are buried in the family cave of Machpelah? Some Jewish writings suggest that she was buried near Bethlehem so that Joseph could pray to her for help, as he goes into Egypt as a slave some years later!

Action Step

There are many places in the Bible that begin with the name Beth, literally 'house of'. In addition to Bethel – House of God, which plays a major part in today's narrative, there is also Bethlehem – House of Bread: Bethesda – House of Mercy: Bethphage – House of Unripe Figs – and many more. They all have a reason for their names such as the one today that marks God meeting Jacob in a special way. So we have the name Beth(house) and El(God). In our culture we often refer to our place of worship or church building as the house of God. I remember as a child when I was rebuked for whistling in church only to be told by an old lady that I shouldn't do that in God's house. I politely asked if it was okay to whistle outside and was told it was. Not being able to let her have the last word I then asked if it was okay because God wouldn't hear me outside! I had to quickly duck as the hand of discipline flew very near my ear! Sometimes we do things in other places or at home that we would never do in church – as though God was partially sighted! He isn't but He isn't just a CCTV camera either! He's there to guide us when our actions may be inappropriate for a Christian.

Parallels Between Joseph And Jesus (Gen 37-50)

JOSEPH	PARALLELS	JESUS
37:3	Their fathers delighted in them	Matthew 3:17
37:2	Shepherds of their fathers' sheep	John 10:11, 27
37:2, 4-5	Testified against men	John 15:18
37:13-14	Sent by their father	John 3:17
37:20	Others plotted to kill them	John 11:53
39:7	Tempted but didn't yield	Matthew 4:1
37:25, 28	Taken to Egypt	Matthew 2:14-15
37:23	Robes taken from them	John 19:23
37:28	Sold for silver	Matthew 26:15
39:16-18	Falsely accused	Matthew 26:59-60
40:2-3	Placed with two other prisoners	Mark 15:27-28
40:21-22	One prisoner saved, the other lost	Luke 23:32
41:46	Similar ages when publicly recognised	Luke 3:23
41:41	Exalted after suffering	Philippians 2:9-11
45:15	Forgave those who wronged them	Luke 23:34
45:7	Saved their people	Matthew 1:21
50:20	God turned bad to good	1 Corinthians 2:7-8

37 - Joseph Sold And Arrives In Egypt
38 - Tamar Has Revenge On Judah
39 - Potiphar's Wife Frames Joseph
40 - Joseph Interprets Dreams Of Cupbearer And Baker

Day 14
Genesis 37-40
14th January

Innocent Joseph Ends Up In Prison!

The Big Picture

Today begins the account of Joseph's adventures that finishes up with him in Egypt. It all begins with his father's gift to him of a special coat. He shares his dreams with his brothers who react violently and determine to kill him but then decide to sell him instead. He is sold and joins Potiphar's household. Meanwhile Judah sins with Shua and abuses Tamar his widowed daughter in law who bears him twin sons. The narrative continues as Joseph prospers with Potiphar until he has to run to escape the amorous advances of Potiphar's wife. He is put in prison but prospers there interpreting dreams for fellow prisoners.

Thinking Step

Joseph's famous 'coat of many colours' was probably a highly decorated ankle length tunic with long wide sleeves. This clearly marked him out as heir to the family fortune. Having long wide sleeves meant it was unsuitable for work – but heirs didn't work anyway! A point not lost on his brothers who were usually working when Joseph visited!

Action Step

Joseph alienates his brothers through no fault of his own. He was his father's favourite and that wasn't his fault! He simply tells his brothers about his dreams naively thinking they would be as excited as he was by the way God was dealing with him! They weren't and he is imprisoned by them. When he is sold he obviously impresses the Midianites and Ishmaelites (both relatives of his father Jacob as descendent of two sons of Abraham – Midian and Ishmael). So much so that they were able to sell him with confidence to Potiphar, Captain of Pharaoh's bodyguard, who was not a man to alienate with a second class slave! Through no fault of his own Joseph finishes up in prison. There he impresses the authorities as well as his fellow prisoners, so much so that he is a trusted prisoner and an esteemed interpreter of dreams. Notice a theme? Even when things go wrong Joseph never grows weary of doing good! It gets him into trouble but doing right is what he believes in. How about you? Are there times when you grow weary of being knocked down for doing the right thing? Why not keep a brightly coloured picture as wallpaper on your mobile phone or computer – to remind you of Joseph's coat and his determination to always do the right thing. A great example to follow!

Day 15
Genesis 41-44
15th January

41 - Joseph Triumphs With Pharaoh's Dream
42 - Joseph's Brothers Call On Him
43 - Brothers Call Again, With Benjamin
44 - Joseph Continues To Toy With His Brothers

Things Get Difficult And Joseph Shines

The Big Picture

Joseph's good reputation gets him released after Pharaoh's cup-bearer remembers Joseph's ability to read dreams. He is taken to interpret the dreams of Pharaoh. With God's help Joseph reveals the hidden meaning of seven good years to come, followed by seven years of famine. He suggests a plan to save the day by appointing a wise man to oversee the next fourteen years and is immediately appointed by Pharaoh as that man! When famine spreads into neighbouring Canaan, Jacob sends his sons to Egypt to buy food and they subsequently bow before Joseph just as he had told them they would. Their full reconciliation is now very close.

Thinking Step

Crying is for real men in the Bible! When Joseph is overcome at the sight of Benjamin he leaves the room to weep then returns having washed his face. Ancient Egyptian nobility wore lots of eye make-up – if the death mask of Tutankhamun is anything to go by! So after crying, some remedial attention would be required!

Action Step

As a result of his indiscretion with one of his father's concubines – 35:22 Reuben has lost his influential position as eldest son. Nevertheless he is the one who pleads for Joseph's life when his brothers capture him and drop him into a pit. When the brothers are told by Joseph that they must bring Benjamin to Egypt, Jacob is not comforted by Reuben when he promises to bring Benjamin back safely. Despite Reuben saying that he will forfeit two of his own sons Jacob totally ignores his gesture. Sadly, sometimes things we do in our lives cannot be wiped away. There are consequences to bear even when God forgives us! The story is told of a preacher who is taking the very first service at a newly built church and finds himself in an impressive pulpit surrounded by the best carved wood he has ever seen. He is preaching about consequences and in order to make his point takes a rough nail from his pocket and with a large hammer proceeds to hammer the nail into the beautiful pulpit! With mock horror he realises his dreadful behaviour and apologises, quickly removing the nail with the claw end of the hammer but the mark would remain – for ever! Don't expect God to remove all the consequences from your previous failures even when He forgives you. Sometimes we need regular reminders not to make the same mistakes again.

45 - The Big Reunion Of Brothers
46 - The Big Reunion Of Family
47 - The Whole Family Settles In Egypt

Day 16
Genesis 45-47
16th January

Sons Re-United

The Big Picture

The whole family is reconciled and united as the brothers forgive and are forgiven. Then their father Jacob comes to Egypt too. They are given suitable land for their sheep, the best pastureland in Egypt. Here they will grow to a mighty nation. The nucleus of the tribes of Israel are together once again. Jacob introduces his father to Pharaoh before settling his whole family in the land of Goshen. As a result of Joseph's diligence Pharaoh prospers as the Egyptians surrender their livestock and then their land in return for food to survive. Finally, Jacob now referred to as Israel, gets a promise from Joseph that he will be buried in Canaan when he dies.

Thinking Step

46:27 SEVENTY – the size of the nation of Israel settling in Egypt. The number of elders of Moses Ex 24:1. The years in exile Dan 9:24. The disciples sent out by Jesus Luke 10:1. The size of the Sanhedrin. The number of scribes employed to translate the Hebrew Old Testament into Greek – the Septuagint.

Action Step

Try to imagine – a shabby old man just in from the desert, meeting the king of the most powerful nation on earth, in his royal palace! That's Jacob meeting the Pharaoh of Egypt. Ironically we know lots about the old man but we don't even know the powerful Pharaoh's name! The Pharaoh asks the old man his age as there was a respect for maturity which has been somewhat diminished in our society today. The ancient Egyptians had a very low life expectancy and that included the Pharaoh and it was probably obvious that Jacob was a very old man. Just imagine the atmosphere as Jacob declares he is 130 years old! I wonder if that's why he blesses Pharaoh twice – maybe with the second one at Pharaoh's request. It is the family of this old man Jacob that would produce a great nation and ultimately the Messiah, King of Kings. It seems appearances were very deceiving – and can be equally deceiving today! So remember to try to look on the inside when you meet people today – because that's how God looks at us. He perceives all believers as cleansed by the blood of Jesus. He sees us as we are in Him and not just as we are today. So try to be inward looking today and your attitude to others will be remarkably different!

Day 17
Genesis 48-50
17th January

48 - Jacob Blesses Joseph's Sons, Youngest First!
49 - Jacob Blesses All His Own Sons, Then Dies
50 - Joseph Buries Jacob In Canaan, Then Dies In Egypt

Nation Of Israel Is Born
But Now We Have To Wait!

The Big Picture

The last three chapters of Genesis record the final events in the lives of Jacob and Joseph before concluding with their deaths. Jacob blesses Joseph's two sons born to him in Egypt, taking the younger first! Just like Isaac instead of Ishmael, Jacob instead of Esau and Joseph instead of Reuben. Jacob's final act is to bless each of his twelve sons the sons who would ultimately become the twelve tribes of Israel. The children of Israel who would fulfil the promises made to Abraham! The book of Genesis closes with the record of Jacob being taken to Canaan for burial as promised, whilst Joseph is embalmed – willing to wait 400 years for his journey into the promised land.

Thinking Step

The Israelites settle in Egypt and bring the idea of worshipping one God only. During the 'New Kingdom' period, henotheism (worship of one god above others) is introduced into Egypt by Akhenhaten, father of Tutankhamun. The Israelites' monotheistic approach could well have been a considerable influence. The idea didn't last long and could have cost Tutankhamun his life as polytheism returned!

Action Step

Do you sometimes wish you were more prominent in your witness for Christ? A Christian who stands head and shoulders above all the others! Well by definition, that simply isn't possible because if we were all prominent none of us would stand out! The book of Genesis closes with the life of the last Patriarch, that giant, Joseph. For the majority of his fruitful life he was very anonymous. We know something of his highlights but that's about it. However, even anonymously his witness continued as a beacon to all who witnessed it. Amongst his brothers he faithfully announced what God was saying to him even if a little more tact might have saved him a lot of unpleasantness! Then in Potiphar's household Joseph continued his moral stance and this got him into real trouble. Whilst in prison he persisted with his witness for God and influenced a number of his fellow prisoners there, not to mention those in charge who recognised in him someone who could be trusted. Wherever he was he was the same – God's man. Wherever you are now are you the same as you will be at Church on Sunday, or tonight at home with your family. Jesus is described in the Bible as the same yesterday today and forever. May that sort of consistency be a mark of our lives too – starting today!

Exodus

Exodus

Exodus continues the history of the Israelites and then a Pharaoh came to the throne who knew nothing of Joseph. Slavery quickly followed and Pharaoh proclaims that all Israelite baby boys are to be thrown into the Nile. A couple from the tribe of Levi have a son who is named Moses. Educated in the courts of Pharaoh he is destined to lead the Israelites. He commits murder then runs away to become a shepherd in the land of Midian. Here he experiences God at the burning bush and eventually agrees to confront Pharaoh with his brother Aaron and demand, "Let My people go!" The Israelites are eventually freed following the tenth plague which results in the Passover. The miracle of the crossing of the Red Sea finally seals their escape. The second half of the book focuses on the Ten Commandments and the Tabernacle.

Below is an acrostic which summarises each chapter of the book.

1. Forced labour for Israel
2. Royal training for Moses
3. Obstinate Moses resists God
4. Moses' excuses are answered

5. Egyptian oppression is increased
6. God's deliverance is promised
7. Yahweh smites the Nile
8. Plagues of frogs, insects
9. Three plagues harden Pharaoh
10. Swarming locusts and darkness

11. Blood required for first born
12. Observance of the Passover
13. National exodus from Egypt
14. Division of Red Sea
15. Adoration song to God
16. Gathering manna six days
17. Extracting water from rock

18. Tribal organisation for ruling
19. Orders at Mount Sinai

Moses Is Born In Egypt
But Quickly Flees!

The Big Picture

In these two chapters we have a brief account of the early life of Moses. We learn of his birth to a couple from the tribe of Levi. Then his concealment at home from the authorities who would have him thrown into the Nile before he is adopted by Pharaoh's daughter and raised in Pharaoh's household to become a well educated leader of men. However, due to murdering an Egyptian, Moses flees to Midian a desert area, probably in present day Saudi Arabia where he settles down marries and has a family. Then the news comes, declaring that Pharaoh has died and God hears His people's groaning. Freedom is calling!

Thinking Step

Pharaoh's plot to kill all Israelite baby boys seems rather brutal! However if he could force these immigrants into mixed marriages then, within a generation the problem of having a nation within a nation would be solved. With no Jewish men available to marry Jewish women the nation of Israel would disappear! It could have worked too, if God had not had other plans!

Action Step

I am constantly surprised by the way God has been preparing me throughout my life for the many things He wants me to do for Him now! When we read about Moses we learn of his education in the best schools of Egypt where he must have learned much from the mathematicians, scientists and philosophers of his day. In fact he probably had his first glimpses of what became the Ten Commandments as he was familiarised with the sophisticated legal and religious rites of the Egyptians. Moses spent a lot of time as the best educated shepherd that the world had ever seen and learned some of the practicalities of leading his troublesome flocks, never dreaming that one day he would be leading troublesome people! Moses learned his lessons well. He became the ultimate "Law Giver" – and a great shepherd holding millions of people together for 40 years. I know church leaders who have failed to hold together a handful of people without factions splitting them into separate groups. I believe all our daily experiences can be used for good and in the case of Moses he did just that using all he had learned to fulfil God's will in his life. Whatever is taking most of your time at the moment why not ask God now to give you opportunities to put this knowledge into practice for the Kingdom? Why not ask Him now?

It Will Take More Than A Burning Bush!

The Big Picture

Moses is confronted by a burning bush as he shepherds his father-in-law's flocks in Midian. Despite a clear call from God, Moses is full of excuses for not following Him. God gives Him miraculous signs to convince Pharaoh. Moses resolves to return to Egypt but relies on Aaron to say God's words, "Let My people go!" Pharaoh refuses to let his slave labour force go free and makes it harder for the Israelites to make bricks by insisting that they find their own straw! The Israelites reject Moses as everything he does seems to make things worse! Downhearted, Moses is recommissioned by God to try again. Moses agrees but only after repeating that he couldn't speak well!

Thinking Step

In Ex 6:20 we learn that Moses came from a marriage between Amram and Jochebed. The Mosaic Law had not yet been declared in detail. However, when it was unions like this were declared illegal and banned! Jochebed was Amram's aunty and this relationship is strictly forbidden in Leviticus 6:20.

Action Step

"If at first you don't succeed – give up!" It's a good job Moses didn't subscribe to this distorted mantra. Sometimes it's so hard to go on and we need to be encouraged. A great and ready source of such encouragement can be the Bible or hymns and songs. I knew a missionary who when exhausted by his church planting activities, would even have doubts about his own salvation and the reality of God – these invariably occurred in the dark of night. Past experience taught him that God doesn't change even when circumstances do. Therefore he would regularly 'lead himself to Christ' using the promises made and confirmed in the Bible. On a recent rough sailing off the Turkish coast my wife who is a poor sailor, was one of the few who was not ill! After the sailing I asked how she endured such an unpleasant trip so well. She shared her secret with me. All she did was to silently sing all the choruses she had learned over the years. The first ones that came to mind were 'Deep and Wide' and 'Will your anchor hold in the storms of life'. Who says God has no sense of humour! When you have a 'Moses Moment', when everything is going wrong, remember God's dependable promise He made at the burning bush, "Certainly, I will be with you..."

Day 20
Exodus 7-10
20th January

7 - Warnings Are Followed By First Plague - Blood
8 - Next Three Plagues – Frogs, Gnats And Flies
9 - Disease On Beasts, Boils And Hail Are Next
10 - Plagues Almost Over With Locusts And Darkness

Nine Plagues
All Judgements On Egyptian Gods

The Big Picture

Moses and Aaron meet Pharaoh again but with no success. Despite the miraculous sign of Aaron's staff turning into a snake and eating the snakes that were produced by the magicians of Egypt from their staffs, it's obvious that the plagues are going to be needed after all! Starting with the Nile turning to blood and progressing through to the plague of darkness. Each of these plagues was specifically designed to show the superiority of Israel's God over the gods of the Egyptians. The stage is now set for the final miraculous act from God – the Passover. One of the greatest events in the whole of world history.

Thinking Step

In our society when you reach sixty you get a free bus pass. When you hit seventy you get free loft insulation. When you reach eighty you go shopping on a motorised scooter. When Moses reached eighty and Aaron was eighty three, the adventure of working out God's plan for them was just beginning!

Action Step

The plagues seem to be like local buses! None for ages and then ten one after the other! However, unlike buses which are all very similar each of the plagues is totally unique. Each one was specifically linked to individual Egyptian gods. Beginning with the gods linked to the Nile such as Hapy – and progressing in our reading today to the penultimate plague against Ra the sun god who was blacked out with the plague of darkness. Notice 12:12 – "I will execute judgement against all the gods of Egypt, for I am the Lord!" It wasn't God punishing the Egyptians. He was simply displaying His power as he challenged their puny gods. Every plague posed a question – Is this god? The answer – No! I AM! This happened nine times and tomorrow we will see the completion of the plagues with the tenth. This raises a penetrating question? What do you think a 21st century plague would be? Could it be natural like a flu pandemic or a tsunami? Or maybe more man-made like a financial or other corporate collapse. I remember a friend who used to respond vigorously to anyone who said they were okay 'under the circumstances'. "We are not under the circumstances," he would say, "We are under God and over the circumstances!" Our God is always the great I AM no matter which plague threatens. Even today!

God of Israel vs. 'gods of Egypt'

PLAGUE	REFERENCE	OBJECT OF EGYPTIAN WORSHIP
1	Polluted Nile (7:14-25)	Hapy - god of the annual flooding of the Nile and it's fertility
2	Frogs (8:1-15)	Heqt - frog headed goddess of childbirth
3	Dust and Gnats (8:16-19)	Isis - goddess makes a beast out of dust
4	Swarms of Flies (8:20-32)	Beelzebub - "Lord of the flies"
5	Death of Domestic animals (9:1-7)	Hathor and Mnevis - gods of cows and bulls
6	Boils (9:8-12)	Sekhmet and Imhotep - gods of healing
7	Hail & Fire (9:13-35)	Tefnut and Set - gods of rain & storms Asbit - goddess of fire
8	Locusts (10:1-20)	Serapia - god of the locusts
9	Darkness (10:21-29)	Ra & Thoth - gods of the sun and moon
10	Death of the Firstborn (11-12)	Pharaoh considered himself a god so his son would be a god too

**"I will execute judgement against all the gods of Egypt,
for I am the LORD!"
(Exodus 12:12)**

Tenth Plague And Then Passover To Freedom

The Big Picture

If this was a boxing match we see the final knock-out blow today as we read about plague number ten and the Passover miracle. This shapes the nation of Israel and ultimately the whole of Christianity for ever. Pharaoh finally tells the Israelites to leave but this only happens after the tragedy of the deaths of the first-born has been experienced. The first ever Passover is now described and we read of 600,000 Israelite men, not counting women and children plus a mixed multitude with their flocks and herds, all leaving Egypt for the last time. All starting the adventure of a lifetime. However, the story doesn't end there...there's so much more!

Thinking Step

Most Christians think it was the angel of death who passed over but he only did the killing! Ex 12:23 says – "For the LORD will pass through...when He sees the blood...the LORD will pass over..." Only God could passover and pardon, just as Jesus did at that special Passover which we call Easter.

Action Step

Every year as Christians celebrate Easter and Jews all over the world give thanks to God for the miracle of the Passover we are reminded of the powerful message and the hope that is bound up in this remarkable historical event recorded in Exodus so long ago and completed two thousand years ago when centuries after the first Passover, Jesus Christ the lamb of God gave His life to free men from the slavery of sin. Matt 27:45 remembers the last plague before Passover – 'At noon, darkness fell across the whole land until three o'clock.' A total of three hours. A symbolic reminder of when darkness fell in Egypt for three days. Have you applied the blood to the door-posts of your heart and claimed the forgiveness that only being covered by the blood can provide? If your answer isn't a resounding "Yes" then you are like an ill person who has the correct effective medicine but refuses to take it! Why not receive Jesus today and be covered by the blood of the lamb. It's as easy as **ABC**.

Accept that you are far from perfect and therefore need to be forgiven.

Believe that Jesus died to forgive your sins to make you perfectly acceptable before God.

Confess Him with your mouth and declare He is your Passover Lamb and Saviour – today! If you do this please contact us via our website www.Bible.org.uk or write to us.

Christ, Our Passover Lamb

PASSOVER	OLD TESTAMENT	NEW TESTAMENT
Instruction to sacrifice	"...take a lamb...and...kill it" (Exodus 12:3, 6)	"Look! There is the Lamb of God who takes away the sin of the world!" (John 1:29)
Condition of sacrifice	"This animal must be a one-year-old male, either a sheep or a goat, with no physical defects" (Exodus 12:5)	"He paid for you with the precious lifeblood of Christ, the sinless, spotless Lamb of God" (1 Peter 1:19)
Reason for sacrifice	"...I will execute judgement..." (Exodus 12:12)	"And just as it is destined that each person dies only once and after that comes judgement" (Hebrews 9:27)
Application of sacrifice	"...each family must choose a lamb or a young goat for a sacrifice..." (Exodus 12:3)	"There is salvation in no one else! There is no other name in all of heaven for people to call on to save them" Acts 4:12)
Result of sacrifice	"...the LORD will pass over your home. He will not permit the Destroyer to enter and strike down your firstborn" (Exodus 12:23)	"So now there is no condemnation for those who belong to Christ Jesus" (Romans 8:1)

"Christ, Our Passover Lamb, Has Been Sacrificed For Us." (1 Corinthians 5:7)

Day 22
Exodus 13-15
22nd January

13 - Guided By Pillars Of Cloud By Day And Fire By Night
14 - Miraculous Path Through The Sea
15 - Worship And Praises For Israel's Deliverer!

God Leads Them Out And Through The Sea

The Big Picture

God teaches the Israelites about sanctifying their first-born to Him. Regular celebrating of the Passover in the future is a great way to tell the next generation what God did for His people so long ago. These are key events for both Jews and Christians today. God led them out and Moses takes the bones of Joseph for burial in Canaan, as promised. They are led by the pillars of cloud and fire and cross the Red Sea (sometimes called the Reed Sea). Following close behind is Pharaoh's army which perishes as the water falls back into place after the Israelites cross. Moses celebrates with a song – but the grumbling soon begins as testing times start.

Thinking Step

So was it the Red Sea with its enormous walls of water which engulfed the Egyptian army? Or was it the Reed Sea in which the whole of Pharaoh's army chariots and all, was drowned in ankle deep water! Which would you judge the greater miracle? Whichever you choose we can clearly see God's hand!

Action Step

The crossing of the Red Sea was a major turning point in the lives of all who experienced it. Something never to be forgotten – but time faded their memories very quickly. Sadly we are just like the Israelites. We have 'forgettories' rather than memories! Like them, we seem to want a fresh revelation every time rather than remembering what happened last time! Next time you are in difficulties take a moment to try to recall if God has handled this sort of thing in your life on a previous occasion. If He has, then try trusting Him from memory rather than asking Him to repeat Himself! Every time I go to the dentist I ask God to keep me safe and keep any pain to a minimum. He never fails me and I always resolve not to doubt Him again – but when the next time comes around my memory is so poor! Wouldn't we be upset if our mature children or grown up grandchildren asked us the same questions seeking the same reassurances every day? So, how do you think God feels? When God answers a prayer for you next time why not write, "Once should be enough!" on a 'post-it' on your fridge or your computer. That way when people ask you why you've done it – you will be able to tell them how good God is – just like the Israelites should have done.

God's Plans For Provision And Protection

The Big Picture

What an example the Israelites are! Never missing an opportunity to grumble! In chapter 16 we have eight references to grumbling in the first twelve verses alone! In reply, God takes care of them and meets their need with fresh quail meat in the evening and manna every morning. Then they complain again that they need fresh water as the patience of Moses is tested to breaking point! They are preserved in a battle with the army of Amalek and erect an altar in remembrance. As pressure grows on Moses he is encouraged by his father in law Jethro, to appoint leaders, able men who fear God and who will act as elders for the people.

Thinking Step

I was once asked by someone what evidence I had for God having a sense of humour! Our reading today provides some evidence. God supplies the Israelites with unique 'bread' each morning – but never tells them what it's called. They just get used to calling it manna which is a Hebrew word meaning "What is it?"

Action Step

Negative complaining is something we don't have to teach our children to do! Nowhere in the Bible are we encouraged to do it – in fact we are urged to do the very opposite. So why do we do it? At the root of it is the thought that "I wouldn't have done it like this!" Listen to a phone-in programme and you will get advice from all and sundry on how to better run the country and reduce taxes. As though their suggestions would never have crossed the Prime Minister's mind previously! This is not a party political point but a simple observation. Isn't it amazing that everyone thinks they can do the job better than the person doing it? Stand at a football match and listen to the 'advice' freely given to the referee and the players. If only they would listen then things would be so much better and far more successful!!! Sheer negativity. The story is told of a new preacher who did everything wrong that it is possible to do on a single Sunday. Then he spotted his predecessor in the congregation! Imagine how he felt when the former pastor shook his hand with the comment, "Thank you – aren't the Scriptures wonderful!" Next Sunday try to be positive and supportive with your leaders (if you are a leader, do the same for members of the congregation!) Try it, you might even like it!

Jesus And The Law

THE 10 COMMANDMENTS	JESUS TAUGHT
"Do not worship any other gods besides me" (Exodus 20:3)	"No one can serve two masters... You cannot serve both God and money" (Luke 16:13)
"Do not make idols of any kind"(Exodus 20:4)	"You must worship the Lord your God; serve only him" (Matthew 4:10)
"Do not misuse the name of the LORD your God" (Exodus 20:7)	"Again, you have heard that the law of Moses says, 'Do not break your vows; you must carry out the vows you have made to the Lord'" (Matthew 5:33)
"Remember to observe the Sabbath day by keeping it holy" (Exodus 20:8)	"The Sabbath was made to benefit people, and not people to benefit the Sabbath. And I, the Son of Man, am master even of the Sabbath!" (Mark 2:27-28)
"Honour your father and mother" (Exodus 20:12)	"But you say it is all right for people to say to their parents, 'Sorry, I can't help you. For I have vowed to give to God what I could have given to you'...As such, you break the law of God" (Mark 7:11-13)
"Do not murder" (Exodus 20:13)	"But I say, if you are angry with someone, you are subject to judgement!" (Matthew 5:22)
"Do not commit adultery" (Exodus 20:14)	"But I say, anyone who even looks at a woman with lust in his eye has already committed adultery with her in his heart" (Matthew 5:28)
"Do not steal" (Exodus 20:15)	"I assure you, anyone who sneaks over the wall of a sheepfold, rather than going through the gate, must surely be a thief and a robber!" (John 10:1)
"Do not testify falsely against your neighbour" (Exodus 20:16)	"And I tell you this, that you must give an account on judgement day of every idle word you speak" (Matthew 12:36)
"Do not covet" (Exodus 20:17)	"Beware! Don't be greedy for what you don't have. Real life is not measured by how much we own." (Luke 12:15)

19 - God's Covenant With His People   Day 24
20 - God Gives The Ten Commandments   Exodus 19-20
24th January

God's Covenant And The Ten Commandments

The Big Picture

The Israelites stop in the Sinai wilderness and face the impressive Mount Sinai. A major encounter between God and mankind is about to take place. Moses ascends the mountain to have a meeting with God and the first thing God says is, "If you will indeed obey my voice and keep My commandments then you will be My Possession or Special Treasure." What an offer! Moses descends and shares with the Elders and the people all that God has said and they all agree to do what God commands. Moses reports the good news back to God. Then he proceeds to tell everyone what God has said. What did God say? – it's better known as the 'Ten Commandments'!

Thinking Step

In chapter 19 Moses goes up and down the mountain at least three times! His final descent brings the teaching of the ten commandments to the people. Then they get them in writing – 32:15. They are destroyed – but quickly replaced. They are proclaimed in Deuteronomy to the next generation. That's a total of four – two audibly and two in writing!

Action Step

Someone once remarked that it's only little boys who have perfected the art of washing just one hand and using a slowly dripping tap to do it! On a more serious note, we have a glimpse today of how important purity is to our Father in Heaven. In today's reading from chapter 19 we read, 'Then the Lord told Moses "Go down and prepare the people for my arrival. Consecrate them today and tomorrow and have them wash their clothing." The same God who required purity from the Israelites requires pure hearts from those who approach Him today. Ps. 66:18 tells us – 'If I had not confessed the sin in my heart the Lord would not have listened.' Whenever you wash your hands today and most of us wash our hands many times each day in these days of being aware of passing on diseases, remember that whilst this cleansing is important it is only the surface – and the effect soon wears off! The purification that our God demands is purification of the heart and we need His help with that because we keep dirtying everything again. So why did God give us the ten commandments? To confirm what He expects from us and show us that we can't reach His standards without His help. Now wash your hands...and ask God to cleanse you from within.

Day 25
Exodus 21-24
25th January

21 - The Rights Of Persons And Property
22 - Proper Conduct With Possessions And People
23 - Sabbatical Year And Annual Feasts
24 - The Covenant Is Confirmed – In Blood

Proper Conduct With People And Property

The Big Picture

Following the giving of the ten commandments, Moses goes into a lot of detail about personal rights and responsibilities. Then he covers the rights of property and outlines the law of God as far as burglary and stealing are concerned. Proper conduct, justice and the Sabbatical year are also covered. God invites Moses and seventy of the elders to come closer. Moses approaches closer than the others. The new covenant is ratified using the blood of bulls and Moses listens to all that God says. All of this is new and will be a real revolution to Israel and other nations. Moses stays up the mountain and spends forty days and forty nights with God.

Thinking Step

Moses brings 70 elders with him to Mount Sinai. How often should we forgive? – 7 times? Matt 18:22 – tells us the answer is 70 times 7. Whilst the Sanhedrin numbers 70 it is actually made up of one High Priest with 3 smaller courts each of 23. All joining together for important trials to make up 70.

Action Step

Before we get lost in the detail I suggest the key thought which should govern your mind today is not "Tell me the rules and I will obey them" but "How can I glorify God in this situation?" Throughout history Christianity has taught keeping to the spirit of the law rather than just the letter. Having said that, the letter is important and today we have lots of them with lots more to come! Remember they were originally written for people who had never seen anything like this before. They are truly revolutionary when viewed in the light of what was going on in other nations at that time. Some people still wear bracelets bearing the initials WWJD to regularly remind them of the question, "What would Jesus do?" I have been tempted on occasions to wear one with WDTBT written on it! Worked it our yet? – "What does the Bible teach?" Notice, it's not what does a verse say but what is the 'concept' that the Bible teaches. May we be preserved from simply quoting texts out of context! In the short prophecy of Haggai he urges the people to "consider this" at least four times in his two chapters. Think, with the help of the Holy Spirit, and work it out…Christianity is truly a thinking person's religion. Whatever you do today will it stand up to the 'Bible Concepts' test?

Eight Hebrew Words For Law

WORD	MEANING	EXAMPLES
Torah	Direction Guidance Instruction	Exodus 24:12
Mitswah	Commandment Command	Genesis 26:5 Exodus 15:26 Exodus 20:2-17
Mishpat	Regulations Judgement Ordinance	Genesis 18:19 Deuteronomy 16:18 Deuteronomy 17:9
Eduth	Testimony Truth	Exodus 25:22
Huqqim	Statutes Laws	Leviticus 18:4 Deuteronomy 4:1
Piqqudim	Orders Commandments	Psalms 19:8 Psalms 103:18
Dabar	Word Terms	Exodus 34:28 Deuteronomy 4:13
Dath	Royal Edict Public Law	Ezekiel 7:26 Daniel 6:8, 12

Arrangement Of The Tabernacle

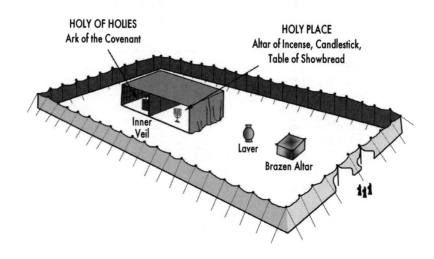

HOLY OF HOLIES
Ark of the Covenant

HOLY PLACE
Altar of Incense, Candlestick,
Table of Showbread

Inner
Veil

Laver

Brazen Altar

The Tabernacle And Temple
A Study In Contrasts

DETAIL	TABERNACLE (Exodus 26)	TEMPLE (1 Kings 6)
Dimensions	45x15x15 feet	90x30x45 feet
Porch	None	30 feet long
Windows	No	Yes
Divider between two rooms	Veil	Veil and doors (2 Chronicles 3:14)
Items in Most Holy Place	Ark with two cherubim (Exodus 25:18-20)	Ark and two separate cherubim (2 Chron. 5:7-8)

25 - The Tabernacle And Ark Of The Covenant
26 - Curtains And Veils Of The Tabernacle
27 - Tabernacle Altar And Courtyard

Day 26
Exodus 25-27
26th January

The Tabernacle Plans In Full Detail

The Big Picture

Nothing left to chance – as we read in 26:30 when God instructs "Set up this Tabernacle according to the pattern you were shown on the mountain." The details may seem a long way away from the 21st century but they truly reflect the world of the Lord Jesus and therefore we need to be familiar with them. The Ark of the Covenant, Table of Shewbread, Golden Lampstand, Curtains, Veil and Bronze Altar. All these details were essential to the Israelites – and their symbolism is all fulfilled in Jesus Christ. Each part of the Tabernacle points to Him. Let's look for Him as we cover these very detailed chapters and – thank God for Jesus who fulfilled them all!

Thinking Step

Tabernacle is a very unfamiliar word today but it was a large tent-like structure inside which God tabernacled with His people – just like the Apostle John tells us Jesus did when He was here on earth. John 1:14 – says "So the Word became human and made His home among us" – literally He tabernacled with us!

Action Step

It must have taken Moses a long time to write all this detail! In our reading today and many of the following chapters we have much detail about the construction of the tabernacle and all the utensils etc. Without this detail the Israelites wouldn't have had a clue how to build the tabernacle. There have been attempts to replicate this structure and each of them is slightly different because the builders tell us that the details we have in the Bible are insufficient! This is where the children of Israel would look and remember who was at the centre of their nation and how important all the utensils etc. were as aids to worship. There are parallels today in our church buildings with the placing of the pulpit, lectern, altar and baptistry. The nearer to the centre an item is – the more doctrinally central it was to those who designed the building. So a sacramental approach puts the altar, or table central whilst a more evangelical approach puts the word in the centre. Even the positioning of the seats or pews in straight lines or arcs declare much of the theology of the fellowship who worship there. Our church buildings say much about us and what we believe just as the tabernacle showed what the Israelites believed. Next Sunday look around and compare what your church fabric builders believed compared to you!

The Appearance And Actions Of The Priests

The Big Picture

More details today which describe the priests and their apparel and consecration for ministry. Little would have changed by the time of Jesus so we are in a real sense learning of the priests with whom Jesus would have had daily contact. The robes and other items of priestly clothing are covered in some detail in our passage today. This also includes the Urim and Thummim, about which we know relatively little other than they were a device used to determine the will of God. We also read today of the consecration of the priests and how they are truly set aside and prepared for ministry of mediating between God and mankind.

Thinking Step

The Urim and the Thummim, literally 'lights and perfections' – were gemstones that were carried by the High Priest and used right up to the end of the Old Testament. They are mentioned in Ezra 2 and Nehemiah 7. It could be something like them that were the lots cast when Matthias was chosen to replace Judas in Acts 1:26.

Action Step

A key element in the consecration of the priests was the sprinkling of blood onto vital parts of the priest's body. You may pause and ask what relevance could this possibly have in the 21st century! Read on – then decide. 29:20 tells us that blood is put on the lobe of the right ear, the thumb of the right hand and the big toe of the right foot. The right ear is where many would have a gold ear ring which was their security in time of need. That's why ear rings were collected from the Israelites in order to make the golden calf. Instead of trusting in ear rings they trusted in the golden calf! What are you trusting in? Next was the right hand thumb, without which we can do very little, this was the reason thumbs were often amputated to disable prisoners in ancient times. Next time you use your right hand and thumb ask yourself, "Is my action glorifying God?" Lastly, blood was put on the big toe of the right foot. If you lose your big toes you have to learn to walk again! Wherever you walk today, is it a place where you would be happy to meet one of your church leaders? Whatever you trust in – everything you do – everywhere you go. Everything is vitally important to your Christian witness – as the Levitical priests knew only too well!

30 - Ministry Of The Priests
31 - Only The Best Is Good Enough!

Day 28
Exodus 30-31
28th January

Priests Are Prepared
And Tabernacle Builders Appointed

The Big Picture

We learn of the altar of incense today, a place where a sweet smell would ascend to Father God in Heaven. This was the forerunner of our eternal flames as it was intended to be used for the burning of incense for all generations. A half shekel coin is to be paid by everyone over 20 years of age, no matter if you are wealthy or poor. So that's where the Poll Tax idea came from! Practical spiritual gifting is recognised in appointing craftsmen Bezalel and Oholiab. Then a reminder to keep the Sabbath as Holy! The tablets of the Ten Commandments are handed to Moses on Mount Sinai, reminding us where all this was taking place.

Thinking Step

Ex 30:13 – Each person over 20 was to contribute to the tabernacle upkeep. Known as ransom money it was a silver piece valued at half a shekel. It's the same for Jesus in Matt 17:27 when Peter finds a coin (a shekel) in a fish's mouth. Enough temple tax for both Jesus and Peter, half a shekel each.

Action Step

Many people think that ministry is what you do as a minister or missionary. I remember when I first sensed God's call to paid ministry (I prefer that description as we are all full-timers!) I went to see my pastor for advice. He simply said I needed to get in touch with a theological college (he specified which!), do the training and then find a church. I said I didn't think that was what God was saying. He said, "Oh, in that case approach a missionary society (again he specified one) and train with them before going to the mission field." Once again I responded by saying that didn't seem the right path either. At this he told me that I obviously wasn't ready. "Pray and come back later!" In our reading today we learn of two men who were in ministry to make the tabernacle furniture. Gifted by God to play their part in ministry by making things! Unusual ministry! What ministry are you involved in? I believe all work, when done to the glory of God at His call and gifting, is ministry. That means your job is probably a task of ministry! You don't have to be 'in the ministry' to minister, you just have to be where God wants you and do what He has gifted you to do. Using this definition what ministry are you going to be involved in today?

Day 29
Exodus 32-34
29th January

32 - Moses Intercedes For Israel But Aaron Leads Them Astray
33 - Moses Talks To God And Sees His Glory
34 - Ten Commandments – Second Set Of Tablets!

Moses Is Faithful But Aaron Is Irresponsible!

The Big Picture

Moses comes down from the mountain remembering all the teaching God has given him with some of it engraved on two tablets of stone, the Ten Commandments. He is distraught when he sees Aaron leading the people in worship of the Golden calf. He smashes the tablets of stone which bore the Ten Commandments in God's own handwriting – and then grinds the golden calf into powder before sprinkling it in the drinking water for everyone to drink! This is only a small part of God's judgement. Moses takes two fresh tablets up the mountain and God writes the Ten Commandments again, returning with his face shining.

Thinking Step

Slow to learn...In Egypt, plagues 5 & 6 are aimed at gods represented by bulls and cows. We have Aaron's golden calf in today's reading; in 2 Chron. 11:15 Rehoboam appoints his own calf worshipping priests, whilst in Hosea 8:5-6 Samaria is told – "Throw out your calf-idol...it is not God."

Action Step

In the immortal words of Arnold Schwarzenegger's character from the 1984 science fiction thriller film 'The Terminator'..."I'll be back". Of course he was only repeating what Moses had said so long before! You would have thought they would have believed Moses wouldn't you? It was Moses who led the rescue out of Egypt, who got them through the Red Sea and who was away meeting God on their behalf. Well sadly they quickly forgot him and turned elsewhere. Of course Jesus said this too, or at least it was said on His behalf on the day He ascended back to Heaven as recorded in the first chapter of Acts of the Apostles. "This same Jesus will return." How many times do we hear on TV "See you next week when we will be here again" or words to that effect. We believe them don't we and they will fail us one day and die, like us, – whereas Jesus is reliable and eternal! Let's live today as if Jesus could come back before tomorrow begins. When we watch our next TV programme that is due to be continued next week let's remember that Jesus could be here before that! He is the One who keeps all His promises and defeated death for us. He said He will return and He will. You can count on it so don't be taken by surprise if today's the day!

35 - Generous Offerings From The People
36 - Great Work From Chosen Craftsmen
37 - The Ark Of The Covenant Is Created
38 - The Altar And Courtyard Are Made

Day 30
Exodus 35-38
30th January

Generous Support
Means Progress With Tabernacle

The Big Picture

Moses begins to teach the Israelites what is required to build the first tabernacle to the design that God has decreed. The offerings come in thick and fast. The craftsmen led by Bezalel and Oholiab have more than enough to do all the work required. The curtains, boards and veils are made to the highest specification. The ark of the covenant is made in acacia wood and covered with gold, this is followed by other items of furniture as well as the altar, laver and work on the surrounding court. Finally we have a summary of all materials used including lots of gold, silver and bronze.

Thinking Step

We see the veil installed in all its splendour. It forms a screen between the Holy Place and the Holy of Holies. This will be replicated in Solomon's temple later. There is also a veil in Herod's temple and it is this which is torn from top to bottom by God, when Jesus is crucified – Matt 27:50-51.

Action Step

Well it's almost a month since we started our reading though the Bible. You may suspect you have heard some of today's reading before – well that's because you have! Maybe God just wanted you and many others to hear it a second time! I remember leading a midweek Bible study in a local church when I covered both chapters of Haggai. Imagine my reaction when told that another visiting preacher had covered this book the previous week! My embarrassment was removed when one of the congregation commented "It must be that God wanted us to hear that again!" It's just the same when God repeats things in the Bible. Sometimes once is just not adequate. When you hear much of Exodus the detail can be very intense. If you think of it as vital, just as vital as an accurate cake recipe – all the details are essential. God is wholehearted in His approach to the Tabernacle knowing that the symbolism and detail would relate directly to Jesus Himself. In the light of this let's make sure we are wholehearted in our approach to our daily life and witness. You've made a great start and in just another day we will be starting our read through two of Jesus' favourite books – Leviticus and Deuteronomy. Ask God now to make them interesting for you – and He will!

Day 31
Exodus 39-40
31st January

39 - Tabernacle And Priests Are All Ready
40 - Tabernacle Is Completed And God Fills It!

At Last – The Tabernacle Is Completed!

The Big Picture

At last the priestly garments are completed and the excitement is at fever pitch as the finishing touches are made to everything that has been so lovingly made – to the glory of God. A final inspection is made by Moses to make sure that everything has been done just as God planned. Then the final act of the Tabernacle being erected! We read of the cloud covering the Tabernacle and the glory of the Lord filling the whole place. A major step has been taken towards the Israelites finally settling in the Promised land but there are more lessons to learn before that happens.

Thinking Step

When you see the priestly robes you know which are God's favourite colours don't you? Blue or should I say Royal Blue, Purple or should I say Priestly Purple – both manufactured by a forerunner of Lydia – Acts 16:14. Finally Scarlet or should I say Blood Red. So many signs of the ultimate Priestly King – Jesus the Christ.

Action Step

Upon completion of the Tabernacle the Israelites resolve to only go where and when God decrees. What a great idea! 40:35 tells us that God filled the Tabernacle to such a degree that there was no room for Moses! Just like John the Baptist was to say so many centuries later – "He must increase and I must decrease." Isn't that true for each of us today? It is many years since I asked Jesus to be my Lord and Saviour and I repented of all my sins and asked Him to forgive me. Since then I have discovered other sins every day and I have had to repent and ask for forgiveness. I remember hearing a preacher say, "I often wonder what I did surrender to Jesus on my conversion because I have had to repent and surrender every day since!" It's called sanctification and it's a process not an event. Whatever He is saying to you now – just do it. The worst that can happen is that you get it wrong! Do you think God can't handle that? Seize the day and promise God today that, as He leads, you will follow. What about that problem you have never ever been able to get to grips with? Only you know what it is. Move over and let Jesus take care of it. More of Him and less of you.

Leviticus

Leviticus

We are now about to look at one of the favourite books of Jesus! He will have learned sections of this at rabbinic school by heart. This is the first of two major teaching books of the Pentateuch, the other one being Deuteronomy. After the action and travelling narratives of Genesis and Exodus we now attend a one month 'event' held at the foot of Mount Sinai. The subject being covered is how to get 'Egypt out of Israel!' How to make God's chosen people into God's Holy people. We begin with the five offerings showing the way to approach a Holy God. Then the seven feasts which show us how to live in fellowship with a Holy God. This book concentrates on the law of the priests rather than all of the Levites as may be inferred by its title, hence the Talmud's title for it is 'The law of the Priests.'

Below is an acrostic which summarises each chapter of the book.

1. Holiness demands burnt offerings
2. Acceptance of meal offerings
3. Necessity of peace offerings
4. Demand for sin offering
5. Burnt offerings for trespasses
6. Offering laws for priests
7. Offering laws for priests
8. Keeping the priest consecrated

9. Offering of Aaron's sacrifice
10. Fire consumes Nadab, Abihu

11. Warning against unclean animals
12. Offerings for birth purification
13. Requirements for unclean lepers
14. Sign of cleansing lepers
15. Hygiene for human uncleanness
16. Institution of annual atonement
17. Prominence of the blood

18. Forbidding of sexual impurities
19. Orders to be holy
20. Restrictions against moral sin

21. Priest's qualifications before God
22. Respect for God's offerings
23. Institution of religious feasts
24. Eating the holy bread
25. Sabbatical year and jubilee
26. Trouble promised for disobedience
27. Seriousness of keeping vows

A Deeper Look At Israel's
Offerings & Feasts

OFFERINGS	LOOKS BACK ON	LOOKS FORWARD TO
Burnt (voluntary)	Payment for sins	The perfect sacrifice of Christ
Meal (voluntary)	All possessions are a gift from God	The greatest gift of all is Christ
Peace (voluntary)	Gratitude for fellowship with God	Fellowship with God through Christ
Sin (required)	Payment for intentional and unintentional sin	All sins forgiven through Christ
Guilt (required)	Repayment and compensation for sins committed	The penalty is paid in full by Christ

AGE	MONTH	DAY(S)	FEAST	LOOKS BACK ON	LOOKS FORWARD TO
CHRIST'S FIRST COMING	1st	14	Passover	Redemption of Firstborn	Christ's Redeeming Death
		15-22	Unleavened Bread	Separation from Other Nations	Communion of the Saints
		16	Firstfruits	Harvest in the Land	Christ's Resurrection
	3rd	50 days after Firstfruits	Pentecost	Completion of Harvest	Sending of Holy Spirit
SECOND COMING	7th	1	Trumpets	New Year for Israel	Regathering of Israel
		10	Day of Atonement	Israel's National Sin	Israel's National Repentance
		15-22	Tabernacles	Israel in the Wilderness	Israel's National Blessing

Day 32   1 - The Burnt Offering
Leviticus 1-3   2 - The Meal Offering
1st February   3 - The Peace Offering

Offerings For Those In Fellowship With God

The Big Picture

These chapters cover the first three of the five offerings. These three are the sweet offerings which are offered to God when you are in fellowship with Him. They are voluntary and serve as a way of showing an individual's devotion to God. The burnt offering was a sign of total commitment to God; everything being consumed on the altar. The level of offering was determined by the wealth of the worshipper. The material nature of the meal offering confirmed that everything you had, all your ma terial wealth, belonged to God. The peace offering or fellowship offering as it is sometimes called was a public sacrifice expressing thanks to God and often included the making of a vow of service by the worshipper.

Thinking Step

Ever wondered why there is so much graphic detail in Leviticus? Well, I heard of a man who found Christ after reading Leviticus! He read the details and marvelled at the accuracy. He then read the rest of the Bible and found Jesus as Lord and Saviour. Oh, I almost forgot to mention – he was a butcher!

Action Step

When we read about animal sacrifices and the like it's hard to relate this to everyday life in the 21st century isn't it? However, the concept of making sacrifices is very much alive today. We often refer to athletes making sacrifices, or congregations giving sacrificially in order to finance a programme they believe God has given them. So the idea of sacrifice is not as alien as it seems at first.
When the Apostle Paul writes to the newly planted Christian church in Rome he pleads with them to offer their bodies as living sacrifices and they knew what he meant. I believe we can understand this too. We need to offer our lives as sacrifices to God in such a way that they are no longer ours but His. Our sacrifices can be very down to earth too. If you are able to financially support something that you are sure is of God – then please do it. Which will you choose of the many seeking your support? Many Christians use prayer letters and funding appeals as Bible bookmarks and prayer reminders – do you? As soon as you can take the opportunity to use one of these 'bookmarks' and make a sacrificial response by sending a gift. The recipient will be so blessed – and so will the giver!

Offerings For Those Seeking Fellowship With God

The Big Picture

These two chapters cover in detail the offerings that are necessary when individual Israelite priests were out of fellowship with God due to an act of unintentional sin. The sin offering of a bull (which was very costly) was to be offered for this wrongdoing. A similar offering must be made when the Israelites as a whole commit unintentional sin. When the leaders or other individuals commit similar sins – then the animal to sacrifice is less – a goat. The guilt offering went a step further and was required when restitution or some recompense is required to be made by the offender.

Thinking Step

Places of sacrifice come and go! Solomon's Temple is destroyed by the Babylonians. Zerubbabel's temple doesn't seem to count as the next one Herod's temple, is always called the second temple! Then the Romans destroy it in AD 70. It is of course our body which is the true temple – 1 Cor. 6:19.

Action Step

Today's offerings in Leviticus are for unintentional sins! They seem very important to God so it gives us a glimpse of how intentional sin must truly offend our Holy God and Father in Heaven. When we do the very things that we know are against what God wants us to do. This is a very difficult subject to teach about as we are all guilty of deliberately going against God aren't we? When the preacher preaches on this subject have you noticed how very appropriate it always is – for the person in front of us or the one behind us but never for you or me! I remember moving into a town to become a pastor at one of the local churches. One day I was irritated by my paper not arriving that morning and decided to visit the newsagents to get things sorted out. Of course by the time I arrived the issue was magnified in my mind and was now a big problem! I should have returned home but I didn't! After 'speaking my mind' I was on my way out when the shop assistant said "I hope it doesn't happen again, what must you think of us as you have only just moved into town to be a Pastor!" Counting to ten may not be in the Bible but it's great advice for you and me today before we act foolishly and sin deliberately!

A Second Look At The Offerings

The Big Picture

The five offerings are covered again in these two chapters but this time addressed specifically to the priesthood. In the Hebrew text this section is a distinct unit and creates a manual of sacrificial procedures. To our eyes it may appear that it is simply a repeat but these chapters tend to form the 'how to' for the priests after the 'what' has been made clear in the earlier chapters. The latter part of our reading seems to be for all the people rather than just the priests and is an exhortation to avoid fat and blood in your everyday diet. Fat was for God and the priesthood alone and blood was the source of life and that made it sacred.

Thinking Step

In the New Testament Zaccheus declares in Luke 18 that he will give back fourfold to all he has defrauded. Our reading today tells us that God only requires full repayment plus one fifth more. Better Bible knowledge could have saved Zaccheus a lot of money – but God does love a cheerful giver!

Action Step

Leviticus 6:7 tells us that the priest shall make atonement before the Lord for the worshipper's guilt offering. Forgiveness for any of the things which they may have done to incur guilt. Now that's a broad sweep of forgiveness! Of course we now have no need for a separate priest as we have direct access to the Lord Himself. I remember inviting a coach driver into a church service only for him to refuse because he couldn't possibly go to church. I pressed him and he confessed that he drank alcohol, smoked cigarettes and gambled on the horses. Plus lots more that he doesn't care to remember! He found it quite incredible that none of these barred him from God and all were forgiveable, even the forgotten ones! Even the sins we have forgotten, God will forgive when we ask for His forgiveness for all our past sins. Of course the devil will remind you of your unconfessed sin every time you are about to be useful to God in specific service. During today when past sins come to mind why not ask God to give you a poor 'sin-memory' but a good 'grateful heart' memory. Once forgiven the only one who can benefit from remembering is the devil himself, now remember that when he comes calling! A prayer worth repeating today is – "Thanks for the reminder of just how much God has forgiven me in my life!"

8 - Preparation Of The Priests
9 - Offerings For The Priests And People
10 - Aaron's Sons - Good And Bad!

Day 35
Leviticus 8-10
4th February

Priests And People Get Ready To Serve God

The Big Picture

Now for three chapters teaching the priests about the law pertaining to them specifically. They need to be cleansed and consecrated using water, blood and oil. The unique ritual involving ear, thumb and toe from Exodus 29 is reviewed again. They also need to wear the correct clothing. Sacrifices are made for the priests and these are followed by offerings for the people. Chapter 10 gets very personal when it retells the account of the four sons of Aaron who were all serving as priests. All are rebuked for not doing their jobs correctly and two of them, Nadab and Abihu, pay for their sins with their lives.

Thinking Step

Nadab and Abihu die before the Lord! The fire they were offering seems to have been theirs rather than from the altar which was the only source of Holy fire. In addition, incense was only to be added by the high priest and then only on the day of Atonement.

Action Step

Aaron has four sons who follow him into the priesthood. Sadly none of them did the job well. Nadab and Abihu are judged by fire and die before the Lord whilst Eleazar and Ithamar sin when making the grain offering. You see, a godly parent doesn't inevitably produce a godly child, even with a godly Uncle Moses! Good parenting is made up of lots of small things. Don't be overawed by the task, let's think of one positive thing and do it – today! Let's take the idea of speaking with love and firmness and meaning what we say. Children without barriers are children who have no indication of where to stop! I clearly remember my wife telling our boys when they were very young, that if they didn't behave better one Sunday afternoon then they wouldn't be attending the special baptismal evening service. They called her bluff being convinced that we wouldn't stop them going to church! They lost! My wife really missed going to the service but it was a lesson well learned and remembered for a long time, particularly by the boys. Constantly changing your mind, until you find the point where your children agree, is a recipe for disaster. Jesus said that we should let our "Yes" be "Yes". Let's try it today – then you will really want your children to be just like their mother or father – firm and reliable!

Take Care With Your Diet
And Rejoice With Your Children

The Big Picture

We now have lots of details about the sorts of food that are permissible for Jews. The first detailed record of what kosher food is. A very comprehensive list that makes interesting reading when you consider this would have been a set of rules that Jesus would have honoured when He was here on earth. The idea of clean and unclean animals actually goes back to Noah who according to Gen. 7, took seven of each clean animal as well as two of each unclean animal into the ark. The second part of today's reading records the laws relating to childbirth and the ceremony of circumcision for each male child. There is also detail of the sacrifice required when presenting a child to the Lord.

Thinking Step

At the birth of a child 12:7-8 tells us that a woman who cannot afford to bring a lamb, must bring two turtledoves or two young pigeons. This is exactly what Mary brought after the birth of Jesus. Luke 2:22-24 serves as confirmation that Jesus gave up everything and lived amongst us in a materially poor family.

Action Step

From our reading today you can see just how important it was to God what was allowed into the Israelite's bodies. We read specific details of which animals could be eaten and which were forbidden. It all reminds us of how pure God wants us to be. Today it is really hard to take in only good things. Of course we can watch our diet by reading food labels properly but what about what goes in through our eyes and ears? I have read that when the original 'walkman' was invented its creator shelved the whole idea commenting, "Who would want music in their ears all day, this is not a good idea!" Well, you can't be right all the time can you! Being careful about what gets into your head is very important if we are not to fill it up with unhelpful, or even worse, ungodly content. So be careful what's on your radio or iPod. Only listen to what you would be happy to have broadcast on a public loudspeaker in your name! As far as filling our minds with visual dross – I was told a story recently about a man who always sent his wife to the newsagents to buy his daily paper. He didn't want to see the magazines and other things that tempted him so he didn't go where he would see such things! We do have choices about what goes into our bodies, so choose carefully.

13 - Keep An Eye On Personal Hygiene
14 - It's All About Ear, Thumb And Toe!
15 - Similar Problems For Men And Women

Day 37
Leviticus 13-15
6th February

Cleanliness Is Next To Godliness!

The Big Picture

These three chapters cover in some detail the laws relating to leprosy and bodily discharges. These conditions were very important in ancient times and reveal a God who is passionately involved with His people and determined that they are given the best information and advice to combat these conditions and diseases. Details of examination of both the people as well as their garments and houses show us how purity and health are issues with our loving Heavenly Father. In chapter 15 we are given the laws regarding bodily discharges from both men and women before a brief summary of the purposes of these laws.

Thinking Step

The detailed procedures involving the ear, thumb and toe as in 8:23 are repeated here in chapter 14 for the cleansing of the people. It's worth noting that as well as blood there is the addition of oil in both passages. We are to be covered by the blood and indwelled by the oil of the Spirit for effective ministry.

Action Step

Have you ever gone to the doctors' surgery with a trivial condition that you found both difficult and embarrassing to describe to the doctor? Well, our reading today reflects some of that as we cover detailed descriptions of bodily ailments and discharges. Of course some of the conditions described in our reading today were serious but many were not. Remember however that God made us and knows how our bodies work – and knows our conditions even before we think to tell Him! He is interested in our small problems as well as the larger ones so don't ever think anything in your life is so insignificant that you cannot talk to God about it. I remember when we were first married and decided to do our first wall papering together. Neither of us had done it before and it was a bit like 'the blind leading the blind'. By midnight, when tempers were getting shorter by the minute – in desperation we decided to ask God to help us with our wallpapering! It worked – and things started to move a lot smoother. Of course, wallpapering is not high on God's agenda but we are! He stepped in to ease our situation because He loves us. When seemingly trivial things are irritating you, mention it to your Father in Heaven. Anything spring to mind? Ask God now to step in and help you through an irritation!

Atonement For The Whole Nation

The Big Picture

The National Day of Atonement. The one day when the High Priest was allowed to enter the Holy of Holies. This occurred six months after Passover. The day when the scape goat was released to symbolically take away the sins of the people. Today this celebration is called Yom Kippur and is celebrated by Jews around Sept/Oct. It is the most sacred of Jewish holidays, the 'Sabbath of Sabbaths'. On Yom Kippur the Jews believe that the Book of Life is closed and sealed and those who have repented for their sins are granted a good and happy New Year. Towards the end of today's reading we have the laws concerning the location of sacrifices and the regulations about the use of blood.

Thinking Step

The reference to the scapegoat in Lev 16:26 of course refers to what happened at the Tabernacle. After the temple is built, this escape gateway is very likely to have been near where we now see the Golden Gate – which is the area where Jesus entered on Palm Sunday and where He will enter when He returns!

Action Step

During one of our recent visits to Israel we had the thrill of visiting a life size replica of the Tabernacle which had been erected to show in a graphic way, what the Tabernacle and all its furniture would have looked like. It was smaller than I had imagined but despite the grandeur of the altar and the sacrificial things, it was the Holy of Holies that touched me the most. Representing the place where the High Priest would be able to make forgiveness available for the whole nation. The guide told us that we couldn't go in for photos, as a reminder of how holy that place was in the original Tabernacle. Of course today this full atonement has been fulfilled in the Lord Jesus Christ whose sacrifice atones for our sins – and not only our sins but the sins of the whole world – according to 1 John 2:2. I have often thought when I see large crowds, representing the whole world if you like, how few individuals will have claimed the forgiveness for which Christ died. A large football crowd or a full shopping centre at Christmas, how many have claimed forgiveness for their sins? All that potential forgiveness and so little received! Why not offer a silent prayer for those next to you when you're next in a crowd. You never know what it may start!

18 - Sexual Purity Is Essential
19 - Social Purity Is Beneficial
20 - Inevitable Penalties That Follow Disobedience

Day 39
Leviticus 18-20
8th February

Sex And The City – As God Wants Them

The Big Picture

We now move from national laws to personal laws. These chapters explain the importance God gives to purity amongst His people and the need for His people to be sanctified. The laws of sexual sin and social order are explained in some detail. Descriptions of the penalties for breaking these laws are also given with a final summary of the reasons why God gave these laws of sanctification to His people. In chapter 20:26 this is summed up beautifully. God said, "You must be holy because I, the Lord, am holy. I have set you apart from all other people to be my very own."

Thinking Step

18:18 says – "While your wife is living, do not marry her sister and have sexual relations with her, for they would be rivals." I think if Jacob had known this he would have said, "Amen" to that. I am sure Leah and Rachel would have agreed too!

Action Step

If you had to sum up the message of Leviticus it would be to get Egypt out of Israel now that Israel was out of Egypt! To become God's holy people. The story is told of a man who came up to that great baptist preacher Charles Spurgeon to declare that after many struggles, he had finally achieved total sanctification and was experiencing totally holy living – the old man was finally dead and the Holy Spirit had total command of his life. Spurgeon mused for a moment and then took a large glass of water and threw it all over him. When the man finally manage to catch his breath and his vitriolic outcry for such an action had ceased, Spurgeon said, "Just as I suspected, the old man is not dead, he was simply asleep!" In chapters 20, 21 and again in chapter 22 we have this declaration; "I am the Lord who sanctifies you." No matter how many sacrifices are offered and no matter how determined an individual may be, only God can sanctify us. Of course that doesn't mean we don't have to try but to try knowing that without God's added input our endeavours are in vain. Today, when you are just ready to give up, remember it's not up to you alone – it is the Lord who sanctifies you! Now ask Him to sanctify you some more today!

Day 40
Leviticus 21-23
9th February

21 - Priests Must Be Responsible
22 - Priests Must Be Obedient
23 - Days To Give Thanks

Live Holy Lives And Celebrate The Feasts

The Big Picture

The standard for conduct amongst the priests is very high and there are many things that they cannot get involved in, otherwise they cannot continue to fulfil their role as God's link with His people. We read today of these laws concerning the priests and the High Priest. There are also details regarding prohibitions on some who cannot be allowed to be priests even though they are of the line of Aaron and would otherwise qualify. Finally we have the laws concerning sanctification of the weekly Sabbath and annual feasts such as Passover, Unleavened Bread, First Fruits, Pentecost, Trumpets, Day of Atonement and Tabernacles.

Thinking Step

23:22 reads – "When you reap the harvest of your land, do not reap to the very edges of your field or gather the gleanings of your harvest. Leave them for the poor and the alien. I am the LORD your God." A repeat of 19:9, anticipating Ruth's visit to Israel many years later as an alien Moabite in need of food.

Action Step

A civilised society has many rules and conventions that keep it together. Leviticus outlines some for the Israelites and they are all aimed at making them God's holy people. I remember witnessing a group of people on a train who realised what they were doing was not lawful. Their leader (an ordained minister as it happened) encouraged them to carry on doing what was unlawful as he told them, "Rules are for fools!" I realise that many in our country believe this mantra but I am convinced that God's people should not. At a ministers' fraternal I was attending many years ago we welcomed a new minister who had been miraculously converted from a life of petty crime and burglary. As the meeting progressed something was said by the new man which raised the question, "Are you still stealing – but just small things now?" The reply was brief and to the point. "Are you still breaking the speed limit?" A discussion ensued regarding which laws it was okay to break! Then the letter of James was quoted – "For whoever keeps the whole law and yet stumbles at just one point is guilty of breaking all of it." In my experience some of the worst drivers are Christians! When you next drive remember that we cannot choose which laws to obey! We must above all others, be seen as lawful people.

Be Good Stewards Of The Land And All It Sustains

The Big Picture

Finally, we have a timely reminder of God's standards in His sanctuary. Then God tells His people how to look after the land and make the most of it, as good stewards. Resting it in accordance with God's laws. Instruction on knowing the difference between right and wrong follows with the urging to do what is right – always. Restoration is promised for those who break the law but who then truly repent. Keeping your word is the final subject to be covered – and how to keep any vows you make to the Lord when it involves such things as your animals, houses or fields. Last but not least, there is very clear teaching regarding the discipline of tithing.

Thinking Step

When Naboth refused to sell his vineyard to Ahab in 1 Kings 21, he was simply obeying God's word in Lev. 25:23 – "The land must never be sold on a permanent basis, for the land belongs to me. You are only foreigners and tenant farmers working for me." Naboth spoke the truth "The Lord forbids it."

Action Step

Did you hear of the man who promised God that he would always tithe his income? Year by year he faithfully gave ten percent to the Lord. As he became more successful, his salary increased until what he was giving to the Lord was more than he had earned when he first made the promise. It seemed such a lot that he asked God if there was something that could be done to help stop the increase in his monthly donations. Without hesitation God said, "Leave it to Me and I will get your salary reduced!" Of course this is only a made up story but can you imagine how the impact of the Church of Christ could be multiplied if all the efforts to raise finance were no longer needed and channelled into other aspects of ministry! I've heard it said that there are two kinds of people in the Kingdom of God. Those who do the work and those who finance it! Of course this is far too simplistic but there is some truth in it. If we all gave at least one tenth of our income – unlike the early disciples who actually sold their possessions and property in order to finance God's work – I am convinced our impact in the world would be amazingly improved. So if you are not giving at least a tenth, ask God today if you should start!

Numbers

Numbers

This great book is called 'In the Wilderness' in Hebrew. It has three distinct parts. The first records a census of the generation that left Egypt, this takes place at the foot of Mount Sinai and is the first step to a nation being formed. The second records their failure to enter the Promised Land and the forty years of wilderness wandering and the amazing way God takes care of them. The third describes the new generation and their preparation to take the step of faith and go into the Promised Land. The whole generation that escaped from Egypt dies in the wilderness, with the exception of Moses, Joshua and Caleb. We learn more about these exceptions before the second generation does the right thing and begins to trust God in preparation for the entry into the land promised to Abraham, Isaac and Jacob..

Below is an acrostic which summarises each chapter of the book.

1. Tallying Israel by tribes
2. Host organized for marching
3. Exchanging Levites for first-born

4. Work of the Levites
5. Instructions for judging adulterers
6. Law of the Nazirites
7. Description of leaders' offerings
8. Emphasis on Levitical cleansing
9. Record of second Passover
10. Nation leaves Mount Sinai
11. Elders and quails given
12. Sin of Miriam's murmuring
13. Spies sent from Kadesh-barnea

14. Judgement on Israel's unbelief
15. Offerings for the land
16. Uprising led by Korah
17. Rod of Aaron buds
18. Necessity of priestly service
19. Eleazar and red heifer
20. Years of wandering end

21. Overthrow of the Amorites
22. Fear of Balaam's donkey

23. Inspiration of Balaam's prophecies
24. Scope of Balaam's prophecies
25. Reward of Phinehas's zeal
26. Audit of Israel's tribes
27. Endorsement of Joshua's leading
28. Law of offerings reviewed

29. Teachings for seventh month
30. Oath and vow laws

31. Conquest of the Midianites
32. Abode of Reuben, Gad
33. Numbering of Israel's journeys
34. Assigning of land borders
35. Appointing cities of refuge
36. Necessity of tribal marriage

Day 42
Numbers 1-4
11th February

1 - Counting The Army For The First Time
2 - Arranging The People In Good Order
3 - Counting Of The Priests
4 - Ministry Of The Priests

The People And Priests Are All Counted

The Big Picture

There's more than one way to look at the first four chapters of Numbers. They can be seen as simply counting the people – but that is only part of the story. Each tribe is allocated a space for their camp when they are not on the move. All the tribes surround the Ark of the Covenant as they are counted and moulded into a nation. Men over 20 years old are counted separately and the Levites were counted separately too. If we add all the numbers together the total number of people were certainly in the millions! Everyone is arranged in family, clans and tribal groups for the first flexing of the muscles of God's people!

Thinking Step

There are over thirty references in the first two chapters of Numbers to the counting of the army – or more accurately the men over 20 years of age. This practice is still popular even when they have no formal army. At the feeding of the 5,000 they once again only count the men (Matt 14:21).

Action Step

God never loses sight of His ultimate plan. In the Sinai wilderness He is looking ahead to the cross and our salvation. He creates the sign of the cross with the spacing of the tribes around the Ark. We see a throng of humanity, God sees a crowd of individuals and loves every one of them. It's the same today, God loves individuals not multitudes! Throughout history some of the greatest leaders in the world have used people as pawns in their power games – but our God treats each one of us as a unique individual! We read in the New Testament that God knows us intimately even down to the number of hairs on our head. The same could be said for these Israelites who form the sign of the cross around the Ark of the Covenant in today's narrative. God doesn't crave the adoration of millions, He wants a relationship with millions of individuals. Throughout your life you will meet people about whom you know nothing – but our Father in Heaven does! Rather than dealing with a taxi driver or a shop assistant today why not do what God does and deal with specific people who are probably living their lives without any knowledge of the living God. It could be your privilege to share something of His love and concern for them. They will be pleasantly surprised and you will have touched the heart of God.

5 - Be Separate And Pure
6 - Nazarite Vow And Aaron's Blessing
7 - The Tribes Support The Tabernacle
8 - The Levites Are Prepared

Day 43
Numbers 5-8
12th February

The Whole Of Israel Is Prepared

The Big Picture

The Israelites are prepared for entry into the promised land little knowing that it is still forty years away! They are sanctified by cleaning up the camp and sending away to the area outside the camp, any of their number who are unclean. Repentance and restitution take place as the people prepare to leave the Sinai wilderness as a nation dedicated to the living God who has redeemed them out of Egypt. Nazirite dedication is fully explained to those who wish to dedicate themselves totally to the Lord. Finally, donations are given and the Levites consecrated. All is now ready for the celebration of Passover before leaving Sinai.

Thinking Step

Christians never retire! Preachers just go on and on! The Levites served for a limited period of time only. In 8:25 we read Levites are to retire from work when they reach fifty years of age. By the time of Jesus they had to have rotas of service so that all could serve for a time. Luke 1:8.

Action Step

Our reading today includes the Aaronic blessing which is still regularly used today in many services. What wonderful words and concepts are contained in these ancient verses. Just three lines; each one longer than the one before. In our reading this blessing follows the Nazirite passage which is addressed to the more committed Israelites who wish to go that extra step and become even more committed to the Lord. Aaron's blessing is specifically for the Nazirites but also for the whole nation of Israel; in other words it is applicable to everyone not just the more dedicated amongst us! Each of the three lines begins with the Lord's Name – Adonai and then has two verbs. The first one requests action from God and the second one details what happens as He acts.

May the LORD bless you and protect you.
When God blesses us we are truly secure.
May the LORD smile on you and be gracious to you.
Living in God's light is real life.
May the LORD show you His favour and give you peace.
Be at peace. He loves you personally!

Try to read this several times today and truly enjoy God's eternal blessings in your life. Remember – whatever your state of mind these promises are for ALL of God's people - and that includes YOU

Day 44
Numbers 9-12
13th February

9 - Passover Celebrated And A Guiding Cloud Appears
10 - Silver Trumpets And 'Off We Go!'
11 - Grumbling People And A Generous God
12 - Miriam And Aaron Rebel But God Is Good

The Long Journey Begins

The Big Picture

Passover is celebrated and they are ready to take the next step. More than a year after leaving Egypt the Israelites set off for the Promised Land. They experience guidance from a cloud and follow it until it stops, marking their camping place for the night. Guidance also comes from the blowing of two silver trumpets. Complaining among the Israelites tries the patience of Moses and even tests God. The people long for the 'good old days in Egypt'. Moses complained too – about the people God had entrusted to him. Quail and manna continue to be the staple diet for these ungrateful people. Aaron and Miriam rebel and Moses has to intercede.

Thinking Step

Numbers 9:12 – is fulfilled in John 19:33. Death by crucifixion was death by asphyxiation. As the victim slumped down in exhaustion, breathing became harder and ultimately they suffocated. As an act of 'kindness' Roman soldiers would break the victim's legs so they could not raise themselves to breath a few more desperate breaths before dying.

Action Step

In the early frustrating days of the journey to the Promised Land as they left the Sinai wilderness, the Israelites began a complaining attitude that they honed to perfection during the next forty years. They tested the patience of both Moses and God but God remained steadfastly faithful to them. Actually, so did Moses but he did lose his temper on more than one occasion! In our passage today we read these marvellous words in 11:23 – when the Lord says to Moses, "Is My arm too short (or lost its power)? Now you will see whether or not my word comes true!" We read that Moses immediately shared this good news with the people because he knew it was accurate and that the Lord could be trusted. In the trials and difficulties that today will undoubtedly bring, try to bear these thoughts in mind. Every time you reach out to touch something or pick something up rejoice that your arm is long enough – just like God's! His word continues to be reliable and every promise we will read as we read through the whole Bible, is as trustworthy today as when it was originally made. He doesn't change and His promises are reliable. Remember that when you can't quite reach things on the top shelf. Unlike ours, God's arm is always long enough!

Twelve Spies Show More Preparation Is Needed

The Big Picture

"Taste and see" says David in Psalm 34. Similarly, the Israelites are urged to send in spies to see just how good this land is. The twelve spies, one from each tribe, vote 10:2 not to enter the promised land because of giants and high walled cities. As a result of this, a whole generation is destined to wander in the wilderness – and a whole generation dies in unbelief. The ten unbelieving spies die almost immediately too. The thank offerings and sin offerings are reviewed along with some teaching about tassels on garments. Rebellion by Korah and Aaron results in judgement from God. Israel rebels too and God has to pass judgement before further progress can be made.

Thinking Step

Tassels are fascinating! A blue thread was the most expensive dye and was a reminder that the commandments are beyond price. They became a mark of authority and social standing. Matt 23:5 tells us of the woman who touched the fringe or tassels of the garment of Jesus. She reached out to tap into His authority, for healing.

Action Step

A whole generation of Israelites missed out on the Promised Land because of fear! 13:28 – "The people living there are powerful and their towns are large and fortified. We even saw giants there, the descendants of Anak!" Often, when God leads us into a new situation it can appear totally beyond us – but that's only because it is – if we try to carry out God's will in our strength. The spies acknowledge that God was correct, the land is fruitful and flowing with milk and honey – however...and there always seems to be a however doesn't there – the spies didn't think they could win, even with God's help! What an insult to our Heavenly Father. Ironically when the next generation goes into the promised land under Joshua they find the well fortified cities surrounded with high walls and God tells them, "Don't touch the walls! I will knock them down without help from you!" In fact He could have knocked them down forty years earlier but the Israelites didn't trust Him. They wasted forty years – be sure you don't! If you have a seemingly impossible obstacle in your way, ask God to do a 'Jericho' for you today – don't just wander off into the wilderness and do something else, only to find years later that God could have solved your problem – if only you had asked!

Day 46
Numbers 17-20
15th February

17 - Supremacy Of Aaron's Rod
18 - Support Of The Priesthood
19 - Sacrifice Of The Red Heifer
20 - Miriam And Aaron Die As Journey Is Delayed

The Priesthood Is Established As Israel Wanders

The Big Picture

Things are not going well since they refused to enter the Promised Land. God confirms the divine call of the priests and how they are to be supported by the rest of the people as they carry out their priestly duties. Chapter 19 gives some detailed teaching on the red heifer. It is to be without blemish, sacrificed totally outside the camp. There are many parallels with Jesus and what He will ultimately do on the cross. Miriam, sister of Moses dies and is buried at Kadesh Oasis, the place where the spies had set out to explore the Promised Land. They travel to Edom but are refused entry, then Aaron dies on Mount Hor.

Thinking Step

At the end of today's reading the Israelites, children of Jacob, are refused access to travel through Edom. The Edomites, children of Esau, are very intransigent even when the Israelites promise to stick to the main road. The family feud that began in Gen. 27 when Jacob tricked Esau out of his inheritance, is still alive amongst their descendants.

Action Step

18:20 – God says to Aaron – "I am your portion and your inheritance." When the land is divided amongst the tribes, the Levites and priests don't get an allocation like the other tribes. Here, before it happens, God tells them what will happen but not to worry as He will be all they need. In years to come when the priests look around at what is happening to the rest of the tribes when they finally get into the promised land, this promise must have been so precious. God is always our portion, He is always sufficient no matter what. Have you ever looked at others in Church and thought, "They seem to have it all together and their Christian faith is so much more balanced than mine." Don't be fooled – often it's just that some people can 'act' better than others! Don't just rely on feelings and emotions, they come and go! God's word is the solid foundation upon which our lives can and will stand firm. We need constant reassuring of this truth. That's probably why the Apostle Paul told believers in Thes. 5:11 "Encourage one another..." and the writer to the Hebrews repeats this in chapters 3 and 10. So, who are you going to encourage with the good news that God is our portion and He is sufficient. Maybe you need to tell yourself first, then share it with someone else!

74

Help Is Sought From Balaam And His Donkey

The Big Picture

The Canaanites attacked Israel with some success but with God's help the Israelites defeat them and destroy their cities. However, they are still destined to wander in the wilderness for more years yet! Following more complaints from the Israelites God tells Moses to create a bronze serpent that will heal all who look at it when they are suffering from snake bites which are a result of their rebellion. Victories over the Amorites and Bashan lead the Israelites to Moab where the locals are terrified by them and their reputation. They call on a prophet called Balaam but thankfully he listens to his donkey who makes more sense than the Moabites!

Thinking Step

Balaam's influence lasts for centuries. Rev 2:14 – part of the letter to the church at Pergamum, "Nevertheless, I have a few things against you, there are some among you who hold to the teaching of Balaam, who taught Balak to entice the Israelites to sin so that they ate food sacrificed to idols and committed sexual immorality."

Action Step

Balaam struggled with putting into practice what he knew in theory. On several occasions he says that he must obey the Lord no matter what He tells him to do. It's only when his donkey rebukes him and things don't work out that Balaam does the right thing and returns home! Doing what you know is right can be hard at times. Did you hear about the new minister who preached his first sermon in his new church and really impressed the enthusiastic congregation with his knowledge and great communication skills. Everyone looked forward to the next sermon from this great orator. The church would surely grow with a man like this at the helm. The following Sunday he preached again but preached the same sermon – much to the embarrassment and annoyance of the congregation. They decided to give him the benefit of the doubt and put this repeat down to him being new and they felt sure next Sunday would redeem the situation. Sunday arrived and he read the same Bible reading. Then he preached exactly the same sermon for a third time! They decided to confront him and this was his reply – "As soon as you are, with the Holy Spirit's help, putting into practice what I have taught – then I will go on to my second sermon!" Why not resolve to put Sunday's sermon into practice this week?

Day 48
Numbers 25-27
17th February

25 - Israel Sins In Moab And Judgement Results
26 - Counting The Army For A Second Time
27 - Joshua Is Appointed Leader

Exodus Generation Now Replaced
By Wilderness Generation

The Big Picture

The Israelites continue to struggle with the Moabites after the failure of Balaam to aide their defeat by cursing them at the request of Barak, king of Moab. Moab would continue to be a thorn in the side of Israel for many years to come. Entry into Canaan is not far away now and a second census is undertaken. This time it is of the new generation of Israelites who have replaced their parents who escaped from Egypt. A whole generation who wandered in the wilderness for forty years because they believed the spies instead of God. After forty years of leadership, Moses is replaced by Joshua who has the privilege of leading the Israelites into the Promised Land.

Thinking Step

Zelophehad had no sons only five daughters who are all named in 27:1. It was decided after Moses consulted the Lord 27:5, to amend the law so that daughters may inherit if they have no brothers. A revolutionary decision at such a time of male domination when women were rarely even mentioned in genealogies never-mind inherit land!

Action Step

How many times do you hear the cry, "How are we going to replace them?" In churches it usually signals the departure of a real stalwart who was a key member of the inner core of the fellowship. When Moses is told by God that his life is coming to an end his replacement is obvious and Joshua is appointed. He had been working with Moses for a long time – Ex 24:13. What an apprenticeship! This is a vital process that is missing from so many churches today. They only act when a vacancy occurs and too often simply look to other fellowships for a replacement rather than planning well and growing their own! Moses did such a great job training Joshua that he was the perfect replacement leader when the time came. A perfect example of how this can benefit your fellowship is in personal evangelism. No matter how many times we are taught from the front, it's still hard to do. I learned how, by visiting with someone who was gifted in this ministry. When the time was right we split and I took someone else and trained them whilst my mentor took another trainee. This approach will work with many other aspects of church life. Why not consider an apprenticeship programme for your church so that you are growing tomorrow's leaders alongside today's? Starting with someone you will train to replace you!

Numbering The People

TRIBE	1ST CENSUS	2ND CENSUS
1. Reuben	46,500	43,730
2. Simeon	59,300	22,200
3. Gad	45,650	40,500
4. Judah	74,600	76,500
5. Issachar	54,400	64,300
6. Zebulun	57,400	60,500
7. Ephraim	40,500	32,500
8. Manasseh	32,200	52,700
9. Benjamin	35,400	45,600
10. Dan	62,700	64,400
11. Asher	41,500	53,400
12. Naphtali	53,400	45,400
Total	603,550	601,730

Day 49
Numbers 28-30
18th February

28 - More Teaching About Offerings And The Passover
29 - More Teaching About Keeping The Feasts
30 - More Teaching About Making And Keeping Vows

Last Minute Teaching For The Next Generation

The Big Picture

The new generation who grew up in the wilderness, are in real need of God's teaching because what was taught to their parents was not passed on during the forty years of wandering. They have arrived at the plains of Moab and need to be prepared for their entry into the Promised Land under their new leader, Joshua. Moses is still alive and will do the teaching even though Joshua has been appointed as the next leader; Moses is still God's man! The whole range of offerings and feasts are reviewed for a people who are hearing them for the very first time. Their response is so much better than that of their forefathers.

Thinking Step

Festival of Trumpets is the ancient forerunner of church bells! Encouraging preparation for the imminent festivals of the Day of Atonement and Tabernacles. All three festivals occur within a period of three weeks in Sep/Oct. Festival of Trumpets begins the celebration of the Jewish New Year. For most of our millennium in 2000 the Jewish calendar was proclaiming the year 5760!

Action Step

A whole chapter is given to the importance of keeping vows that you make. 30:2 "A man who makes a vow to the Lord or makes a pledge under oath must never break it. He must do exactly what he said he would do." When we don't, it saddens God – but our salvation is still secure. I remember teaching in a large church and towards the end of the event I asked the folk to promise to read the Bible and pray daily for the next 30 days. The positive response to this question usually results in up to 100% on the response forms collected at the close of the day. Imagine my sadness when relatively few 'ticked the box'. It had been a good day and I couldn't understand why there was such a disappointing response. Seeing me looking perplexed the pastor came over and said, "Let me explain what's happened, I have been teaching for the last month or so, that promises should only be made when you are sure you can keep them, in fact try wherever possible to sleep on it before making a promise!" All was clear now! It's almost impossible to go through a day without promising something to somebody – so when you do be sure it's a 'vow' as to the Lord and not just 'words'!

31 - Midianites Are Destroyed - Along With Balaam!   Day 50
32 - Some Tribes Choose To Settle On The East Bank   Numbers 31-33
33 - Walk Through The Story So Far   19th February

Looking Back Before Going Forward

The Big Picture

One of the last tasks for Moses was to deal with the Midianites. As well as soundly defeating them the prophet Balaam is also killed. There is no record of what happened to his donkey! Distribution of the spoils of war, preceded by purification by Eleazar the priest, brings this action to a close. Agreement is reached for the land east of the Jordan river to be divided amongst the tribes of Reuben, Gad and Manasseh, provided they cross the Jordan river and help the other tribes to conquer the Promised Land first, then they may return to the east side. Chapter 33 is the first of many summaries of the story so far – an early 'Walk Through'.

Thinking Step

As Manasseh settles on the east side you will also learn later that they settle on the west side too. They are the only tribe that settles on both sides of the Jordan river. That's two portions for Manasseh and one for Ephraim, the two sons of Joseph. Jacob's favourite son Joseph finishes up with three portions of land!

Action Step

If a job's worth doing – it's worth doing well! How many times have you heard that? Well, there must be something to it as God says it to the Israelites in 33:55 – "If you fail to drive out the people who live in the land, those who remain will be like splinters in your eyes and thorns in your sides. They will harass you in the land where you live." Well, the Israelites didn't conquer all the inhabitants of the land and they lived to regret it for many centuries. There is a sense in which half a job is worse than no job at all. Just doing part of what God asks but not finishing it, is dishonouring to Him and a slur on your good name too. When I am introduced to someone who has done a bit of everything I am not impressed but simply conclude – they couldn't stick at anything! I remember when we celebrated 25 years of ministry with Walk Through the Bible in 2009 an old friend of mine said to me, "Well done for sticking with it – there are so many good starters but not enough good finishers." What about you? Today is a great chance to confirm that you will continue your reading the Bible through! Ask God now for the strength to continue. You've survived Leviticus and almost finished Numbers. "Well done you!"

Day 51
Numbers 34-36
20th February

34 - This Is How Big The Land Is
35 - These Are The Safe Places To Go
36 - Safeguards For Future Generations

Preparations Carried Out – Entering Is Imminent!

The Big Picture

Details of boundaries and borders are now described as the Israelites are almost ready to enter the promised land. The Levites get no land areas but are given cities to live in. Some of these are allocated as refuge cities. Places of safety for the people who find themselves in need of protection after accidentally killing someone. Inheritance problems are raised about land allocations when marriages take place between men and women from separate tribes. The solution is that no land areas are transferable so the original land allocations will remain the same. This is the last teaching from Moses before his final three sermons which we call Deuteronomy – and then, off to Jericho!

Thinking Step

Forty eight Levite Cities. Each city in the shape of a square and designed to be self sufficient. Six of these cities are for refuge to protect man-slaughterers but not murderers. Such individuals could find refuge until the chief priest died and then they were set free. Six cities for non-murderers – and the commandment not to kill is number six!

Action Step

Have you ever been in a position where the outcome expected just seems too good to be true? I remember going to see my home town football team, Hartlepool United playing Barrow in the old fourth division. Almost immediately we were winning 1-0. The goals kept going in and by half time we were winning 7-0! As the team went off at half time someone in the crowd said in a very loud voice, "We haven't won yet!" As the second half began the opposition scored to make it 7-1 and the voice was heard again, "I told you, we are going to get beaten!" We didn't; we won 10-1! The crowd couldn't believe the outcome could be as good as it appeared. Isn't that true of you and me sometimes! Centuries ago the Israelites were being prepared to get a land of their own, a land flowing with milk and honey. Too good to be true – but it wasn't! God promised the Israelites what they really needed – a land to live in – and He delivered, in full. He promises us a fulfilled life everyday but it's a process that we need to be involved in too. As today progresses play your part, whenever you find yourself smiling, thank God! Whenever you are floundering, ask God to undertake for you – and believe He can – and play your part and rejoice – with smiling!

Deuteronomy

Deuteronomy

The final book of the Pentateuch is the book of second chances, summed up in its title meaning 'second law' or 'repetition of the law.' It takes place on the plains of Moab and is the final preparation from Moses before he dies and the Israelites go into the Promised Land. The new generation which succeeds the one that wandered in the wilderness, now hears the final three sermons of Moses which make up the whole of this book. These sermons can be broadly summarised with three simple titles. Chapters 1-4 : 'What God has done for Israel' – (a short Bible Walk Through!). Chapters 5-26 : 'What God requires from Israel'. Chapters 27-34 – 'What God has in store for Israel.' The laws and regulations of Deuteronomy are primarily aimed at the ordinary people and contain some of the most favourite passages of Judaism and of Jesus Christ Himself.

Below is an acrostic which summarises each chapter of the book.

1. Retelling of Israel's failures
2. End of Israel's wanderings
3. Possessing Gilead and Bashan
4. Exhortation to obey God
5. Applying the Ten Commandments
6. Teaching children the law
7. Idolatry to be destroyed
8. Necessity of God's testing
9. God's grace after intercession

10. Tablets for the ark
11. Heritage for obeying God
12. Exhortation to holy separation

13. Lying prophets must die
14. Animals suitable for eating
15. Way of remitting debts

16. Feasts listed and explained
17. Obliteration of all evildoers
18. Rights of the Levites

19. Involuntary killer given refuge
20. Strategy for God's warfare
21. Rights of captive women
22. Adultery and morality laws
23. Exclusions from the assemblies
24. Leaving a mate legally
25. Summary of civil laws

26. Offering of firstfruits
27. Building the Ebal altar
28. Extended blessings and cursings
29. Disobedience will bring curses
30. Initiative for following God
31. Establishment of Joshua's leading
32. New song of Moses
33. Conferring the tribal blessings
34. End of Moses' life

The Influence Of Deuteronomy
In The Gospels

DEUTERONOMY	GOSPEL
(8:3) "'...He did it to teach you that people need more than bread for their life; real life comes by feeding on every word of the LORD.'"	**(Matt 4:4)** "But Jesus told him, 'No! The Scriptures say, People need more than bread for their life; they must feed on every word of God.'" **(Luke 4:4)** "But Jesus told him, 'No! The Scriptures say, People need more than bread for their life.'"
(6:16) "'Do not test the LORD your God as you did when you complained at Massah.'"	**(Matt 4:7 & Luke 4:12)** "Jesus responded, 'The Scriptures also say, Do not test the Lord your God.'"
(6:13) "'You must fear the LORD your God and serve him. When you take an oath, you must use only his name'".	**(Matt 4:10)** "'Get out of here, Satan', Jesus told him. 'For the Scriptures say, You must worship the Lord your God; serve only him.'" **(Luke 4:8)** "Jesus replied, 'The Scriptures say, You must worship the Lord your God; serve only him.'"
(6:5) "'And you must love the LORD your God with all your heart, all your soul, and all your strength.'"	**(Matt 22:37)** "Jesus replied, 'You must love the Lord your God with all your heart, all your soul, and all your mind.'" **(Luke 10:27)** "The man answered, 'You must love the Lord your God with all your heart, all your soul, all your strength, and all your mind and Love your neighbour as yourself.'"
(24:1) "'Suppose a man marries a woman but later discovers something about her that is shameful. So he writes her a letter of divorce, gives it to her, and sends her away.'"	**(Matt 5:31)** "'You have heard that the law of Moses says, A man can divorce his wife by merely giving her a letter of divorce.'" **(Mark 10:4-5)** "'Well, he permitted it,' they replied. 'He said a man merely has to write his wife an official letter of divorce and send her away.' But Jesus responded, 'He wrote those instructions only as a concession to your hard-hearted wickedness.'"
(5:16) "'Honour your father and mother, as the LORD your God commanded you. Then you will live a long, full life in the land the LORD your God will give you.'"	**(Mark 7:10-11)** "'For instance, Moses gave you this law from God: Honour your father and mother, and Anyone who speaks evil of father or mother must be put to death. But you say it is all right for people to say to their parents, 'Sorry, I can't help you. For I have vowed to give to God what I could have given to you.'"
(5:16-20) "'Honour your father and mother, as the LORD your God commanded you... 'Do not murder. Do not commit adultery. Do not steal. Do not testify falsely against your neighbour.'"	**(Matt 19:18-19)** "And Jesus replied: 'Do not murder. Do not commit adultery. Do not steal. Do not testify falsely. Honour your father and mother. Love your neighbour as yourself.'" **(Mark 10:19 & Luke 18:20)** "'But as for your question, you know the commandments: Do not murder. Do not commit adultery. Do not steal. Do not testify falsely. Do not cheat. Honour your father and mother.'"
(19:21) "'You must never show pity! Your rule should be life for life, eye for eye, tooth for tooth, hand for hand, foot for foot.'"	**(Matt 5:38-39)** "'...If a tooth gets knocked out, knock out the tooth of the person who did it. But I say, don't resist an evil person! If you are slapped on the right cheek, turn the other, too.'"
(19:15) "'Never convict anyone of a crime on the testimony of just one witness. The facts of the case must be established by the testimony of two or three witnesses.'"	**(Matt 18:16)** "'But if you are unsuccessful, take one or two others with you and go back again, so that everything you say may be confirmed by two or three witnesses.'"

Looking Back At What God Has Done!

The Big Picture

This first sermon of Moses looks back at how gracious God has been with His people over the past forty years. It traces their journey from Mount Sinai or Mount Horeb as it is sometimes called, all the way to their current location – Moab. It covers their journey to Kadesh Oasis and their encounters with the Moabites, Edomites and Ammonites. The conquest of the eastern side of the Jordan valley when King Sihon and King Og are defeated and their land given to the two and a half tribes of Gad, Reuben and Manasseh. The people are also reminded of the leadership change from Moses to Joshua. Finally the whole of chapter four summarises the terms of God's covenant with Israel.

Thinking Step

It took the children of Israel forty years to cover a journey that should have taken only eleven days! It's like taking forty years to travel from London to Yorkshire (that's if you would like to!). All that wasted time and unnecessary suffering and hardship! All that rebellion from the people and all that faithfulness from God!

Action Step

Have you ever sent a teenager upstairs to find something that they have lost? In no time at all they return saying, "Sorry, I have looked everywhere but can't find it!" Then as soon as you go up to have a look, there it is in the middle of the floor! In our passage today God promises His people that if they truly seek Him they will find Him. We read in 4:29 as part of the prophecy given to them, confirming that the future will not be easy "...and if you search for him with all your heart and soul, you will find him." Looking like a teenager isn't enough, you have to look as though your life depends on it – because it does! The reading continues, "In the distant future when you are suffering all these things, you will finally return to the Lord your God and listen to what he tells you. For the Lord your God is a merciful God. He will not abandon you or destroy you or forget the solemn covenant he made with your ancestors." When you next see an advert for insurance remember that our God is more reliable. When you see a great guarantee on your next car, remember our God is more reliable. All we have to do is seek Him and we are guaranteed to find Him! Start looking today... with success guaranteed!

5 - The Law Is Explained For A Second Time   Day 53
6 - Be Sure To Teach Others This Law   Deuteronomy 5-7
7 - The Promised Land Awaits   22nd February

The New Generation Receives The Old

The Big Picture

The Ten Commandments are reviewed next, after confirmation that this covenant is with the people of the day, not their Fathers! A timely reminder that God has no grandchildren! Some of the most famous words in the Old Testament are to be found in chapter 6 and are repeated throughout the Old Testament – "Hear, O Israel!" In our reading the Israelites are commanded to teach the law to future generations. A wise precaution when you consider that their forefathers didn't teach them when they were children during the wilderness wanderings. They are also commanded to conquer Canaan, a task they never accomplish completely and which causes them endless trouble.

Thinking Step

Today many hotels and houses in Israel and around the world have a small box pinned to their doorway. It's called a mezuzah and it contains chapter 6:4-9, the Jewish confession of faith which is recited twice daily by the faithful. This is what Jesus uses in Matt 22:37 to confirm which is the greatest commandment.

Action Step

Last minute advice is not always the best but in this instance it is, as Moses shares some of his last thoughts. 5:1 says, "Hear, O Israel, the decrees and laws I declare in your hearing today. Learn them and be sure to follow them" – and in 6:1 we read "These are the commands, decrees and laws the LORD your God directed me to teach you to observe in the land that you are crossing the Jordan to possess." In the Hebrew language the word to learn and the word to teach have the same core and can in a real sense, be said to be the same word. So when a Hebrew speaker asks you to learn him something, he is not speaking poor English but good Hebrew! The two main points today are as relevant as ever they were. We need to learn to follow – and teach others how. How long have you attended church? Are you a learner only or a teacher as well? Are you putting into practice what you learn or are you simply storing up knowledge? It's not how much you know but who you share it with, that will extend the Kingdom of God. No matter how inadequate you may feel, keep an eye open for a sharing opportunity today – be ready to share something of what you believe today and you will be the most blessed!

Day 54
Deuteronomy 8-11
23rd February

8 - Continue To Remember God's Goodness
9 - Remember What Happened With That Golden Calf!
10 - Remember What God Expects From You
11 - Continue To Study And Obey The Commandments

Don't Forget Lessons Of The Past!

The Big Picture

The second sermon of Moses continues as the Israelites are taught what God expects of them right now. A familiar plea is heard to remember God as they enter the land. They are reminded that this land is only going to be theirs because God promised it and because He loves them. There as an awful reminder of their rebellion when the Ten Commandments were given to them and the tablets of stone were smashed to pieces. They must remember that God forgave them because He is a merciful God. Be sure to love God and keep His commandments and He will be very dependable even down to regular rainfall in a dry land.

Thinking Step

8:4 "For all these forty years your clothes didn't wear out and your feet didn't blister or swell." God cares for the big things in life like the exodus out of Egypt but He also cares for the very small things too, like providing everlasting clothing and comfort for a people who have turned their backs on Him!

Action Step

Isn't God fortunate to have you and me on His side! How would He manage without us...All too easily we only turn to God when we need His help – but in between times we don't bother Him because we don't need any help! The Israelites are reminded in our reading today that 9:4-5 says, "After the Lord your God has done this for you don't say in your hearts, 'The Lord has given us this land because we are such good people!' No, it is because of the wickedness of the other nations that he is pushing them out of your way. It is not because you are so good or have such integrity that you are about to occupy their land. The Lord your God will drive these nations out ahead of you only because of their wickedness and to fulfil the oath He swore to your ancestors Abraham, Isaac, and Jacob." It's the same today! However God blesses you today please remember it's only because He loves you! Remember this when someone annoys you today and you are tempted to think, "They don't deserve me to be nice to them!" When you are tempted to think like this, thank God that He doesn't think like this and neither should we!

86

Details For Holy Living In The Promised Land

The Big Picture

This is a section of detailed laws for everyone. The Israelites are warned not to do what is right in their own eyes but do what God demands. There is a constant problem with idolatry and warnings not to worship false gods but to be loyal to the true living God. Test what is said by itinerant prophets to check if it is from God. A list of clean and unclean animals repeats what has already been told to the generation that perished in the wilderness wanderings. Money and slavery laws are also explained. Finally we have details of the law concerning the first-born and then the feasts and a start on the appointment and practice of judges.

Thinking Step

14:21 tells us, "...but you are a people holy to the LORD your God. Do not cook a young goat in its mother's milk." This later became the foundation for what we have in modern Judaism today i.e. that milk and meat shall never be mixed or taken together, even to the extent of having separate kitchen utensils.

Action Step

If you want to irritate a congregation it's easy, just preach about giving! Some of us are so holy we never mention money and some of us are so worldly that we only talk about money! Seriously, money has its place in all our lives. Remember it's the love of money that is a root of all kinds of evil, not money itself, 1 Tim 6:10. Did you notice what today's reading said? In 16:16-17 we read "Three times a year all your men must appear before the LORD your God at the place he will choose, at the Feast of Unleavened Bread, the Feast of Weeks and the Feast of Tabernacles. No man should appear before the LORD empty-handed, each of you must bring a gift in proportion to the way the LORD your God has blessed you." Were these feasts only about money? No! Nevertheless, money was part of each of them. Can you imagine what would happen to your fellowship if everyone handled money as God would like them to? Would missions be short of funding? Would outreach be limited by lack of money? If your answer to these questions is "No" then play your part by including money in your spiritual life. Ask God to lay a project on your heart – NOW! Learn more about it. Pray for it. Share the vision. Support it. God wants you – not just your money! He wants both!

Day 56
Deuteronomy 17-20
25th February

17 - You Will Want A King Ruling Over You
18 - The Lord Will Judge Any False Prophets
19 - Cities Of Refuge Will Be Available To All
20 - The Lord Will Lead You When You Go To War

God Will Be At The Centre Of Society

The Big Picture

The rules continue! Just think, how else would they know what God wants? Remember also that these rules are not to cramp His people but to bring them to real fruitfulness. More details on Judges and then information about Kings even though they don't have one at the time! God knew they would come one day but He wanted His people to know that they would be very costly. Priests' and prophets' duties and how they are to use the cities of refuge, already described in Numbers 35 are repeated here. When crimes occur witnesses are vital to justice and one isn't enough. Finally God even offers teaching on the unlikely subject of warfare!

Thinking Step

19:19,21 – "Then do to him as he intended to do to his brother...life for life, eye for eye, tooth for tooth, hand for hand, foot for foot." At a time when whole cities were often raised to the ground because of the sin of one person we have a glimpse here of the forgiving heart of God.

Action Step

Have you ever preached and had someone query something they say you said but which you know you didn't say? I remember it happening to me some time ago and I suggested we listened to a recording of my sermon as they were all recorded. "No need" was the reply "I know what you said – I don't need to hear it again!" What he alleged I said was only heard by him and was the exact opposite of the main message I was giving! I believe this was a small insight to how God must feel when He is misquoted. 18:20 talks about false prophets who quote things that God has not declared. I believe sometimes the language we use can lead others to believe that we are not just stating our opinion but declaring the mind of God. We need to be very careful and never misquote God. A seasoned pastor friend of mine said of one of his congregation, "He's had more leads from God than you will find at Cruft's Dog show this year! Harsh but I knew the person in question and had to agree. If it's your opinion then say so. If it's God's mind then say that too – just be certain of your facts. So think back, have you misquoted God lately? Talk to Him now and apologise. Then with His help repair the damage!

Stable Relationships Result In A Civilised Society

The Big Picture

The second and longest sermon of Moses comes to a close with our reading today. In the days of Moses when marriage in other nations was very vague, sadly rather like the twenty first century in the UK, God lets His people know exactly what His thoughts are about marriage and separation. How to handle rebellious children and what to do about your neighbours property are included too. We also have strict rules about acceptance into the Tabernacle which will ultimately hold good for the temple too. Finally we have God's mind on how to settle disputes and honour the concept of giving a tithe.

Thinking Step

23:13-14 – 'As part of your equipment have something to dig with and when you relieve yourself, dig a hole and cover up your excrement. For the LORD your God moves about in your camp to protect you and to deliver your enemies to you. Your camp must be holy...' God even has plans for your toilet arrangements!

Action Step

21:18-23 is the foundational passage for the story that Jesus tells many centuries later. The story is of the prodigal son, which I think should be called the story of the forgiving father. The point of Jesus' parable and the other two He tells in Luke 15 is that our Heavenly Father is constantly looking for us and rejoices when we return to Him. There could have been a rabbinic story based on this passage in Deuteronomy in the days of Jesus, which was designed to deter possible wanderers from leaving for fear of what could happen to them. It could even be that Jesus starts to tell this story but to the surprise of His hearers, changes the end and makes His unforgettable point. God longs for you to come back – He is not longing to have the chance to punish or reject you! Most of us slide away from God sometimes, it's human nature. However, it's God's nature to want you back. Does the distance between you and God seem greater lately? He hasn't moved and doesn't need to – but you need to! Not tomorrow but now! If you return to God today, you can actually imagine God running out to meet you so you don't have to cover the whole distance yourself! That's how important you are to Him.

Day 58
Deuteronomy 27-30
27th February

27 - Build An Altar
28 - Anticipate Blessings And Curses
29 - Covenant Conditions Explained
30 - Covenant Details Declared

Commitment To God's Covenant

The Big Picture

This final section of Deuteronomy is the third and last sermon of Moses. The people are encouraged to build an altar as a matter of urgency as soon as they cross the Jordan and enter the promised land. Moses tells them that when they cross the river they are to split into two groups, one proclaiming curses and the other proclaiming blessings, underlining the consequences of ignoring or keeping the law. They can trust God for the future but in many ways it is in their hands too. God's covenant is based on His power and is meant for this generation and those that follow. Hard times are prophesied but there is also assurance that Israel will finally be restored.

Thinking Step

27:12 – "When you have crossed the Jordan these tribes shall stand on Mount Gerizim to bless the people: Simeon, Levi, Judah, Issachar, Joseph and Benjamin." All sons of Jacob's wives Leah and Rachel. All to stand on the same Samaritan mountain where Jesus later meets the woman at the well to share more blessings with her about living water.

Action Step

I hadn't been a pastor long when I attended a local fraternal of church leaders from most of the denominations in the town. The subject of a proposed mission to be led by Billy Graham was raised. I was amazed to hear one of the ministers comment that he wasn't a fan of Billy Graham. He continued, "Billy Graham seems to be talking in black and white terms all the time, you're either saved or not, you're either going to heaven or hell! There was a sharp intake of breath before an interesting discussion followed! Our reading today list lots of consequences both good and bad, of ignoring God's commandments and going your own way through life. They seem very black and white to me! I believe the whole of mankind is in one of two camps, saved or unsaved. Thankfully it is not me who is on the throne of judgement over these matters and I trust God will not only be fair but seen to be fair on the last day. A simple question – "Which camp are you in?" Today is an excellent opportunity to trust God and know for sure. You only have to look inside and repent of your sin, look to Jesus and accept His gift of eternal life, Look to God and thank Him for His forgiveness.

31 - Israel And Joshua Are Addressed By Moses
32 - Thanksgiving Is Lead With The Song Of Moses
33 - The Tribes Are Blessed By Moses
34 - Moses Dies And Joshua Steps Up

Day 59
Deuteronomy 31-34
28th February

Moses Completes His Work For God

The Big Picture

In these last chapters of Deuteronomy the book of second chances, Moses solemnly charges both Joshua and the people to be strong and courageous and trust God as they enter the Promised Land. The book of the law is to be placed next to the Ark of the Covenant as a permanent reminder of the Israelite's stubbornness and rebellious behaviour which must stop with Moses dying. A song is then composed and read to the people, the Song of Moses. Finally Moses blesses each of the tribes and has a last look from Mount Nebo, into the land he will not enter with his people. Moses is buried in a secret place in the nearby valley opposite Beth-peor.

Thinking Step

34:6 – 'The Lord buried him in a valley near Beth-peor in Moab but to this day no one knows the exact place.' God knew the tomb of Moses could become 'the holy place' for Jews – a shrine. A graphic reminder that we are to worship the living God not the tombs of His faithful followers.

Action Step

Moses' closing remarks, then his urging to the people to remain faithful to the Word of God, then a song followed by a blessing. Sounds like a normal Sunday service doesn't it! Seriously, there is a sense in which Moses is summing up everything that really matters to the people and the key verse is 31:12 – 'Call them all together men, women, children, and the foreigners living in your towns – so they may hear this Book of Instruction...' Verse 13 continues – 'Do this so that your children who have not known these instructions will hear them and will learn to fear the Lord your God.' He urges them not repeat the failure of their parents who didn't pass on their faith! Recently a Bible Explorer presenter (one of hundreds of volunteers who are trained by Walk Through the Bible to teach the Bible in UK schools) was teaching about the birth of Jesus. One of the pupils called out, "I don't believe in Bethlehem!" It seems she had been told by her parents that everything in the Bible was untrue. So her rejection even included hard geographical facts of present day cities! That's how 'written off' the Bible is for many. If this concerns you then take some action. You can train to be a Bible Explorer presenter by contacting Walk Through the Bible or you can prayerfully and financially support what others are doing. Just do something, please!

Joshua

Joshua

With the firm foundation for the whole of the Bible, the Pentateuch, now solidly in place – all is ready for entry into the promised land at last! Of the twenty four chapters that make up this book exactly half concentrate on the conquering of the people who live there already. The remaining second twelve detail the settling of the twelve tribes into the promised land. This book takes the name of its major character Joshua, who was one of the spies along with Caleb who believed the Israelites should have gone into Canaan forty years earlier. Joshua and Caleb are the only two adults who left Egypt with Moses in the Exodus and survive to enter the promised land and settle there. His Hebrew name Joshua, given to him by Moses is the same as that of the Greek name Jesus. Both can be translated as Yahweh is Salvation.

Below is an acrostic which summarises each chapter of the book.

1. Prosperity promised for obedience
2. Rahab protects two spies
3. Onward through the Jordan
4. Memorial stones are set
5. Israel's circumcision at Gilgal
6. Successful conquest of Jericho
7. End of Achan's coveting
8. Defeat of Ai's army

9. Lying by the Gibeonites
10. Attack of five kings
11. Northern kings are conquered
12. Diary of defeated kings

13. Method of land division
14. Expectations of Caleb rewarded
15. Apportionment to Judah's sons
16. Niche for Ephraim tribe
17. Selfishness of Manasseh satisfied

18. Victory proclaimed in Shiloh
19. Inheritance given to Joshua
20. Cities of refuge named
21. Towns of Levites named
22. Offence of the altar
23. Rehearsing of the law
24. Years of Joshua end

Day 60
Joshua 1-4
1st March

1 - Joshua Is Commissioned As New Leader
2 - Spies Are Helped By Rahab
3 - Jordan River Is Crossed
4 - Memorial To The Crossing Is Erected

Israelites Enter Canaan Miraculously

The Big Picture

A smooth transition from Moses to Joshua. The last words of Moses were to encourage the Israelites to read the Word of God. The first words of Joshua have the same imperative. Joshua handles wisely the requests from the tribes who want to settle east of the Jordan River. Then he sends out spies, only two this time and with the help of Rahab leads Israel to victory over Jericho. It could be that the two spies represent the tribes whose spies were 'believers' last time i.e. Judah and Ephraim. So Judah could have been represented by Salmon who fathers a child by Rahab. The child is named Boaz and he ultimately marries Ruth to become an ancestor of Jesus Christ.

Thinking Step

3:15-16 – 'As soon as the priests who carried the Ark reached the Jordan... the water from upstream stopped flowing. It piled up in a heap a great distance away at a town called Adam...so the people crossed...' Adam is still there twenty miles north! It wasn't a single file crossing they crossed as a nation!"

Action Step

Our reading today contains one of the most famous miracles in the Old Testament – the crossing of the Jordan River – but it's not the most important part of the reading. It's more than just interesting that Joshua takes up the emphasis of Moses in Deuteronomy and stresses the importance of reading the word of God – 1:8 – "Do not let this Book of the Law depart from your mouth, meditate on it day and night so that you may be careful to do everything written in it. Then you will be prosperous and successful." When two great leaders like Moses and Joshua agree on something I think we should listen don't you? We have made great progress in our reading through the whole Bible even though some of it has been far from simple! Very well done. I remember a man asking me where I found, as he put it the 'interesting bits' in the Bible! The bits that were intriguing and thought provoking. I told him – no secret – just read the Bible. He responded "Oh I understand that but which additional books do you use?" My reply of "Just the Bible" didn't satisfy him. You see, he was looking for a shortcut but there is no shortcut to reading the Bible through – you just have to do it. Keep at it and make Moses and Joshua proud of you!

5 - Circumcision Re-Introduced And Manna Ceases   Day 61
6 - Jericho Falls And Joshua Pronounces A Curse   Joshua 5-8
7 - Sin Catches Up With Israelites At Ai Defeat   2nd March
8 - Restoration Of The Nation And Then Ai Falls

Jericho Falls As Israelites Begin To Conquer

The Big Picture

After the amazing crossing of the Jordan River the surrounding nations feared the Israelites. God tells Joshua to reintroduce circumcision that had not been practised for the past forty years. Passover is celebrated north of Jericho at Gilgal. Manna is no longer needed and so it stops. Then Jericho falls to the unique strategy of the Israelite's God. Sensing they are 'on a roll' they approach the next city Ai, with over confidence and fail to take it due to the sin of Achan. At the second attempt after Achan and his family have paid for their wrongdoing with their lives, Ai falls and is razed to the ground and the people renew their covenant with God.

Thinking Step

There are two cities of Jericho in the Bible. There is the city in our narrative today which was completely destroyed and then cursed by Joshua – 6:26. Then there's the city of Zaccheus and Bartimaeus in the New Testament. Both are now archaeological digs near to the modern city of Jericho which is number three!

Action Step

Have you ever sensed God working in your life to such a degree that you felt you could cope without Him in future! Doesn't make sense does it? So why when we see that one way works and another way fails, do we insist on trying the failure route over and over again? Stupidity or sinfulness, you choose! The overall strategy of taking Jericho was perfect the only glitch was that God used humans to do it! He must sometimes feel like the schoolteacher who confessed just how good school would be if only there were no students! The instruction in 6:19 to put the valuables they would find into the treasury of the Lord, was too much for Achan! It would have given him financial security if it had worked so must have seemed a very attractive addition to God's plan – but sin's like that it is attractive. I remember a preacher asking his congregation if they sinned then asked them if they enjoyed it! Like good Christians they said they sinned but didn't enjoy it at which point the preacher shouted "You're not doing it right!" Sin can be enjoyable but it is never fulfilling. Are you facing a Jericho moment today? Then count to thirteen (that's how many times they marched around the city!) and resist the temptation to amend God's guidance in any way. It's perfect just as it is!

Day 62
Joshua 9-12
3rd March

9 - Gibeonites Deceive The Israelites
10 - Amorites Fall As Joshua Conquers The South
11 - North Crumbles As Joshua Conquers
12 - Lots Of Defeated Kings

Land Is Conquered, South Then North

The Big Picture

Having entered the land in the middle so to speak at Jericho, there is a need to firm up the defeat of the central belt which included Jericho and Ai before Joshua turns to the south. Here he encounters problems with the Gibeonites who trick the Israelites into signing a covenant with them. Victory over the Amorites is only achieved thanks to the miraculous heavenly intervention of God. Then Joshua turns north for more victories. In conclusion we have a summary of the territory conquered and details of the kings who were conquered too. With this we come to the end of the 'conquering section' of Joshua and we are exactly half way through the book.

Thinking Step

Some things are so amazing you would doubt them even if you were there at the time! The account of the moon and sun stopping and standing still comes into this category – but does that mean it didn't happen? All I know is that if God is God then He could have done it – no problem! So rule it out at your peril!

Action Step

I still remember starting my first job and the man who was training me telling me to ask him about anything no matter how trivial if I was unsure about anything. Of course I did for a while and then the pride of a sixteen year old kicked in and I only asked him if I was really stuck or couldn't make a decent guess as to what he would say anyway. Many of us still treat God like this. Just like I treated my trainer Barry! Only for real emergencies! When the Gibeonites came with their devious plan in chapter 9, it had the ring of truth and was such a 'no-brainer' that the men of Israel took an executive decision themselves to save God the trouble! 9:14 – 'The Israelites tried some of the food but they did not ask the LORD if he wanted them to make a treaty.' Despite leaving God out of the consultation process within a few verses we learn that the Israelites had made the covenant with the Gibeonites in the name of the Lord God! The lesson to be learned is that asking God every time will keep us out of trouble. Taking some of the decisions ourselves will sooner or later get us into trouble. When you next ask yourself "Should I?" – no matter how trivial try asking God and then you know the answer will be right!

13 - Reuben, Gad And Manasseh Settle In The East   Day 63
14 - Caleb Takes On A Big Challenge   Joshua 13-15
15 - Remainder Of Judah Settles In The West   4th March

Tribes Begin Settling Into The Land

The Big Picture

Joshua is no longer a young man but there was still much to do. There still remained some areas of the promised land that had not been conquered. These were still in the hands of Philistines and the Geshurites. The Philistines were still occupying the area which can be broadly described as the Gaza Strip today. Their name was subsequently attributed to the whole land of Canaan as it later becomes known as Palestine. God reassures Joshua that these areas will be available for settling and encourages Joshua to go ahead with the allotting of areas to the tribes as well as to Caleb. Detailed descriptions of the boundaries of the tribal areas conclude today's reading.

Thinking Step

Caleb was one of only two who survived the wanderings and entered the Promised Land. This is even more remarkable when you consider he was a Gentile! In Numbers 32:12 we read that he was a Kenizzite (a Canaanite tribe). His family must have converted to Judaism. From the very beginning God's heart was for the whole of mankind.

Action Step

The Israelites settle into the land but not as a nation rather as a gathering of tribes. It takes many centuries before they become a nation united under King Saul. In the meantime they live as individual groupings under the general umbrella of 'Children of Israel.' The independent tribes of Israel even fought each other and as we will see later in the Bible one of them – Benjamin – was almost wiped out in these inter-tribal wars. It seems to me that many of our churches are a bit tribal especially in these days of multi services and a massive array of worship styles, giftings and ministries. So many activities that you can't attend or be involved in everything so before you know where you are, you only know folk who are involved in the same things as you. Think about your church now. If you normally attend the early service try the later one just to see how many people you know! If you only attend the morning service try the evening one. Try your best to meet others in your fellowship who you don't normally fellowship with. Sit in an area you don't normally frequent. If you have a church directory try putting a face to all the entries and the ones you don't know, look for them next Sunday. One way or another play your part in consolidating your fellowship rather than fragmenting it.

Settling Of Remaining Tribes Into The Land

The Big Picture

The allocation of land continues with the tribe of Joseph, through his sons Manasseh and Ephraim who were born to him and his wife Asenath in Egypt, receiving the lion share of the Promised Land. The boundaries show again that their joint land areas spread across both the east and the west sides of the Jordan River. Despite being described as half tribes these sons of Joseph are at least as populous as many of the other full tribes. We also see sadly, that one of the tribes Simeon, is almost indistinct now and has virtually become part of Judah. Finally a city is given to Joshua, as God had promised.

Thinking Step

19:24 – 'The fifth lot came out for the tribe of Asher...' Much of this area is now Lebanon but notice the name Kanah in v28. Some claim this is an alternative site to Cana of Galilee for the town of the first miracle where water was turned to wine! The Bible confirms that Jesus travelled this far north – Luke 4:26.

Action Step

Given the choice between the easy and the hard road we instinctively choose the easy one don't we? Well I have been known to! When things get tough we often give up. A friend of mine was having all sorts of trouble finalising details for a preaching tour to the USA some years ago and his wife asked him "What do you think the Lord is trying to tell you?" Without hesitation he replied "He's probably telling me to try harder!" That wasn't the answer she was expecting and probably not the answer most husbands would have given. In our reading today we are given information about the allocation for the tribe of Dan in 19:40-48. The places mentioned are all in the south west of Israel – but isn't the city of Dan in the north? (From Dan in the north to Beersheba in the south!) It seems God's plan for Dan seemed too difficult for them so they travelled north and seized the city of Laish (Leshem) and renamed it Dan. As a result they probably felt safe from the Philistines but they couldn't have known that they were prime targets for the Assyrians who attacked Israel from the north a few centuries later! If you are going through a particularly hard time right now don't opt out, stick with it. Remember God doesn't want the toughest option for you He just wants the best one for you!

Cities Of Refuge And Cities For Levites

The Big Picture

God reminds Joshua about the cities of refuge which were planned with Moses in Numbers chapter 35. Of the forty eight cities allocated to the Levites, six of them are strategically placed to act as places of refuge for those in fear of their lives. These are to act as places of protection for all who kill accidentally and need a place to hide. They will be safe there and will finally be freed when the Chief Priest dies. The Levitical families, descendants of Kohath, Gershon and Merari, sons of Levi, have specific cities of refuge assigned to them. This completes the allocations and settlement details of the Children of Israel into the Promised Land.

Thinking Step

20:4 – 'Upon reaching one of these cities the one who caused the death will appear before the elders at the city gate and present his case...' Justice at the gates just like Boaz achieved in Ruth 4 and 1 Kings 22:10 shows 'courtroom at the gates' idea continued for a long time.

Action Step

21:45 reminds us – 'Not a single one of all the good promises the Lord had given to the family of Israel was left unfulfilled, everything he had spoken came true.' Of course when we read that all the good promises made by God came true we need to remember that this trustworthy nature of God holds true even when His promises are not what we would choose ourselves or do not seem to be to our benefit. He is a God who always says what He means and always means what He says and we misinterpret His words at our peril. I don't know about you but there are chunks of the Bible that I don't fully understand (in fact there are parts that I don't understand at all!) but that means God is cleverer than I am, which comes as no surprise to those who know me! When a particularly difficult passage is important for us to comprehend God will enable our understanding, in the meantime let's concentrate on what we do understand. I have quoted Mark Twain many times when he said "Most people are bothered by those passages in Scripture which they do not understand. The Scripture which troubles me most is the Scripture I do understand." Let's spend the rest of today thanking God for His promises which are all kept, even the ones which we secretly wish we could change!

Day 66
Joshua 22-24
7th March

22 - Eastern Memorial Misunderstood
23 - Joshua Challenges Israel To Keep The Covenant
24 - Joshua's 'Walk Through' Of How Good God Has Been

Joshua Dies And The People Are Ill-Prepared

The Big Picture

The time comes for the armies of the tribes who have chosen to settle on the east side of the Jordan River to return home. Joshua reminds them that the covenant is for them too and they must keep true to it in the same way as the rest of the tribes on the west side. The returning tribes build an altar near the river as they cross over and civil war threatens to break out! The other tribes misunderstand why the altar was built and much diplomacy is required by both sides. A brief 'walk Through' the story so far and an emphasis on the importance of serving the Lord brings this book to a close.

Thinking Step

Joseph had waited nearly 500 years but finally we read – in 24:32 – 'The bones of Joseph which the Israelites had brought along with them when they left Egypt were buried at Shechem, in the parcel of ground Jacob had bought from the sons of Hamor for 100 kesitahs. (Ironically nobody knows the value or weight of the kesitah today!)

Action Step

When I lived in the northeast of England many years ago a colleague came into the office one morning to tell everyone that he had become a father. After his lunch break on the same day he proudly declared that he had registered the lad with Sunderland AFC supporters' club. No matter how many times we told him that his son would have to make up his own mind he simply repeated that he was a Sunderland supporter now! Wouldn't life be easier if we could determine what our children believed when they grew up? Not surprisingly they have to decide for themselves. Joshua knew that as some of his last words were – "So fear the Lord and serve him wholeheartedly. Put away forever the idols your ancestors worshipped when they lived beyond the Euphrates River and in Egypt. Serve the Lord alone – but if you refuse to serve the Lord then choose today whom you will serve. Would you prefer the gods your ancestors served beyond the Euphrates? Or will it be the gods of the Amorites in whose land you now live? As for me and my family we will serve the Lord." Now spend a few moments thinking of friends and members of your family who as far as you know are not yet believers. Pray that they will choose the best and determine you will do all you can to influence them in that direction.

Judges

Judges

The Israelites are settled in the promised land but the man who took them there, Moses plus the one who settled them there Joshua are both dead. There is no obvious leader now and the nation of Israel is in danger of imploding. This book records the deeds of the thirteen judges who rule for almost 400 years. Some in great detail like Deborah, Gideon and Samson whilst the others like Shamgar may only get a single verse. The book is dominated by the repeating of the same mistakes with the same consequences, the 'Cycles of the Judges.' Surrounding nations attempt to conquer Israel but with the help of Godly Judges they are reprieved over and over again. The period of Judges is summed up at the end with – 'In those days there was no King in Israel everyone did what was right in his own eyes.

Below is an acrostic which summarises each chapter of the book.

1. Territories Israel left unconquered
2. How God tested Israel
3. Ehud slays Moab's king

4. Jabin overcome by Deborah
5. Uplifting song of Deborah
6. Determination via Gideon's fleece
7. Gideon's army routs Midianites
8. Ephod causes Gideon's downfall
9. Shechemites make Abimelech king

10. Oppression by the Ammonites
11. Fighting Jephthah subdues Ammonites

12. Gileadites overcome the Ephraimites
13. Oppression by the Philistines
14. Deceit over Samson's riddle
15. Samson kills thousand Philistines

16. Philistines find Samson's secret
17. Ephraimite hires own priest
18. Offences committed by Danites
19. Perversion of Levite's concubine
20. Levite's vengeance on Benjamites
21. Existence of Benjamin assured

Some Poor Leadership Results In Chaos

The Big Picture

The first two chapters make sad reading, recording the failure of Israel to fully conquer the land that God has given them. So begins the 'Cycles of Judges' under Othniel, Ehud, Shamgar and Deborah. We see four of the seven cycles in these chapters. Othniel and Ehud defeat the Mesopotamians and Moabites but Shamgar's influence warrants only one verse! The most influential Judge at this time is Deborah, the only female Judge. As a prophetess Deborah calls Barak to fight the Canaanites but he says that he won't go without her! Jael plays an important part too! A victory song is sung and the land has peace for the next forty years.

Thinking Step

3:15 – 'When the people of Israel cried out to the Lord for help, the Lord again raised up a rescuer to save them. His name was Ehud son of Gera a left-handed man...' A right-handed man would never have got through Eglon's security who would frisk visitors on their left, Ehud's sword was on the right – v21.

Action Step

How many times have you made a mistake just the once and never repeated it? Usually we tend to make the same mistakes over and over again. The ancient book of Judges sums up modern man and woman very well indeed. The cycles of events in Judges reflect this repetition and each has five steps. The first one is SIN by ignoring God and doing what you want to do; this is quickly followed by SLAVERY to that sin which just seems to take over! Then, in desperation, a SHORT PRAYER is offered to God for help. When God intervenes He brings SURE FREEDOM which in the book of Judges, only lasts as long as the current Judge, nevertheless there is a period of SILENT PEACE. Then the whole cycle starts again as they slip into sin once more. Ask yourself, 'Where am I on this cycle and where do I long to be?" Being at peace with God is the target isn't it? So where are you? Once you discover this, then you know the next step to take. If you are at step one, repent. If you are at step two, repent. If you are at step three, you are repenting. If you are at step four you have repented. Step five is where you are as long as you keep repenting. Do you see a trend here? Now you know what to do – so just do it!

The Judges Of Israel (Judges 3-16)

JUDGE	YEARS OF PEACE	YEARS PUT DOWN	MEMORABLE ACT(S)	OPPRESSOR	REF.
Othniel	40	8	Was victorious in war against King Cushan-rishathaim	Mesopotamia	3:7-11
Ehud	80	18	Plunged a dagger, with his left hand, so deep into King Eglon's belly even the handle disappeared	Moab	3:12-30
Shamgar	-	-	Slaughtered 600 of the invaders with a long sharp cattle prod	Philistines	3:31
Deborah	40	20	The only female Judge. General Sisera defeated by a woman with a tent peg	Canaanites	4-5
Gideon	40	7	Used a fleece to determine God's will, defeating 135,000 Midianites with just 300 men	Midianites	6-8
Tola	23	-	Judged Israel for 23 years	-	10:1-2
Jair	22	-	Had 30 sons who rode 30 donkeys and owned 30 towns	-	10:3-5
Jephthah	6	18	Made a rash vow ending in the death of his daughter	Philistines and Ammonites	10:6-12:7
Ibzan	7	-	Had 30 sons and 30 daughters	-	12:8-10
Elon	10	-	Judged Israel for 10 years	-	12:11-12
Abdon	8	-	Had 40 sons and 30 grandsons, all 70 had his own donkey	-	12:13-15
Samson	20	40	Killed a lion with his bare hands, attacked Philistines with a donkey's jawbone, betrayed by Delilah - but strengthened by God in one last mighty act	Philistines	13-16

6 - Gideon Is Summoned And Tests His Call With A Fleece

7 - Gideon Defeats Midianites With A Reduced Army!

8 - Gideon Is Asked To Be King But Remains A Judge

Day 68

Judges 6-8

9th March

Gideon Defeats Midianites And Israel Has Peace

The Big Picture

This is the fifth of the seven cycles of Judges. Gideon was challenged by the Angel of the Lord whilst threshing wheat at the bottom of a winepress. After this miraculous encounter Gideon asks the angel for a miraculous sign to confirm God's call! This is when a fleece is laid on the threshing floor twice to provide him with confirmation. Gideon's army is found to be too big and God gets him to reduce it to just 300! With this small number victory is assured and the Midianites are defeated. Gideon is invited to be King and renamed Jerubbaal but refuses the throne declaring that it belongs to the Lord. However his son Abimelech has other ideas after Gideon's death.

Thinking Step

6:11 – '...Gideon...was threshing wheat at the bottom of a winepress...' A very poor place to do this. This operation should have been out in the open on a threshing floor so that the wind could blow away the chaff but 'Mighty Hero' Gideon was hiding from the Midianites.

Action Step

How many times have you heard people say that they have laid a fleece out so that God could confirm His call. In 6:36-38 – we see that when Gideon wanted the fleece wet, verse 38 says – '...and that is just what (naturally) happened.' However when Gideon asked for the fleece to be dry, verse 40 says – 'So that night God did as Gideon asked.' The second one, with opposite results had to be a miracle! If you are tempted to lay down a fleece for confirmation please be sure to ask for something that if it happens, will truly reveal the hand of God. Remember when Gideon meets an angel he is not persuaded even when in 6:21 the angel 'zaps' a meal into a burnt offering and then disappears! Then Gideon asks for a miraculous sign!! I remember having a conversation some time ago as two of us looked out of an office window to a distant hill. "If that moved to the other side of the window while we are away at lunch" my colleague said "Then I would believe there is a God!" "Would you really" I asked. "Not really" he said honestly "I'd look for a scientific explanation!" We are not persuaded by miraculous signs; there are times when we simply have to bow the knee and admit our intellect is inadequate and just believe!

Day 69
Judges 9-12
10th March

9 - Abimelech Briefly Becomes King At Shechem
10 - Tola And Jair Judge With Little Impact
11 - Jephthah Is Called With Better Results
12 - Ibzan, Elon And Abdon Judge Next

Many Judges
But Only One Makes A Godly Impact

The Big Picture

Abimelech son of Gideon is anointed King of Israel and rules for three years. His end comes when a woman drops a millstone onto his head but he insists his armour bearer kills him so that he was not killed by a woman! Next Tola and Jair judge Israel then the sixth cycle begins as the Philistines and the sons of Ammon begin to dominate Israel. Jephthah is persuaded to be a Judge despite his mother being a prostitute. He makes a foolish promise which results in his daughter's death. Ephraim is conquered because its people couldn't say "Shibboleth" properly! Finally three Judges about whom we know virtually nothing rule over Israel, Ibzan, Elon and Abdon.

Thinking Step

Ask most people and they will tell you Saul was the first King of Israel. 9:6 tells us that Abimelech was made King by men of Shechem. The difference was that Saul whose name means 'chosen by God' was God's choice whilst Abimelech was chosen by the men of Shechem!

Action Step

How many times have you said "You got yourself into this mess so you have to get out of it!" During the sixth cycle of judges we read that God calls the bluff of the Israelites in 10:14 after they have turned from Him to worship the Baals of the Philistines and the Ammonites. This isn't the first time they have gone astray like this and even true repentance can't pass without a challenge this time – "Why don't you cry out to the gods which you have chosen..." Wishful thinking is so often mistaken for stepping out in faith. If you seem to be making one wrong decision after another, slow down and read James 1:5 – 'If any of you lacks wisdom he should ask God who gives generously to all without finding fault and it will be given to him.' Remember when they looked for the first deacons they chose men who were full of the Spirit and wisdom – Acts 6:3. Making mistakes is not unforgivable but it is second best to getting things right! Making repeated poor judgements is the mark of a disciple who isn't grounded in the Word and Spirit led. If you know you're heading in the wrong direction today why not repent before God, start again, ask for an infilling of the Spirit and wisdom – and trust Him to be as good as His Word!

106

Samson – The Strong Man Who Was So Weak!

The Big Picture

In these four chapters we have the account of the strongest yet weakest of all the Judges, Samson. God gives a baby to a barren woman and he is dedicated as a Nazarite in accordance with Numbers 6:2-5. Later when he grows up Samson is to be married but loses his wife to his best-man! His amazing strength is the mark of his leadership but his answer to everything seems to be rooted in brute force. The infamous story of his girlfriend Delilah and his unfortunate hair cut are recorded here followed by his ultimate demise as he destroys the place where the Philistines are worshipping their god Dagon. This breaks his own record for killing Philistines!

Thinking Step

16:3 – 'Now Samson lay until midnight and...arose and took hold of the doors of the city gate and the two posts and pulled them up along with the bars, then he put them on his shoulders and carried them up to the top of the mountain which is opposite Hebron.' A journey of over 30 miles!

Action Step

What is your philosophy of life? In the case of Samson I think he would have said something like "If in doubt kill them!" Each of the three chapters recording his adult life has at least one reference to violence by Samson. Any brave friends he had should have gathered all their courage together and challenged him with the question "Don't you ever learn Samson?" At the very end of his life he is blinded and then set to work with the menial task of grinding corn. The added insult to such a strong macho man was that this work was usually done by women! The Philistines decide to ridicule him even more by bringing him out to amuse them but they get more than they bargained for! It's probably been some time since Samson prayed to God but with the help of a young lad he is led to the supporting pillars of the temple. There he prays his last prayer and as he starts he asks God to remember him! How God must have longed for a different prayer! After a life of violence Samson asks for one last thing from God – strength to kill all the Philistines in the temple! He appears to have learned nothing! What about you? Are you still showing the same weaknesses now that you showed when you were younger? Pray today that you will 'grow up' in your Christian faith!

Day 71
Judges 17-19
12th March

17 - Story Of A Levite For Hire
18 - Story Of A Whole Tribe Going Astray
19 - Personal And Tribal Immorality

A Little Wickedness Can Go A Long Way!

The Big Picture

Despite having five chapters remaining in the book of Judges Samson is the last Judge we will read about. The familiar saga of failure through idolatry and immorality continues however. The story of Micah and his appointment of a young Levite as his own personal priest is an interesting cameo in this book of cyclic failure for so many centuries. We learn more details of Dan's failure to conquer their allocated land and their travelling north to settle in Laish. Finally we have the account of a Levite who takes a concubine into his home but she is unfaithful to him and returns to her father only to die a grisly death after the Levite follows her.

Thinking Step

The sum of 1,100 pieces of silver are mentioned on two totally unrelated occasions in 16:5 and 17:2. It seems this could have been a way of saying "A vast fortune more than 1000 pieces!" In weight about 10 stones, the weight of an average adult – in silver!

Action Step

I am not to blame I'm a product of today's society. This is typical of the excuses we hear when some people are challenged about their poor life style. That's what they were saying repeatedly during the period of Judges but their exact words were "It's all because we have no king ruling in Israel!" People often say "If only my circumstances were different, if only I could win the lottery, if only my health was better, if only I had had better parents etc etc." When are we going to accept that we have a very big hand in shaping our own destiny and when Jesus is our Saviour we are empowered by the Holy Spirit! We are more than the product of our environment and gene pool we can be new creatures in Christ. As the apostle Paul wrote in 2 Cor. 5:17 'Therefore if anyone is in Christ he is a new creation, the old has gone the new has come!' No matter what you were you are new and have amazing potential when you are in Christ. It was said of Augustine of Hippo, when a woman of low morals from his past shouted to him "Augustine it's me!." He replied "Yes but it isn't me!" He changed radically and so can you! So what are you going to ask God to help you change in your life today?

Benjamin Escapes Extinction – But Only Just!

The Big Picture

Civil war erupts between Israel and Benjamin following the death of the concubine of the Levite. Benjamin was hopelessly outnumbered with an army of only 26,000 against Israel's 400,000! Despite some severe defeats and large casualties Israel continues to trust God. The final battle resulted in the tribe of Benjamin being virtually wiped out. Only 600 escape and find refuge at Ramon in the wilderness. Despite the men of Israel all taking an oath not to let their daughters marry men from Benjamin they long to help their brother tribe. Following a battle at Jabesh-Gilead Israel takes 400 virgin women as prisoners and gives them to Benjamin. With more women from Shiloh the tribe of Benjamin once again became viable.

Thinking Step

20:2 quotes 400,000 soldiers only a short time after 5:8 mentions 40,000 – how come? Counting in those days was not the exact science it is today and sometimes only the men were counted as in Numbers, sometimes only the clans or families and sometimes only the officers in charge.

Action Step

Have you ever noticed that even when you are doing what God wants you to do things don't always go without problems and failures? I am sure the Apostle Paul would confirm this and even the Lord Jesus was tempted immediately after His Father in Heaven confirmed that He was very pleased with His Son at His baptism. Even after God had confirmed the action to be taken regarding the tribe of Benjamin there were still considerable fatalities for Israel in 20:21, then after that another heavy defeat with extensive deaths in 20:25. Even after confirming things with God again the third battle with Benjamin was initially going far from well. Then the breakthrough came and victory followed – in God's good timing. Being a believer doesn't insulate us from problems it simply gives us the guarantee that God will see us through it. Like with David in Psalm 23 – 'Even though I walk through the valley of the shadow of death I will fear no evil for you are with me.' So what about today? When problems loom up try to remember that your life is a journey and that you will come out the other end of each experience. Be assured that God will not have caused this trouble – He's not like that! Try asking yourself "What can I learn?" rather than "Why me?"

Ruth

Ruth

A family saga which includes a touching love story involving a non-jewish woman. It is firmly rooted in the period of Judges – 1:1. In those Godless times few people followed the God of Israel. When a famine hits the land a married couple Naomi and Elimelech, with their two sons decide to move to neighbouring Moab. It's not a long way off geographically – little more than a couple of days journey but as a Gentile land it is far away from Jewish culture. God moves in amazing ways so that years later Naomi returns to Bethlehem with no husband or sons – all have died in Moab and she brings with her one of her daughters-in-law Ruth. Despite Ruth being a Moabite, who were hated by the Jews and who hated them in return, God uses her and rewards her with a unique place in history.

Below is an acrostic which summarises each chapter of the book.

1.   Ruth returns with Naomi
2.   Unlimited gleaning from Boaz
3.   Time for kinsman redeemer
4.   Husband redeemer for Ruth

Day 73
Ruth 1-4
14th March

1 - Ruth Marries But Ends Up In Bethlehem As A Widow
2 - Ruth Gleans And Is Protected By Boaz
3 - Boaz Desires To Be Ruth's Kinsman Redeemer
4 - Ruth Brings Grandfather Of David Into The World

The Love Story Of A Jew And A Moabite

The Big Picture

An ordinary couple leave Bethlehem to find refuge in Moab. They take with them their two sons. They probably chose Moab instead of the more popular Egypt because the Moabites would be less familiar with the Hebrew language and they wanted wives for their two sons called Mahlon and Kilion whose names meant 'Sickly' and 'Wasting Away' in the Hebrew language! Only Naomi and Ruth return and to survive Ruth gleans in the field of Boaz who becomes her Kinsman-Redeemer and husband. They have a son called Obed. That could have been the end if Obed had not had a son called Jesse who became the father of David who was a key ancestor of Jesus the Christ.

Thinking Step

The mother of Boaz is the infamous Canaanite Rahab – Matt 1:5. His father is Salmon – Matt 1:5 (who may have been one of the spies in Jericho where Rahab lived). Ruth is a Moabite. This means these two direct ancestors of Jesus Christ were half Jewish and non-Jewish respectively.

Action Step

I think one of the biggest barriers to salvation is church! We give the impression so many times that you have to be good to be a Christian. More than that you have to be respectable to be a follower of Jesus! May we be forgiven for such a distortion of the truth. Our reading today confirms, if it needed confirming that 'Gentile Canaanites,' 'Children of Lot Moabites' and 'Mixed Race People' are all acceptable to God! Surely not! – well, this short book of Ruth makes it clear so the only way around it is to reduce the Old Testament to 38 books (but you will need to reject a few others too before we get to Malachi if you take this route!) It's very clear salvation is for everyone! Rejoice in this truth and make sure you are one who has received Jesus as Lord and Saviour. If you haven't already then the first step is simply repenting and saying you're sorry for all the wrong you have done. Next, accept Jesus as Lord and Saviour and finally live the rest of your life empowered by the Holy Spirit within the fellowship of a local church. What's more, it means everyone you know is eligible too! Everyone you meet today qualifies! Remember this when you are irritated by someone today or someone is particularly obnoxious! You and I probably only qualified for salvation because it's open to everyone!

1 Samuel

1 Samuel

Emphasis now moves from tribal rule by Judges to kingdom rule by Kings. Samuel has been described as the last Judge and the first prophet. Hannah is a barren woman who miraculously has a son and names him Samuel and dedicates him to God, leaving him to be raised by Eli. Eli's sons are rejected as his successors and the whole family die leaving Samuel as priestly successor. The cry that began during the period of Judges is shouted again "We want a King!" and guided by God, Samuel anoints Saul as the first King of Israel but he fails to fulfil the role well. Soon afterwards David is anointed as King and kills Goliath whilst visiting his brothers who are in Saul's army. Saul makes several attempts on David's life but with the friendship of Saul's son Jonathan, David survives to become King when Saul dies in battle.

Below is an acrostic which summarises each chapter of the book.

1. Birth of Hannah's son
2. Immorality of Eli's sons
3. Revelation of Eli's judgement
4. Tragedy of ark's capture
5. Heavenly glory leaves Israel

6. Offerings with returned ark
7. Foreign gods are removed

8. Stubborn request for king
9. Appointment of Saul arranged
10. Making Saul Israel's king
11. Unified defence of Jabesh
12. Exhortation against demanding king
13. Lesson of Saul's foolishness

14. Triumph of Jonathan's attack
15. Hopelessness of Saul's disobedience
16. Record of David's anointing
17. Overthrow of giant Goliath
18. Unfriendly Saul threatens David
19. Guarding David from Saul
20. Helpful Jonathan shields David

21. David demands priests' provisions
22. Ahimelech killed by Saul
23. Victory over the Philistines
24. Integrity shown by David
25. Death of Samuel mourned
26. Saul spared by David

27. Exile in Philistine territory
28. X-rated seance with witch
29. Integrity of David challenged
30. Loss of Ziklag avenged
31. End of Saul's life

Samuel Is Called And Responds Positively

The Big Picture

Hannah's barrenness ends when Samuel is born. She brings him to Eli as promised and declares a prophetic prayer to God. Samuel is raised as a Nazirite, according to Numbers 6:5 and hears God's call whilst still a child. He quickly grows to be all that Eli's sons are not. The Israelites are defeated by the Philistines when the sons of Eli carry the Ark of the Covenant into battle with them and the Ark is captured. Shortly afterwards Eli is told of the death of both of his sons and he collapses and dies too. Israel is despondent, sure that God has left them and Ichabod, meaning 'no glory', is born to Eli's son Phinehas.

Thinking Step

2:12-13,17 'Now the sons of Eli were scoundrels who had no respect for the Lord or for their duties as priests...so the sin of these young men was very serious in the Lord's sight.' – Why? All because they did not live according to the written Word of God!

Action Step

The story is told of a very able swimmer who is struggling to reach the coast after a long and arduous swim. It's very cold and misty so she can see only a few yards ahead. She is in pain and despite the encouragement of those in her support boat she decides to surrender to the circumstances and give in. Imagine her despondency when the mist lifts and she sees the shore only a short distance away. "I wish I had kept going" she cried. "I couldn't believe my distress would have ended so soon." When Eli's sons are both killed whilst working as priests it is little wonder that Eli is staggered. He collapses and dies of a broken neck but many would suspect of a broken heart too. When his daughter in law widow of Phinehas gives birth it is a sad occasion. So sad that she burdens the poor child with a name that means 'No Glory' – Ichabod. Life seems so dark it could never be good again! In deathly dark days we need to remember that above the dark cloud that envelopes us is the same shining God who loves us no matter what. He is much closer than He seems. The reality is much more reassuring than our perception at times like this. We simply need to hold on to our Father in Heaven who is always holding on to us!

Day 75
1 Samuel 5-8
16th March

5 - The Philistines Seize The Ark - And Sin
6 - The Israelites Retrieve The Ark - And Sin
7 - The Israelites Repent And Conquer The Philistines
8 - Samuel's Sons Are Rejected As Judges

Samuel Is Great Judge But Poor Father!

The Big Picture

The Philistines still have the Ark. They decide to put it in Dagon's temple in Ashdod but with calamitous consequences as Dagon's statue falls and is then broken into pieces! Tumours and mice infestation spreads through the population of the town so the ark is removed to another town with the same consequences. This happens again so the ark is loaded onto a cart also carrying golden replicas of tumours and mice. The cart journeys to the Israelites and there is rejoicing. However another move soon becomes essential. The Ark finally settles for the next twenty years. Samuel's sons are rejected as his successors and the cry for a King once again is sounded out.

Thinking Step

6:10-12 '...Two cows were hitched to the cart and their newborn calves were shut up in a pen and sure enough without veering off in other directions, the cows went straight along the road toward Beth-shemesh lowing as they went.' Cows would normally return to calves but God honoured the Philistine's fleece!

Action Step

Before hire-purchase and credit cards the only way to buy an expensive item was to save up for it and wait! Of course as a child that didn't stop me asking and asking for what I wanted for Christmas – months before December 25th. Just because we wait a long time and just because we really want something – it doesn't mean it will give us pleasure or benefit. The Israelites looked around at their neighbours and realised they were the only ones without a King. That didn't seem fair so they did what we all do sometimes, ask and ask and ask! I think they asked so long that they were concentrating on the asking rather than what they were asking for. Even when the consequences and costs of getting a King were explained to them they still responded like children. I can just see them stamping their feet and shouting their mantra "We want a King, we want a King" – so loudly that nothing else could be heard. I know the Bible says pray without ceasing but I don't think this necessarily means for ever. I understand it to mean fervently and regularly until an answer is received. Check your prayer list today to see if God has answered some of your long term prayers but not in the way you were hoping and replace them with some other needy causes.

9 - Saul - Chosen By God
10 - Saul - Anointed By Samuel
11 - Saul - Hailed As King By Israel
12 - Saul - Urged By Samuel To Follow God

Day 76
1 Samuel 9-12
17th March

Saul Seems To Have Everything Going For Him!

The Big Picture

Saul comes into the picture now as this tall handsome man experiences difficulties finding his father's donkeys! He decides to consult Samuel to see if he can help and Samuel after some protestations from Saul anoints him King of Israel! His main calling God said was to deliver his people from the Philistines. However not all the people are convinced until there is a cry for help from a city further north on the east side of the Jordan River. Saul gathers a great army of fighting men. The city is freed from the Ammonites and the Israelites all want Saul as their King! Samuel warns them that they must support Saul as their King otherwise both will lose out.

Thinking Step

Three times we see 'worthless' in 1 Samuel – previously in 1:16 and 2:12 and today in 10:27. It literally means 'sons of Belial' (or sons of the devil). It's still around centuries later – Paul writes in 2 Cor. 6:15 'What harmony is there between Christ and Belial? – or what does a believer have in common with an unbeliever?'

Action Step

In today's reading Saul was simply looking for his father's donkeys. He knew what he was doing even if he wasn't doing it very well this time. It was probably something he could do without a lot of thinking. However he is having no success so decides to ask for help. Well, Samuel finds Saul's donkeys for him but at the same time he finds a new King for Israel! Wow – now that's a challenge and a half! I think this amazing news maybe hadn't sunk in when Saul talks to his uncle. He is asked a straight forward question in 10:15, "... what did he (Samuel) say?..." Saul's answer is rather vague to say the least. He said the donkeys had been found but didn't tell his uncle that Samuel had anointed him to be King. Samuel later has difficulty finding Saul who was hiding in the baggage! It seems he was a very reluctant King! I believe there are many of us who turn a deaf ear to a call from God just like Saul seems to do in today's reading. It may be that you are rejecting a move because it will take you out of your comfort zone. You are plodding along quite nicely thank you. Don't reject what God has called you to do. Accept the challenge today and enjoy what God has for you. Remember a rut can so easily become a narrow grave!

Day 77
1 Samuel 13-15
18th March

13 - Saul - The Slide Begins
14 - Saul - He Plans To Succeed But Neglects God
15 - Saul - The End Is In Sight

Saul Fails – All By Himself!

The Big Picture

Saul is told that God regrets making him King and that his reign is to end! The number of years of his reign are omitted from the Hebrew text in 13:1. Thankfully Acts 13:21 tells us it is forty years. His early conflicts with the Philistines bring him some success but once, when Samuel fails to arrive to make the offerings – Saul offers them himself! This brings condemnation when Samuel arrives and also God's declaration that Saul's kingdom would not endure. Saul makes a foolish oath about not eating until he has success over the Philistines and it causes lots of problems within his army and family. Saul acknowledges his failures but it's too late the kingdom is slipping away!

Thinking Step

The Amalekites in today's reading appear in several passages of the Old Testament but finally disappear by the hand of the tribe of Simeon – 1 Chron. 4:43. Their homeland was probably south of Judah and they were a nomadic people. They probably came from Eliphaz a son of Esau, who had a son called Amalek Gen. 36:12.

Action Step

I was told years ago that there are only three answers to prayer – yes, no or wait! I can agree with this as an academic exercise but in practice it's so much harder! One of the hardest things to endure is being ignored! Now I don't believe God ignores our prayers but in today's reading He doesn't give Saul a clear 'Yes or No' response, so Saul impetuously acts anyway! See 13:9 and 14:38. Of course all prayers don't need an answer of confirmation. Praying for your family or friends or colleagues in mission etc. etc. doesn't require a definitive answer every time. Some of our prayers are for guidance or wisdom or confirmation – and we need specific answers, just like Saul. If a clear 'No' is the answer then that's easy, don't move! I know it's never as easy as that but at least it's clear! If 'Yes' is clearly received then you can step out into whatever God has confirmed. Again it is rarely as easy as that but once again, at least it's clear! Now for the tricky one...no response. I think we should take no action, pray without ceasing until we get a definitive response. Saul thought his timing was better than God's and went ahead anyway – God's timing is always right, just live with it!

David Selected And Protected By God

The Big Picture

Half way through 1 Samuel and Saul has lost the kingdom, even if it takes a while before he is replaced by David. We begin with a repeat of the previous verse stating God's regret at making Saul King. Then Samuel sets off to find a replacement and anoints David but only after checking all his brothers first! David is appointed Saul's musician and becomes his armour bearer. Following a very generous reward scheme Goliath is defeated by David. Jonathan and David bond as life-long friends. Saul goes back on his unique reward scheme and tries to kill David on two occasions. David becomes very popular and finally marries a daughter of Saul! Saul keeps trying to kill David.

Thinking Step

17:40 – 'He picked up five smooth stones from a stream and...started across the valley to fight the Philistine.' Only one Philistine, so why five stones? Goliath was only one of five giants from Gath. The others must have run away but David and his men get them in the end – 2 Sam 21:15-22.

Action Step

Many years ago when our sons were young boys we used to be visited by my parents who made a journey of about 10 miles by car to visit us for tea every Thursday. One evening as they returned home, their car broke down and in the days before mobile phones, they could have been stranded for some time. They were encouraged when another car pulled up beside them but their encouragement quickly turned to apprehension when they saw the driver. He was 'all hair, tattoos and earrings' (according to my Dad!). Of course we didn't hear about this until they were safely home and were able to telephone us. "He couldn't have been more helpful" my Mum said. "He took us home first, then returned with your Dad to our car and waited with him until the breakdown truck arrived", he certainly didn't live up to his appearance – thankfully! In our reading today Samuel learned a similar lesson when he was looking for a new King. 16:7 tells us – 'The Lord said to Samuel "Don't judge by his appearance...The Lord doesn't see things the way you see them. People judge by outward appearance but the Lord looks at the heart."' Try wearing x-ray specs today! Try looking further than their skin with people you meet today – and remember they have similar limitations when they look at you!

Day 79
1 Samuel 20-23
20th March

20 - Saul Is Determined That David Will Die
21 - David Protected And Fed By Priests
22 - David Parents Safe In Moab; Saul Massacres Priests Of God
23 - David Attacks Philistines - Then Flees From Saul

David Honours Saul And God Honours David!

The Big Picture

On the run from Saul, David meets priests at Nob near Jerusalem and asks for food. When he confirms that he and his men have not slept with a woman recently he is given consecrated bread to eat. David also receives Goliath's sword and then heads for the security of Gath – of all places! There, when recognised, he feigns insanity! Moving on David goes to Moab to seek safety for his parents who he leaves there. Sadly the priests who earlier helped David are killed by order of Saul. Under the guidance of God, David attacks and conquers the Philistine invaders at Keilah but upon learning that Saul is coming he leaves for the caves of Engedi.

Thinking Step

20:31 – "As long as that son of Jesse is alive you'll never be King. Now go and get him so I can kill him!" Saul wanted David dead so that Jonathan would succeed him as King! Succession could have been a problem for David when the throne was vacated but Saul and three of his sons die together – 31:8

Action Step

In these days of people living longer and an enormous growth in care homes I often talk to folk who feel guilty that they are unable to take their ageing parents into their own home and look after them. Instead they have to arrange for them to go into a retirement home. Actually in Essex where we leave, some of these homes are difficult to tell apart from hotels! We have tried to make it easy for our sons by telling them that when circumstances dictate, we will willingly go into a retirement or nursing home. My one proviso is that our room must have wireless internet access and my laptop and laser printer be kept in good working order! Seriously, we want our children to enjoy life to the full and share much of it with us as they do now. We don't want to spoil things by squeezing two families into a house that is designed for one! It's interesting that with seven older brothers, David still has to take responsibility for his ageing parents. For him it's not possible to look after them himself but he still undertakes to keep them safe and well looked after. Resolve today to make it easy for your family when these decisions have to be made for you and tell them when you next see them! It could improve your relationship with them for ever!

24 - David Spares Saul - But Not His Robe!
25 - Abigail Wiser Than Her Husband Nabal
26 - David Rejects Another Opportunity To Kill Saul

Day 80
1 Samuel 24-26
21st March

David Refuses To Kill The Lord's Anointed

The Big Picture

Saul takes 3,000 men to Engedi where David was hiding in a cave. When Saul entered to use it as a toilet David refused to kill him but cuts off the bottom of his robe and waives it when he leaves shouting "My Lord the King". David and Saul are reconciled. The news of Samuel's death only takes up one verse, this is followed by the story of Nabal and his wife Abigail and how they deal with David and his men. When Nabal dies David marries Abigail. David moves west but news reaches Saul and he brings his 3,000 men again. David has another opportunity to kill Saul but refuses once again. They are reconciled again!

Thinking Step

Within Judaism the hem or bottom of the robe represents the authority of the wearer and is the place where fringes may be found indicating social standing etc. It's significant that Saul has his hem removed by David in 24:4 and earlier when it is torn by Samuel in 15:27. Link this with Luke 8:43.

Action Step

I used to serve on an eldership where one of my colleagues could not accept a decision going against him. I remember a particular issue when he was in a minority of one! We debated, reasoned, then prayed the issue through before having a show of hands. The result was predictable, with him being the only dissenter. Graciously he acknowledged that he would accept the majority as the Lord's will and the meeting continued. A month later it was like the film "Groundhog Day." It all happened again – with the same outcome! He relived this whenever he could and never as far as I can recall, actually accepted that he simply got this one wrong. It seemed to me that his 'conviction' had turned sour and needed to be dropped. In our reading today I think Saul is like that. Never really changing his mind just saying that he had and always looking to get his own way the next time. I think we all like to think that our opinions are the same as God's but when they aren't we must show due humility and stop being a barrier to what the Lord wants. It can be a sign of strength when we change our minds and agree with others who have God on their side! Try it! Just because you are in a minority it doesn't mean it's a cause to fight for!

Day 81
1 Samuel 27-31
22nd March

27 - David Finds Refuge With The Philistines
28 - Saul Consults Medium When God Doesn't Answer Him
29 - Philistines Don't Need Help From David
30 - David Has Revenge On The Amalekites
31 - Saul And His Sons Die On Mount Gilboa

Saul Dies And Is Replaced By David

The Big Picture

David retreats to Gath and lives in Ziklag. From there he waged guerilla attacks on Philistine cities leaving King Achish to incorrectly think that he was loyal to the Philistine cause! God is silent for Saul who in desperation consults the witch of Endor to raise up Samuel and is told his sons will die tomorrow! The Philistines are about to attack Saul but as the people don't trust David, he is not included in the army. David returns to Ziklag to find it ransacked. With God's encouragement he pursed the attackers, the Amalakites, and retrieves all that was taken. Meanwhile the Philistines engage with Saul on Mount Gilboa. Saul and his three sons are killed. Now David is King!

Thinking Step

11:1-11 records Saul's rescuing of the city of Jabesh-gilead from the Ammonites. This deed was never forgotten and it is the men from this same city who recovered Saul's body as well as those of his sons from the degradation of being displayed on the walls of Beth-shan – 31:11-13.

Action Step

I don't understand how fortune tellers make a living! If the news is good then I can wait and will enjoy it when it happens! If the news is bad then I really don't want to know and am happy to wait for it to come in the fullness of time. I suppose it's the eternal nature in all humans that naturally thinks of life after death. It's the way we are made! It always saddens me that newspapers and magazines as well as many websites constantly waive the astrology flag and it is accepted as perfectly okay – just a bit of fun! The true life giver Jesus Christ, is shunned and locked away in case any offence is caused to unbelievers! There is no doubt that there is a life hereafter – the only questions are where will we will spend it and with whom! I believe quality of life in the here and now is what most people long for and need. Life lived to the full as Jesus put it. If we get our priorities right here on earth and accept Jesus as Lord and Saviour, our future is assured, it's with Him! Whenever you come across any astrological propaganda why not offer a short prayer for the soul of the first unsaved person who comes into your mind? At least that way we can use this astrological dross for a good positive purpose.

2 Samuel

2 Samuel

The changeover from Saul to David takes about seven years but finally David is established as King and rules initially from Hebron and then Jerusalem. There are more issues with the Ark of the Covenant before it is housed in the home of Obed-edom from Gath! David plans to build a temple but is told that he will not – his son will – and he praises God! David has many victories over the surrounding nations but then his adultery with Bathsheba and the murder of her husband Uriah is a great setback. Nathan confronts David and he repents. His successor, Solomon, is born to him and Bathsheba is his mother. Absalom who was born to David in Hebron attempts to take the kingdom from his father but is murdered by Joab as he hangs in a tree caught by his hair. David is devastated but again praises God.

Below is an acrostic which summarises each chapter of the book.

1. **H**eaviness of David's heart
2. **I**shbosheth made Israel's king
3. **S**adness over Abner's death
4. **T**orture of Ishbosheth's killers
5. **O**utset of David's reign
6. **R**emoving ark to Jerusalem
7. **Y**earning to build temple

8. **O**ppressors subdued by David
9. **F**avour shown to Mephibosheth

10. **T**riumph over Ammonite alliance
11. **H**ypocrisy of David's adultery
12. **E**ffects of David's sin

13. **R**eproach placed upon Tamar
14. **E**xiled Absalom comes home
15. **I**nsurrection by son Absalom
16. **G**ravity of Ahithophel's advice
17. **N**ature of Hushai's counsel

18. **O**pposition by Absalom ends
19. **F**orgiving of Absalom's followers

20. **D**eath of rebellious Sheba
21. **A**vengement on Saul's sons
22. **V**ictory psalm by David
23. **I**dentity of David's men
24. **D**avid's census brings plague

David Is Finally Established As King Of Judah

The Big Picture

The account of Saul's death is repeated and David curses Mount Gilboa where it happened. David's reign begins in Hebron where he rules over Judah for just over seven years. Abner is the leading light for the house of Saul and under his guidance a surviving son of Saul, Ish-bosheth is anointed King of Israel but rules for only two years. War between Saul's army led by Abner and the army of David continues. A truce is attempted but fails when Abner is killed by Joab the leader of David's army. The surviving son of Saul is murdered but Mephibosheth son of Jonathan, comes into the picture now. David's reign in Judah is about to increase to include Israel.

Thinking Step

Instead of being buried with his father and brothers in Jabesh – 1 Sam 31:13, Ish-bosheth is buried in Hebron with Abner. Old enough – as he was 40 years old when crowned King 2:10 – yet not fighting on Mount Gilboa with his father and brothers when they die. Was there already a plot for him to replace Saul?

Action Step

So often we expect our children to do what we say rather than do what we do. How many times have you looked at your children and seen yourself especially when they are less than well behaved! In our reading today when David fasts in 3:36 the people are very impressed and the text goes on to say that they were pleased with everything else the King did! Of course this would be spoilt when David sins with Bathsheba but usually David's actions were very influential for good. A friend of mine was travelling on a local bus. It was only after he had paid the driver and sat down that he realised he had been given too much change. As the bus filled he resolved that it was too much trouble to give the excess money back to the driver and would simply put it in the offering next Sunday. When he was about to get off, his conscience wouldn't let him leave with the extra money so he made his way towards the driver. "You gave me too much change" my friend said. The driver answered "I know I just wanted to see if you would live up to your sermon last Sunday when you talked about honesty!" Try living today as if you were role playing for your children or someone else's children. I think you'll be surprised by how many changes you have to make!

Day 83
2 Samuel 5-7
24th March

5 - David Anointed King Of Israel
6 - Moving Of Ark Results In Rejoicing And Sadness
7 - David Is Told He Cannot Build A Temple

Finally David Rules Israel And Judah

The Big Picture

David is anointed King over Israel and rules Judah and Israel for a total of forty years. His headquarters are now in Jerusalem as he establishes his kingdom with victories over the Philistines. Whilst bringing the Ark into Jerusalem it is incorrectly handled and Uzzah dies, David then leaves the Ark with Obed-edom for three months. Finally it is taken into Jerusalem with much rejoicing and some criticism from David's wife Michal. It is at this high point in his life that David is told by Nathan the prophet that the honour of building God's temple in Jerusalem will fall to his heir and not David. David responds positively and praises God anyway!

Thinking Step

The death of Uzzah is a problem for David and may seem unfair but 1 Chron. 3:13-15 looking back at this, clearly states the Ark should have been carried by Levites and not placed on a cart. The correct method of movement as laid out by Moses in Ex 25 and Numbers 4, was followed in 6:13.

Action Step

Of all places for the Ark of the Covenant to find rest it was the house of the Gittite Obed-edom a citizen of Gath. The Bible clearly states that the household of Obed-edom was blessed by the Lord as a result. No details are given of how this took place but it is clear that Obed-edom did things right and God blessed him. There is no mention of thanks from David but as Obed-edom's actions were for the Lord I am sure that God's blessing was all that he needed. It's reasonable to conclude that the Ark of the Covenant which represented God Himself was given the appropriate place within the household and I think this is the key. When God is in His rightful place in our lives then He is able and willing to bless us. More than that when God is in His rightful place in our families, He is able and willing to bless us. The question for today is "Is God in the centre of your life and family or is He simply an addition which dominates Sundays but takes a back seat for the rest of the week." Try leaving one of your Bibles (most of us have several) in a prominent place where you will see it every day as a reminder of putting God in His rightful place – at the centre of everything we do.

8 - David Has Many Victories
9 - David's Compassion Over Mephibosheth
10 - Ammonites Insult Results In Their Defeat

Day 84
2 Samuel 8-10
25th March

David's Victories Mean He Can't Build The Temple

The Big Picture

David continues to conquer his enemies, confirming why God wants His temple built by a King with less blood on his hands! For the sake of his good friend Jonathan, David seeks out any of his relatives. He is put in touch with Jonathan's son Mephibosheth, who is disabled in both feet. In fear and trembling he comes to see David and falls at his feet. David greets him warmly and offers him accommodation and regular dining at his royal table in Jerusalem. David tries to pay his respects to the new King of the Ammonites upon the death of his father. The offer of friendship is rejected and David's messengers are disgraced. A battle follows with victory for David.

Thinking Step

Imagine Ziba's suspicions when David enquires if any other members of Saul's family are still alive! It could easily have been a ruse to get the opportunity to kill a rival for the throne. That's probably why he twice tells David that Mephibosheth is disabled in verses 3 and 13 therefore no threat to David.

Action Step

Twice in our short reading today we read the same words – 'So the Lord made David victorious wherever he went' – 8:6 and 14. When you first read this whole passage you get the impression that it was the brilliant David or his amazing army that gained his many victories – but it was the Lord! I have heard some great preachers preaching some great sermons but if they use the word 'I' too often, I am afraid I lose interest! Whatever we do for the Lord has to be acknowledged as a joint venture. The sooner we can lose the 'I-Self' approach to ministry and enjoy the 'We-team' approach, the more God can use us. I think these lyrics from a Don Francisco song of several years ago just about sums it all up -

The Lord's the one who makes the choice of the instrument He's usin'
We don't know the reasons and the plans behind His choosin'
So when the Lord starts usin' you don't you pay it any mind
He could have used the dog next door if He'd been so inclined.

It is truly amazing that God does use us isn't it? Just be grateful today that you are not on your own. So next time you think "I could do that for God" – pause and ask God if 'we' should do it together.

Day 85
2 Samuel 11-13
26th March

11 - David Sins With Bathsheba
12 - David Repents Before Nathan
13 - Tamar Is Revenged By Absalom

Sin Has Inevitable Consequences

The Big Picture

We have a very personal narrative now. The adultery of David with Bathsheba and the plotting of David to get her husband Uriah killed in battle. Uriah shows himself a very faithful man whilst David and Bathsheba blatantly betray him. After being confronted by Nathan, David acknowledges his sin against God and repents. Sadly his child by Bathsheba dies but David turns to God in worship accepting God's judgement. They have another son, his name is Solomon. Absalom a favourite son of David arranges for his brother Amnon to be murdered after his despicable treatment of their sister Tamar. Absalom then flees the country only to be sorely missed by his loving father David.

Thinking Step

Ironically bathing is a cleansing ritual within Judaism. Yet it is the act of bathing that caused the downfall of David and Bathsheba. Her name means 'daughter of an oath' so it could be that her adultery broke her faithful parents hearts too! On a lighter note, my computer spellchecker offered only one alternative for Bathsheba – it was 'bathtub'!

Action Step

Of course there are always extenuating circumstances when I sin, whereas when others do wrong it's just that they are weak and cannot withstand temptation! I know we rarely would put it in such stark terms but...it is close to the truth isn't it! David seems to be very willing to condemn the sinner in Nathan's story but never sees that it could be him! We knew a couple who many years before, had married because she was pregnant. He was already married to someone else and had to be divorced in those days when divorce was the unforgivable sin for many people. They had repented and put all this behind them and had a full and faithful relationship together for many years. Of course God had forgiven and forgotten their deeds of so long ago. Sadly however, they had forgotten them so well that they were always the first to criticise others in similar plight. They never saw themselves in other people's circumstances even when they were very similar! Unfortunately that can be true for each of us and we quickly take the high moral ground forgetting that we are forgiven sinners too! Please remember today what Jesus taught in the prayer we call the Lord's prayer – "Forgive us our sins as we forgive those who sin against us!" Do you have some forgiving to do today? Why not do it as though your own forgiveness depended on it...

14 - Absalom Returns To Jerusalem

15 - Absalom Schemes With Help From Ahithophel

16 - Absalom Declared King

Day 86

2 Samuel 14-16

27th March

David's Problems With His Son Absalom

The Big Picture

Joab sends a wise woman to see David with a story that is very similar to the David and Absalom situation. David agrees to allow Absalom to return. He returns to Jerusalem but doesn't see David for two years. Absalom raises support amongst the people and devises a plan to replace David as King. David recognises his support is slipping away in favour of Absalom and leaves the city even leaving the Ark behind. Ahithophel is now advising Absalom rather than David but Hushai remains faithful. David discovers that Mica son of Mephibosheth, is hoping to be King and is already in Jerusalem. Prophecy of 12:11-12 is fulfilled as Absalom is advised to take his father's harem.

Thinking Step

15:29 – 'So Zadok and Abiathar took the Ark of God back to the city and stayed there.' An act of faithfulness from the priest Zadok who later anoints Solomon as King and replaces Abiathar as Chief Priest. Many believe the Sadducees in the days of Jesus are followers of this Zadok and derive their name from him.

Action Step

Our reading today includes a very unusual account of two instances of stone throwing 16:6 and 16:13. The usual response would have been that suggested in 16:9 – 'Abishai son of Zeruiah demanded. "Let me go over and cut off his head!"' – and that would have been an end to it. It's interesting that David forbids them taking any such hasty action because what is happening could be from God! These instances take place on the Mount of Olives where centuries later, Jesus' disciples witness the arrest of Jesus and want to fight to rescue Him but He forbids it as He knows for certain it is the will of His Father in Heaven. Nevertheless Peter almost cuts off the head of Malchus – John 18:10 but has to be satisfied with an ear! It's at difficult times like this that it is hardest to follow and trust God, when things happen that confuse us, when the next step is not obvious. Doubts come into your mind and you are tempted to rationalise and veer off the pathway that God has previously made clear. If you are having particularly difficulties this week don't act in haste, they could be from God even though it may not appear so! God moves in mysterious ways – just remember that!

Rival Regime Is Removed – And David Weeps!

The Big Picture

Ahithophel suggests an immediate attack be made to take David's camp by surprise but only kill David. Hushai suggests a better plan would be to have a proper battle out in the open with large armies on both sides. The prayer of David that Ahithophel's counsel would appear foolish, is answered – 15:31. Hushai's advice is accepted by Absalom and Ahithophel is so shocked that he returns home and hangs himself! David splits his army into three and tells his men to deal gently with Absalom! Sadly when they find him trapped by his head in a tree, Joab kills him. When the news reaches David he simply replies "I wish I had died instead!"

Thinking Step

18:15 – 'Ten of Joab's young armour bearers then surrounded Absalom and killed him.' Why ten? Could it be because of 15:16 – 'So the King and all his household set out at once. He left no one behind except ten of his concubines to look after the palace.' One killer for each of the concubines abused in 16:22!

Action Step

17:23 tells us the very sad account of Ahithophel who for the first time, has his advice rejected. The text says 'When Ahithophel realised that his advice had not been followed he saddled his donkey, went to his home town, set his affairs in order and hanged himself. He died there and was buried in the family tomb.' Sure signs of immaturity and misplaced pride. If at first you don't succeed throw all your toys out of the pram and stamp your feet as hard as you can! One of the blights of the church today is just how many immature believers it contains. The story is told of a long standing Christian who applied for a paid post in another church but was told that she was not experienced enough for the position. She complained that she had been a Christian for twenty years whereas the person who was appointed had only been a believer for five years. She was told that whilst the other had only been a Christian for five years that was significantly longer than her, as it appeared she had been a believer for just one year – twenty times! Are you prone to having 'Ahithophel moments' ? Acting immaturely when real maturity is called for. Why not change the wallpaper on your mobile to show the face of a baby as a reminder not to be one yourself!

Trying Times For David

The Big Picture

David is devastated by the death of Absalom, so much so that Joab rebukes him for neglecting everyone else! Support from the northern tribes proves difficult to secure but the southern tribes claim David as 'one of theirs' – of the tribe of Judah! Joab is replaced as commander of the army by Amasa. David returns to Jerusalem only to learn of another revolt against his leadership. Sheba the Benjamite mounts a coup and wins over the northern tribes but his dominance is abruptly ended by an unnamed wise woman who cuts off his head and throws it to Joab in order to save her city from attack. David is back in control now and the kingdom is united – but not for much longer.

Thinking Step

It seems that David was so upset by the death of Absalom that we have to ask the question "Was Absalom David's first choice to succeed him as King?" Was he destined to rule in peace after David had finished the subduing of the enemies of Israel? Is that why he was called Absalom – 'Father of Peace.'

Action Step

19:33, 37 – "Come across with me and live in Jerusalem" the King said to Barzillai. "I will take care of you there." "...here is your servant my son Kimham. Let him go with my lord the King and receive whatever you want to give him." In our reading today faithful Barzillai, from Mahanaim, was offered so much by King David but preferred Kimham to receive the blessing. Stepping aside to allow a blessing to go to another is something that is not natural! 'If we have done the work we deserve the glory!' is the mantra for too many in our churches today. At a prayer meeting some time ago attended by leaders of the local churches, much prayer was offered for more souls to be saved and added to local churches. Then one man stood up and prayed "Please bring more into your Kingdom and expand your Church here in this town – even if it isn't in my fellowship!" Let's think in broad concepts rather than being limited to our church or denomination. When you hear of something happening that glorifies God but it's happening in another fellowship, thank God that at least it's happening! Then ask God to bring more into His Kingdom and to use YOU. That way your fellowship is more likely to be the one that grows – but if it results in another Church fellowship increasing in numbers, then praise God anyway!

No Matter What – God Is Worthy Of Praise

The Big Picture

There is a famine in the land and God tells David that it's because of the killing of Gibeonites by Saul. These are not recorded in the Bible. The solution is gruesome. Seven sons of Saul have to be sacrificed! In fact it finishes up being two sons and five grandsons. Rizpah, mother of the two sons, stays to protect the bodies which have been left unburied. David is so touched by this act that he lays to rest the bones of Saul and Jonathan in the tomb of Saul's father, Kish. A brief report of several wars with the Philistines and what happened to the four other giants of Gath is followed by a repeat of Psalm 18.

Thinking Step

21:15-22 – Here we have a list of the giants who escaped the four unused stones when David killed Goliath. It seems David is getting old now as he grows weary and needs help – see 21:15. In fact David kills none of them but relies on his servants to act for him.

Action Step

In Psalm 18 David gives us a glimpse of how God sees him and how He sees us. Phrases like – "He rescued me because He delights in me, I have kept the ways of the Lord, I have not turned away, I have never abandoned His principles, I am blameless before God – I have kept myself from sin." At first reading it seems that David is a bit above himself but the reality is that God sees us as we are in Him not as we see ourselves. That's difficult to comprehend for sinful people. I attended a seminar some time ago and the leader asked us to make a note of three things that would best describe us, then three things that our spouse would use to describe us! The lists were different of course but contained many similarities around the room. When summing up the responses the question was asked "How many of you described yourself, or thought your spouse would describe you as Holy?" Next time you feel unworthy or generally down in the dumps, try reading this Psalm and get a glimpse of how God sees David – and you! Of course the devil will tell you it's not true for you – but it is true when you are a child of God, just like David.

Last Words Of David As He Buys A Plot Of Land

The Big Picture

The last words of David constitute his final oracle and it is very like his Psalms. The list of David's Mighty Men contains names we have come across before but there are some about whom we know nothing. It begins with the main three, then two who don't quite make the top three. Lastly there is a considerable list but some of the names are difficult to clarify as one person or more, so counting is difficult. David takes a census of the whole of Israel then there is a plague when many people die. The plague stops when David buys Araunah's threshing floor to build an altar. Ultimately this is where Solomon builds the temple.

Thinking Step

Any names jump out at you apart from the last one, Uriah the Hittite? Did you see where Ira the son of Ikkesh came from? – Tekoa, which would later be the home of Amos the prophet. Did you notice Eliam, son of Ahithophel, the Gilonite? Eliam was one of David's mighty men whilst his father supported Absalom against David!

Action Step

Hidden in the list of David's Mighty Men is a beautiful account of three of his mighty men risking their lives in order to get him some water to drink. When he receives the water from his beloved Bethlehem well, he pours it out on the ground as an offering to the Lord. It says a lot for David's heart but it says a lot about his men too. Their devotion to David and to the Lord is admirable. When I was sent to Sunday school as a child, my Mum always gave me my collection and I always faithfully put it in the offering plate. There was no sense of sacrifice or dedication, I was just giving my collection like everyone else. When I became an adult attender my offering remained similar, larger but not sacrificial. Many people never move on from this point. Loose change is for the offering! I smile when occasionally, I hear from the front "Let's take up our offering now – and let's make it a completely silent one!" (Only paper money is silent!) David gave what he treasured most at that time. We are allowed to keep nine tenths of what we earn so we shouldn't begrudge God one tenth! Carry some loose change with you to remind you that God deserves His portion and should have first call on your money. The loose change is yours to keep and use wisely!

1 Kings

1 Kings

After the books of 1 & 2 Samuel which relate the accounts of the first two Kings of the United Kingdom Saul and David, this book covers the life of the third and last of the three Kings of the United Kingdom – Solomon. In many ways it is the climax of the United Kingdom with the Kingdom increasing its borders to the largest it will ever be. The amazing account of Solomon's temple being built is another significant event. Sadly Solomon's life is very much made up of two halves and after his two major building programmes, to build the temple and his own palace, Solomon fades away. Significantly because of that, his life only takes half of this book! The remaining half is dominated by lots of Kings, both north and south after the kingdom divides. During this period of division the greatest prophet of Judaism, Elijah strides onto the scene.

Below is an acrostic which summarises each chapter of the book.

1. **S**olomon anointed Israel's king
2. **O**pponents of David killed
3. **L**ord gives Solomon wisdom
4. **O**fficers of King Solomon
5. **M**aterials for temple requested
6. **O**uter temple is completed
7. **N**ature of Hiram's work

8. **S**olomon's prayer of dedication
9. **I**nstruction for Solomon's covenant
10. **N**ature of Solomon's riches
11. **S**olomon's wives bring idolatry

12. **I**nsurrection of northern tribes
13. **S**in of unnamed prophet
14. **R**eign of King Jeroboam
15. **A**bijam and Asa reign
16. **E**vildoers Omri and Ahab
17. **L**ord provides Elijah food

18. **S**overeignty shown on Carmel
19. **P**rophet Elijah calls Elisha
20. **L**oss by Syrian army
21. **I**njustice in Naboth's vineyard
22. **T**ermination of Ahab's life

Day 91
1 Kings 1-4
1st April

1 - Solomon Succeeds The Fading David
2 - David Counsels Solomon - Then Dies
3 - First Signs Of The Wisdom Of Solomon
4 - Wisdom Gives Way To Army Building!

Great Start By King Solomon

The Big Picture

'Favourite' son Absalom is now dead and Adonijah, son of David's wife Haggith, prepares to seize the throne and so a coup begins to develop. Meanwhile Nathan confers with Bathsheba about her son Solomon, being the next King and with David's blessing, Solomon is anointed King. As soon as David dies Adonijah, Joab and Shimei are executed whilst Abiathar the priest is dismissed. With this clean slate, Solomon in a dream, asks God for wisdom to rule well and uses this received wisdom immediately when two women argue over a child. Solomon appoints eleven Deputies or District Governors and twelve Princes or High Officials to help him rule the land. Solomon's fame was spreading and admirers came from far and wide.

Thinking Step

Solomon's wisdom lets him down! 4:26 – 'Solomon had 4,000 stalls for his chariot horses and he had 12,000 horses.' This is exactly what God didn't want! Deut 17:16 – 'The King must not build up a large stable of horses for himself or send his people to Egypt to buy horses...'

Action Step

Today we read of one of the many marriages of Solomon. 3:3 – 'Solomon loved the Lord and followed all the decrees of his father David, except that Solomon too offered sacrifices and burned incense at the local places of worship.' This is an early example of adding to what God had said and done. Today, there are many following in the steps of Solomon and adding to what God has said. I remember training counsellors for a Billy Graham event when one of them asked to have a word with me. He said he couldn't continue the training as we were only preaching half a gospel! He said that we needed to add that in order to be saved, you have to be baptised, in water by immersion as a believer. As a Baptist I knew where he was coming from but told him he was adding to the simple gospel something that is good and Biblical but not essential for conversion otherwise millions of converted Anglicans and Methodists, not to mention the thief on the cross, are destined to miss out on Heaven! When Jesus shouted "It is finished!" that is exactly what He meant. Ask yourself with the Bible as your authority, are you adding things to the gospel? If so, promise yourself now that you will stick to what the Bible teaches as your authority – with no add-ons!

Solomon's Temple 960-586 B.C.

"When Solomon finished praying, fire flashed down from heaven and burned up the burnt offerings and sacrifices, and the glorious presence of the Lord filled the temple. The priests could not enter the temple of the Lord because the glorious presence of the Lord filled it. When all the people of Israel saw the fire coming down and the glorious presence of the Lord filling the temple, they fell face down on the ground and worshipped and praised the Lord, saying **'He is good! His faithful love endures forever!'"**
(2 Chron. 7:1-3)

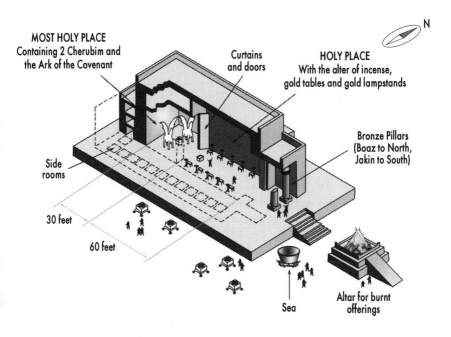

MOST HOLY PLACE
Containing 2 Cherubim and
the Ark of the Covenant

Curtains
and doors

HOLY PLACE
With the alter of incense,
gold tables and gold lampstands

N

Bronze Pillars
(Boaz to North,
Jakin to South)

Side
rooms

30 feet

60 feet

Sea

Altar for burnt
offerings

Day 92
1 Kings 5-8
2nd April

5 - The Temple Project Begins
6 - After Seven Years - The Temple Is Completed
7 - After Thirteen Years - Solomon's House Is Completed!
8 - Temple Furnished And Solomon Preaches, Prays & Rejoices

God's Temple And Solomon's House Completed

The Big Picture

Solomon contacts his father's friend in Lebanon, King Hiram, to arrange for a supply of good cedar wood. Labourers are recruited from Israel and each of them works for a month and then has two months off. The temple stones will be cut and dressed away from site so that the holy place is not desecrated. The project takes seven years. The next fourteen are taken up with the building of Solomon's house. Back at the temple with the help of Hiram a craftsman in bronze work, the pillars and utensils for the temple are added bringing the project to an end. The Ark is installed and the Glory of God fills the temple! Solomon preaches and prays and Israel rejoices!

Thinking Step

6:2 – 'The Temple that King Solomon built for the Lord was 90 feet long, 30 feet wide and 45 feet high.' 7:1-2 – '...Solomon's...Palace...was 150 feet long, 75 feet wide and 45 feet high' – nearly four times larger! Original measurements were in cubits. From the King's fingertip to his elbow – about 18" – the first ruler!

Action Step

8:27 As Solomon preaches he makes a very profound statement – '...but will God really live on earth? Why, even the highest heavens cannot contain you. How much less this Temple I have built!' Many, many times our God is too small and we need to, literally, magnify the Lord. I believe this is the root to much liberal thinking. When we read the Bible and we read of things that are frankly impossible for us to achieve, we then deduce that it is impossible for God too. I was told of an overheard conversation in a large cathedral when a young person saw a magnificent statue of the Virgin Mary holding the Baby Jesus. The youngster said "They have a small Jesus but we have a big Jesus!' There's so much truth in this childish statement. When you read the Bible try not to presume on God's ability by likening Him to you! God is so much bigger and more capable than we can ever imagine. Did you hear about the little girl who told her parents that she had been told of something that God couldn't do! He can't make a snowball so big that He can't lift it! On a serious note, if you have a small pocket testament why not put it in your pocket or handbag today to remind you that we have pocket size Bibles but we do not have a pocket size God!

9 - Covenant Renewed And Kingdom Expands   Day 93
10 - Queen Of Sheba Pays A Visit   1 Kings 9-11
11 - Solomon's Many Marriages Result In God's Rebuke   3rd April

All Seems To Be Thriving, Then Failure Comes!

The Big Picture

The temple is completed and Solomon makes a covenant with God. His building programme continues and includes a fleet of ships based in Ezion-geber, now Aqaba. The Queen of Sheba visits Solomon and is amazed by his wisdom and opulence. Solomon's harem grows and grows! Old adversaries of King David, Hadad the Edomite and Rezon son of Eliada, now look for revenge against David's son. A more formidable rebel was Jeroboam. Recruited by Solomon he soon hears a prophecy that he will rule over the ten northern tribes! Solomon threatens to kill him and he has to run to Egypt for safety. Rehoboam then comes to the throne and it is now safe for Jeroboam to return!

Thinking Step

11:3-4 – 'He had 700 wives of royal birth and 300 concubines...and sure enough they turned his heart to worship other gods...' Solomon writes in Eccl. 2:8-11 – '... and I had many beautiful concubines. I had everything a man could desire!... but...it was all so meaningless. There was nothing really worthwhile anywhere.'

Action Step

11:41 A summary of Solomon's final twenty years...'The rest of the events in Solomon's reign, including all his deeds and his wisdom, are recorded in The Book of the Acts of Solomon.' What sad words! Nothing of real merit worth recording in the Bible. We don't know exactly how old Solomon was he came to the throne but he was probably about 20 years old. If this is so, then this latter part of his life was when he was 40 – 60 years old. The prime of life! As a pastor I have met many lovely Christian folk who when they retire from secular work, feel they can retire from being an effective part of the Church of Christ! Some say "I was very active in my last church and I would like to simply 'fill the pew' now!" May God save us from ever being happy to fill the pew! Occasionally I am asked to fill a pulpit, I always respond by saying that I cannot but I am happy to come and preach! I knew a man many years ago who lived most of his adult life totally incapacitated, due to a long term illness. He was one of the greatest prayer warriors I have ever known. I am sure God has something for you to do no matter what your age or ability. Why not ask Him what it is NOW, then do it!

The Kings Of Israel

NAME	KEY EVENTS	YEARS	NATURE	REFERENCES
Jeroboam	Revolted against Solomon & Rehoboam Influenced by Ahijah the prophet	22	Bad	1 Kings 11:26-14:20 2 Chron. 9:29-13:22
Nadab	Worshipped idols like his father Killed by Baasha in Philistine land	2	Bad	1 Kings 15:25-28
Baasha	Spoken against by prophet Jehu "Dogs will eat those belonging to Baasha..."	24	Bad	1 Kings 15:27-16:7 2 Chron. 16:1-6
Elah	Killed by Zimri, one of his officials	2	Bad	1 Kings 16:6-14
Zimri	Ousted by the army choice, Omri Died as he burned down the palace	7 days	Bad	1 Kings 16:9-20
Omri	Fought for Kingship with Tibni Built the city of Samaria	12	Bad	1 Kings 16:15-28
Ahab	Married Jezebel the Baal worshipper Challenged by Elijah on Mount Carmel Dogs licked up his blood	22	Bad	1 Kings 16:28-22:40 2 Chron. 18:1-34
Ahaziah	Died by falling through latticework in an upper room of the palace Death prophesied by Elijah	2	Bad	1 Kings 22:40-53 2 Kings 1:1-18 2 Chron. 20:35-37
Jehoram (Joram)	Idolatrous but tore down Baal's pillar Numerous contacts with Elisha Shot with an arrow by Jehu	12	Bad	2 Kings 3:1-9:24 2 Chron. 22:5-7
Jehu	Killed off the family of Ahab Removed all traces of Baal worship	28	Bad	2 Kings 9:1-10:36 2 Chron. 22:7-12
Jehoahaz	Prayed to God for help with oppression but continued to worship idols	17	Bad	2 Kings 13:1-9
Jehoash (Joash)	Wept over a dying Elisha Defeated King Amaziah of Judah	16	Bad	2 Kings 13:10-14:16 2 Chron. 25:17-24
Jeroboam II	Recovered previously lost territories as God had promised through Jonah	41	Bad	2 Kings 14:23-29
Zechariah	Refused to turn away from idolatry Assassinated in public by Shallum	½	Bad	2 Kings 14:29-15:12
Shallum	Assassinated by Menahem	1 month	Bad	2 Kings 15:10-15
Menahem	Destroyed a town for not surrendering Paid Assyrian King Tiglath-Pileser to support his kingship	10	Bad	2 Kings 15:14-22
Pekahiah	Killed in a conspiracy by Pekah	2	Bad	2 Kings 15:22-26
Pekah	Lost cities in attacks by Tiglath-Pileser Assassinated by Hoshea	20	Bad	2 Kings 15:27-31 2 Chron. 28:5-8
Hoshea	Defeated by Assyrians under King Shalmaneser	9	Bad	2 Kings 15:30-17:6

The Kings Of Judah

NAME	KEY EVENTS	YEARS	NATURE	REFERENCES
Rehoboam	Ten northern tribes revolted Invaded after rejecting the law	17	Bad	1 Kings 11:42-14:31 2 Chron. 9:31-12:16
Abijah	Defeated Jeroboam in God's name but didn't remain faithful to God	3	Bad	1 Kings 14:31-15:8 2 Chron. 13:1-22
Asa	Battled Israel's King Baasha Complete faithfulness to God	41	Good	1 Kings 15:8-24 2 Chron. 14:1-16:14
Jehoshaphat	Formed an alliance with Israel Fought against the local nations	25	Good	1 Kings 22:41-50 2 Chron. 17:1-20:37
Jehoram	No one was sorry when he died Buried outside the royal cemetery	8	Bad	2 Kings 8:16-24 2 Chron. 21:1-20
Ahaziah	Allied with Israel's King Jehoram Both killed by Jehu	1	Bad	2 Kings 8:24-9:29 2 Chron. 22:1-9
Athali-ah (Queen)	Tried to destroy Judah's royal family Lost her throne to her grandson	6	Bad	2 Kings 11:1-20 2 Chron. 22:1-23:21
Joash	Seven years old when crowned Repaired temple but killed priest's son	40	Good	2 Kings 11:1-12:21 2 Chron. 22:10-24:27
Amaziah	Succumbed to idolatry Challenged Israel but lost	29	Good	2 Kings 12:21-14:22 2 Chron. 25:1-28
Uzziah	Burned incense on the altar Struck with leprosy by God	52	Good	2 Kings 15:1-7 2 Chron. 26:1-23
Jotham	Pleased God with his actions but the people remained corrupt	16	Good	2 Kings 15:32-38 2 Chron. 27:1-9
Ahaz	Re-instated idolatry and pagan altars Closed the doors of God's Temple	16	Bad	2 Kings 16:1-20 2 Chron. 28:1-27
Hezekiah	Opens and dedicates God's Temple Diverts water to avoid destruction	29	Good	2 Kings 18:1-20:21 2 Chron. 29:1-32:33
Manasseh	Made a carved idol for the temple Pulled in to exile by a nose ring	55	Bad	2 Kings 21:1-18 2 Chron. 33:1-20
Amon	Even more idolatrous than Manasseh Assassinated by his own officials	2	Bad	2 Kings 21:19-26 2 Chron. 33:21-25
Josiah	Hilkiah discovers God's law Josiah brings devotion back to God	31	Good	2 Kings 22:1-23:30 2 Chron. 34:1-35:27
Jehoahaz	Deposed by the King of Egypt	¼	Bad	2 Kings 23:31-33 2 Chron. 36:1-4
Jehoiakim	Led to Babylon in bronze chains by King Nebuchadnezzar	11	Bad	2 Kings 23:34-24:5 2 Chron. 36:5-7
Jehoiachin	Taken along with temple treasures to Babylon by King Nebuchadnezzar	¼	Bad	2 Kings 24:6-16 2 Chron. 36:8-10
Zedekiah	No humility shown to Jeremiah Temple desecrated	11	Bad	2 Kings 24:17-25:30 2 Chron. 36:11-21

Day 94
1 Kings 12-16
4th April

12 - Rehoboam Seems As Foolish As Solomon Was Wise!
13 - Prophetic Warnings For Jeroboam
14 - Rehoboam's Sin And God's Judgement
15 - Abijam's As Bad As Rehoboam, Asa Is As Godly As David!
16 - Kings Of Israel, Not A Godly One Amongst Them!

After Solomon Dies, The Kingdom Splits

The Big Picture

The United Kingdom splits, resulting in ten tribes in the north (Israel) and two in the south (Judah). Judah is loyal to Rehoboam son of Solomon. Israel talks to Rehoboam at Shechem but he tells them that things will be tougher with him than with Solomon! Unsurprisingly Israel chooses to go with Jeroboam who sets up golden calves for the people to worship instead of going to Jerusalem in Judah. His bad example is followed by his successors and Israel and Judah continue to fight no matter who is King! Towards the end of Jeroboam's reign in Israel, Asa becomes King of Judah – he was a Godly King, as was his son Jehoshaphat. Meanwhile Ahab becomes King of Israel.

Thinking Step

13:2 – '...this is what the Lord says "A child named Josiah will be born into the dynasty of David. On you he will sacrifice the priests from the pagan shrines who come here to burn incense and human bones will be burned on you." A prophecy that will be fulfilled but not for another 300 years when Josiah reigns!

Action Step

Rehoboam rejected the advice of the older men "If you are willing to be a servant to these people today and give them a favourable answer, they will always be your loyal subjects" and instead asked the opinion of the young men who had grown up with him and were now his advisers.' Did you hear about the young man who rebelled against his parents because they didn't understand him and were embarrassingly ignorant. He left home but returned quickly and repentant and was amazed how much his parents had learned while he was away! Being old doesn't make you right but it doesn't make you wrong either! Generation gaps are not new, as today's reading shows. They are usually caused by youngsters thinking the older generation is out of touch and knows nothing. They are also caused by the older generation forgetting that they used to be the younger generation! Young people are not the church of tomorrow and pensioners are not yesterday's church – they are both members of today's church. Do whatever you have to do to relate to those who are not of your generation. Try a smile first – it can work wonders!

17 - Elijah Steps In And Announces A Drought

Day 95

18 - Victory On Carmel And Drought Finally Ends

1 Kings 17-19

19 - Elijah Runs And Runs And Runs!

5th April

Israel's Greatest Prophet Arrives On The Scene!

The Big Picture

Onto the stage today strides that giant of a prophet Elijah. He performs miracles with the weather and with a widow's son in Zarephath as well as being fed by ravens. His confrontations with Ahab and Jezebel result in him running the equivalent of several marathons. Elijah challenges the prophets of Baal on Mount Carmel and God wins in spectacular fashion. Knowing Ahab and Jezebel are after him again he runs south to Beersheba, more than 100 miles away! Then on to Mount Sinai which is another 100 miles! After yet another long run to anoint two new Kings he continues his journey and challenges Elisha to follow him. Elisha responds positively and follows obediently.

Thinking Step

17:1 Elijah declares that there will be no more rain until he says so! This was a real 'red rag to a bull' when you consider the Baal worshipped by Ahab and Jezebel, which they imported from the Sidonians and whose full name was Baal-Melkart, was the god of land fertility, weather and especially rainfall!

Action Step

Standards are dropping everywhere and we are becoming more and more an ungodly country. I am one of a dying race who believes and trusts in the living God. Ring a bell? You would be quite unusual if you have never had thoughts like these rush through your mind. I wonder if that was in Elijah's mind when he uttered that immortal line "I alone am left and now they are trying to kill me too" – 19:10 and 14. In verse 18 of the same chapter, God reminds Elijah that "I will preserve 7,000 others in Israel who have never bowed to Baal or kissed him." So Elijah was not humanly alone and neither are we, usually! I know we always have the Holy Spirit to rely on but if we keep our spiritual eyes open, it's amazing how often we meet a fellow believer who will encourage us. I remember being approached by a stranger standing by my car and pointing to a 'religious' sticker in the rear window. "You don't believe all that stuff do you?" "I do as it happens!" I responded. "So do I" the stranger said "God bless you today". In a stress filled day this was pure living water that refreshed me just when I needed it! Why not look for an opportunity to encourage a fellow believer today? It will make their day – and yours!

Day 96
1 Kings 20-22
6th April

20 - Big Victories Over Aram For Israel
21 - Naboth Murdered For Vineyard - Ahab Humbled
22 - Godly South And Ungodly North - As Usual!

North Is Godless Whilst South Is Godly!

The Big Picture

Attack from Ben-hadad King of Aram, is threatened and heavy demands are made on King Ahab. A prophet tells Ahab that God will give him victory if he attacks first. The initial attack is very successful. The following spring a second confrontation also results in victory but ultimately Ben-hadad is wrongly spared. Ahab is told he will die instead of Ben-hadad! Meanwhile Ahab makes a move for a vineyard owned by Naboth but he refuses to sell. With Jezebel's encouragement Naboth is killed and the vineyard taken. Elijah condemns the whole family of Ahab. King Jehoshaphat of Judah plans war with the Arameans and Ahab agrees to support him. Ahab is killed in battle.

Thinking Step

21:19 – "...because you (Ahab) have done this, dogs will lick your blood... where they licked the blood of Naboth!" 22:37-38 – ' ...Then his (Ahab's) chariot was washed...and dogs...licked his blood... This was the ancient 'chariot wash' where chariots were cleansed of blood after battle. So the dogs consumed the blood of Naboth and Ahab as prophesied!

Action Step

God's man who dominates this book is Elijah and yet, when God wants a man to be His spokesman to Ahab regarding the wars with the Arameans, an unnamed prophet – 20:13 – is used instead of Elijah! This underlines that it is what God says that is important and not who says it. I remember at the beginning of a new year, a college lecturer of mine told his students about a church service he attended at Christmas in a church near his home. He said that as soon as the Bible passage was read, a predictable one as it was Christmas, he thought to himself "I can't imagine anything here that will be new to me!" Then the speaker apologised that their minister was unable to speak as a sudden illness had incapacitated him but that he, as the church secretary was willing to stand in at the last minute!" "So not even a theologically trained speaker!" The sermon had not progressed far when he made a point that took my college lecturer friend by surprise. "It was a new concept I had never seen before" he told his class. It is the Word of God that has the power and not the speaker! No matter how inadequate you may feel, God can use you to great effect. When an opportunity presents itself today why not take it – even though you are probably no Elijah!

2 Kings

2 Kings

The two Kingdoms that were once one, continue to fight with each other and the surrounding nations. The land that was given to them by God knows little rest and peace. Elijah is replaced by Elisha but the people reject his overtures just as they had those of his predecessor. Israel becomes so rotten as its final tally of Kings reaches nineteen, all Godless! Judgement comes with the Assyrians from the northeast when all ten northern tribes are dispersed and mixed up to create a new group of mixed race people – the Samaritans. Only two tribes are left now and as Benjamin is virtually part of Judah, essentially only one tribe remains! This southern Kingdom of Judah benefits from being ruled by more Godly Kings but judgement reaches them too when the Babylonians invade and carry them away into exile for 70 years..

Below is an acrostic which summarises each chapter of the book.

1. King Ahaziah is judged
2. Intern Elisha receives mantle
3. Northern kingdom conquers Moab
4. Gehazi and Elisha's miracles
5. Seven dips restore Naaman

6. Army invisible but ready
7. News of Syrian departure
8. Dire predictions of Elisha

9. Commissioning of King Jehu
10. Ahab's seventy sons killed
11. Priest Jehoiada crowns Joash
12. Temple repairs are made
13. Ill Elisha prophesies victory
14. Victory proclaimed over Judah
15. Idolatrous kings of Israel
16. Temple heathenised by Ahaz
17. Yielding Israel to Assyria

18. Opposing Assyria by Hezekiah
19. Fall of Assyrian army

20. Illness reversed for Hezekiah
21. Sins of Manasseh abound
22. Recovery of God's law
23. Annals of Josiah's purification
24. Exile of King Jehoiachin
25. Last siege of Jerusalem

The North Continues To Slide Despite Elisha

The Big Picture

Elijah condemns Ahaziah son of Ahab, who suffers a fall and enquires of Elijah whether or not he would recover. He didn't but it cost the lives of a lot of his men! Elijah ascends to heaven in a whirlwind and Elisha receives a double portion of his spirit. Elisha's early miracles which are very similar to those of Elijah, concern the everlasting jar of oil and the healing of the son of the Shunammite woman. The final miracle in this section is the multiplication of loaves to feed 100 men, a small version of the Lord's miracle when He fed 5000 men plus women and children which takes place many centuries later.

Thinking Step

The Old Testament town of Shunem is the place where the only son of a prominent woman is raised from the dead through the ministry of Elisha. Centuries later and within a few miles of Shunem, is the New Testament city of Nain where Jesus raises from the dead, the only son of a widow.

Action Step

The fiery chariot of Elijah has caused many folk to stop and think but thanks to a book called 'Chariots of the Gods' (Was God an Astronaut?) too many have come to the wrong conclusion. It seems to me that when we look for a rational explanation for God, we are often looking for an alibi for not taking God seriously! It's on a par with condemning the church as being full of deluded people or full of hypocrites or fanatics. Every one of these theories is an attempt to create a water tight reason for rejecting God without having to think any deeper. If God was an astronaut – fascinating – but the story ends there, unless you are sharp enough to write a book about it in the 1960's! However if God is truly God – then that is mind blowing and demands some serious thought that could change your life for ever. I remember someone saying to me years ago "So, if you are wrong and there is no God then when you die that's the end – right?" "If you are correct, when you die you go to be with Him – right?" You win both ways! As a teenager I 'graciously' gave God one year to prove Himself! It was the best idea I ever had! Long before the year was up I had found Him! Know someone who needs to hear this today?

Day 98
2 Kings 5-8
8th April

5 - More Miracles Through Elisha Including Naaman's Healing
6 - Aram's Army Is Sent Home But Return To Besiege Samaria
7 - Lepers Discover Arameans Have Fled And Siege Ends
8 - Elisha's Ministry To Arameans Whilst Jehoshaphat Reigns In South

Elisha Influences Commoners And Kings

The Big Picture

The healing of Naaman in the Jordan begins our reading today but Gehazi is afflicted with the same leprosy. There's an amazing miracle as the prophets' accommodation is enlarged! Elisha confounds the Arameans by knowing all their plans so troops are sent to capture him but they fail miserably and blinded go to Samaria! King Ben-hadad later besieges Samaria and famine follows. A group of lepers discover that the Aramean army has deserted and the siege and famine are over. There was widespread famine in Israel for seven years. Then Ben-hadad asks Elijah if he will survive his current illness. Elisha tells him "Yes but no!" He does but only to be murdered by his successor Hazael!

Thinking Step

A fresh start...8:2 – 'So the woman did as the man of God instructed. She took her family and settled in the land of the Philistines for seven years.' When she returned she had no debts to repay. Deut 15:1 – 'At the end of every seventh year you must cancel the debts of everyone who owes you money.'

Action Step

Sometimes we miss the whole point! Naaman did at first! It wasn't the washing that would heal him but his willingness to obey the word of the Lord given to him through Elisha. Which river to choose was not the issue, it was accepting that being obedient was the key. It wasn't the physical blood on the doorposts of the Israeli homes at Passover that saved them and got them out of Egypt, it was the fact they were willing to put the blood there and believe. We do many things in our Christian lives where if we are not careful, we think it's doing the thing itself, in the right way and at the right time that brings results. In reality it is our obedience to God that moves us on in our growing ever more like Jesus Himself. Of course it's so much more comfortable thinking that it's the way we do things etc. because that puts us in control. Obedience is the action of a servant and obedience is all God requires of us! So what are you kicking against at the moment? Which issue is being delayed by your stubbornness and pride? In the immortal words of NIKE, "Just do it!" and God will respond in His usual loving way and that's when it usually makes sense...like it did for Naaman.

Godless Athaliah Replaced By Godly Joash

The Big Picture

Newly anointed King Jehu of Israel travels to Jezreel where King Joram and Judah's King Ahaziah are meeting. Both Joram and Ahaziah are killed. Jezebel meets a grisly death – 9:33 – as prophesied by Elijah – 1 Kings 21:23. Jehu systematically destroys Ahab's entourage. He did the same with relatives of Ahaziah. He also wiped out all worshippers of Baal in Samaria. Athaliah mother of Ahaziah kills her way to the throne of Judah! Only Joash survives. He is crowned King when he is seven years old and Athaliah is assassinated. The temple of Baal and it's priests are killed and the forty year reign of Godly Joash begins. During his reign he repairs the Temple.

Thinking Step

Two outstanding women of the Bible but all for the wrong reasons! Queen Jezebel rules in the north with Ahab and twelve years later Queen Athaliah rules in the south with no King. Neither lives up to her name! Jezebel means 'unmarried and chaste' while her daughter Athaliah has a name meaning 'Yahweh is exalted'.

Action Step

It's nothing short of amazing that wicked Jezebel has a mass-murdering daughter called Athaliah who has a Baal worshipping son called Ahaziah, who has a Godly son called Joash! So whilst Godly parents don't always have Godly children, it seems the opposite is equally true. Sometimes ungodly parents can produce Godly offspring. Notice the 'behind the scenes' character who is instrumental in getting Joash on the right path, it was the High Priest Jehoiada. A good influence can benefit other lives! A Godly influence can change lives for ever. I am sure there are 'Jehoiadas' in your life, men and women for whom you thank God whenever you think of them. Why not thank God now for the Godly people who helped shape you for the better, into the person you are today? Having done that what about your influence? I bumped into a man recently who thanked me for visiting him so many times when I was a church pastor. I have to say I saw few signs of regeneration in him when a friend and I visited him as part of our organised evangelism outreach. You just can't see what is going on inside people can you? He told me that we had played a major role in him finally finding Christ. He is the leader of a Godly family now. What a privilege to be involved! Who will you be influencing for good today?

Judgement Comes As The Assyrians Invade

The Big Picture

Godless Kings continue to reign in Israel with a few Godly ones in Judah. Elisha dies after a prophetic meeting with Jehoash King of Israel. Amaziah King of Judah, challenges Jehoash to fight. Jehoash is victorious and goes on to attack Jerusalem inflicting much damage to the city wall. Uzziah (or Azariah) succeeded his defeated father Amaziah whilst, in Israel Jeroboam II reigns and his prophet is Jonah! Meanwhile Assyria gets closer as Tiglath-pileser invades, followed by Shalmaneser who completes the task. This is how Assyria conquers the ten northern tribes of Israel. Peoples from other nations are mingled with the children of Israel to produce a unique group of half Jew/half Gentile people – the Samaritans.

Thinking Step

14:25 – 'Jeroboam II recovered the territories of Israel...just as the Lord the God of Israel, had promised through Jonah son of Amittai, the prophet from Gath-hepher.' Nazareth and Gath-hepher are neighbouring villages. Jonah went to Gentile Nineveh in Assyria and centuries later Jesus ministered to Gentiles too. Hence "Can anything good come from Nazareth?" – John 1:46.

Action Step

15:7 – 'When Uzziah died he was buried with his ancestors in the City of David and his son Jotham became the next King.' Compare this with – Isaiah 6:1 – 'It was in the year King Uzziah died that I saw the Lord. He was sitting on a lofty throne and the train of his robe filled the Temple.' In the midst of civil war and threats from a neighbouring super power Assyria, God is still working His purposes out! Sometimes we can be so blinded by the bad things that are engulfing us that we fail to see the good things that are happening too. This was not an excuse for Isaiah and other faithful people like him to be downhearted. In fact they were very positive and faithful. It could be that you are going through a particularly dark patch at the moment and wonder where God is! He is still here with you working His purposes out. In good times we can see God is in control but in bad times it takes a little more looking! Whenever you hear depressing items in the news try saying to yourself "My God is still in control!" Just because He is!

Hezekiah's Godly Rule In Judah

The Big Picture

Hezekiah a great Godly man is now king of Judah. The Assyrians desperately want to conquer Judah and next turn to Jerusalem. Hezekiah consults Isaiah who is given assurances from the Lord – 19:6-7 and 19:21. Ultimately the Assyrians did return home and Sennacherib is assassinated. Hezekiah becomes gravely ill but after appealing to Isaiah, God grants him a further fifteen years of life. A letter is delivered from the King of Babylon and Hezekiah foolishly shows his future enemy all his treasures. On Hezekiah's death his son Manasseh a wicked man, becomes King, followed by Amon who was just as bad and then his son Josiah, a Godly King with reformation in his heart.

Thinking Step

Why did the Assyrians and after them the Babylonians and then the Persians and then the Greeks and then the Romans, all want this sliver of land? It's the unique land bridge that links Asia, Europe and Africa. It linked all the major world powers for centuries and they all wanted the land God had promised to Abraham.

Action Step

A very good friend of mine, John Hoover, died when he was just mid forties. He was my mentor at Walk Through the Bible and taught me how to teach my first OT events when I first trained in the summer of 1984. At his funeral everyone in attendance was wondering why he had died so soon – in fact, too early! At the start of the service everyone was reminded that he had not died early, he had died at the right time, we just didn't understand how it could be the right time but it was! In our reading today Hezekiah pleads with God to give him more time and he gets fifteen years more. In 21:1 we read that his son Manasseh, was only twelve years old when he succeeded his father to the throne so he must have been conceived during this 'life-extension.' It's interesting to consider that it was Manasseh, in 21:9, who – '... led them to do even more evil than the pagan nations that the Lord had destroyed when the people of Israel entered the land.' So here's the question to ponder – is God's timing better than man's? When your timetable seems out of sync. with God's, try to remember this narrative and be reminded that God's timing is not only better than ours but is perfectly better and ours is only as good when we agree with Him!

Day 102
2 Kings 22-25
12th April

22 - Josiah Repairs Temple And Rediscovers The Law
23 - Josiah Makes Fresh Covenant With God
24 - Nebuchadnezzar Threatens Judah
25 - Judah Deported Into Babylonian Exile

More Spiritual Progress
Then Nebuchadnezzar Attacks!

The Big Picture

During Josiah's temple repairs the 'book of the law' is found. When it is read to Josiah he repents and all Judah with him. Then Pharaoh Neco kills Josiah at Megiddo. Nebuchadnezzar invades, ransacks the Temple and takes thousands back to Babylonia to begin the exile period. After the reigns of Jehoahaz and Jehoiakim, Jehoiachin becomes King and is exiled to Babylonia. Zedekiah is King for those who remained in Judah but revolts and Jerusalem is under siege for over two years. The royal family tries to escape but are executed in front of Zedekiah who is blinded and exiled to Babylonia. A governor is appointed for those who remain but is killed by rebels who flee to Egypt.

Thinking Step

Assyrians destroyed captives, Babylonians used them. Daniel remembers it like this – Dan. 1:4-7 The King said "Select...strong, healthy,...good-looking young men,"... Daniel (called Belteshazzar.), Hananiah (called Shadrach) , Mishael (called Meshach) and Azariah (called Abed-nego) were four chosen to be trained in the language and literature of Babylon.

Action Step

In our reading today – 23:22 – 'There had not been a Passover celebration like that since the time when the Judges ruled in Israel, nor throughout all the years of the Kings of Israel and Judah.' Sadly it seems they had forgotten how to celebrate Passover – it was obviously not an habitual part of their lives! Moses believed in habits! – Deut 6:6-9 '...commit yourselves wholeheartedly to these commands...Repeat them again and again to your children. Talk about them when you are at home and when you are on the road, when you are going to bed and when you are getting up...' In other words make them habitual. Jesus believed in habits too! Paul reminds us in 1 Cor. 11:25 – 'In the same way, he took the cup of wine after supper, saying "This cup is the new covenant between God and His people – an agreement confirmed with my blood. Do this to remember me as often as you drink it."' What have you forgotten to do regularly? Think now...pray, read the Bible, attend Church, meditate on Jesus. Whatever it is why not resolve today to develop one good habit and maybe another tomorrow? You may need to jettison some old ones to make room!

1 Chronicles

1 Chronicles

Centuries after the historic events of Samuel 1&2 and Kings 1&2, after the exile in Babylonia, the Chronicler possibly Ezra looks back with the advantage of hindsight and records a priestly view of what happened before the exile. Much of this book is dominated by the genealogies that were so important, particularly after the exile. Beginning with Adam, the royal line of David is meticulously traced. Then the Chronicler records a view from God's perspective, of the life of David who was a man after His own heart. The account of David begins with the death of Saul, then 'happenings' with the Ark of The Covenant. A detailed record of David's military victories is followed by David's preparation for The Temple which he is destined not to build. Finally the last days of David and the coronation of Solomon bring this book to a close.

Below is an acrostic which summarises each chapter of the book.

1. **D**escendants Adam to Edom
2. **E**ach descendant of Judah
3. **A**ll of David's sons
4. **T**ribes of Judah, Simeon
5. **H**ouses of Reuben, Gad

6. **O**ffspring of Levi's sons
7. **F**our sons of Issachar

8. **S**ons of Benjamin's tribe
9. **A**ssigned positions for Levites
10. **U**gly end of Saul
11. **L**eaders in David's army

12. **T**ribal totals of army
13. **H**and on ark disciplined
14. **R**aids of Philistines repelled
15. **O**btaining ark for Jerusalem
16. **U**nited celebration at tabernacle
17. **G**od's covenant with David
18. **H**armony through David's reign

19. **D**efeat of Ammon, Syria
20. **A**ssault against the Philistines
21. **V**erdict against David's census
22. **I**nstructions to build temple
23. **D**avid organizes Levitical duties
24. **S**ervices assigned temple priests

25. **R**esponsibilities of temple musicians
26. **E**mployment of gate keepers
27. **I**sraelite army division commanders
28. **G**uidelines for building temple
29. **N**ecessary materials given gladly

1 - Adam To The Early Patriarchs
2 - Historic Lines Of The Sons Of Judah
3 - David's Sons And Descendants

Day 103
1 Chronicles 1-3
13th April

Adam To The House Of David

The Big Picture

The first nine chapters of 1 Chronicles have been described as the most boring chapters in the Bible! I don't agree and hopefully by the time you have read them over the next few days, neither will you! Remember the comedian who said "It's the way I tell 'em!" Well it's very much 'the way you read 'em!' These genealogies were written for the exiles who needed to know where they came from. They helped re-form the Israelites into a nation again as they return to the land that God gave to their ancestor Abraham so long ago. Beginning with Adam, these three chapters trace the family history of the Jews up to David and his line.

Thinking Step

2:34 states Sheshem had only daughters. Society of the day saw women as second class citizens. Nevertheless Tamar is included in 2:4 and later, in the genealogy of Jesus – Matt 1:3. God has always had a high regard for women. Gen. 1:27 – '... In the image of God he created them, male and female he created them.'

Action Step

Lots of the names we have just read are names only! We know little if anything, about many of these essential building blocks that God used to create His chosen people and through them to bring His Son into the world as its Saviour. I remember, in my thirties, when the church I was active in resolved to create an eldership and I became one of them! About the same time we had reason to clear out many of the rooms in that church building and discovered photographs of deacons long since departed. Being mature men of faith, we started laughing at these austere men dressed in such formal stiff clothing! Only to be reminded by our oldest deacon that these were men of real faith and vision even if their names had been lost in history – as ours would be too! These two events seemed to go together. It reminded us all that we had a call to action today and for some of us it would bring some kind of temporary 'fame' but we were all tiny fragments in the majestic plan of God. Do all you can to the glory of God today because you are part of the foundations for future work in the Kingdom. Do everything you need to today to make that foundation firm and strong.

155

Day 104
1 Chronicles 4-6
14th April

4 - Tribes Of Judah And Simeon In Detail
5 - Tribes Of Reuben, Gad And Manasseh
6 - Tribe Of The Levites And Priests

History Of The Tribes Of Israel – Part 1

The Big Picture

Having traced many family histories from Adam to David we now go back to the twelve tribes of Jacob, or should I say Israel! Initially these tribes simply bore the name of each son but it's not quite so straight forward now. Remember that Chronicles was written probably only about four hundred years before the birth of Jesus Christ! We only cover half of these tribes in our reading today but it's already evident that there are some differences from the list of sons born to Jacob in Gen. 35 – with the inclusion of Manasseh instead of Joseph. There is detail on each tribe but even more on the tribe of Levi and the refuge cities.

Thinking Step

5:26 gives us a summary of what happened to those who settled east of the Jordan. 'So the God of Israel caused King Pul of Assyria (also known as Tiglath-pileser) to invade the land and take away the people of Reuben, Gad and the half-tribe of Manasseh as captives.' Israel is only on the west side today.

Action Step

What seems to be an endless list of names is suddenly interrupted with a mini overview of an otherwise unknown Bible character, Jabez. All we know about Jabez is covered by just two verses but what we do know about him is potentially life changing even after so many centuries have passed since he lived.

4:9-10 'There was a man named Jabez who was more honourable than any of his brothers. His mother named him Jabez because his birth had been so painful. He was the one who prayed to the God of Israel "Oh, that you would bless me and expand my territory! Please be with me in all that I do and keep me from all trouble and pain!" and God granted him his request.' The prayer of Jabez in verse 10 can be summed up with four simple headings -

1. Ask God to bless you.
2. Ask God to expand your influence.
3. Ask God to be with you in everything you do.
4. Ask God to protect you.

Since the publication of a small book called 'The Prayer of Jabez' by Walk Through the Bible – literally millions of lives have become even more effective for God as this prayer was used to focus thoughts for each day. Why not try it for a month – starting today – and let us know if it makes any difference!

7 - Tribes Of Issachar, Benjamin, Asher And Sons Of Joseph
8 - More Details On Benjamin
9 - Genealogies Of Those Who Returned

Day 105
1 Chronicles 7-9
15th April

History Of The Tribes Of Israel – Part 2

The Big Picture

We continue with tribal genealogies. There is another summary for Manasseh, it seems 5:23-26 was for the eastern part of the tribe whereas this one is for those who settled to the west of the Jordan River. There is no Dan or Zebulun but it's possible that some of the names in 7:12 could be from Dan and as Zebulun usually follows Issachar in many listings it is possible that some of the names in 7:6-12 could be from Zebulun. By the exile period several of the tribes had merged and consequently parts of some lists could have merged too. Genealogies for the Priests, Levites and King Saul bring this section to a close.

Thinking Step

It seems that some of the twelve tribes of Israel persevered better than others! Centuries have passed since they began with the twelve sons of Jacob. Some stood the test of time better than others. It's similar with the twelve apostles of Jesus Christ, some of them seem to fade away from the pages of Scripture too.

Action Step

In these last nine chapters the Chronicler has whisked us through history and now we stand at the threshold of the reign of King David. The story-line pace slows considerably and many of the returnees from exile must have breathed a sigh of relief as this part of the writings came to a close and maybe you did too! So what next? Well as far as the Jews were concerned, they would continue to read of God's opinion on the life of King David. They have already been shown how faithful and sadly how unfaithful, their ancestors had been and yet God had remained faithful, as He always did. History records that the returnees from exile in Babylonia resolved to do better this time and they did for a while! Sadly not for too long...and before they knew where they were Alexander the Great swept in and another series of challenges beckoned. They had little breathing space and we can't rely on having more, or even as long. When Paul wrote to the church in Corinth he said '...Indeed, the "right time" is now. Today is the day of salvation.' 2 Cor. 6:2. In other words, you don't know what the future holds so act today! That was true for those coming back from exile – and it's true for you and me too. Whatever God is telling you to do – do it now, don't delay!

Day 106
1 Chronicles 10-14
16th April

10 - Demise Of Saul
11 - David And His Mighty Men
12 - Mighty Men Of Ziklag And Hebron
13 - The Ark Is On The Move
14 - David Builds A House

Reflections On The Reigns Of Saul And David

The Big Picture

King Saul fails to honour God and is replaced by David. David is anointed as King with a similar narrative to that in 1 Samuel. It takes place in Hebron and the Chronicler uses the same phrase used in 2 Samuel when Israel addressed David 'Behold we are bone of your flesh.' When you get such a great saying it would be a shame not to repeat it! The story of the conquest of the city of Jerusalem is re-told. The account of the Ark being taken into what is now David's city of Jerusalem is related too and we are reminded of David's house being built and his victory over the Philistines.

Thinking Step

10:14 & 13:10 clearly state that God killed both Saul and Uzziah! It's a bit like saying that God sends unbelievers to hell, whereas it is their actions or inactions, that result in people going to hell. Saul dies in battle and Uzziah dies next to the Ark – both having disobeyed God – now pay the price.

Action Step

12:22 – 'Day after day more men joined David until he had a great army, like the army of God.' It didn't happen overnight it was a process not an incident. His army grew gradually which is a great way to grow. New recruits could be grafted onto a strong functioning band of men and in no time they would be so tightly grafted on to the main body that the join would be invisible! That's how it should be with the church of Jesus Christ. Just like the church described in Acts 2:47 – '...and each day the Lord added to their fellowship those who were being saved.' More and more churches today are offering opportunities to have what the Christian life is all about, clearly explained. This is a great initiative but...what happens afterwards? I remember the first time I used a launderette when we were on holiday years ago. A lovely lady took me under her wing and showed me the ropes, from operating the machines to folding the clean clothes. After a few visits I was an expert! So much so that I was able to help another newcomer later that same week! Of course it's not as instant with Christian believers but the principle's the same...So, who will you be helping to disciple this week? We need to be discipling disciples until they become disciplers!

15 - The Ark Is Moved Joyfully
16 - David's Psalm Of Praise
17 - David Wants To Build A Temple
18 - David Accepts His Son Will Build The Temple

Day 107
1 Chronicles 15-18
17th April

David Praises God No Matter What!

The Big Picture

David decides that moving the Ark is essential and requires spiritual preparation. The joyful procession that is described in 1 Samuel 6 is recounted. Sacrifices are offered and musicians appointed, then a Psalm of Asaph is used (including portions of Psalms 105, 96 and 106). Asaph and others are charged to minister regularly before the Ark. David longs to build a suitable house for the Ark but God confirms, as in 1 Samuel 7, that whilst David cannot build such a place, his son will. David rejoices and praises God. Victories over enemy armies show what a great warrior David is but also how unsuitable he is to build the new Temple! He is a man of war not peace!

Thinking Step

There are several mentions of Obed-edom in 1 Chronicles. His name means 'servant of Edom' (or Esau – brother of Jacob) so it could be a very common name but equally all the references could point to the same man! If so, he was a faithful man – 13:14, a musician – 16:5 and a gatekeeper – 26:4.

Action Step

Have you ever really wanted something to happen in your life but it never did? It could be something humanly important like getting married or being a parent, or something spiritually important like being a gifted preacher or counsellor. It could be almost anything but the vital thing is how we react when it doesn't happen! It can destroy you, it can weaken your faith or it can positively build you up! Look at the life of David in our reading today – how he really wanted to build a temple for God but because he had been a faithful warrior for God, he couldn't! Similarly he had so wanted his first son by Bathsheba to live but sadly he died. David could have become such a bitter and twisted individual but no, his response both times was so positive – to praise and worship God! 2 Sam 12:20 and 1 Chron. 17:16-27. When things don't live up to your expectations how do you react? There is much in the life of David that it would be best not to emulate but in this respect there is no better model. Is there anything that springs to mind for you that you have wrestled with but which you need to accept will not happen now and praise God anyway! Whatever it is – thank God that He is still sovereign and always know best – and praise Him!

159

Day 108
1 Chronicles 19-22
18th April

19 - David Continues To Conquer The Land
20 - More Victories For David
21 - Testing Times For David
22 - David Prepares For Temple Building

David Conquers
And Temple Preparations Are Made

The Big Picture

Several events from David's life from 2 Samuel are repeated here, the humiliation of David's servants and his military victories. The census and the plagues of 2 Samuel 24 are also recounted. Whenever 'repeats' are made they are from God's perspective and thought worthy of inclusion by the Chronicler. When the temple site is purchased there is a slight difference in the name of its owner, with 2 Samuel 21 preferring Araunah whilst here in 21:18 it's Ornan but it is nothing unusual for people to have more than one name and it's worth remembering that the Chronicler had access to the historic accounts when he wrote. David charges both Solomon and the leaders to build the temple well.

Thinking Step

The site of the temple on Araunah's threshing floor in 21:22 is linked with Mt. Moriah in Genesis where Isaac is almost sacrificed by Abraham – Gen. 22:2. Both are brought together in 2 Chron. 3:1. A threshing floor needs wind and mountain tops are usually windy, both could easily be descriptions of the same place.

Action Step

In 2 Samuel 11:1 we read – '...David sent Joab and the Israelite army to fight the Ammonites. They destroyed the Ammonite army and laid siege to the city of Rabbah. However David stayed behind in Jerusalem.' This is followed by the account of David and Bathsheba's adultery. The parallel passage we have read today is 20:1 – '...Joab led the Israelite army in successful attacks against the land of the Ammonites. In the process he laid siege to the city of Rabbah. However David stayed behind in Jerusalem.' This time the account of David and Bathsheba is conspicuous by its absence. To understand why, just remember that the books of Samuel and Kings were written as historical accounts whereas the books of Chronicles were written to reflect God's viewpoint. Isaiah 43:25, Jeremiah 31:34 and Hebrews 8:12 & 10:17 all declare "Their sins I will remember no more!" So God never reminds the Chronicler of the David and Bathsheba episode because it is remembered no more! Note carefully, it does not say that God forgets our sins – it says He remembers them no more! To forget is a sign of weakness but to remember no more is an act of God's love. Do you have something you would like your Father in Heaven to remember no more? Tell him now and it will be remembered no more. You have His word on it.

Temple Ministries Are Described In Detail

The Big Picture

Solomon becomes King and sets about organising the Levites for their duties. They are split into three main groups taking their names from the three sons of Levi – Gershon, Kohath and Merari. Now that the Tabernacle is stationary, the Levites will assist the sons of Aaron rather than transport the Tabernacle. Of course all the descendants of Aaron are of the tribe of Levi anyway so they are all one family. Aaron's descendants from two of his sons Eleazar and Ithamar, draw lots to determine their duty rotas. We're given details of a well developed music ministry as well as how the gatekeepers and officers are organised by the drawing of lots.

Thinking Step

23:30 – '...and each morning and evening they stood before the Lord to sing songs of thanks and praise to him' – worship groups are not new! When the apostle Paul lists some spiritual gifts in 1 Cor. 12 and Ephesians 4 he does not include music, strongly suggesting that his lists do not include all gifts.

Action Step

Some churches think that if things are organised then they can't possibly be spiritual! You know the sort of thing "Oh, we haven't organised anything we just want God to have His way!" As though He couldn't if we had arranged something! Others want everything scripted and timed which for some, runs the risk of squeezing out the ministry of the Holy Spirit. Of course this varies from church to church, some are more structured than others but in my experience being organised no matter how loosely, can facilitate the work of the Holy Spirit, not hinder Him. Today's chapters reflect organisation that aids spirituality. 23:13 '...set apart to dedicate the most holy things, to offer sacrifices in the Lord's presence, to serve the Lord and to pronounce blessings in His name forever.' 23:31-32 'The required number of Levites served in the Lord's presence at all times, following all the procedures they had been given.' I think the apostle Paul sums it up very well in 1 Cor. 14:39-40 – 'So, my dear brothers and sisters, be eager to prophesy and don't forbid speaking in tongues – but be sure that everything is done properly and in order.' In other words be spontaneously organised – or – plan in a very flexible way! To the organised, "Don't be afraid to be spontaneous sometimes!" To the spontaneous "Don't be afraid to plan something in detail occasionally."

Day 110
1 Chronicles 27-29
20th April

27 - Commanders And Officers Appointed
28 - David Speaks Plainly To The People And Solomon
29 - Solomon Succeeds David As King

Final Preparations For Solomon's Reign

The Big Picture

We approach Solomon's accession to the throne and are given lists of the twelve military commanders and tribal leaders. In addition there is a fascinating list of royal officers who are responsible for David's various property and commercial interests. We are also given the names of David's counsellors including Ahithophel and Hushai about whom we learned much when we read 2 Samuel. David assembles all of these men, who were responsible for the nation's religious and secular life, to be addressed by him in Jerusalem. He reminds them that he had wanted to build the Temple but now Solomon would do it. Financial implications for the Temple are outlined, then David prays publicly and sees Solomon crowned before dying a contented man.

Thinking Step

Did you spot an interesting comment in 29:22? – '...and again they crowned David's son Solomon as their new King.' He was previously 'made King' by David in 23:1 when David declared his choice of successor but the actual coronation took place some time later and that's what we have read about today.

Action Step

In David's prayer at Solomon's coronation he shows much wisdom. 29:19 – "Give my son Solomon the wholehearted desire to obey all your commands, laws and decrees and to do everything necessary to build this Temple, for which I have made these preparations." Isn't it interesting that David prays for Solomon to be Word centred first and then build the Temple second. When we are in the Word of God and it is in us, our priorities will be God's priorities and God's Word will be our constant encouragement and guide. I remember hearing a preacher say "Of course this is not my opinion, it is what the Word of God says. My opinion is no better than yours." I cannot stress enough how sad I feel when we debate parts of Scripture as though we and its writer are on equal terms and of equal intellect! It is God's Word and at times will inevitably be hard to understand but I have found that regular reading of the Bible results in fresh revelations every time. Passages that were closed last time are a little clearer this time – that's when I look forward to reading them next time, when they will be even clearer! We have come a long way in our reading of the Bible and are about one third of the way through – well done! Be encouraged to persevere!

162

2 Chronicles

2 Chronicles

2 Chronicles continues the story of 1 Chronicles, which is not surprising as they were originally one book. Solomon dominates the first quarter of 2 Chronicles as the Temple is completed in all its splendour and he reigns with pomp. Sadly Solomon's rule ends rather abruptly. The book of 1 Kings tells us about the Kingdom splitting with Israel in the north and Judah in the south. The Chronicler however, with the benefit of knowing that Israel is now but a distant memory, follows the Kingdom of Judah only tracing its story all the way to the final demise. One King after another follows Solomon and their reigns are viewed through God's eyes rather than as history. Unlike Samuel and Kings, Chronicles takes the story further and ends with the call from Cyrus King of Persia, for the Jews to end their exile and return home to the promised land.

Below is an acrostic which summarises each chapter of the book.

1. **R**equest for God's wisdom
2. **E**nlistment of Hiram's help
3. **I**nitiation of temple construction
4. **G**arnishments of the temple
5. **N**ew home for ark

6. **O**ffering temple dedication prayer
7. **F**illing temple with glory

8. **S**olomon's cites and sacrifices
9. **O**bservations by Sheba's queen
10. **L**eaders reject Rehoboam's harshness
11. **O**ffences strengthened by Rehoboam
12. **M**istake of Rehoboam judged
13. **O**vercoming Israel under Abijah
14. **N**arrative of Asa's faith

15. **T**emporal reforms of Asa
16. **H**ypocrisy and Asa's death
17. **R**evival under King Jehoshaphat
18. **O**ffences done by Jehoshaphat
19. **U**se of impartial judges
20. **G**od's victory over Moab
21. **H**orrible reign of Jehoram

Day 111
2 Chronicles 1-5
21st April

1 - Solomon's Wisdom And Wealth
2 - All Is Ready To Build The Temple
3 - The Temple Is Built At Last
4 - Final Touches To The Temple
5 - The Ark Is Installed And God's Glory Descends

At Last – The Temple Is Completed

The Big Picture

We begin with the wealth and wisdom of Solomon which leads us into the account of the construction of the Temple. Full dimensional details are once again given for the Temple in 3:3. Solomon faithfully follows the plans made by his father David. Little mention is made of Solomon's house which 1 Kings 7 describes as four times the size of the Temple! Details of the utensils for the Temple are once again described in some detail. These, along with the things already made by his father David are installed in the Temple. The Ark is set in place and we read that the glory of the Lord filled the Temple!

Thinking Step

3:17 – 'Then he set up the two pillars at the entrance of the Temple' He named the one on the south Jakin, (God Establishes) and the one on the north Boaz (Strength). Some suggest that these two pillars represented David's strength as he conquers the enemy and the establishing of Solomon's peaceful reign of Israel.

Action Step

What would you give to have had an invitation to this opening! When all had been finished and the temple was furnished and the Ark installed – then 5:14 – 'The priests could not continue their service because of the cloud, for the glorious presence of the Lord filled the Temple of God.' Wow! Isaiah had a vision similar to this when in Isaiah 6:1 – 'It was in the year King Uzziah died that I saw the Lord. He was sitting on a lofty throne and the train of his robe filled the Temple.' Sheer awesome magnificence! I remember a debate at a Christian conference that asked the question "What would you do if Jesus Himself walked into this room?" Some said they would raise their hands in worship, some said they would sing His praises, some said they would clap and shout with joy. Only one man I believe got it right when he said "I would simply fall on my face as a sinner and not dare to look!" In these days of informality I believe we have lost some of the sense of the Majesty of God which our reading today brings to light for us. Just imagine the service couldn't continue because of the glorious presence of the Lord filling the Temple of God. Why not ask Him to give us a fresh glimpse of just how glorious and majestic He is – now!

The Rise And Fall Of Solomon

The Big Picture

As part of the consecration of the Temple, Solomon preaches and then prays. He dedicates the people and himself to living Godly lives with God's help. When Solomon finished his prayer, fire from Heaven came down and consumed the burnt offerings and sacrifices and the glory of the Lord filled the Temple. An enormous number of sacrifices are made over the next seven days as they celebrated the Feast of Tabernacles. The building programme ends and the Lord confirms His covenant with Israel as He appears to Solomon. Solomon races ahead of God to enlarge his Kingdom, marry foreign wives and grow very wealthy. Then it all comes to an end and Rehoboam becomes King.

Thinking Step

9:1 – 'When the Queen of Sheba heard of Solomon's fame, she came to Jerusalem to test him...' 1,000 years later Jesus recalls it in Matt 12:42, "...and now someone greater than Solomon is here and you refuse to listen to Him!" Sheba is Yemen today and is 99% Muslim but the story about the Queen of Sheba lives on – in the Koran!

Action Step

All covenants have two sides. We preach a distorted Gospel if it stops at salvation. God saves us but we are to live for Him in return. Solomon is reminded of this in 7:17 'As for you, if you faithfully follow me as David your father did, obeying all my commands, decrees and regulations, then I will establish the throne of your dynasty...' Solomon had his part to play. It's the same with us. God offers us the gift of eternal life just because He loves us and because without it we are lost. The Bible is very clear on this – Gal 2:16 'Yet we know that a person is made right with God by faith in Jesus Christ, not by obeying the law and we have believed in Christ Jesus, so that we might be made right with God because of our faith in Christ, not because we have obeyed the law...' Jas. 2:14 – 'What good is it, dear brothers and sisters, if you say you have faith but don't show it by your actions? Can that kind of faith save anyone?' It's like so much in the Christian life, a matter of balance and understanding everything in the light of the complete picture of Scripture. God plays His part and we must play ours, everyday. He died for us, we must live for Him. Be balanced!

Day 113
2 Chronicles 10-12
23rd April

10 - This Is How Big The Land Is
11 - These Are The Safe Places To Go
12 - Safeguards For Future Generations

Rehoboam Fails And Judah Is Weakened

The Big Picture

Rehoboam travels to Shechem where he tells the tribes of Israel that life will be even more difficult than it was under his father Solomon and the result is the same as recorded in 1 Kings 12, he is rejected in favour of Jeroboam who becomes King of the northern Kingdom, leaving Rehoboam to rule the significantly smaller southern Kingdom of Judah. The united Kingdom is divided never to be united again. Civil war breaks out as Judah considers trying to bring Israel back into a united Kingdom by force. This is condemned by God and Rehoboam obeys and does not attack! Shortly afterwards they are attacked by Egypt and the temple and palace are ransacked.

Thinking Step

11:16 – 'From all the tribes of Israel, those who sincerely wanted to worship the Lord the God of Israel, followed the Levites to Jerusalem, where they could offer sacrifices to the Lord, the God of their ancestors.'
Those loyal to God begin travelling south. When the Assyrians invade later, most of the faithful Israelites are safely settled in Judah.

Action Step

12:1 – '...but when Rehoboam was firmly established and strong, he abandoned the Law of the Lord and all Israel followed him in this sin.' A good start but then a slide! When the books of Chronicles were being written the northern tribes had already been conquered and scattered by the Assyrians, they are now known as Israel. The Bible has many examples of people who started well and then decided they could succeed without the help of God. Rehoboam was one, just like his father Solomon. What about you? Was there a time when God was fresh and relevant to you as you established your life in Him and on His Word? Then perhaps you decided that you could cope by yourself! Just like Rehoboam. Ironically he must have seen his father slide away but must have thought he would be different! He was an exception! The devil deceives many of us into thinking that we are exceptions to the rules of inevitability. For certain, if we fail to continue to walk with God and regularly read His Word, we are bound for a dry existence when things go smoothly and a rough ride when things get tough. Isn't it about time that you got back on track with Him? Why not tell Him now that you really do need Him and ask Him to rule your life again and get back to the good old days!

13 - North And South At War
14 - Victory Over The Ethiopians
15 - Asa Reforms The South With Help From Azariah
16 - Asa Is Rebuked By Hanani

Day 114
2 Chronicles 13-16
24th April

Asa Reforms The South

The Big Picture

Now that Rehoboam is dead, Abijah is King of Judah. He takes up his father's conviction of uniting all the tribes and challenges Jeroboam to join Judah because that is what God wants! Their armies fought, the victor was Abijah and Jeroboam dies. For a while Abijah thrives but then he dies too and is succeeded by his son Godly Asa. During his reign Asa is challenged by the prophet Azariah and carries out many reforms and more Israelites migrate south to join him. After a twenty year period of peace, Israel attacks Judah with the help of the Arameans but with no success. Hanani condemns Judah for relying on the Aramean army rather than on God

Thinking Step

If in doubt the answer is Azariah! The Azariah of 15:1 is one of 26 Azariahs in the Old Testament! A very well known Azariah is better known by his Babylonian name Abed-nego. You will find him in Dan:1 as part of the famous trio of Shadrach, Meshach and Abed-nego. Keep an eye open for the other 24!

Action Step

The words of Azariah – 15:2 – '...The Lord will stay with you as long as you stay with Him! Whenever you seek Him you will find Him but if you abandon Him, He will abandon you.' This is one of my favourite verses in the Bible. When you explore the phrase – 'Whenever you seek Him, you will find Him' – what it actually means is so much deeper than the words we read here. It means 'If you seek Him, He will let you find Him.' Aren't those last six words quite breathtaking? The creator God of the whole universe will not only let you find Him but He won't make it too difficult! Guidance is such a problem for some people. It's as though they are trying to discover what God wants of them whilst God is hiding His plans so that they can't find them! Just search, God wants us to know... so He makes it easy! A perfect example to follow when guidance seems hard is to emulate the Apostle Paul on his second missionary journey. In Acts 16 he couldn't preach in Asia, then he was unable to visit Bithynia but he kept moving on until he got a vision about Macedonia. He kept moving. God can guide a moving object easier than He can budge a static one! If in doubt, step out – then God can fine-tune your direction. Usually you need to move first!

Day 115
2 Chronicles 17-20
25th April

17 - Jehoshaphat Spreads The Word
18 - Jehoshaphat Makes A Pact With Ahab
19 - Jehoshaphat Organises His Kingdom
20 - Jehoshaphat's Reign Summarised

Jehoshaphat – A Godly Reformer

The Big Picture

King Jehoshaphat sent out itinerant teachers who taught the 'Book of the Law.' He ruled in peace and the surrounding nations feared him. Sadly he formed an alliance with King Ahab which we first learned about in 1 Kings 22. Ahab persuades Jehoshaphat to join him fighting against Ramoth-gilead but disguises himself during battle so that he will not be recognised as a King! Despite this however, Ahab is fatally wounded and dies by the end of the day. Following the battle Jehoshaphat returns to Jerusalem where he appoints Judges and re-organises his Kingdom. Enemy threats to invade cause Jehoshaphat to lean on God for an amazing victory. Truly the battle was not his but the Lord's!

Thinking Step

18:2 – 'Some years later he went down to visit Ahab in Samaria...' Travelling north to Samaria is described as going down! Leaving Jerusalem built on seven hills, was always descending, going to Jerusalem was always ascending. Hence the Psalms of ascents, 120-134. Fifteen songs for pilgrims to sing as they go up to the Temple from all directions.

Action Step

I worry sometimes when I hear Christians say that they are waiting on the Lord because they seem to be doing nothing whilst waiting for God to act! Inactivity is often mistaken for spirituality! 20:15-16 says "Listen all you people of Judah and Jerusalem! Listen, King Jehoshaphat! This is what the Lord says: Do not be afraid! Don't be discouraged by this mighty army, for the battle is not yours but God's. Tomorrow, march out against them..." No inactivity here, don't be afraid, don't be discouraged, the battle is God's – now, march out! Trusting is not always passive it is often active. I remember looking for a new office for Walk Through the Bible and both my wife and I were convinced God had a larger place for us. I suppose we could have stayed at home continuing to pray but we decided to 'march out' instead. Just that week, a landlord had decided to reduce his rent on a unit that was just right for us. Twice as big but half the rent rate – which meant twice as much space for the same money! I suppose we could have discovered this property in some other way but I like to think that our faith was active and that we played our part. The battle was the Lord's of course but we had to march out. Where do you need to be pro-active today?

21 - Warnings Go Unheeded
22 - Athaliah's Son Becomes King
23 - Athaliah Is Killed As Promised
24 - Joash Becomes King - Aged Seven!

Day 116
2 Chronicles 21-24
26th April

Jezebel's Bad Influence Lives On In Athaliah

The Big Picture

Jehoram reigns in Judah with his wife Athaliah. Edom and Libnah revolt as a sign of God's judgement on Godless Jehoram. A letter from Elijah pronounces judgement which results eventually in the death of Jehoram. His son Ahaziah comes to the throne but is eventually killed by Jehu at God's command. His mother Athaliah then takes the throne for about six years before it passes to her son Joash who becomes the king, aged seven years! Reformation under the priest Jehoiada takes place with Josiah eventually being active in repairing the Temple. On the death of Jehoiada the priest, Joash starts to slip into idolatry and suffers defeat by the Arameans. On his death his son Amaziah becomes King.

Thinking Step

The passion of your heart will show no matter what. It did with Joash. There are double figures of references in chapter 24 to the project of his life – 'the Temple of the Lord.' The first one is verse 4 then verse 5 then verse 7 then verse 8 then two in verse 12. Can you spot the others?

Action Step

24:9-12 – 'Then a proclamation was sent throughout Judah and Jerusalem, telling the people to bring to the Lord the tax that Moses the servant of God, had required of the Israelites in the wilderness. This pleased all the leaders and the people and they gladly brought their money and filled the chest with it. Whenever the chest became full, the Levites would carry it to the King's officials. This went on day after day and a large amount of money was collected.' Did you notice it was an offering not a collection! The difference being a collection is taken but an offering is given. Did you notice they were pleased when they were asked for money! There is no record of "All they seem to want is my money!" or "Where's my small change, here comes the collection plate!" They knew that giving was a natural part of worship. 24:14 tells us that there was money left over after the craftsmen had been paid so that even more things could be added to the Temple. They had the Temple and were happy to give with thanksgiving. We have a life changing Saviour so shouldn't we be even happier to give, especially to spread the good news of Jesus or get more people into the Bible! There's no time better than now to review your giving but remember, do it with a smile!

Day 117
2 Chronicles 25-28
27th April

25 - The Life Of Godly Amaziah Reviewed
26 - The Life Of Godly Uzziah Reviewed
27 - The Life Of Godly Jotham Reviewed
28 - The Life Of Ungodly Ahaz Reviewed

A Run Of Godly Kings Comes To An End

The Big Picture

Amaziah reigned for twenty nine years and was one of Judah's Godly Kings. Far from perfect – he even killed his servants who had murdered his father! For a time he turned to idolatry and challenged Israel to a war which he lost. The Temple was ransacked and the wall of Jerusalem was damaged as a result. The historic account is in 2 Kings 14. His young son Uzziah is another Godly King. He repairs the wall but then slides into sin too and dies a leper. His son Jotham reigns as the third Godly King in a row. He is succeeded by his son Ahaz who leads Judah into making child sacrifices as the run of 'Godly Kings' comes to an abrupt end.

Thinking Step

In 26:6 – we read of the Philistine city of Jabneh which is called Jabneel in Josh 15:11. Today it is called Yebna (Greek version of Jabneh). It's famous as the place where rabbis met shortly after the fall of Jerusalem in AD70 to confirm and re-affirm the canon of the Old Testament.

Action Step

25:14-15 – 'When King Amaziah returned from slaughtering the Edomites, he brought with him idols taken from the people of Seir. He set them up as his own gods, bowed down in front of them and offered sacrifices to them! This made the Lord very angry and He sent a prophet to ask "Why do you turn to gods who could not even save their own people from you?"'. It may seem strange that when God gave Amaziah victory over the Edomites it encouraged him to worship the gods of those he had defeated! So why did Amaziah do this? It could be that he did it just in case these gods could help him in future! Have you ever made a 'plan B' even before 'plan A' had failed? I had little faith that Walk Through the Bible would succeed, as it did, in 1989 when my wife and I stepped out in faith with no financial safety net! I even looked into part-time jobs and part-time pastorates to help bolster our income. Amazingly there was never any need, looking back, the financial numbers just didn't add up!! – but they did...! Don't 'over analyse' your plans before stepping out. Many a Godly idea must have been assigned to the shelf as not being viable, when all the time God had made provision for it to succeed! Think! Is there such a plan in your life?

172

29 - Temple Becomes A Place Of Worship
30 - Extended Passover Celebrated
31 - Idols Destroyed And Priests Stimulated

Day 118
2 Chronicles 29-31
28th April

Reformation By Hezekiah

The Big Picture

Hezekiah comes to the throne bringing a Godly reign back to Judah. He purified the Temple after the Godless acts of his father Ahaz and reintroduced Temple worship. Invitations to come to Jerusalem to celebrate Passover were sent to all the tribes but had mixed responses. Despite some ridicule, many of the faithful came to Jerusalem to celebrate. Many were not ready to celebrate Passover as they were ceremonially unclean but King Hezekiah himself prayed for them. Such days were unknown since the reign of Solomon and they extended the feast for another seven days. All the idols and high places were eradicated before everyone returned home, rededicated to their God.

Thinking Step

31:1 – '...the Israelites...went to all the towns of Judah, Benjamin, Ephraim and Manasseh and they smashed all the sacred pillars, cut down the Asherah poles and removed the pagan shrines and altars.' This was the first time in the history of Judah that there were no pagan high places and then, the pagan Assyrians invaded!

Action Step

About this time Assyria conquered Israel, so for many in the north it was their last chance to turn to God. Many ridiculed Hezekiah's messengers, thinking there was plenty of time to take religion seriously but time was more limited than they knew! A friend of mine who was converted in his later years was amazed that his family and friends were so dismissive of him and his new found faith. "They don't know what they are missing!" he often told me. I had to remind him of how many times he had heard the 'good news' before he responded positively! It's not just making a decision to accept Christ that many believe can be put off for another day, it's also steps of obedience by God's people that are deferred to a future unknown date. Benjamin Franklin said "The only things certain in life are death and taxes." Well, taxes will be the least of your worries when you die! We all have to face physical death, unless the Lord comes soon but we don't know His timetable. When people put off following God's guidance they are really saying "I think God has something worse for me so I will not move!" God isn't like that, He loves us! He has probably already shown you what He wants you to do next – so just do it – you'll be so glad you did!

Day 119
2 Chronicles 32-33
29th April

32 - Assyria Invades But Hezekiah Holds Firm
33 - Manasseh Becomes King - And It's Bad!

Assyria Invades But God Protects Judah

The Big Picture

Just when the land had been cleansed of paganism, the pagan Assyrians pour in and besiege the fortified cities of Judah! Under the leadership of Godly Hezekiah and his prophet Isaiah the people are encouraged to trust God and not fear Assyria. They trust and they are miraculously delivered as we read earlier in 2 Kings 18-19. We also have an abbreviated account of how Hezekiah had his life extended – 2 Kings 20. Hezekiah's tunnel is built and still exists today. Hezekiah one of Judah's most Godly Kings is succeeded by his son Manasseh, perhaps the most Godless! Wonderfully we read of Manasseh turning to God before his death. His son Amon then becomes King but not for long!

Thinking Step

33:11 – '...they took Manasseh prisoner. They put a ring through his nose and led him away to Babylon.' This is exactly what God said He would do to the invading Assyrians, through His prophet Isaiah! – 2 Kings 19:28 – '...I will put my hook in your nose...I will make you return by the same road on which you came.'

Action Step

33:13 – '...and when he prayed the Lord listened to him and was moved by his request. So the Lord brought Manasseh back to Jerusalem and to his Kingdom. Then Manasseh finally realised that the Lord alone is God! He returned to Jerusalem to undo some of the wicked acts he had previously carried out.' This account of the conversion of Manasseh is not found in the historical records of 2 Kings! So it could be that the writer was unaware of it. As a pastor I have regularly had to console people who have lost a loved one and didn't know whether they were a believer or not. My advice was always the same. "If you don't know for certain, just trust that it was so!" I heard a true story some time ago that underlined this trusting approach. An American farmer was badly gored by a bull and was rushed to hospital on the brink of death. His wife, a devoted Christian was distraught because she knew he had spent his whole life ridiculing her faith. You can imagine her surprise, when he did finally regain consciousness, to discover that he was a believer! When challenged about his conversion he replied "The bull threw me up as an unbeliever but on my way down I accepted Christ!" Is it time you accepted Christ? Don't delay any longer – take a look at the Jan 21st page to see how.

34 - Josiah Discovers The Law
35 - Celebrate Passover Like Never Before!
36 - Exile Becomes A Reality Until Cyrus Is King Of Persia

Day 120
2 Chronicles 34-36
30th April

Exile, Until Cyrus Comes To The Rescue!

The Big Picture

The last of the Godly Kings takes the throne. His name is Josiah. His reforms began when he was just sixteen years old, when the book of the law was discovered as the Temple was being repaired – also in 2 Kings 22. Renewal begins and Passover is celebrated with great rejoicing – also in 2 Kings 23. Following Josiah's death at the hands of Pharaoh Neco, his son Jehoahaz takes the throne. The Egyptians replace Jehoahaz with his brother Jehoiakim. Then Nebuchadnezzar attacks and takes the next two Kings, Jehoiachin and later Zedekiah (2 Kings 25:7), into exile. Seventy years later Cyrus offers to return them to the promised land!

Thinking Step

The Israelites had failed to keep Sabbaths during this long chaotic period. Lev. 26:34 warns about this! So God claims them all at once! 36:21 – 'So the message of the Lord spoken through Jeremiah was fulfilled. The land finally enjoyed its Sabbath rest, lying desolate until the seventy years were fulfilled...'

Action Step

34:30-32 – '...There the King read to them the entire Book of the Covenant that had been found in the Lord's Temple...He pledged to obey the Lord by keeping all his commands, laws and decrees with all his heart and soul. He promised to obey all the terms of the covenant that were written in the scroll and he required everyone...to make a similar pledge...' In our reading today Josiah gives us three great points to bear in mind about reading the Bible. One of them he repeats!
1. Firstly read the whole book
So many folk only read bits of the Bible and wonder why it doesn't make sense. "The Word, the whole Word and nothing but the Word" – now that has a ring of truth doesn't it?
2. He pledged to obey – and promised to obey
When rabbis talked about hearing their teaching they would only accept that you had heard when you did what they had taught! – and if it was important they would repeat it, just like here!
3. He required everyone '...to make a similar pledge...'
Encourage others to take the Bible seriously and to read it for themselves and obey what the Holy Spirit reveals to them. As we continue our reading through the Bible let our prayer be "Please show me something each day that will stimulate me spiritually and enrich my daily life!"

Ezra

Ezra

With Ezra we begin exploring what happens to thousands of Israelites as they return home from exile. The first six chapters give the account of the return led by Zerubbabel when the largest number come back, having said that it was only a tiny portion of those living in exile in Babylonia, which became part of the Persian empire. Then there's a break of about sixty years before chapter seven recounts the return led by Ezra. During the sixty year gap the remarkable life of Esther takes place in far away Persia. Under the leadership of Zerubbabel, aided and abetted by the prophets Haggai and Zechariah, the temple is rebuilt but it's not a patch on Solomon's Temple! Ezra prepares the people for restoration with a big emphasis on being married to Jews only. Foreign wives had sadly become the norm but Ezra gets the people back on track with his exposition of the Law.

Below is an acrostic which summarises each chapter of the book.

1. **T**emple proclamation by Cyrus
2. **E**xiles return under Zerubbabel
3. **M**aking the temple foundation
4. **P**ostponement of the work
5. **L**etter written to Darius
6. **E**xiles finish the temple

7. **W**arrant authorizing Ezra's return
8. **O**utline of Ezra's return
9. **R**epentance prayer by Ezra
10. **K**eeping foreign wives judged

The Big Return Begins

The Big Picture

The prophecies in Isaiah 44:28 and Jeremiah 29:10 are fulfilled and returning to the promised land is now possible after seventy years in exile in Babylonia. Our reading begins with the decree from Cyrus and we also learn of the gifts from supporters who would not be returning but who were very supportive of the venture, as King Cyrus obviously was. Then we have lists of names – doesn't the Bible love its lists!! Lots of names in different categories show us the variety of the people who return with Zerubbabel, with the common aim of rebuilding the temple in Jerusalem and beginning afresh to follow the God who had remained faithful to them during their exile in Babylonia.

Thinking Step

Zerubbabel or Sheshbazzar. Do we simply have two names for the same person? – like Daniel (Hebrew) who was also known as Belteshazzar (Babylonian). The weakness in this argument is that Zerubbabel and Sheshbazzar are both Babylonian names. However it is hard to perceive that Sheshbazzar would later lay the foundation stone of the temple rather than Zerubbabel – 5:16.

Action Step

It is inconceivable that without God stirring up Cyrus, the thought would have entered his head to arrange for the temple to be rebuilt in Jerusalem! Of course God regularly stirs up the hearts of unbelievers otherwise none of us would be able to respond to His gift of salvation! Today's reading reminds us that the Jews needed to be stirred up. 1:5 tells us that not just the heads of families and the priests and Levites but everyone had their spirits stirred up. Having said that, only a small fraction responded and returned. I wonder if those who remained later regretted not returning? At the end of a crusade, Billy Graham was asked by a woman "What should I do Billy?" – I know I rejected God's call to the mission field many years ago and now I am old and it's too late." He assured her that God still had work for her to do. It was not too late. What a shame to have lived a 'second rate' life when God had a 'first rate' one in mind for her. I can honestly say that I am unaware of rejecting God's guidance on major issues in my life. Many times this was only due to the wise advice from my wife, for whom I thank God regularly. Respond today to God's stirring in your heart – you will never regret it.

Good Start But Then It Stops!

The Big Picture

Work begins with the building of an altar where sacrifices are offered. This marks the climax of the Jewish year as they celebrate the Festival of Tabernacles. Cedar wood is purchased from Lebanon just as Solomon had done. So work on the Temple begins with much praising and singing mixed with weeping from those who remembered the grandeur of Solomon's Temple. The enemies of Judah offered their help but it was refused. This resulted in threats and propaganda that stopped progress for many years. A letter written in Aramaic is sent by the enemy to Artaxerxes informing him that the returnees are rebuilding the walls and will declare independence as soon as it's completed. The King's reaction was to stop all building work!

Thinking Step

3:8 tells us that the Temple reconstruction began in the second month. No coincidence that 1 Kings 6:1 tells us that Solomon began his Temple in the second month too. There was a real effort to follow the timetable and design of Solomon's Temple and to rebuild it rather than just build a new one.

Action Step

3:12 – '...but many of the older priests, Levites, and other leaders who had seen the first Temple wept aloud when they saw the new Temple's foundation.' The foundation would probably have been more like a framework for the whole building rather than just a flat footprint. So when the older generation saw it they would have been thinking of the splendour of Solomon's Temple and this effort was a disappointment. Have you noticed as you grow older, how many times you look back using rose tinted spectacles and make quick negative judgements on new ways of doing things today? We don't want to lose our heritage or good traditions. There are often real benefits in looking back but remember what the apostle Paul said in his letter to the Philippians – 3:13 – "...Forgetting the past and looking forward to what lies ahead, I press on..." Remember, if you look back too much you tend to bump into things! Are you struggling today with the "it was so much better in the old days" syndrome – well snap out of it, it probably wasn't! Or are you a young person who doesn't have much to look back on yet? Well be understanding and patient with the older generation because all things being equal, you will suddenly discover that you are one of them!

Initial Doubts But Temple Is Completed

The Big Picture

The next building action takes place after more than twenty years have elapsed. It is when Darius is King of Persia. The prophets Haggai and Zechariah are present to support this vital work of completing the rebuilding of the temple. Each of them has a specific message for the people which we will learn more about when we look at their books later. A letter is sent to Darius by his governor Tattenai requesting confirmation that the rebuilding could take place. A reply came back confirming not only that the building activity was approved but also confirming that Persia would cover the cost as promised long ago by Cyrus! The temple is completed and dedicated. Passover is celebrated with great rejoicing.

Thinking Step

There is a mention of Tattenai (probably) and his office (certainly) in an uncovered Babylonian record dated 502 BC which speaks of Ta-at[-tan-ni] governor of Ebernari (i.e. of Beyond the (Euphrates) River). Judah would have come under his jurisdiction of Syria and Palestine. Nice to see that archaeology once again affirms the Word of God.

Action Step

I remember being at a church meeting when the subject of funding for a particular project was raised. The response was very predictable. "There are lots of members who simply cannot afford to give any more, we will have to look outside for loans etc." The chairman, with a real twinkle in his eye, suggested that we first consider selling all the customised number plates out of the church car park and then see how much we still needed! So often when we pray for something God's response is "Great, you have the funds and/or opportunity, you go and get on with it!" We can be the answer to our own prayers! In our reading today we read in 6:4 – '...all expenses will be paid by the royal treasury.' Music to a fund raiser's ears! In 6:8 we read '...you must pay the full construction costs without delay...' Confirmation they would pay! Then the twist at the end – the verse continues, '...from my taxes collected in the province west of the Euphrates River...' In other words the funding was coming from their own taxes! A generous gesture from the King because he could have used this money for other purposes but nevertheless the settlers were funding the project themselves. They were the answer to their own prayers! What are you praying for? Consider the possibility that you could be the answer to your own prayers too.

Ezra Returns And Things Get Moving Again

The Big Picture

We are more than half way through his book and finally Ezra makes an entrance! The events of Zerubbabel are almost sixty years ago and during this intervening period Esther has been Queen of Persia! Ezra is a direct descendant of Aaron which gives him real credibility. He is an accomplished teacher of the law. All his expenses are covered by Artaxerxes and what is more, tax exceptions for returning religious workers are also given. A relatively small group returns with Ezra and they are listed in our reading today. A specific attempt to fully equip and staff the temple is made so that it can function effectively under Ezra's guidance, as he teaches the law.

Thinking Step

Many of the large remnant who remained in Babylon will have remained true and faithful to their Jewish roots but simply didn't wish to return to the land of their fathers. Their hope of a coming Messiah lived with them. Significantly it is from this area in the east that Magi travel to see Baby Jesus centuries later.

Action Step

The story is told of a man who died and went to Heaven. As he was being shown to his place that had been lovingly prepared for him, he passed a large barn-like building. He enquired about it and was told it would be better if he ignored it. However he insisted on seeing inside. His request was granted and the large doors were opened. He rushed inside to find nothing but racks of boxes – all identical except for a label on each which bore a person's name and the boxes were in alphabetical order. He ran to 'his rack' and found 'his box'. He asked if he could open it and was told it would be better if he didn't but if he insisted, he may. He ripped open the ribbon that secured the box and removed the top. Inside the box he discovered all the blessings he could have had whilst on earth, if only he had asked – but he hadn't. After a few moments he sadly replaced the lid and asked if he might leave. 7:6 tells us that Ezra received all he asked for because God was with him. Don't be afraid to make your requests to your Heavenly Father. Of course, you probably won't get everything you ask for because we sometimes ask for the wrong things! I don't know about you, I want to find my box empty when I get to Heaven!

Ezra Leads Revival In Israel

The Big Picture

Mixed marriages between the Jews and people from other nations is a big problem that Ezra has to resolve. Ezra is distraught by this flagrant breaking of God's law and prostrates himself before God on behalf of himself and his fellow exiles – and repents. Others join him and together they make a covenant to resolve the whole situation of foreign wives. It's a mess! Leading priests and Levites are involved too. All the exiles gathered together in the pouring rain probably in December, in the open square next to the Temple and resolved to separate from their foreign wives immediately. Many of the transgressing senior priests and Levites are named as well as many other exiles. The story continues in Nehemiah...

Thinking Step

Even though Ezra is blameless, notice how an 'I' turns to a 'we' or an 'our' when Ezra prays. O my God, I am utterly ashamed, I blush to lift up my face to you. For our sins are piled higher than our heads and our guilt has reached to the heavens, ...we have been steeped in sin.

Action Step

Too often we have rules for ourselves and different rules for others. This is particularly true in the church where too many times there seems to be a higher standard expected of those 'in ministry' whilst the congregation are more easily excused. The situation that Ezra discovers is one where the 'clergy' of the day are no better than the 'laity'. I remember clearly a lady talking to my wife at the church door one Sunday after service and saying how wonderful it must be to be married to a believer. She agreed and said that she had never known me as an unbeliever as we were both converted before we met. "Oh how lovely!" the conversation continued "Just imagine, married to another believer...no arguments or disagreements..." It took all of Margaret's considerable self-control not to burst out laughing but to gently correct this false assumption! God's standards are the same for all of us and temptations are as powerful for each of us. Holding a particular position in church does not cocoon you from problems – it often attracts them! This seems a very appropriate time to remember all your church leaders and to pray for them and their families that they would remain faithful to God and His calling and that all couples would remain true to their spouses in these days of growing marital and family breakdown.

Nehemiah

Nehemiah

We've looked at the return led by Zerubbabel, then the return with Ezra and now Nehemiah leads the third and final return. In the Hebrew Bible the books of Ezra and Nehemiah are one. We take up the story with Nehemiah acting as the cupbearer for King Artaxerxes I of Persia whose step mother was Queen Esther! The office of cupbearer was very influential as we saw with Joseph's cupbearer friend who had direct access to Pharaoh in Gen. 41:9. Upon hearing of the dire straits of Jerusalem and its walls, Nehemiah is granted royal approval to travel and organise repairs. Nehemiah's actions take place about a dozen or so years after Ezra had arrived in Jerusalem. This fresh activity creates animosity just as it did when previous building programmes were attempted. However with support from the prophet Malachi, the walls are completed in record time and Jerusalem is established and safe.

Below is an acrostic which summarises each chapter of the book.

1. **J**erusalem's tragic plight mourned
2. **E**nlisting the king's support
3. **R**ecord of all workers
4. **U**ndermining attacks by Samaritans
5. **S**elling Jewish children renounced
6. **A**ssembling wall despite opposition
7. **L**edger of returning Jews
8. **E**xplanation of God's law
9. **M**aking confessions of sin

10. **W**itnesses to signed covenant
11. **A**ccount of Jerusalem's leaders
12. **L**evites lead temple dedication
13. **L**evites restored to temple

Operation 'Wall Build' Is Underway

The Big Picture

Nehemiah hears about the problems in Jerusalem and responds with fervent prayer – for several months! One day he is attending to his duties serving wine to King Artaxerxes when the King comments on Nehemiah's sad face. An 'arrow prayer' is offered by Nehemiah before he responds and tells the King about the urgent need in Jerusalem, to rebuild the walls. Artaxerxes offers help and before he knows where he is Nehemiah is on his way to Jerusalem supported by a group of armed soldiers! On his arrival, local dignitaries, Sanballat and Tobiah, challenge his authority but Nehemiah gets work started almost immediately. This is seen as an act of treason even though Nehemiah insists he is simply about God's work

Thinking Step

In 5:1 we have an interesting beginning to Nehemiah's prayer. "O Lord, God of heaven, the great and awesome God..." It seems this format lasted many centuries as when Jesus is asked how to pray, His response in Matt. 6:9 is very similar but a little more intimate – "Our Father in heaven, may your name be kept holy... "

Action Step

There is no room for arrogance in the Kingdom of God and when we hear Nehemiah's reply to the challenge of his enemies, there is no hint of any arrogance – just certainty and trust in his Father in heaven. 2:20 says "The God of Heaven will help us succeed. We His servants, will start rebuilding this wall..." It's important that we don't appear arrogant when asserting our beliefs so we must be very careful – just as Nehemiah was. I remember watching Billy Graham being interviewed on TV and being asked if he was certain he would go to heaven when he died. Without hesitation his response was a firm "Yes" which brought the accusation of "Isn't that rather arrogant Dr Graham, how can you say you are good enough to get into heaven?" I will never forget the considered response. "I have car insurance and I believe what is written in my policy and I trust the insurance company to keep their word – I am simply trusting." He continued "It's just the same with my place in heaven, I have in writing, assurance from someone whose word I trust – I am simply trusting." There's a big difference between arrogance and trusting God, one is supreme over-confidence in self and the other is supreme realistic confidence in God. I'm too unreliable but God is totally reliable. So it's a no-brainer for me. Who will you choose to trust!

Work Proceeds But With Some Opposition

The Big Picture

Our reading begins with a detailed list of the builders involved and where they were building. Most of the gates mentioned no longer exist but the very first one, where it all began, is now called St Stephen's Gate and is the entrance right next to the Pool of Bethesda in Jerusalem today. It has continued to be used as a sheep market and the gate is still known as sheep gate. As the building work proceeded, Sanballat resorted to ridicule in his efforts to curb the progress. Enemies of the wall banded together to cause disturbances but with little success. The builders work with one hand, holding a weapon in the other.

Thinking Step

Did any of Ezra's returnees help Nehemiah re-build the wall? Very few of Ezra's 1,754 are named, however there are at least two duplicates mentioned. Ezra 8:33 and Nehemiah 3:4 record Meremoth son of Uriah. Whilst Malchijah son of Harim is in Ezra 10:31 and Nehemiah 3:11. I'm sure there would have been others unnamed.

Action Step

4:18 – 'All the builders had a sword belted to their side...' Doing the Lord's work and at the same time, defending themselves against their enemies. I remember when I was an elder in a church which also had a deacons' court. Folk who didn't know much about the structure of church life, would ask what the difference was between an elder and a deacon. My stock reply was that deacons did the work and elders prayed about it! Not true of course but there is some truth in it! They wanted to know which was the most spiritual – caring for the building or pastoring the people. In these days of marked divisions between paid and unpaid ministry, clergy and laity, full-time and volunteer, secular and spiritual – we need to remember that all work is ministry when done in the name of Jesus. What Nehemiah's builders were doing was ALL spiritual. I believe all occupations can be seen as spiritual – when done in the Name of Jesus. I remember hearing a preacher say that his ideal job would be fixing wheel caps to motor vehicles in a car factory. With each one, he said he would say a prayer and slip in a tract that an angry motorist would find just when they were changing a wheel – to let them know that Jesus loved them! Enjoy what you do today – or should I say enjoy today's ministry!

Despite Opposition
Wall Building Record Is Broken!

The Big Picture

After the excitement of the wall building and seeing it get higher and higher – reality sets in! Food is scarce and money even scarcer. Mortgages and loans are everywhere but paying them back will be another issue! 5:7 – "You are hurting your own relatives by charging interest when they borrow money." Nehemiah makes the accusation that Lev. 25:36 is being broken. He says that he will not claim his food allowance or charge interest and the people promise 'no interest' too. News reaches Sanballat that the wall is complete except for the gates. He accuses Nehemiah of wanting to become King! Considerable pressure continues but the wall is completed in the record time of 52 days!

Thinking Step

I spent many years working in the construction industry in the north east of England and regularly had to give promises to architects or structural engineers for delivery of materials to site. The usual was 6-8 weeks or about 52 days! That was for only materials to site whereas Nehemiah finished the whole job in 52 days!

Action Step

6:17-19 It seems Tobiah was an avid correspondent with the nobles of Judah. Unlike Sanballat, who was very open in his disputes with Nehemiah, Tobiah's opposition was quiet and mostly unseen. We know from his name that he was probably a supporter of Yahweh (his name means 'Yahweh is good') and his son is called Jehohanan (which means 'Yahweh is gracious') and it becomes very popular with Jews and is translated 'John' in the New Testament. So he had all the right credentials but was against what God was doing through Nehemiah and the exiles. I have encountered open opposition, indeed sometimes outright hostility, in my years of church leadership but give me this anytime rather than sly back biting negativity which is done subversively – like that of Tobiah. Church politics are a barrier to many of God's plans for His local church and the Devil loves them! If you can't be open with your opposition to anything going on in your church today ask yourself should you be opposing it! Openness and straightforwardness should be marks of every gathering of God's people. Jesus said in Matt 10:16 "...so be as shrewd as snakes and harmless as doves..." and in Matt. 5:37 – "Just say a simple "Yes I will" or "No I won't"..." You don't need to plot – and if you are – stop it now! – and let the Holy Spirit do His work, maybe using you!

Now Ezra Comes On The Scene

The Big Picture

Another list of names but if you have a good memory for this sort of thing you will find that Nehemiah 7 is virtually identical to Ezra 2! Nehemiah saw this listing as the glue to hold together the generations who had re-settled the land over the past 100 years or so. Ezra comes to the fore again after seeing Nehemiah lead the re-building of the wall with such drama. On a wooden platform Ezra teaches for about six hours and the people repent with weeping. The next day they act on what God had said and celebrate the Festival of Tabernacles in meticulous detail that had not been witnessed since the days of Joshua, 1000 years ago!

Thinking Step

Thirteen priests and thirteen Levites are listed in 8:4, 7 as helpers for Ezra. The Bible usually favours sevens or twelves or forties but uniquely there are thirteen here – twice! I believe this was such a radical re-start for Israel that ALL the tribes were included who settled the land – in thirteen areas – both sides of the Jordan.

Action Step

I have preached in many churches of different denominations and the one question I always ask is "When do you want me to stop my sermon?" There is such a variety and wide expectation from church to church that not to ask could be inviting trouble! My record for enforced brevity is seven minutes and I only found out as I was heading for the pulpit (this was the moment I resolved to always ask in future when I was to finish!). In our reading today Ezra was speaking for about six hours – in Hebrew – to a gathering who probably only spoke Aramaic! That's why he needed the thirteen Levites and their colleagues to help with translation! – 8:8. It was so effective that they gathered several more times – 8:18. I am not suggesting sermons of six hours! I am suggesting that it is the Bible which needs to be taught and applied regularly – just like Ezra did. Make sure all you say is grounded in the Word. I remember hearing someone ask a preacher how does he know for certain that what he preaches is the right word for that occasion. Without hesitation he replied "I always preach from the Bible and if you do too, you won't go far wrong!" Make the Bible your inspiration whenever you preach or teach and YOU won't go far wrong either!

Looking Back Before Moving Forward

The Big Picture

The Israelites separated themselves from foreigners and stand as an act of confession. They worshipped and praised for many hours, still standing. The Levites teach the people a 'walk through' of how God has cared for them and their ancestors all the way back to the choosing of Abram. A covenant is then agreed and signed by the leaders, Levites and priests. There is agreement to no more mixed marriages. Further practical promises about keeping the Sabbath and the paying of taxes and the giving of tithes are made. The final pledge to care for God's house in future brings these momentous events to a close.

Thinking Step

The Levites' address begins with two statements that are reflected in two great hymns today. Both in 9:5 – 'Stand up and praise the Lord...May it be exalted above all blessing and praise...' 'Stand up and bless the Lord...' by James Montgomery and 'Above all...' by Michael W Smith. You can even download 'Above all' as a ringtone! Thanks Levites!

Action Step

The Levites here, not surprisingly take the Jewish approach to teaching by giving a general overview so that seeing the big picture will enable the people to get everything into perspective. This is a theme you will see many times in the Bible. So many of today's errors are a result of taking Scripture out of context and thereby magnifying something or reducing it beyond the original intentions of the Bible authors under God's guidance and inspiration. There is also the problem of people not thinking through and forming their own doctrine and theology but simply adopting the views of their favourite preacher. I remember talking to a lady during one of the breaks at an OT event I was teaching and she asked me what my opinion was, regarding the ministry of women in the church. I simply responded by enquiring what hers was. "Oh she said, I don't have one, that's why I wanted to know yours because what you have said today has made a lot of sense to me, so I thought your opinion on women in the church could be mine too!" Always explore the Scriptures for yourself as well as benefiting from the exploring of others. I hope you are encouraged by your progress so far! Well done! – and remember – it's not too late to encourage someone else to join you. 'Step by Step' can begin at any time of the year.

Day 131
Nehemiah 11-13
11th May

11 - Resettlement Within And Without
12 - The Wall Is Dedicated
13 - Restoration Of The People And The Law

People Resettled In The Promised Land

The Big Picture

Ordinary people cast lots to see if they could move into Jerusalem where the leaders lived. Meanwhile the rest of the people continue in other cities. There was singing and purification ceremonies for the priests and Levites who in turn, purified the people. The sound of praise and worship could be heard for miles around. The Word of God was read out loud like in the days of Ezra and the commands about foreigners were heard again. Nehemiah realised that the people had fallen back into their old ways and commanded that the law about mixed marriages and the Sabbath must be honoured this time. He thanked God for the way He had been used to re-establish the people.

Thinking Step

Only the wealthy and those of noble birth would normally live in the cities, within the walls. The rest, generally the poor people lived outside the security of the walls. These folk were known as the daughters of Jerusalem or whichever city it was. Like young girls, they were the most vulnerable and the first casualties of enemy attacks.

Action Step

Nehemiah did some great jobs. He re-built the walls of Jerusalem and saw the people respond so well to the teaching of Ezra. Then he corrected the people as they slipped back from the standards that Ezra had established as they re-settled into the Promised Land. Not bad for a senior civil servant whose main job was to taste wine for the King before serving it to him as safe to drink! Ironically if Nehemiah had taken the safe route in life we would know nothing of him, the walls would have been re-built by someone else and he would have been totally unfulfilled in his life, deep down knowing that there could have been so much more. So what about you and me? Are we taking the best steps in life or are we even now, on a detour that we know will lead to disappointment because God isn't in it? Looking back at some of the steps we have taken as a family, they wouldn't have made sense if God hadn't been in them. However, He was and they did! It's never too late to stop and turn around. When God is in it you will reap the benefit for the rest of your life and for eternity. Has the Holy Spirit brought something to mind? – then act on it and keep in step with the One who knows the best route to take.

Esther

Esther

We step backwards with our story-line today as we begin reading Esther. She lived between Zerubbabel who re-built the Temple (Ezra 1-6) and Ezra who re-built the people (Ezra 7-10). She was one of the many Jews who never returned to the Promised Land. Her story takes place when Ahasuerus was King of Persia. Ironically God's influence is everywhere in this narrative but His Name is never mentioned! Ahasuerus has a celebration so big that it is recorded by the secular historian Herodotus! The party that followed resulted in him foolishly losing his favourite wife! Through the amazing acts of God, Esther replaces her and is in the right place at the right time with the help of her cousin Mordecai, to rescue the Jews from the schemings of Haman. The Jews give thanks for Esther every year on the Feast of Purim.

Below is an acrostic which summarises each chapter of the book.

1. **P**ersian decree against Vashti
2. **U**ncle Mordecai saves king
3. **R**evenge plotted by Haman
4. **I**ntercession made to Esther
5. **M**aking dinner of Ahasuerus

6. **F**avour shown to Mordecai
7. **E**sther requests her life
8. **A**hasuerus gives Mordecai promotion
9. **S**ons of Haman hanged
10. **T**estimony to Mordecai's greatness

Commoner Makes It Big And Becomes Queen!

The Big Picture

This book was probably written before the Greeks dominated the world which would explain why the King is called Ahasuerus rather than his Greek name, Xerxes. His wife Vashti wouldn't obey a drunken request to come to him immediately, so she is dismissed! When he sobers up he realises he has lost his favourite wife! A replacement is found in the beauty competition that followed. Her name is Esther. She gets twelve months of beauty treatments before she is allowed to be with Ahasuerus! However she quickly becomes his favourite wife. Meanwhile Mordecai overhears an assassination plot to kill the King and reports it to Esther who tells Ahasuerus. It is duly recorded in the official records kept by the Palace.

Thinking Step

God's chosen people have had many names. For example Hebrews, Children of Israel and Israelites. Today we call them Jews which is a name they were given in exile. Esther calls them Jews all the time and so a shortened version of Judah, becomes their name up to today.

Action Step

Are there some things that you will never change your mind about even though you are not as convinced now as you used to be? Don't mistake stubbornness for commitment. A friend of mine would often say after a church meeting "Well that's something else decided that will quickly become one of the laws of the Medes and Persians!" He meant it would never be changed and could easily become a problem for future generations. In our reading today we are looking at the very people who have this intransigent law code. When Vashti was dismissed from her privileged place as favourite Queen, this is recorded in 1:19 – ...'let it be written in the laws of Persia and Media so that it cannot be repealed...' The laws of the Medes and Persians should be consigned to history where they belong. Today we need to be sensitive to the Spirit's guidance and respond with flexibility. Do you have something that needs a 'change of mind?' Why not explain how you feel now, to your Father in Heaven. Then go to any other people involved and explain your heart change to them. This action could clear the air in many homes and it could be a real step forward in many churches. It could be a giant step for you spiritually and a liberating experience that will revolutionise the way God will use you. Don't delay, do it now...

Maniac Plans Massacre – Is There No Escape?

The Big Picture

Haman comes into the picture now as he is promoted by the King to a position that demanded everyone must bow down to him whenever he passes. Mordecai refused and Haman 'declared war on all Jews' because Mordecai was Jewish! For twelve months he casts lots until he has determined the best day to massacre them all. He explains the idea to the King who agrees and offers financial support! News gets to Mordecai who is devastated. The only one who can help is Esther but she explains that she can't just walk into the King's presence without an invitation. People have died for less! However she knows she is in a unique position so she is determined to try.

Thinking Step

In the days of mass illiteracy a signet ring often replaced the signature of influential people and carried great power and responsibility. Ahasuerus gives his to Haman – for bad. In Genesis a signet ring had been passed to Joseph – for good. In the New Testament a signet ring is given to the Prodigal Son – for love.

Action Step

Some of the most famous words in the Bible were in our reading today. 4:14 – often paraphrased as 'Perhaps you are here for such a time as this.' I believe this is true for all of us – not just the select few. We are here to play our unique part in God's plan. Sometimes we know what He wants but we would prefer He called someone else! The old "Here I am Lord, please send someone else" syndrome. I have done things over the years that I was convinced I would never be able to achieve but with the help of a faithful wife and the strength of God we have seen a ministry grow from nothing. We had no initial setup finance from Walk Thru in the USA. I was not pleased at the time but rejoice now! We sensed we were in the right place to make an impact for God no matter how small. It's the same for you! Can you imagine what would happen to your church if everyone said "We have a vision to fulfil now and I want to play my part – so I'm going to do it!" If it's only you who moves, you could be the catalyst to encourage others. Take a risk for God! You are in a place for such a time as this – so make the most of it.

Pride Comes Before A Fall – For Haman

The Big Picture

Esther approaches the King and he welcomes her! She invites him and Haman to a couple of banquets. Haman is delighted by such honours! However on his way home he sees Mordecai and all his contentment disappears. He resolves to have a giant gallows built to have Mordecai hanged! During a sleepless night the King reads his Palace or Chronicle records to discover that Mordecai was never rewarded for uncovering an assassination plot. The King seeks Haman's advice about how to honour such a man and Haman thinks it's him! When he discovers it's Mordecai he is devastated! Esther finally has the opportunity to explain the Jewish massacre plot and reminds him that she is a Jew! Haman dies – on his own gallows!

Thinking Step

One of the seven eunuchs sent to bring Queen Vashti is called Bigtha – 1:10. One of the eunuchs whose assassination plans were uncovered by Mordecai was called Bigthana – 6:2. Variations of the same name which means 'Gift of God'. What a name for someone who played such a significant if involuntary, role in Esther becoming Queen!

Action Step

5:13 – "...but this is all worth nothing as long as I see Mordecai the Jew just sitting there at the palace gate." Poor old Haman he had so much but it wasn't enough. For him today was just a planning day for tomorrow! So many people miss the blessings of today because they are chasing the blessings of tomorrow. As the old hymn says 'Count your blessings, name them one by one and it will surprise you what the Lord has done.' So what are you looking forward to today? Might I suggest you make it the best day you have ever had rather than worrying about tomorrow? If you're preparing a sermon, make it the best one you've ever done! If it will be a quiet day alone or with a friend – enjoy it to the full. If you will be spending the day with your children or grandchildren, do all you can to make it the best day ever! Get the point? Whatever you are doing today enjoy it in the fullest sense, by doing the best you can to the glory of God. Just think how different Haman's life could have been if his aim had been to have a fruitful life today rather than getting rid of Mordecai tomorrow! James. 4:14 – 'How do you know what your life will be like tomorrow?...' You don't, so let's trust God for tomorrow and enjoy Him today!

Day 135
Esther 8-10
15th May

8 - Counter Decree From Ahasuerus
9 - Feast Of Purim Is Established
10 - Mordecai Is Honoured

The Great Escape With Much To Celebrate

The Big Picture

Now that Haman is dead, King Ahasuerus gives his signet ring to Mordecai to show his trust in him. Esther pleads with the King to somehow stop the Jews being wiped out. As a result the King makes a law that allows the Jews to retaliate if they fear attack. This situation resulted in many turning to Judaism for fear of being attacked themselves. The Jews are saved – but around 75,000 of their enemies were killed but no plunder was taken. This rescue is celebrated every year by Jews at the Feast of Purim (the word purim meaning lots, it's a reminder of how Haman originally determined the date for the Jews to be wiped out).

Thinking Step

The Feast of Purim is a synagogue highlight for Jewish children every year. It involves readings from the book of Esther and every time Haman's name is mentioned, everyone makes as much noise as possible to drown his name out. Use of voice, feet, hands and groggers (like old fashioned football rattles) all help to make a great noise of condemnation.

Action Step

Who would ever have guessed that God would use the casting of lots as a key element in His people's amazing escape from a massacre? As you read through the Bible you constantly see instances of God surprising His people by the way He chooses to act. He is a God of infinite variety. Sometimes when we are asking God to work in our lives, we can only imagine one way. Whereas He has something altogether different in mind. I remember a low point in our lives when both of our sons had suspected cancer. Gary showed the symptoms first and we prayed for his healing and he was healed by the skill of the medical profession – and we thanked God! Later when Paul showed similar symptoms we prayed for him too and he was healed without needing any treatment and we thanked God again! So why did God treat two brothers with similar conditions in such diverse ways? We just don't know but there's a verse that is helpful when an answer is hard to come by – Psalm 115:3 – 'Our God is in the heavens and He does as He wishes.' Are you asking God to work in your life and expecting it in your way but nothing is happening? It could be that you are trying to squeeze God into your plans. Trust God to work it out in His way. He knows best!

196

Job

Job

Considered by many to be the oldest book in the whole Bible. Job was probably a contemporary of Abraham and his life story slips nicely in between Genesis chapters 11 and 12. It addresses the old dilemma of why do good people suffer, sometimes more than wicked people? We see the beginning of an early form of prosperity theology i.e. – 'If you love God He will see to it that you prosper. If you disobey God or sin in other ways, then you will be stripped of all your personal wealth and even suffer from ill-health.' There are many people who believe this today! The main theme of his book is the sovereignty of God, nothing happens that takes God by surprise. Job undergoes all sorts of trials despite living a blameless life and as for his friends – who needs enemies when there are friends like Job's!

Below is an acrostic which summarises each chapter of the book.

1. **J**ob's prosperity and tragedies
2. **O**utbreak against Job physically
3. **B**irth cursed by Job

4. **G**ather what is sown
5. **O**rdinary case of chastening
6. **D**enial of Eliphaz's charge
7. **S**upplication against God's mistreatment

8. **S**uffering befalls only wicked
9. **U**nfortunate helplessness of man
10. **F**airness of God questioned
11. **F**inite man must repent
12. **E**vident truths animals know
13. **R**esolution to debate God
14. **I**nsignificance of man's destiny
15. **N**ecessity of sin's punishment
16. **G**od's affliction for innocence

Day 136
Job 1-3
16th May

1 - With Permission Job Is Attacked By The Devil
2 - More Attacks From The Devil
3 - Speaks Out Before His Friends

God Knows That Bad Things Happen To Good People

The Big Picture

The opening chapter of Job can be hard to believe at first reading but I always bear in mind the ways that Jesus dealt with the devil as an individual. Jesus knew confrontations with the devil but He always knew victory over him – every single time. From the start it's clear that the devil is subordinate to God – nevertheless he is able to strip Job of everything! Even his children. Job's response? – "The Lord gave me what I had and the Lord has taken it away. Praise the Name of the Lord". Physical sickness came and to make matters worse his friends arrive. Finally in frustration, Job curses the day he was born.

Thinking Step

Job is cast aside and finishes on the rubbish heap – 2:8. Everyone thought he was with all the other dead rubbish because of sin and that he was as good as dead! This explains his wife saying "Curse God and die" and why his friends sit with him for seven days (which was the required period of mourning) – Gen. 50:10.

Action Step

The first challenge of the book of Job is this – do you believe in the devil? Believers tend to fall into one of two camps – the devil is a primitive myth and therefore can be ignored or he is to blame for everything that goes wrong and there is potentially a demon around every corner. Quite clearly Jesus believed in the devil and as far as I am concerned that is good enough for me! Jesus believed in a personal devil who conversed with Him and in essence that is what happens in our reading today. A conversation between God and the devil. It shows the devil has limited power and that God is sovereign all the time. You may ask "Why did God create a being who does so much harm?" Well He created mankind as well, didn't He and they can do some dreadful things! As soon as freewill is allowed, creatures have the power to do wrong as well as right. In our fallen world we often do the devil's job for him, we don't need him to get us into trouble! However sometimes things go wrong as a result of his work so remember Paul's advice in Ephesians 6 – "Put on all of God's armour so that you will be able to stand firm against all strategies of the devil." If you haven't already, I suggest you put it on now!

4 - Eliphaz Declares That Only The Wicked Are Punished   Day 137
5 - Eliphaz Tells Job To Appeal To God   Job 4-6
6 - Eliphaz Is Challenged To Point Out Job's Sins   17th May

Some Believe Only The Wicked Are Punished!

The Big Picture

One of Job's friends Eliphaz, responds to Job's first utterance by making the point strongly that the innocent never perish, it's only the wicked who do. He accuses Job of being foolish and tells him he must appeal to God. He says that in Job's position that's what he would do. He tells Job that he is being disciplined by God and needs to bear it and not despair. Job answers Eliphaz's accusations and asks him for sympathy. He needs some encouragement from his friend. Then Job says this in 6:24 – 'Teach me and I will keep quiet. Show me what I have done wrong' and v28 – 'Look at me, would I lie to your face?'

Thinking Step

6:15-17 – "...as unreliable as a seasonal brook that overflows its banks in the spring...when the hot weather arrives, the water disappears..." Job was likening his friends to the wadis of the Jordan rift valley. When they are dry, they are 'desert like'. In the wet season the water is suddenly a raging flood that sweeps everything away.

Action Step

6-24 "...show me what I have done wrong." Notice it's to his friends who know him very well indeed. Surely there must have been something they could have pointed out but it seems not. It appears 1:1 was accurate after all '...He was blameless – a man of complete integrity. He feared God and stayed away from evil.' Very often it is the appearance of wrongdoing that can damage a reputation that's why it's important to 'stay away from evil'. I know a man whose job it was to look after Billy Graham whenever he visited the UK. Unfortunately when he was due to collect Billy from the airport one time, he was unavoidably tied up and asked his wife to do the run instead. He and his wife were personal friends of Billy and his wife so they didn't anticipate a problem. When she turned up, Billy wouldn't get in the car but got a taxi instead. He was so protective of his reputation that he would not run the risk of being seen getting into the car alone with a lady who was not his wife! Even the appearance of wrongdoing is to be avoided. Are there things in your life that could be misinterpreted by others and thereby damage your reputation and that of your Saviour? If the Holy Spirit has brought something to mind now – please do something about it before it's too late.

Day 138
Job 7-9
18th May

7 - Job Keeps Questioning God
8 - Bildad Challenges Job
9 - Job Refutes Bildad's Argument

Bildad's No Help And God Isn't Listening!

The Big Picture

Job continues to ask questions. He pleads with God to end his distress and says he will soon be dead but he would like God to give him some respite before he dies. Bildad the Shuhite a friend of Job tells him to get real! His children must have sinned and that's why they died but as God does not punish the just there's still hope! Job argues that it sounds great in principle but how can you put your case before God Himself? He is so powerful He'll win every time! In his frustration Job concludes that it makes no difference anyway because God simply treats innocent and guilty the same. What Job really needs is a mediator.

Thinking Step

Bildad the Shuhite was a descendent of Shuah. In Gen. 25 we have a list of sons born to Abraham by his second wife Keturah and one of them is Shuah. The meaning of Shuah is interesting – it means prosperity. Mr. Prosperity, what a name for someone who was called to help his friend who had lost everything!

Action Step

9:33 – "If only there were a mediator between us, someone who could bring us together." These amazing words from Job to his friend Bildad are so prophetic. So long ago and yet Job realised that he needed someone to bridge the gap between a Holy God and sinful man. Before our conversion in our more rational moments, we can sometimes understand our need of an intermediary. Jesus our intermediary, does not discriminate between those who are 'respectable' and those who are the dregs of society and all shades in between. He is the go-between for everyone and sometimes we find that hard to swallow. Try this today but be warned it is not for the feint hearted. With everyone you meet today try to begin with the thought "Jesus died for this person too!" If at all possible when you have been the 'old grump' again, lacking in love and compassion for everyone – remind yourself that Jesus is still your go-between too! Just imagine the frustration of Job when he longs for someone to negotiate with God on his behalf but there is no one! God must have been thinking "No one yet Job but it's all in hand!" Why not thank God now for your mediator Jesus Christ. When you meet another 'Job character' looking for a way to communicate with God, why not recommend your mediator?

Why Are You Picking On Me God?

The Big Picture

Job tells God that he cannot understand why a created being is having such a hard time from his creator. Why does it appear that God is just waiting for Job to make a mistake and then He will destroy him? Why bother to let Job be born alive in the first place? Another of Job's friends Zophar, tells Job to be quiet and listen to God. "He is so much greater than you!" "Bow down before Him and confess your sins, that's the answer." Job reacts with sarcasm and tells Zophar that he's saying nothing new. Job knows that God is supreme and knows everything and can outwit even the cleverest people on earth but why is he suffering?

Thinking Step

Job lived in Uz which was next to Midian where Moses worked as a shepherd for forty years. It is a distinct possibility that Moses picked up the scroll of Job, all about suffering, when he was suffering in exile himself after murdering an Egyptian. Moses and Job, both wondering where God was when they needed Him!

Action Step

Job addresses his friends in 12:2 – "You people really know everything don't you? When you die wisdom will die with you!" I feel like this after watching some debating programmes on TV! Sometimes like Job, our unbelieving friends drive us to distraction the way they try to counter everything we say with what they think is a sound historical or scientific argument against believing. We sometimes forget that they are blinded by the powers of this world and simply can't see what is very obvious to you and me. I remember resorting to saying "I feel sorry for you!" when I couldn't think of another argument to put before a work colleague to persuade him that my faith could be just as relevant to him as it was to me. He had an argument ready for everything I said and in those days I acted as though I believed that it was possible to argue someone into the Kingdom. Of course you can't! I'm sorry I dismissed him the way I did. I have a suggestion for you when you are next debating your faith and if you never do, I recommend it as a way to strengthen you! Don't get in the way of the Holy Spirit as He works in other people's lives. Sometimes a simple "Sorry, I don't know!" can confirm to an enquirer that you don't need to know everything before you believe!

No One Understands,
So Job Speaks Direct To God

The Big Picture

Job continues his argument and puts Zophar in his place by telling him that he isn't the only one who knows a lot, Job is quite learned too! He accuses him of not listening and deliberately misunderstanding Job's situation. He tells Zophar that he is in danger of God's judgement himself if he insists on saying what is not true. Finally he asks Zophar to shut up, he's heard enough! Then he asks God directly why is He subjecting him to such suffering. He tells God that life is brief enough without all this suffering. He asks God to forget him and treat him as if he was dead until God's anger has subsided and life can return to normal!

Thinking Step

Each of Job's friends travelled 150 miles. Eliphaz came from Teman east of the Jordan. Bildad came from west of the Jordan. Zophar came from Naamah also west of the Jordan. All three would have travelled south on the east side of the Jordan down towards the Red Sea to meet up with Job in Uz. Considerable journeys even today!

Action Step

I have always found praying in a language other than my daily language quite difficult. I remember visiting an elderly lady who I prayed with before leaving her. She interrupted my prayers by asking me would it be possible to pray with more reverence and refer to God as Thee and not You! I did my best whenever I visited her but only for her sake because I believe we should use exactly the same language when praying, as talking. Of course leading public prayers can be different but even then I do try to be "me" rather than 'sounding false.' 13:23-24 – shows us how Job prayed. "Tell me what have I done wrong? Show me my rebellion and my sin. Why do you turn away from me? Why do you treat me as your enemy?" Earthy language that communicates just how Job felt. I remember talking with a man who had just heard his father had died. The man had not been a believer long and had hoped to witness to his Dad to bring him into the Kingdom too but now, it was too late. "I am so angry with God" he said. I suggested he told God what he thought but he said he couldn't in case he swore! Try to be "you" when you pray rather than just getting the language right. After all, God does know our thoughts as well!

15 - Eliphaz Continues To Counsel Job
16 - With Friends Like You...
17 - God Finds Job Useful!

Day 141
Job 15-17
21st May

Don't Look Down On Job's Youthfulness

The Big Picture

Eliphaz continues the conversation after Job has finished talking to God. He challenges Job to have more respect for God. Then he tries to explain where Job is going wrong. He says that wiser men than Job have struggled with life and it's injustices. Job responds "I have heard all this before!" "I like to think that I would be more comforting than all of you if our roles were reversed!" Then he turns again to God and tells Him how distraught he is with the way he is being treated. He is at the end of his tether and doesn't know how much more he can take. He is convinced he has been made an example to warn others!

Thinking Step

16 15 - "Here I sit in sackcloth. I have surrendered and I sit in the dust." When Job sits in sackcloth, it is unlikely that he has a fresh change of clothes at hand! More than that, the text could mean that Job has sewn himself into the sackcloth clothing because he can see no end to his suffering!

Action Step

15 10 - 'On our side are aged, grey-haired men much older than your father!' This may be roughly translated as "I am old enough to be your father!" It seems Eliphaz is an older friend of Job, perhaps old enough to be his father. Isn't it strange that sometimes we think we simply acquire wisdom by getting older. We confuse wisdom and knowledge. I asked a friend of mine who was a church pastor, who did he take his problems to? Without hesitation he told me he always went to the local postman in his congregation! There were lots of people in his church who knew much more about the Bible, theology, doctrine and a thousand other subjects but if he wanted a wise response, the postman was by far the best person to go to! Education is a wonderful thing and should not be under estimated – after all wisdom is knowledge guided by understanding. James 1:5 says 'If you need wisdom, ask our generous God and He will give it to you...' and when they were seeking deacons in the early church, Acts 6:3 says '...so, brothers, select seven men who are well respected and are full of the Spirit and wisdom...' Don't rely on your grey hair my friend (if you have any hair!). Get the Bible into you and ask God for wisdom. There are no upper or lower age limitations.

Day 142
Job 18-19
22nd May

18 - Bildad Tells Job - Words Are Not Enough!
19 - Job Responds - I Need Your Help!

Why Can't Family And Friends Support Me?

The Big Picture

Bildad comes into the conversation now and says Job has talked enough! It is so obvious that the wicked will be snuffed out and that's an end to it. Job replies "More words..." "Whichever way you look at it I have had a rough deal from God and everyone is rejecting me!" "God is punishing me so why can't you my friends and family, stop – to give me some respite?" Job closes with that amazing declaration "I know that my Redeemer lives" and adds a warning that those who are persecuting him will one day have to stand before God and explain why they didn't support him in his hour of need!

Thinking Step

Job gives us one of the best known quotes about 'our Redeemer' – in 19:25 – "... as for me, I know that my Redeemer lives and that He will stand upon the earth at last." What a declaration for a non Jew to make! Many years before Moses lived or the Pentateuch was written, God revealed Himself to Gentile Job.

Action Step

Have you noticed how many times we put others into our own made-up categories and then make all sorts of assumptions about them? I have to say though, that I am less likely to do so now – having made so many mistakes! When we first moved to the south of England I knew very few folk outside my denomination and was therefore suspicious of many people I came into contact with. One such man was the local catholic priest called Donald. The more I got to know him the more I was sure he was a real brother in Christ. Humorously he was mistaken for a member of the local Brethren assembly one time after he prayed in a local prayer meeting! He told me about his first funeral at the nearby crematorium. Before each service they played pleasant background music to suit each occasion and the duty manager took some pride in getting it right. When he knew the next service was to be lead by a catholic priest he immediately selected a sure winner 'Ave Maria'. After the service the duty manager asked Donald if everything was alright. Donald's response was a jaw dropper. "Very nice thank you but could I have something more uplifting and thought provoking next time – I suggest 'I know that my Redeemer Liveth!'" If you are tempted to make assumptions about the folk you meet today, remember my friend Donald!

206

Don't Tell Me That God
Doesn't Judge The Wicked!

The Big Picture

Zophar steps into the debate for a second time. He has heard enough and is insulted by much that has been said. "Don't you understand?" he says. "The success of wicked people has always been short-lived!" "No matter how much the wicked man achieves, it's never enough." "God will punish him, he will not escape!" Job answers Zophar by telling him that wicked people do live long and enjoy life, he doesn't know what he's talking about! In fact Job suggests that God gives the wicked an easy ride. The suggestion that God will punish their children doesn't sit well with Job at all. He is determined that wicked men do prosper and his friends are all wrong!"

Thinking Step

'Hell Fire and Damnation – Zophar style' 20:7, 14, 15, 16, 25 give his thoughts. 'Thrown away like his own dung, the food he has eaten...turns into poisonous venom, he will vomit the wealth he swallowed, he will suck the poison of snakes, the viper will kill him, the arrow is pulled from his body, the arrow head glistens with blood.'

Action Step

Those of you who are parents will understand 21:2-3 better than the rest of our readers! "Listen closely to what I am saying. That's one consolation you can give me. Bear with me and let me speak. After I have spoken you may resume mocking me." Job is totally exasperated by Zophar and his other friends. They appear to be listening but they don't hear what he is saying! Have you noticed how often a word of witness just seems to evaporate into mid air? I remember talking to a new convert who was being prepared for believer's baptism. I asked her who had been the biggest influence in her life and a major factor in her accepting Christ as Lord and Saviour. She filled up as she answered "It was a girl at school many years ago who first said things that got me thinking." She went on to say that she never showed any outward signs of interest and right to the end of attending the same school, she never told her fellow pupil how some of her comments had been so thought provoking, even though she was always ridiculed for saying them. "I have never seen her since we left school and would love to let her know that I was listening!" Don't be discouraged today when your words seem to fail to have an impact. Trust the Holy Spirit to hammer them home!

Day 144
Job 22-24
24th May

22 - Just Admit It Job!
23 - These Trials Will Purify Job
24 - Everything Will Come To An End

Same Old Stuff From Eliphaz
But Job Is Determined!

The Big Picture

Eliphaz joins in once again and condemns Job for his sins which he is now denying but which God is well aware of. "Job, just admit your sins" urges Eliphaz "Then you will know peace." Job repeats his longing to have a meeting with God when everything could be explained and he would then understand why all this is happening to him but he can't find Him! However Job is convinced that God is ultimately in control. Job declares that there is wickedness all around and he can't understand why God does nothing. "Having said all that, both good and bad will ultimately perish" says Job "...that's an end to it!"

Thinking Step

22:6 – "For example, you must have lent money to your friend and demanded clothing as security..." An accusation from Eliphaz which would later contravene the law in Ex. 22:26-27 – 'If you take your neighbour's cloak as security for a loan, you must return it before sunset. This coat may be the only blanket your neighbour has...'

Action Step

22:21 – "Submit to God and you will have peace then things will go well for you." There comes a time for all of us when we have to acknowledge like Job, that God really knows best even when we don't understand why things are happening. There is so much unnecessary bitterness eating people away because their lives haven't worked out the way they would like them to have done. I have visited many a home where the resentment against God is like a suffocating blanket ruining what could still be a wholesome life. Being convinced that you have had a rough deal and holding God responsible will not improve your lot! I have a friend who is totally blind following an operation on a brain tumour many years ago. He has no bitterness in him and still talks about watching TV and bidding you goodbye by saying "See you later!" He once told me that it must be terrible to be deaf and how grateful he is that he only lost his sight! I remember visiting him one day to find him painting the garage door! "It's easy when you get the hang of it" he said. Why not resolve today that things that you don't understand will not mar the rest of your life and that you will enjoy it knowing that God still has work for you to do – and enjoy!

25 - Let Me Repeat Myself...
26 - Pardon Me For Interrupting!
27 - I Really Believe That I Am Right!
28 - Wisdom Only Comes From God

Day 145
Job 25-28
25th May

God Is Still In Control
And The Fount Of All Wisdom

The Big Picture

Next, Bildad the Shuhite joins in the conversation and tells Job that there is no way anyone can meet God face to face. Job declares just how powerful God must be to do all He does but why can't He see that Job is innocent! He asks God to punish his enemy as well as the wicked. He knows that they all know about God's power and that everything will catch up with them someday. Finally he muses that man is so gifted and can do so many amazing things but no one seems to know where to find wisdom or understanding. Job re-affirms that wisdom and understanding can only be found in God.

Thinking Step

The brevity of Bildad's third talk in 25:1-6 leads some to believe that Job interrupts him because he has heard it all before! 25:3-6 does sound similar to Eliphaz in 4:17-19. With the twin themes of 'How can a mortal be innocent before a Holy God' and 'People are of little worth before God!'

Action Step

Chapter 28 brings us some teaching on wisdom. A quality that cannot be found simply by searching and cannot be purchased no matter how much money or wealth you might have. Wisdom comes from God and He encourages us to ask for it when He inspired Paul as he wrote to the Ephesian church 1:16-17 – "I have not stopped thanking God for you. I pray for you constantly, asking God the glorious Father of our Lord Jesus Christ, to give you spiritual wisdom and insight so that you might grow in your knowledge of God." Sadly we are tending to rely more and more on knowledge rather than wisdom. Too many times we change the order of words and make them knowledge first and then wisdom will follow! Job saw the folly of this and it was one of his main problems with his friends. I can still remember talking to an experienced minister who told me "For seven years I studied the Bible in Hebrew, Greek and Latin as well as many of the writings by great men like Martin Luther but I was never taught how to communicate with people or apply what I was learning to everyday life i.e. to seek wisdom." In other words, lots of education in the hope that wisdom would follow. Our churches need to be led by believers who are wise and not just well educated – starting with YOU!

Day 146
Job 29-30
26th May

29 - It Was So Much Better When I Was Young!
30 - Things Aren't What They Used To Be!

Job Yearns For The Good Old Days
When He Was Respected By All

The Big Picture

Job continues to speak "I long for the good old days when I was respected and was able to do good things that mattered." He fondly looked back to the days before his suffering when his reputation was still intact and his opinion carried a lot of weight. He was saddened by the fact that even the young men had no respect for him now. In fact they taunt him and laugh out loud when they see him. Losing his wealth was hard to take but losing all respect was even harder. Is this all because God is punishing him and he doesn't know what for?

Thinking Step

We used to have a God fearing society. It was safe to go out at night. Youngsters had manners. People knew their place. We had a caring society. There was integrity. Criminals were correctly punished. Today youngsters are out of control and their parents are no better. I don't like their music. So says Job 4000 years ago! Sound familiar?

Action Step

Have you noticed, doing the right thing does not protect you from things going wrong? How many of us 'did the right things' with our children but they still went astray? How many of us took the path that God seemed to be showing us very clearly – only for it to turn out to be a cul de sac? God knows that there are times if we were given all the details of His will, we wouldn't be able to grasp it anyway – so He doesn't tell us! Did you hear of the young man who was totally confused as to why his mother treated him so badly when he was little more than a baby? She tied him to the bed for hours on end and he didn't know why. Now she was dead and he had no one to ask. Finally a friend of the family helped him. She told him that his mother loved him so much that she tied him to the bed to stop him tearing at the infection he had on his face. She bathed him with olive oil all night. This went on for weeks but at the end of it he had a pure clean skin, unblemished, thanks to his mother. "If only I had known that" he said. How many times would we say that too? In the end we just have to trust Him who knows the whole story.

The Old Men Have Failed,
Let A Young Man Try Now!

The Big Picture

"I have made promises to God and kept them" says Job. Before there were Ten Commandments Job obeyed them! He is at a loss to know what he has done wrong and why God has it in for him! His insistence on his innocence silences his friends. Then along comes Elihu to try to get Job to see sense! He has not intervened until now because he is just a young man and he was sure the older friends of Job would be able to answer all Job's questions. Young Elihu is certain he has the words to put to rest all Job's concerns once and for all!

Thinking Step

Job anticipates Moses and shows he did live a Godly life! 31:13 – "If I have been unfair to my male or female servants...how could I face God?" Deut 24:14 "Never take advantage of poor and destitute labourers..." 31:16 – "Have I ... crushed the hopes of widows?" Exodus 22:22 "You must not exploit a widow..."

Action Step

Elihu bides his time before speaking out. However in frustration – some might say arrogance – he finally steps in and has much to say to Job and one assumes Job's friends too. One of my many weaknesses is that I rarely have Elihu's patience, I tend to think that everyone is waiting to hear my opinion and so voice it whenever I can!! A bit like Simon Peter I suppose and often just as wrong as him too! Having said that, I believe we have a duty to speak out whenever the time seems right. It's judging when it is the right time that gives many of us problems. Only today, at home, our doorbell rang and it was the Jehovah Witnesses! Me simply saying "Thank you and goodbye" didn't seem enough but I knew I wouldn't argue them into the kingdom either – so I challenged them to read the whole of the Bible and stop picking verses here and there. I hoped they would see that what they are teaching does not stand up to the 'Whole Bible' test. Then I smiled and bid them "Farewell" hoping that what I said was a word in season for them and trusting God that I had said the right thing. I had obviously done something right because they thanked me for being polite and smiling! How will you handle your next opportunity to speak out today?

Day 148
Job 33-34
28th May

33 - Let's Debate This...
34 - Let's Try Again To Debate This...

You Are Not A Special Case, Job!

The Big Picture

Elihu continues to speak to Job by telling him that they are both the same, made from clay. They are equal. However Elihu challenges Job's claim that he is innocent and God is simply picking on him! He tells Job that when he says God does not speak he is not taking into account dreams and visions. He adds "... and many are ill but recover, showing God is compassionate." Pausing for Job to respond but hearing nothing – Elihu continues to speak to Job and his friends. He declares God can do no wrong and He treats people the way they deserve. Elihu tells Job because of his intransigence, he has now added rebellion and blasphemy to his list of sins.

Thinking Step

33:11 – "He puts my feet in the stocks and watches my every move." This is a direct quote from what Job has said previously in 13:27 – "You put my feet in stocks. You examine all my paths. You trace all my footprints." So it seems Elihu was listening earlier when Job thought no one was!

Action Step

34:12 – 'Truly, God will not do wrong. The Almighty will not twist justice.' So why is it then that insurance policies often have a 'catch-all' clause known as 'act of God'? This clause only ever covers bad things never good ones! Actually I was told that even during the soviet period in Russia there was an 'act of God' clause in policies even though the official line from the government was that there was no God! I suppose God always comes in handy for someone to blame – even if you don't acknowledge He exists! Seriously, when things go well why do we give the credit liberally to anyone other than God but when things go bad, the buck stops at God's desk? Not one of us is responsible – we are all innocent! A friend of mine went to a football match some years ago and his team scored a wonderful goal. As he had just finished theological training the only word he could come up with as he celebrated the goal was 'Hallelujah!' This resulted in him getting some strange looks and having a little more space on the terraces than he usually had. Nevertheless God got the glory! What do you have to thank God for today? Next time something good happens to you, try thanking God first. It doesn't have to be out loud but if it is, it could be a great conversation starter!

35 - Elihu Tries For A Third Time To Win The Argument   Day 149
36 - Job Is Reminded That God Is Great   Job 35-37
37 - God Really Is Wonderfully Powerful   29th May

Remember How Great God Is And Fear Him

The Big Picture

Elihu asks Job if it is right for him to continue claiming he is righteous and yet question if it's worth all the effort! Elihu wonders if it makes any difference to God if we sin or not but concludes it must, as God sees everything. A rather pompous Elihu continues to defend God who he says is merely trying to attract Job's attention and stop him sinning further. "Every time we hear thunder or see the mighty acts of creation, we are reminded of how powerful God is" says Elihu. Then he suggests that everything God does is a punishment or a sign of love and people who are truly wise should show God reverence no matter what happens.

Thinking Step

When his other friends speak, Job interrupts but when Elihu speaks, Job listens. Elihu invites Job to debate with him but he never does. The words of a man called Elihu, whose name means 'He is my God' seem sufficient to prepare Job to have another conversation with God Himself.

Action Step

36:26-30 – "Look, God is greater than we can understand...He draws up the water vapour and then distils it into rain. The rain pours down from the clouds and everyone benefits. Who can understand the spreading of the clouds and the thunder that rolls forth from heaven? See how he spreads the lightning around him and how it lights up the depths of the sea." Elihu points Job to the creator by remarking on the creation and wondering how great God really is! I regularly watch the news and weather forecast on TV but when the weather forecaster says something like "Unfortunately the weather didn't do what it should have done yesterday" I find myself musing "I think it's God's job to determine what will happen, it's your job to try to forecast it!" It's the same with some natural history programmes where I recently heard the 'expert' telling us all that the caterpillar forms a chrysalis and then turns itself into a butterfly. I think once again, you will find that it's God who does the transformation, not the caterpillar. Am I being unnecessarily picky? I think not. As soon as we only look at the creation and never the creator, we will soon fall into the trap of thinking that we can explain it all away without mentioning God at all. Look out of a window now and remind yourself, how great is the God we worship!

You Are Seriously Out Of Your Depth, Job!

The Big Picture

God speaks to Job and has some questions for him! He acknowledges Job's questions and then bombards him with some that only God can answer. He asks about the making of the world, the weather, the seas, light and dark and many more. Taking a breath, God then says "Of course you know all this because you are so old and very experienced!" By now Job's shoulders must be rounder than they have ever been. He would have been able to enter any friend's tent without lifting the flap! God isn't finished yet. What about the stars and the many diverse animals that exist? So many profound questions that Job must have been wondering, could there possibly be any more!

Thinking Step

Job talks about God in 9:7-10 – 'He made all the stars...Bear, Orion, the Pleiades and the constellations...' "Only to have God later remind him of this by asking in 38:31-32, "Can you hold back the movements of the stars? Are you able to restrain the Pleiades or Orion...or guide the Bear...across the heavens?"

Action Step

We take so much for granted every day. Having enough air to breathe, enough food to eat, enough water to drink...the list could go on and on. Job is reminded of many of the miracles of creation in our reading today and they can serve as reminders for us too. Our God is totally dependable and amazingly creative but must not be taken for granted. As a parent there is nothing more galling than our children not acknowledging what we do for them and just assuming that it will continue even if they don't acknowledge us. Well, how do you think God feels? Assuming that you are breathing and you probably are as you are reading this – you have much for which to thank God. Just pause now and thank the God of creation, who made everything out of nothing – for being concerned about you! Our lives would be so much richer if we looked up regularly to see the amazing sunsets and rainbows that God creates all the time. I don't know about you but I notice these things so much more when I am on holiday or away in another country. Surely we don't need to be away from home before it dawns on us what a wonderful God we have and how worthy He is to be worshipped. Thank Him for another day today and resolve to serve Him better than you did yesterday!

All's Well That Ends Well

The Big Picture

"So do you still want to argue with Me?" says God to Job. Job is repentant and puts his hand over his mouth. Then God asks him if he is powerful enough to do the mighty things that God does or create the amazing animals that God has created? If he is then God would praise him! God declares people are afraid of a crocodile so they should be very afraid of its creator! Job concedes that God is totally powerful and unstoppable and sits in the ashes repenting. His friends are condemned by God but spared after Job prays for them. Finally Job receives from God twice as much as he had taken away from him.

Thinking Step

Job names his three daughters this time but not his sons and also includes them in his will! His original children were all unnamed and are replaced but not doubled like his livestock. Thus leaving us to conclude that Job would see them again. He lost his initial livestock for ever but his children – for a short while only!

Action Step

Our saga of the life of Job comes to a happy ending. We often hear about the patience of Job but I didn't notice he was that patient, did you? I think this book is more accurately about the sovereignty of God rather than anything to do with Job. Over all the things that happen to Job there is a loving God who guaranteed that Job would survive and that his present day sufferings were only temporary. What a reminder for us, especially when we are going through hard times – God is still sovereign and in control. No matter how dark the days may be God radiates His goodness over us all. Remember too that Jesus said He would never lose those who the Father had given Him, so we are truly blessed. It also reminds us to be better friends than Eliphaz, Bildad or Zophar ever were and you can include Elihu in that list too! How can we be better than Job's 'comforters?' By listening, by being sympathetic and empathetic and most of all by praying for those in trouble and in need of our support. If you haven't already thought of it yourself, let me give you a tip. I am using my 'to-do-list' on my mobile phone as a prayer reminder. Why don't you join me and together we can be the sort of friends that Job would have really appreciated and benefited from.

Psalms

Psalms

Often thought of as the 'Temple Hymnbook' the book of Psalms is very special today to both Jews and Christians alike. Of the 150 Psalms it is generally acknowledged that David wrote approximately half of them. The rest were written by various writers from Moses onwards – covering about 1000 years in total with several compilers bringing them together over the centuries. Psalms is a collection of songs that fall into five separate sections. Each of these individual books of Psalms relate to the five books of the Pentateuch. Initially this song book had no name but it gradually became known as the 'Book of Praises.' As the Old Testament was translated into Greek and Latin the title of the "Book of Psalms" became the norm. It has been a source of inspiration and challenge for hundreds of years and we can with confidence, anticipate the same as we read the Psalms today.

Below is an acrostic which summarises each chapter of the book.

1. Brief description of Godliness
2. Life of God's Anointed
3. Expression of God's deliverance
4. Security in God's presence
5. Safety of God's protection
6. Evil of David's enemies
7. Divine judgement for enemies

8. Image of God's son
9. Song of David's praise

10. Tongue of the wicked
11. Heaven test the righteous
12. Emptiness of flattering words

13. Mercy for the Faithful
14. Appraisal of man's sin
15. Nature of God's people

16. Teaching about Christ's resurrection
17. Hope for disappointed Christians
18. Affirmation of the righteous
19. Truth of God's Word

20. Where trust is placed
21. Assets of the King
22. Lapse of God's presence
23. Keeper of the sheep
24. Seal of God's salvation

25. Necessity of being forgiven
26. Outline for Church attendance
27. Truth for troubled times

28. Intercession for Israel's salvation
29. Nature reveals God's glory

30. Turning mourning into joy
31. Help through deep depression
32. Embracing the Lord's guidance

33. Counsel of the Lord
34. Occasions to Praise God
35. Uncovering lies and deception
36. Names of God's attributes
37. Collection of wise advise
38. Inquiry into David's sin
39. Lesson in keeping silent

40. Opportunities to share God
41. Fruit from showing compassion

42. Thirsting for God's presence
43. Healing for heavy souls
44. Embracing of God's purpose

45. Unearned grace of God
46. Nature under God's control
47. God is greatly exalted
48. Occasion for great joy
49. Death of decadent people
50. Limitation of burnt offerings
51. Yoke of yesterdays sin

52. Nonsense of loving evil
53. Occupation of sinful men
54. Rescuing David from trouble

55. Salvation in impossible situations
56. Tears are God's tools
57. Aspirations of God's help
58. Nightmare of wicked people
59. Deeds of wicked people
60. Separation of the disobedient

61. Intent of David's heart
62. Nurturing dependence on God

63. Tuning in to God
64. Habits of God's enemies
65. Efficiency of God's creation

66. Prayers the Lord hears
67. Assembly called to praise
68. Tribute to the Messiah
69. Humiliation of the Messiah

70. Wisdom of knowing God
71. Holiness in old age
72. Elation of all nations
73. Reward for the corrupt
74. Eminence of God's judgement

75. Source of future promotion
76. Impact of God's wrath
77. Notice of God's mercy
78. Nation of Israel remembers
79. Elimination of the heathen
80. Request for God's return
81. Solution for Israel's problems

82. Wisdom of God's judgement
83. Attackers of Israel's security
84. Lord's house comes first
85. Kindness of God returns

86. Need for God's presence
87. Owner of Zion's gates
88. Request for answered prayer

89. Song of God's mercy
90. Importance of time management
91. Treasures of God's presence

92. Deep things of God
93. Omnipotence of the Lord
94. Wicked workers are condemned
95. Notes about proper worship

96. Worship as a lifestyle
97. Heavens declare His righteousness
98. Excitement over His coming
99. Realizing God is Holy
100. Entering into God's courts

101. Theme of personal purity
102. Hope of human hearts
103. Essence of God's mercy

104. Sovereignty of God's creation
105. Covenant recalled with Abraham
106. Offences committed by Israel
107. Redeemed of the Lord
108. Necessity of God's help
109. Fate of the wicked
110. Understanding the Messiah's reign
111. Looking at God's works

112. Glimpse into God's gifts
113. Admonition to praise God
114. Terror of God's presence
115. Help comes from God
116. Evidence of loving God
117. Remembering the Lord's Kindness

118. Builder's stone becomes Messiah
119. Usefulness of God's Word
120. Trusting God for deliverance

121. Hope comes from God
122. Importance of Jerusalem's peace
123. Song for God's mercy

124. Difficulty comes before deliverance
125. Enduring presence of God
126. Labouring with literal tears
127. Instructions for new families
128. Generosity of God's favour
129. Hardships of Israel's beginning
130. Thirst for God's forgiveness

Psalms In The Gospels

PSALM	MESSAGE	MATT.	MARK	LUKE	JOHN
8:2	You have taught children and infants to give You praise	21:16			
22:1	My God, my God, why have You abandoned me?	27:46			
22:18	They divide my garments among themselves and throw dice for my clothing	27:35	15:24	23:34	19:24
31:5	I entrust my spirit into your hand			23:46	
34:20	For the Lord protects the bones of the righteous; not one of them is broken				19:36
35:19	Don't let my treacherous enemies rejoice over my defeat. Don't let those who hate me without cause gloat over my sorrow				15:25
41:9	Even my best friend, the one I trusted completely, the one who shared my food, has turned against me.				13:18
69:9	Passion for Your house has consumed me...				2:17
69:21	...they offer me sour wine for my thirst.				19:28
78:2	I will speak to you in a parable.	13:35			
78:24	...He gave them bread from Heaven.				6:31
91: 11-12	...He will order His angels to protect you...	4:6		4: 10-11	
110:1	...Sit in the place of honour at My right hand until I humble your enemies, making them a footstool under your feet.	22:44 26:64	12:36 14:62	20:43 22:69	
118: 22-23	The stone that the builders rejected has now become the cornerstone.	21:42	12:10	20:17	
118: 25-26	Bless the one who comes in the name of the Lord...	21:9 23:39	11:10	13:35 19:38	12:13

Whoever You Are
Worship The Lord And Pray To Him

The Big Picture

Psalms begins by contrasting two ways of life, the Godly and the ungodly. This is followed by a declaration of the Lord's Anointed One and an appeal for all to worship Him whether you are a King or a commoner. Then we have a Psalm of David written after he ran away from his son Absalom as David rejoices in victory in the face of defeat – thanks to God – 2 Sam 15. The last three Psalms are all about prayer. Evening prayer for deliverance, morning prayer for guidance and in conclusion, a prayer for God's mercy which could be our daily prayer.

Thinking Step

After the introductory first Psalm, the next Psalm – the first by David, proclaims "The Lord's Anointed will rule!" Jesus Himself quotes from this Psalm as He speaks to the church at Thyatira in Rev. 2:27 when He declares ultimate victory for faithful believers, in His revelation to the Apostle John.

Action Step

"Answer me, listen, don't turn me away" – these are the initial thoughts of the first verses of the last three of our Psalms today. They remind us that no matter what – God will answer, listen and never reject us. In good times we rarely need these assurances but in bad times they can be music to our ears. Oil to our wounds. I remember hearing of a man diagnosed with cancer, being urged to get things right with his God before he died. I was amazed when he said that he had given God no thought at all during his life and therefore he had no intention of turning to Him when he felt desperate! It was a matter of pride and a fear of being rejected. Has the Holy Spirit brought someone to your mind today who has not been to church for ages? Someone who used to be a part of your fellowship but who slipped away? Why not give them a pleasant surprise and take time today to make contact with them. Don't rush in to inviting them to church but invite them for coffee. Let them know that you are interested in them as a person and not just as a number on your church membership role. Remind them that God loves them and that it's never too late to return to Him – in the knowledge that He will never turn them away.

God Is Dependable And Fair

The Big Picture

In times of trouble when the tribe of Benjamin is creating problems, at about the same time as David is having difficulties with Absalom, David turns to God for reassurance and justice in our first Psalm. In Psalm 8 God is declared majestic and His creation confirms it everywhere you look. Psalm 9 praises God for victory over the enemy and the certainty that they will be judged for their wickedness in due course. God's judgement is yearned for as the ultimate solution for wickedness in Psalm 10. In times of testing, God's Word is pure and His righteousness can be relied upon forever, declares Psalms 11 and 12.

Thinking Step

The heading for Psalm 7 describes it as a 'Shiggaion' which comes from the verb shagah "to reel about through drink." A related word describing 'out of control emotion' is used in 1 Sam 26:21 – 'Then Saul confessed "I have sinned... I have been a fool and very, very wrong." God's people often experience very strong emotions!

Action Step

I worked with a man many years ago who said the answer to every problem in the world would ultimately be found in science. When I mentioned God to him he laughed and said that no one of any intellect believed any of that stuff now! That attitude is far from modern as our reading today reveals in 10:4 – 'The wicked are too proud to seek God. They seem to think that God is dead.' Of course God gets many mentions in daily life but sadly, almost all of them are exclamations rather than expressions of reverence! My pet theory is that God gets more mentions on the average makeover programme on TV than He does on Songs of Praise! We need to redress the balance with positive references to God, Christianity and the church, in our normal everyday conversations. I was in the hairdresser's just a week or so ago and the barber asked me what I was doing with my time. I told him about the book I was writing – this one! He told me his parents were born again believers and that he used to go to church. We covered Alpha courses and reading the Bible before my time was up. Try just dropping a 'Godly word' and see what happens next time you have your haircut!!

Day 154
Psalms 13-18
3rd June

13 - Please Answer, Now! - David
14 - Unbelievers Are Fools! - David
15 - Believers Are Wholesome - David
16 - Believers Are Assured - David
17 - Believers Are Protected - David
18 - David Is Thankful For Deliverance - David

Unbelievers Have Nothing
Believers Have Everything!

The Big Picture

Today's reading begins with David longing for God to answer his prayers and become even more real to him. In Psalms 14 and 15 the Godless and the Godly are once more compared and contrasted – with the Godly winning, yet again! Psalm 16 is one of assurance as it confirms that eternal life waits for those who are trusting in the living God. Psalm 17 describes the God who protects His people 'in the shadow of His wings.' The final Psalm reflects David's thanksgiving for being delivered from his enemies and in particular, from Saul who tried so many times to kill him.

Thinking Step

In ancient times bodily parts were used to portray emotions, a bit like today we use words like – 'heart.' 16:7 – '...even at night my 'heart' instructs me.' Here David used the word 'kidneys.' A similar use of bodily parts is found in 16:9 – 'No wonder my 'heart' is glad and I rejoice...' Here the actual Hebrew is 'liver'.

Action Step

17:4 – 'I have followed your commands which have kept me from going along with cruel and evil people.' Of course simply reading the Bible is not enough – as you already know. David doesn't say that he is familiar with God's word or that he has read it several times – he says he has followed God's commands. In other words he has applied the truths of the Word to his life and daily experience. I have taught in many different settings – and congregations vary greatly but broadly they fall into three categories. The most common one is the group who will take your word for anything! They never check anything with their Bible and are seemingly untouched by you and the Holy Spirit. The opposite to this is the congregation who listen primarily to check your soundness! They are not listening to what God may say to them but feel they have a mission to check that you are on the straight and narrow, or at least on the same path as they are – which isn't necessarily the same thing! The best congregation are those who check what you are saying, in their own Bible, in order to apply it to their lives as a word from God through you. Which of these best describes your approach? Get into the third group as soon as you can – and grow!

Our God Creates Us, Suffers For Us And Reigns In Us

The Big Picture

We begin with praising the virtues of God's Works and Words in Psalm 19. Then in the next Psalm a dire warning that we must trust in God not in horses and chariots for our security. Psalm 21, written for a choir, tells how much King David rejoices in God and knows victory in Him. The next Psalm is 'the Psalm of the cross' which begins "My God, My God, why have you forsaken me?" which is quoted by Jesus on the cross. Psalm 23 needs little comment as the most famous Psalm. Our last Psalm is the 'King of glory' Psalm which ends "Who is this King of glory? The Lord of Hosts, He is the King of Glory!"

Thinking Step

20:7 – 'Some nations boast of their chariots and horses but we will boast in the Lord our God.' David disabled chariots rather than re-use them – 2 Sam. 8:4 – 'David captured 1,700 charioteers... then crippled all but 100 of the chariot horses.' Solomon does the opposite, 1 Kings 10:26 – 'Solomon ...had 1,400 chariots and 12,000 horses... and built chariot cities...'

Action Step

23:4 – 'Your rod and your staff protect and comfort me.' What warming words to read, words of real assurance and certainty. However we need to remember that the shepherd's rod was a defensive aid used to ward off enemies of the sheep – so protecting them. On the other hand however the staff was a disciplinary tool that the shepherd often used to prod and poke the sheep if they misbehaved. So David tells us that he is comforted by the protection and the discipline of the Lord! I welcome protection all the time but I can't say the same about discipline! What about you? I hear parents often saying that they don't discipline their children because they want to be their friend. We need to remember we are parents not friends, when children are growing up. They need us to be protectors and where necessary, discipliners too. I don't mean poking them with a shepherd's staff because there are many better ways to discipline a child but failing to discipline is not a sign of love, it's the opposite. When we are good parents our children will usually be good friends to us – when they grow up.

Day 156
Psalms 25-30
5th June

25 - An Alphabet Of Guidance - David
26 - Examine Me O Lord - David
27 - The Lord Is Trustworthy - David
28 - Answered Prayer Joy - David
29 - God's Powerful Voice - David
30 - God Is Always Faithful - David

Much To Learn And Much To Be Thankful For

The Big Picture

We begin with an acrostic Psalm which has 22 verses, one for each letter of the Hebrew alphabet. This made the theme on guidance easier to memorise. It is a format repeated in several other Psalms. We then continue with Psalms 26 and 27, which proclaim David would welcome God's testing because he continues to trust Him and will always be faithful. We are reminded that God answered David's prayers and He will answer ours too. God is powerful and we need to acknowledge that He is worthy of our worship. Finally in Psalm 30, entitled 'at the dedication of the house', David praises God for a dramatic deliverance.

Thinking Step

According to the Septuagint translation of the Old Testament, Psalm 29 was used as part of the celebration of the Feast of Tabernacles – Lev. 23. Later however the Talmud prescribes it for the Feast of Pentecost which was when God through Peter, increased the church by 3,000 souls – Acts 2.

Action Step

27:14 – 'Wait patiently for the Lord. Be brave and courageous. Yes wait patiently for the Lord.' These words are so challenging in our society where 'instant' is the order of the day. My Mum would often say to me, "Just be patient and wait then you will appreciate, whatever you are waiting for so much more." That may well be true but it doesn't make waiting any easier does it? Every new computer gadget that comes on to the market promises things will be quicker! Every small window of waiting is being filled up. TV screens in waiting rooms, adverts whilst you wait on the phone and so it goes on. David tells us here "Wait patiently... yes wait patiently..." The art of waiting is something that needs to be practised if we are ever going to be any good at it. It seems they weren't much better at it in David's day than we are now as he has to repeat himself! It's interesting that the two requests to wait are divided by two very positive commands – be brave and be courageous. Maybe this is the key. As we wait we need to trust that God has everything under control. His timing is perfect. So wait and be brave and courageous – and see God take action!!

31 - Rise Up And Bless The Lord - David
32 - God Forgives And Cleanses - David
33 - Creator And King - Uncertain
34 - Desperate Times Call For Desperate Measures - David

Day 157
Psalms 31-34
6th June

God Is Great, Even When Times Are Difficult

The Big Picture

In Psalm 31 we are urged to not be downhearted but trust in the Lord and take courage. Psalm 32 continues the theme – when we do so, He will bless us with all the forgiveness we need. We need to acknowledge our sins and He will take care of it all and refresh us for life. Psalm 33 encourages us to worship the Lord with stringed instruments and consider His creation. The Lord looks down from Heaven and knows all that is happening. Psalm 34 was written at a time of great stress for David as he feigned madness in order to escape Abimelech. However he finds God is more than able to take care of him.

Thinking Step

31:6 – "I hate those who worship worthless idols. I trust in the Lord." This Psalm was obviously well known to Jonah as it came to mind when he found himself in the fish's stomach. Jonah 2:8 – 'Those who worship false gods turn their backs on all God's mercies.'

Action Step

32:3+5 – 'When I refused to confess my sin, my body wasted away and I groaned all day long... Finally I confessed all my sins to you and stopped trying to hide my guilt. I said to myself "I will confess my rebellion to the Lord" – and you forgave me! All my guilt is gone.' Doesn't this ring true? Despite knowing that it simply doesn't work, we wrestle with our sins hoping they will just go away! Is there something in your life that you know needs to stop but persists and just won't go away? David sums it up so well when he remembers that he refused to confess and it gave him no peace at all. Then he stopped hiding his sin. Lastly he confessed it to God and received forgiveness. So it's that simple! Uncover it and confess it. I am sure this was the thought in the mind of the Apostle John when he wrote in 1 John 1:9 – '...if we confess our sins to Him, He is faithful and just to forgive us our sins and to cleanse us from all wickedness.' The remedy is there for us – all we have to do is uncover and confess. If the Holy Spirit has brought something to your mind whilst you have been reading this, you know what you need to do don't you? Uncover and Confess.

Day 158
Psalms 35-37
7th June

35 - Please Help Me With My Enemies - David
36 - God Is All We Need - David
37 - Rest In The Lord - David

When In Trouble – Rely On The Lord

The Big Picture

As David often does, he prays for his enemies in Psalm 35. He is remarkably honest in asking God to act against those who are troubling him. In Psalm 36 he speaks in great detail of God's unfailing love and how vital it is for sinful mankind. He speaks of a God who never fails us. David's hectic life results in Psalm 37 where he implores all of us to take time to rest in the Lord. Even when wickedness is all around, our God can give us security and rest. We need to trust God even when our enemies seem so powerful, knowing that God loves justice and will deliver those who trust Him.

Thinking Step

David asks God to put on armour – 35:1-3 – 'O Lord, ...put on your armour and take up your shield... lift up your spear and javelin...' The Apostle Paul tells us we can do this, thanks to Christ – Eph. 6:13 – 'Therefore, put on every piece of God's armour so you will be able to resist the enemy...'

Action Step

37:12-13 – 'The wicked plot against the godly, they snarl at them in defiance but the Lord just laughs, for He sees their day of judgement coming.' There have been many times during my life when I have longed to intervene rather than trust the Lord that He knows best and as David tells us here, God actually laughs at the futility of those who oppose Him. I think that's great! As Director of Walk Through the Bible for many years I was constantly amazed at the ethics, or lack of them amongst some Christians. I have heard folk say that it's okay to break parts of the law, especially copyright law because it is for the Kingdom! My reply has always been "Well that makes my fundraising easier, all I have to do is rob a bank and we are sorted for many years!" There are also those who sign agreements with you and then, sometime later tell you – without a blink – that they signed in good faith but now don't feel obliged to keep to their word! I expect this sort of thing in the world but not in the Christian world. Maybe I am just naive. I am glad it doesn't cause God problems! He just laughs and knows that 'their day of judgement is coming.' Make sure you aren't caught up in any of this because God wants ethical believers not opportunists!

Do Good And Care For The Helpless

The Big Picture

With our reading today we complete the first of the five books that make up the Book of Psalms. David explains that he knows what it's like to be a sinner but rejoices in the fact that God is his salvation. Psalm 39 describes man's all too brief life but David confirms that his hope is totally in the Lord. God's will is something David finds real satisfaction and delight in doing – in Psalm 40. He declares that the law is within his heart. The last Psalm of Book One, Psalm 41, reminds us all that helping others has its own reward.

Thinking Step

Jeduthun is mentioned in the title of Psalm 39 (and also the titles of Psalms 62 and 77) He is probably the Levitical musician appointed by David and mentioned several times in 1 Chron. 16:37-43. His name has a very appropriate meaning for a musician – it means 'praising!'

Action Step

41:1 – 'Oh, the joys of those who are kind to the poor! The Lord rescues them when they are in trouble.' Of course there are many ways to be poor. It can be financial, social or even emotional. Generally any of us who are in need may be described as poor. Don't limit your thoughts to those across the sea or those in the inner cities of the poorer European countries or even our own. We are surrounded by a mission field and are often a needy part of it ourselves. As soon as we get this perspective in our mind then being kind to the poor is being kind to EVERYONE we meet. Remember that Jesus said "You will always have the poor among you and you can help them whenever you want to but you will not always have me." So it's not just a blanket 'help everyone' but respond to the leading of Jesus. You simply cannot help everyone – so don't feel guilty when you find you can't! You can be kind to all you meet but you will only be able to 'really' help relatively few. Ask Jesus now who it is He wants you to help and then take care of those He gives you. If everyone did this we would have a world where government help could be rendered obsolete! So who are you helping today, do you know yet?

Day 160
Psalms 42-48
9th June

42 - Longing For God - Korah
43 - Hoping In The Lord - Uncertain
44 - We Continue To Trust In God - Korah
45 - Prepare For The Wedding - Korah
46-48 - Our God Reigns - Korah

Longing For Our God Who Is All-Powerful

The Big Picture

The second book within Psalms begins with a Psalm by the sons of Korah which brings us those beautiful words 'As the deer pants for the water...' This is followed by Psalm 43 confirming the Psalmist's hope in the Lord. The next Psalm is anonymous and stresses our continued trust in the Lord. Psalm 45 includes the line 'My tongue is the pen of a ready writer' which is a very well known part of this beautiful love song. Psalms 46 to 48 remind us that God reigns as our refuge, strength, ruler and King.

Thinking Step

Six of today's seven Psalms are attributed to the sons of Korah. Thanks to the genealogies in 1 Chronicles we know that these were included in the listing of men assigned to lead the music in the House of the Lord after the Ark was placed there – 1 Chron. 6:31-32.

Action Step

46:1-2 – 'God is our refuge and strength, always ready to help in times of trouble. So we will not fear when earthquakes come and the mountains crumble into the sea.' Such uplifting words when our world seems to change by the minute! Of course as well as these cataclysmic changes there are also the very small ones too – which seem to be the ones that often threaten us the most. When I became a Christian in the 1960s the church was an unchanging docile creature compared to the rampant image some fellowships enjoy today. In fact we often parodied a popular hymn of that time 'Like a mighty tortoise moves the church of God. Brothers we are treading where we've always trod!' Almost everything has changed since then. Worship styles, hymns, dress code, Bible translations, sound systems and other technology in churches, church offices... I could go on! I occasionally get invited to speak to fellowships which seem to have evaded most of these changes and are living in a 'time bubble!' It's nostalgic but serves to remind me that if the church isn't pliable it soon becomes dry and irrelevant. Thank God for all changes that result in life-change, even the changes that really irritate us! Where would a bit of bending enable God to work even more in your life and fellowship? A bit of flexibility can go a long, long way!

God Loves A Cheerful Repenter!

The Big Picture

Our reading today begins with a warning that riches don't bring redemption, then a reminder that everyone will be judged by God at the end of time. The next Psalm number 51, was written as a result of Nathan confronting David over his adultery with Bathsheba – 2 Sam 12, which reveals a Godly side of David by the way he reacts to the judgement of God. Then Psalm 52 continues the theme of God's judgement. If you think you have already read Psalm 53 – you have! Or more accurately, you have read Psalm 14 which is almost the same. Bringing our reading to a close Psalm 54 tells us that God is our helper in good times and bad.

Thinking Step

Why does Psalm 53 appear identical to Psalm 14? Well there are some differences and this one could explain why. In Psalm 14 the word for Deity is 'Yahweh' (The Lord) whereas it is 'Elohim' (God) in Psalm 53. This probably reflects cultural or personal taste, like some of us use 'Thou' and others 'You' when we pray.

Action Step

When David commits adultery with Bathsheba he confesses, thanks to the intervention of Nathan, that he has sinned against the Lord. Not Bathsheba or her husband Uriah but God Himself. When you read Psalm 51 don't you sense just how much David appreciated Nathan's intervention? Are you aware of anyone you know who is living their life in open contradiction to God's laws? Then you need to 'do a Nathan!' A friend of mine was chatting to a young woman who told him that she was going to be married soon and just how thankful she was to God that she and her future husband were believers. It then became obvious that they were living as man and wife already! So my friend gently shared a few Scriptures with her. She responded rather tentatively and said "I am sure my pastor would have said something of the kind if it was important!" My friend then showed them to her in the Bible, to substantiate what he was saying was actually taught in the Bible! She was staggered and asked "Why didn't my pastor say something?" It could be he didn't want to create a barrier for them at such a sensitive time but he should have! Don't hold back but be gentle and others could benefit from a 'Nathan interruption!'

You Are Always Safe In God's Hands

The Big Picture

We have five Psalms of David today and he follows some familiar themes when he praises and worships God. First of all in Psalm 55 he declares that there is no more reliable place than with God. Psalms 56 and 57 remind us that when you are afraid, remember that God has you safely in His possession so trust Him and talk to Him in prayer. Psalm 58 tells us to console ourselves in the knowledge that the wicked will be judged one day and finally in Psalm 59, remember God will rescue you from all evil men when you continue to trust Him in all circumstances.

Thinking Step

Four of the Psalms today have the heading 'michtam' or 'mikhtam.' There are two others, 16 and 60, making six in total all ascribed to David. This term indicates they are very special Psalms. It means to be engraved on a durable tablet, possibly of gold, for preservation. This would explain why some commentators refer to them as 'Golden Psalms.'

Action Step

55:20-21 – 'As for my companion, he betrayed his friends, he broke his promises. His words are as smooth as butter but in his heart is war. His words are as soothing as lotion but underneath are daggers!' There are few things more hurtful than being lied to but it's the bending of truth, or should I say 'spin' that can be the most divisive. We never set out to deviate from the truth but we meander away without being aware of it. When we train people to teach Walk Through the Bible events or Bible Explorer lessons in schools, we regularly remind them to check and re-check their Bible narratives to make sure that when they teach they teach the Bible rather than their version of the Bible! I know a preacher who has a tendency to elaborate stories or events to increase the impact when they are told. I remember we were discussing a particular subject of controversy and he said that a number of people had spoken to him and expressed similar views to his. When asked how big the number was, he had to admit that it was only one person but he added quickly, one is a number isn't it? It's a very short slip from truth to untruth isn't it? Keep vigilant and always stick to the truth, no matter what!

God Is Always There When You Need Him

The Big Picture

2 Sam. 8 tells us of David's victory in the Valley of Salt and Psalm 60 records his thanks to God. A timely reminder that we need not be overwhelmed but can be faithful and patient as we wait on God in our daily lives – is found in Psalms 61 and 62. From his wilderness experiences David writes of his thirst for God in Psalm 63 and God's protection over him in Psalm 64. God's amazing creation is the source of David's praise and worship in Psalm 65. An unknown writer looks back in Psalm 66 at how faithful and reliable God has always been.

Thinking Step

The heading of Psalm 60 records a different number of casualties to 1 Sam. 8:13. This reveals the variations in counting that are marks of ancient history. Discrepancies usually reveal different criteria when counting. One number could be the injured and the other, those killed, as the word 'smite' does not necessarily mean killed but could mean injured.

Action Step

I don't know about you but my world is regularly shaken and my faith tested in many ways. Often these crises pass quickly but sometimes they last a long time and leave an indelible imprint in my life. So, when I read 62:2 – 'He alone is my rock and my salvation, my fortress where I will never be shaken.' – I had to delve a little deeper. I found that the Hebrew text goes into a little more detail than some of the English translations. The amplified Bible for instance – 'He only is my Rock and my Salvation, my Defence and my Fortress, I shall not be greatly moved.' This agrees with the more formal NASV – 'He only is my rock and my salvation, my stronghold, I shall not be greatly shaken.' A small word is used in both of these translations that is really significant – it is 'greatly.' So the text confirms we will not be greatly shaken but there may be some minor tremors! When this happens, God is not picking on us and we have not necessarily done anything to deserve it. We live in a fallen world so just get used to it! You may be being shaken at the moment – if you are, just hold tight and remember that God is holding on to you too, so even if you feel you are losing your grip, God won't!

Day 164
Psalms 67-72
13th June

67 - God Of The Whole Earth - Uncertain
68 - Father Of The Fatherless - David
69-70 - Please Come Closer, God - David
71 - Prayer For The Elderly - Uncertain
72 - Messiah Will Reign - Solomon

God Rules Over The Whole Earth

The Big Picture

Our reading today brings to a close the second of the five books that make up the Book of Psalms. An unknown author confirms that God rules the entire world – then David brings us to the intimate thought that God is the Father of the fatherless, in Psalm 68. Drawing closer to God is the thought that David brings to us in Psalms 69 and 70. An unknown writer urges us to remember the older members of society – before Solomon closes this second portion of Psalms with a great Messianic Psalm which could date back to one of the anniversaries of his coronation.

Thinking Step

72:15-16 – '...May the gold of Sheba be given to Him (Messiah)... May there be abundant grain ... May the fruit trees flourish like the trees of Lebanon...' Remember Solomon was Israel's richest King and had gold from Sheba and cedars from Lebanon and the word translated 'abundant' is a unique word in the Old Testament and actually means 'superabundant.'

Action Step

71:18 – 'Now that I am old and grey, do not abandon me, O God. Let me proclaim your power to this new generation, your mighty miracles to all who come after me.' This is a passage we have used many times when training Bible Explorer presenters to teach the Bible in schools. Preparing folk of all ages often in their later years, to go into schools to teach children the exciting story-line of the whole Bible. This programme is totally unique in the way it presents the Bible to an increasingly Biblically illiterate generation today. If you would like to know more, please contact us via our website – www. Bible.org.uk The unknown Psalmist is telling us just how important it is for each generation to pass on the Bible to the next generation. This is more important today than ever before because in these days of the demise of Sunday Schools, the only children who get a positive exposure to the Bible are 'church kids' rather than neighbourhood children. We have a duty to do our part otherwise lots of children when they grow up, do so with a totally stunted spiritual part to their personality. Please consider supporting/joining us. Would you please include us in your prayers as we continue to reach children in this mission field we call the United Kingdom? Thank you.

Our Almighty King Reigns And Rules

The Big Picture

All five of our Psalms today were written by Asaph as we begin the third section of the Book of Psalms. He dominates this third section. The old theme of how the wicked prosper is raised again in Psalm 73 because it is a difficulty for everyone. We're reminded in Psalm 74 that God has made a covenant with us and He will honour all He has promised. Psalm 75 celebrates that God is judge, He is absolutely fair and to be trusted. Psalms 76 and 77 declare that our God is a mighty God and is all powerful. There is no one like Him in all creation.

Thinking Step

Asaph was a very prominent musician and his family was very influential. Neh. 12:46 – 'The custom of having choir directors began long ago in the days of David and Asaph.' Fancy being linked with David! Ezra 3:10 – 'When the builders completed the foundation of the Lord's Temple... the Levites, descendants of Asaph... praise the Lord.'

Action Step

In 73:13-14 we read – 'Did I keep my heart pure for nothing? Did I keep myself innocent for no reason?' 'I get nothing but trouble all day long, every morning brings me pain.' Whilst the world around us seems to be going from success to success, some of us are struggling to stay on course. I have a simple question for you "Are you struggling to fulfil your plans or God's?" I knew a baptist minister who had something of a novel approach to the appointment of all office bearers and department leaders at the annual church meeting. He would get all leaders to lay out a plan for their local church ministry in the next twelve months and report on fruit and progress over the past twelve! This enabled everyone to re-appraise what they were doing – why they were doing it and whether God wanted them to continue doing it! Ask yourself why are you doing what you are doing and does God want you to be doing something else? Make a note in your diary to ask yourself this question every year – maybe on January 1st or on your birthday! That way you can be sure you are doing God's will for your life. The success of the world around you will now be of little or no consequence because you will be so excited working with God and seeing Him act in your daily life.

Day 166
Psalms 78-80
15th June

78 - Look Back With Thanksgiving - Asaph
79 - God Will Help At The Right Time - Asaph
80 - Our God Is A Merciful God - Asaph

God Has Been Faithful In The Past And Still Is Today

The Big Picture

Psalm 78 is the second longest Psalm with 72 verses. It is in the form a wistful 'looking back' at how God has been faithful from the days of the Exodus right up to the reign of David when this Psalm could have been written. Psalm 79 moves forward and looks back to the invasion of Jerusalem by Nebuchadnezzar and his Babylonian army. It was probably used by those who remained, after many were taken into exile in Babylonia. The last of our three 'Asaph Psalms' today, is a plea for mercy on behalf of the whole of Israel. It contains several pleas for restoration adding 'and then we will be saved!'

Thinking Step

Like several others Psalm 78 has the heading 'Maskil', which the Septuagint (the OT in Greek) translates as 'Psalm of understanding.' Possibly written to teach the many folk who could not read or write. Just like the long hymns of Charles Wesley were used to teach the early Methodists.

Action Step

78:9-12 – 'The warriors of Ephraim ...did not keep God's covenant and refused to live by his instructions. They forgot what he had done – the great wonders he had shown them, the miracles he did for their ancestors on the plain of Zoan in the land of Egypt.' You would think that seeing the amazing miracles with which God blessed Israel over the years, no one would need to be reminded of them. However their memories were as poor as ours! In Psalm 78 Asaph looks back at a whole chunk of Bible history and 'walks them through it' so they were able to see the big picture! Moses was the first one to use this method in Deut. 1-4 with many others repeating the concept – including Joshua in Josh. 24 and Jesus Himself in Luke 24 – not forgetting Stephen in Acts 7. Many folk think that the whole idea of Walk Through the Bible was a discovery of brand new teaching methods, whereas it was a rediscovery of ancient Biblical methodology. Bible study without the 'Big Picture' as our backcloth is a two dimensional experience – so be sure you get regular refreshers and take others with you when you attend our live events. Full details of venues and how you can arrange one for your own church may be found on our website – www.Bible.org.uk We look forward to our paths crossing in the near future.

236

81 - God Wants Obedience - Asaph
82 - Leaders Are Responsible - Asaph
83 - God's Enemies Are Doomed - Asaph
84 - The Joy Of God's Presence - Korah
85-86 - Revive Us O Lord - Korah

Day 167
Psalms 81-86
16th June

Obey God And Enjoy His Refreshing Presence

The Big Picture

Psalm 81 was probably used at the Feast of Tabernacles with a clue in verse 3 about the blowing of the horn before this feast – Lev. 23. It is a call to obey God bearing in mind that they had not always been obedient where this feast is concerned – Neh. 8:17. In Psalm 82 Asaph condemns the poor leadership of some in Israel – which will bring God's judgement. A cry for protection from their enemies is made in Psalm 83 before the sons of Korah write Psalms 85 and 86 rejoicing in dwelling with the Lord and praying to Him for revival.

Thinking Step

Psalms 8, 81 and 84 use the word 'gittith' in their titles – probably describing a stringed instrument. It's the feminine form of 'gath' which was the Philistine city home of Goliath. Gath means 'oil/winepress' and is used to describe the place of Jesus' suffering prior to the cross – Gethsemane. Even the headings of the Psalms point to Jesus!

Action Step

84:6 – 'Won't you revive us again, so your people can rejoice in you?' Massive revivals have occurred throughout history but don't be misled – they are simply a time when a lot of individuals experience revival in their own hearts and lots of others do at the same time. I remember seeing an enormous engraving in one of America's mega churches in Texas. It read "Reaching the Whole World for Christ," I found myself swallowing hard at an apparent over-statement before I continued to read "One at a Time." Yes that's how we reach the world and that's how we are revived too. I have celebrated communion in many ways and in many places over the years and there are special blessings attached to each of the variations. However there is still something special in taking the bread as individuals and then all drinking the wine together. Signs that we are personally responsible before God but we also have the privilege of being members of a vast family, the church. Do you remember the old hymn by Albert Midlane? 'Revive Thy Work O Lord' Sadly the end of the first verse gives me a problem! – 'and make Thy people hear...' I don't think so! If we are to be revived people we need to listen, then obey. God won't make us but He longs for us to respond. What do you need to respond to today?

Day 168
Psalms 87-89
17th June

87 - Zion, City Of Our God - Korah
88 - Lord, Lift Me Up - Heman
89 - When Things Are Bad, God Is Good - Ethan

The Lord Is Worthy Of Our Praise

The Big Picture

Psalm 87 brings us some thoughts on the beautiful city of Jerusalem. Despite its many troubles it is still a special place in God's sight. The theme was popularised in the hymn, 'Glorious Things of Thee are spoken...' by John Newton, set to a tune by Haydn which is the tune of the current German national anthem. Psalm 88 has been described as the saddest of all Psalms with its tune called 'The suffering of affliction' – it is the only one attributed to Heman. Psalm 89, unique to Ethan, lifts up God as the supreme ruler of the whole universe and a real comforter in times of trouble. This concludes book three of the Book of Psalms.

Thinking Step

Both Heman and Ethan are described as Ezrahites. As they are mentioned in 1 Kings 4:31 as wise men who have been surpassed by Solomon, they cannot be related to Ezra who came much later, after the exile. Their clan name was probably to show they were of the family of Ezrah of whom we sadly know nothing.

Action Step

Psalm 88 reminds us that God meets us at our lowest ebb and can empathise with us as one who suffered much and gave His only Son for us. If like me you have asked many folk how they became a Christian, an all too familiar theme is that many of us turn to God when we feel we have no where else to turn. Very few people turn to God when they feel good – it's usually when they feel awful. Why not resolve today to share your good times with your Father in Heaven, as well as your low times? What have you enjoyed today? Something at home, at work, amongst your family... thank God for that experience now. On a human level can you imagine how galling it must be for God when lots of people who come to Him only do so because they want something to make them feel better! Did you hear about the pastor who decided he would systematically ring his deacons to express his appreciation for all they do? He rang the first one whose wife answered the phone. When he spoke to her husband he simply expressed his thanks and rang off. The deacon's wife couldn't believe that the pastor had rung but didn't want anything! Remember the idea – next time you ring a deacon, or even your pastor. They will be pleasantly surprised and the idea might even catch on!

Our God Is Gloriously Majestic And Worthy Of Praise

The Big Picture

In the fourth section of Psalms the first Psalm is traditionally attributed to Moses who lived to 120 years old but look at verse 10! Unnamed Psalmists have penned six of the next seven Psalms and relish the thought of being protected by God's wings, proclaiming how good it is to worship our loving God, declaring how majestic is our Heavenly Father, affirming that God is just and will see to it that justice is always done, shouting out that God is glorious and reigns for ever! Wow, what a list! We also have tucked in between two of these anonymous Psalms, a beautiful call to worship in Psalm 95 by the greatest Psalmist of all, David.

Thinking Step

Psalm 95 must have been a favourite of the writer of the letter to the Hebrews. Look at chapters four and five and you will need both hands to count the number of times this Psalm is quoted! When you re-read the Psalm you will understand why – it's hard to read it without beaming from ear to ear!

Action Step

We are encouraged to 'Sing a new song to the Lord' – 96:1. For many of us that happens every Sunday but for some of us it's only when we go to Spring Harvest or the Keswick Convention! It doesn't seem many years ago that each church had its own hymn book and they changed very little from year to year. Then people discovered the overhead projector and more recently, the multi-media projector and a plethora of songs and hymns exploded onto the church scene. Of course, just because a song is old it doesn't mean it's good and similarly just because it's new it doesn't mean it's bad. I am one of those who believes if it has a good tune then people will sing it irrespective of the words! Otherwise, why would normally sane adults sing "Ding dong merrily on High, in Heaven the bells are ringing..."! Of course some of the modern ones are no better. What about "Jesus we love You, we worship and adore You..." with the last verse including "Spirit we love You, we worship and adore You, glorify Your name..." I don't think so! Jesus said "He (the Spirit) will glorify Me..." – John 16:14. So sing a new song but be sure it's Biblical!

Day 170
Psalms 98-103
19th June

98 - Serve The Lord With A New Song - Uncertain
99 - Serve The Lord With Reverence - Uncertain
100 - Serve The Lord With Gladness - Uncertain
101 - Serve The Lord With A Holy Life - David
102 - Serve The Lord In Your Weakness - Uncertain
103 - Serve The Lord With Blessings - David

Serve The Lord With All You Are

The Big Picture

As with Psalm 96 we are again urged to sing a new song in Psalm 98. The tone of worship and praise continues through Psalms 99 and 100 where the anonymous Psalmists encourage us to lift up our God and serve Him gladly. Then David steps in with Psalm 101 to continue the idea of living a holy life and being fully committed. Psalm 102 is a great aid when we are overwhelmed with problems and fears – with those immortal words from the KJV "Hear my prayer O LORD and let my cry come unto thee." The repeated exclamation "Bless the Lord" concludes today's reading.

Thinking Step

103:12 – 'He has removed our sins as far from us as the east is from the west.' Look at a globe and you will see that if you travel north or south you eventually reach your goal. If you travel east or west around the equator, you never reach your goal. That's how far our sins are removed!

Action Step

Psalm 103:15-17 – 'Our days on earth are like grass, like wild flowers, we bloom and die. The wind blows and we are gone – as though we had never been here but the love of the Lord remains forever with those who fear him...' David takes up Job's thoughts from Job 14. Whenever I attend a funeral it is always poignant to get a glimpse of any flowers that have not been cleared away from earlier. Already they are drooping as a reminder of how short our lives are. I don't see this is a depressing thought but as a reminder to make the most of today. When the flowers are at their best they are at their most effective in encouraging us and bringing a sweet perfume into our lives. A wise person asks "Why put off until tomorrow what you can do today?" My wife and I have led many tours to Israel and have lost count of the number of people who say "I wish I had done this when I was younger." It's the same with everyday life. I remember a lady who came to Christ when she was almost eighty. She made the most of her short Christian life on earth but with no bitterness at all she often said "If only I had responded to Jesus years ago!" Whatever the Holy Spirit is saying to you – don't delay.

104 - Our God Is The Creator God - Uncertain
105 - Looking Back At The Pentateuch - Uncertain
106 - Our God Forgives And Forgets - Uncertain

Day 171
Psalms 104-106
20th June

God Creates, Remembers, Forgives And Forgets

The Big Picture

An anonymous Psalmist writes Psalm 104 to remember God's creation and finishes with a resounding "As for me, I will praise the Lord!" Psalm 105 is another teaching Psalm even though it is not described as such. It goes back to Genesis and covers most of the storyline of the Pentateuch, up to Numbers. Psalm 106 echoes this theme of looking back with gratitude and amazement as its author goes back to Genesis and covers the storyline of the Bible up to the period of Judges — remembering that we are all sinners. This concludes the fourth section of the Book of Psalms.

Thinking Step

Psalm 104 has been likened to a popular ancient song 'Hymn to the sun", attributed to Akhenhaten who was the first monotheistic Pharaoh of Egypt and father of Tutankhamun. The main difference is that Akhenhaten points to the sun god whilst the Psalmist points to the Living God. It seems the Psalm could be a corrective for Arkenhaten's popular hymn!

Action Step

105:25-36 reviews the plagues of Egypt but does not refer to them as plagues! The first event mentioned is darkness which was number nine in Exodus 10. Could it be that the act of darkness looking back, was the pivotal action that tipped the scales and led to the Israelites coming out of Egypt? The plagues of Exodus were not punishments they were signs from God, which the Egyptians and probably many of the Israelites too were slow to recognise. In our everyday lives we are often so close to the current event that we have difficulty rising above it and seeing what God is revealing to us. We see events as plagues rather than signs. The Psalmist in Psalm 105 reveals the end first when he begins with darkness, whereas life tends to start at the beginning and proceeds to the end! A former pastor of mine never talked about problems. He always described them as opportunities! How many opportunities have you shunned today because you thought they were problems? Wind back the video recorder of your mind and see if I am correct. Of course we can't wind back life even if we can rewind live TV! Just say to yourself, now "When a problem occurs today I am going to ask God to change it to an opportunity." You'll be amazed how many times He will do it for you!

God Is All We Need – Praise Him Daily!

The Big Picture

And so we begin the final section of the Book of Psalms. We begin with a real heart warming truth "Give thanks to the Lord for He is good! His faithful love endures for ever." The unknown Psalmist of Psalm 107 tells us that God knows what we need and will not see us in distress without rescuing us. Psalm 108 brings us some fundamental thoughts from David. He says he will worship and praise from the very beginning of the day. He relishes the fact that he has a God who rules the heavens and is the same God who gives him victory over his enemies.

Thinking Step

Psalm 107 – 'And can it be?'
v10 -'Some sat in darkness and deepest gloom, imprisoned in iron chains of misery.' Inspired – 'Long my imprisoned spirit lay fast bound in sin and nature's night.'
v14 – 'He led them from the darkness and deepest gloom, he snapped their chains.' Inspired – 'My chains fell off, my heart was free. I rose, went forth and followed Thee.'

Action Step

107:2 – 'Has the Lord redeemed you? Then speak out! Tell others He has saved you from your enemies.' Is this just a word for the ancient Israelites or does God want us to speak out today too? I believe there are many ways to speak out and giving tracts out on street corners and/or carrying a large sandwich board are methods only for those who are specifically called to that kind of public ministry. What about the rest of us? How do we speak out? When I was a trainer for Evangelism Explosion our team saw many folk come to Christ using this unique and attractive method of personal witness and evangelism. There was a specific framework that guided you through a Gospel presentation and was in my opinion, one of the most effective evangelism programmes ever devised. It equipped so many ordinary folk to do an extra-ordinary job of bringing people to an understanding of having a living faith in Jesus Christ. The very first step was both vital and easy to miss. It was top of the list – 'making friends!' It has been described as pre-evangelism and that's what it is, except I would include it as part of evangelism rather than something that happens before you get to 'talking gospel.' We need to befriend before we can effectively communicate. Whatever you are doing today – making friends is preparing the way for making converts!

The All-Powerful God Protects And Cares For Us

The Big Picture

David addresses the problem of protecting our reputation in our first Psalm today. Verse 4 tells us that "I love them but they try to destroy me – even as I am praying for them!" This is followed by a beautiful messianic Psalm 110 which declares that the Lord will sit at the right hand of God and rule in power. This Psalm is quoted many centuries later in Acts 3:34-35 as Peter speaks on the day of Pentecost and 3,000 souls are saved – shortly after Jesus ascended back to Heaven. The last two Psalms today remind us that our God cares for us and wants us to fear Him and trust Him completely.

Thinking Step

Psalm 110 is a very special Psalm, Jesus uses it as He debates with Jewish leaders and firmly confirms David's authorship. Mark 12:36 – For David himself, speaking under the inspiration of the Holy Spirit, said 'The Lord said to my Lord "Sit in the place of honour at my right hand until I humble your enemies beneath your feet."'

Action Step

Psalms 111 and 112 – each one has 22 lines. Both Psalms are in the form of an acrostic with each of the twenty two lines beginning with successive letters of the Hebrew alphabet. So I wonder why they were written like this – it must be that they were intended to be memorised rather than just read! Psalm 111 concentrates on 'The ways of God' whilst Psalm 112 covers the 'Man of God'. In other words it is important to know about God and His ways and not to be shaken when God takes a route that you don't expect. You can do this best when you are a man or woman of God and trust your Lord totally. So the two Psalms overlap and complement each other, like two sides of a coin. So what about you? Does God still do things that surprise you? Of course He does! As you mature as a man or woman of God your faith will grow strong enough to trust Him even when you don't understand. All of us are on the same road of becoming people of God, constantly trying to understand the ways of God. Next time something happens that at first shakes you – use it as another stepping stone in your understanding of the ways of God and you will grow as a man or woman of God – a little more prepared for what lies ahead.

Day 174
Psalms 113-118
23rd June

113 - God Is Gracious - Uncertain
114 - God Is Our Deliverer - Uncertain
115 - To God Alone, Be Glory - Uncertain
116 - God Has Done Marvellous Things - Uncertain
117 - God Of All Nations - Uncertain
118 - Trust God, Not Man - Uncertain

Six Hallel Celebration Psalms Of Praise

The Big Picture

Psalms 113 and 114 would usually be said or sung before Passover each year. They remind us of the continuing grace of God and His deliverance of the Israelites from Egypt so long ago – in the unforgettable exodus. The exodus that is celebrated in the Passover which is remembered by the Jewish faithful worldwide every year. After Passover Psalms 115, 116, 117 and 118 would be said or sung. Psalms 115 and 116 confirm that God alone deserves our praise and worship for He has done wonderful things. Psalm 117 calls all nations to praise God and Psalm 118, thought to be Martin Luther's favourite urges us to trust in God above all things.

Thinking Step

Mark 14:26 – 'Then they sang a hymn and went out to the Mount of Olives.' This marks the last time Jesus sang on earth. His last singing could have been the words – "Give thanks to the Lord, for He is good! His faithful love endures forever." How appropriate as He left for the Garden of Gethsemane and then Calvary.

Action Step

As you probably know the Book of Psalms marks the centre of our Bible. So be encouraged we are about half way through reading the whole Bible! Psalm 118 is the central chapter and verse 8 is the very centre of the Bible. 'It is better to trust the Lord than to put confidence in people.' As the Old Testament was arranged into verses in 1448 by Rabbi Nathan – and the New Testament was given similar treatment by Robert Estienne more than 100 years later in 1558 – it must be that God deliberately arranged it that way as these two men couldn't have colluded. So what is the central idea of the Bible? 'Trust in the Lord'. If this was at the core of everything we do and say, wouldn't the world be a different and better place? I believe trusting in the Lord is active and not passive. We misconstrue the truth when we sit back and say "I am trusting in the Lord!" Are you trusting in the Lord today? It's so much easier when you know what He expects of you. How can we know that? By reading the Bible through and through until it is part of us and is reflected in all aspects of our daily life. Let the central verse of the Bible be at your very centre as you 'trust in the Lord' today.

God's Amazing Word

The Big Picture

The first eleven letters of the Hebrew alphabet are covered in these 88 verses of this acrostic Psalm. Eight verses for each letter. 'Aleph' emphasises the joy of walking with the Lord. 'Beth' explains the only way to be pure is to follow the Word. 'Gimel' says "I need God's help to understand His Word.' 'Daleth' tells us it can be a struggle but God helps. 'He' asks for God's guidance, to keep focussed. 'Vav' declares devotion for God's Word. 'Zayin' reminds us our only hope is God's Word. 'Heth' says "I love the God of the Word." 'Teth' declares "I want to know more!" 'Yodh' says "God's Word is my guide." 'Kaph' concludes "I will trust God forever."

Thinking Step

The first letter of all eight verses of each set is the same letter of the alphabet. Thus the first eight verses begin with the first letter, the next eight verses all begin with the second letter and so on. Not only that but the syllables of each verse had to perfectly match each other because it was set to music!

Action Step

It seems to me that the UK and many other countries want the morals and ethics of the Bible without God! That's impossible of course. We wouldn't be what we are without the Bible and its standards. Schools, hospitals, health care, charities and so many other good things, came from men and women of faith and these ventures were rooted in the Word of God. I read recently of a university professor who said that in her opinion the Bible needed to be taught in all schools no matter what the cost. She said that our society was so firmly established on the Word of God that a lot of what we say doesn't make sense unless we have a good knowledge of the whole of the Bible. Sayings such as 'David and Goliath contest' – 'Eye for an Eye' – 'Turn the other cheek' – are simple examples. Concepts of fidelity, honesty, morality and fairness are more vital ones. We cannot throw the Bible out without impoverishing our society but we continue to try. It's usually done in the name of not wanting to offend people of other religions but I believe that's just an excuse being used by atheists who want all religion removed from our country. Playing off one group with another is a ploy that is working really well at the moment. Why not pray right now that God will strengthen His Church to stand firm – starting with you!

God's Life-Changing Word

The Big Picture

The second eleven letters of the Hebrew alphabet are covered in these 88 verses of this acrostic Psalm. Eight verses for each letter. 'Lamedh' – God's Word protects you from the wicked. 'Mem' – God's Word educates us for daily life. 'Nun' – God's Word guides you all the time. 'Samekh' – God's Word keeps you upright in a crooked world. 'Ayin' – God's Word is totally complete. 'Pe' – God's Word explains everything you need to know. 'Tsadhe' – God's Word will last forever. 'Qoph' – I will always obey God's Word as long as I live. 'Resh' – God's Word rescues me from evil. 'Shin' – I love God's Word every day. 'Tav' – We need to continue to feed on God's Word.

Thinking Step

Interesting Bible Facts

*   1189 chapters in the whole Bible
*   Shortest chapter – Psalm 117
*   Middle chapter – Psalm 118
*   Longest chapter – Psalm 119

Action Step

Verse 105 – 'Your word is a lamp to guide my feet and a light for my path.'
At first glance this seems to be the same promise expressed in slightly different ways but it is two separate promises. We have God's promise that He will be our personal lamp. He guides our daily steps and shows up imminent pot-holes. This is essential as we move on and it also implies strongly that moving on is a vital part of Christian living. Living as we have done for many years in a small town on the Essex coast – we see many folk moving in to enjoy their retirement. It saddens me however when new folk come to church and declare with real feeling, that they have come to retire and not to get involved in church life! They were very involved in their last church and now they want to take it easy! This leads to stagnation and stunts Christian experience and should be avoided at all cost. The second thing this verse tells us is that we have a broader light to illumine our whole path. Sometimes we get so overcome by what our lamp shows us that we don't look up to see the broader view as God lights our path. Keep these two concepts in mind today. God guides in detail but He also has a big plan for you to enjoy. Look up as well as down!

Ascending In Peace And With Thanksgiving

The Big Picture

Our reading today is the first eight of the fifteen Psalms of ascent. Cherished by many as the songs that pilgrims sang as they came up to Jerusalem to celebrate the Feasts. These short songs would prepare worshippers to enter in the right frame of mind, often after a long hard journey. The songs begin with a cry for peace and protection and then a Psalm of David, 122, giving thanks and praying for the city of Jerusalem. Psalms 123-125 are reminders of God's mercy, His constant presence with us and also how trustworthy He is. An anonymous Psalmist reminds us that God restores His people. Finally a Psalm attributed to Solomon which mentions spiritual house building and gives thanks to God for children.

Thinking Step

Today you can approach the now blocked Temple entrance (Huldah Gates) in Jerusalem by going up the rabbinic steps at the southern wall. In the 1970's Neil Armstrong, the first man on the moon, visited these steps. Realising that Jesus had walked there he said he was more excited to stand there than on the moon!

Action Step

Psalm 127:1 – 'Unless the Lord builds a house the work of the builders is useless.' I remember being pointed to this verse by someone who believed I shouldn't consider money, just ministry! He was in insurance and I asked him if he just thought of insurance policies at work – or did he think of money as well. "Of course we have to consider money in insurance but that's different to church!" I believe our standards at home, work and in church should be the same. What we believe on Sunday is what we believe the rest of the week, isn't it? Therefore what we do during the week should be done in the same spirit as Sunday. Just think how your conduct would change if you always had someone with you from church, wherever you went! What do you need to change today to become a little more consistent? Your attitude at work, with your children, with those in your housegroup or those who... You fill in the blank!

Going Up To Jerusalem To Worship

The Big Picture

Today we are reading the remaining seven Songs of Ascent. These songs were often used to remember God's deliverance of His people from exile in Babylonia and their return home to Zion. The thrill of approaching Jerusalem after being in an alien land for so many years is hard to imagine. The emphasis of trusting God, being thankful and having a childlike faith are the subjects covered in Psalms 128 – 132. With real unity, Jerusalem was approached with reverence and praise – and these attributes are addressed by Psalms 133 and 134.

Thinking Step

The steps leading to the Temple entrance are called the rabbinic steps today and are the place for teaching that would have been used by rabbis including Jesus and Peter on the Day of Pentecost. They are uneven in depth and width so that you have to look down as you climb – so, approaching the Temple with head bowed.

Action Step

130:5 – 'I am counting on the Lord, yes, I am counting on Him. I have put my hope in His word.' When a Jew really means to make a point it is repeated. I said, when a Jew... you get the point I trust! You see this in the teaching of Jesus as well as in the Apostle Paul and the Gospel writers. In this Psalm an unknown writer pours out their heart to emphasise their reliance on God. They then add that as well as relying on God they will also rely on His Word. Right from the beginning of the church there were those who questioned negatively the accuracy of the Word of God. I have no problems with the questioning – I just want it to be positive with a view to building up our faith rather than knocking it down. Has anyone ever said to you, "Surely you don't believe all that Bible stuff – I thought you were an intelligent person!" I've heard it many times but I always respond by saying that what I do understand in the Bible is very important to me and the rest I will work my way through – into heaven and beyond! After all I haven't figured out how a car or a TV or a computer or an iPod works yet but I still enjoy what they do for me! Count on God and trust His Word. You're on firm ground.

God Cares – Home And Away

The Big Picture

Our first two psalms are anonymous and proclaim that looking back God is great and even today, He continues to be just as great! Psalm 137 is firmly rooted in the exile as it reminds us of the futility of being away from what God has for you. All they can do is sit and cry! They can't sing! So why was this Psalm such a hit as a song in the charts for 'Boney M' many years ago? Our final two Psalms are from David as he reminds us that God continues to answer prayers and wants us to be His holy people but remember, we must want Him to work in our hearts to achieve this.

Thinking Step

135:19-20 – 'O Israel, praise the Lord! O priests – descendants of Aaron – praise the Lord! O Levites, praise the Lord! All you who fear the Lord, praise the Lord!' First, all the tribes except Levi. Then the family of Aaron from the Levites – then the rest of the Levites – and finally non-Jews who fear the Lord. Everyone's included!

Action Step

Psalm 137 reveals some of the frustration and desperation of being out of God's gracious plan for you. The Israelites are in Babylonia but God has an amazing plan to get them back into the land that He promised to Abraham, Isaac and Jacob so long ago. When the Babylonian empire falls to Persia, that's the time they are offered a chance to get back on track. The tragedy is that most of them are so used to being away from the Promised Land that they refuse to return with Zerubbabel, Ezra or Nehemiah. Are there parts of your life that you have held on to for so long that you simply can't surrender them to God even when the opportunity presents itself? What is the Holy Spirit bringing to your mind right now? Whatever it is, trust God with it rather than holding on to it as though it was important! I remember I hadn't been a Christian very long when God made it clear that I had to stop smoking. In the 1960's smoking was a very social thing to do but God said that it wasn't for me. I found excuses, I even tried to do a deal with God that I would read my Bible more if I could continue to smoke! In the end I agreed with God and stopped. I have never regretted it and neither will you, whatever He is asking of you.

140 - Lord, Keep Me Safe! - David
141 - Protect Me And Guard My Mouth - David
142 - Lord, I Need Your Help Now! - David
143 - I Need You To Teach Me, Lord - David
144 - Mankind Is So Insignificant - David
145 - God Is Great! - David

We Need God's Help Every Day

The Big Picture

Here are the last six Psalms of David. In the first David pleads for protection from a God whom he knows to be faithful. Psalm 141 is one for us all – please guard what I say! We have a touch of self pity in Psalm 142 written when hiding in a cave. In Psalm 143 David acknowledges that he continues to need wisdom from God. Next he recalls that man is so unworthy of God's attention but re-affirms that he will continue to praise Him. The last of David's Psalms is his final acrostic on the Hebrew alphabet. The 'missing' verse which completes the 22 verses required is only in some manuscripts and falls between verses 13 and 14.

Thinking Step

Even the Godly have fears! A cry of desperation from David in 143:7 – "Come quickly, Lord and answer me, for my depression deepens. Don't turn away from me, or I will die." This is very reminiscent of his cry in 28:1. In the ups and downs of life – doubting is natural!

Action Step

Psalm 142 is a teaching Psalm from David, a maskill and comes when David is under severe pressure, hiding from King Saul in fear for his life. The heading for this Psalm tells us that it was written in a cave which was a regular place of refuge as he ran from King Saul. It is a Psalm where David cries out to God for help because he is in trouble! Along with David we have a tendency to use God for emergencies too but don't feel guilty about that – it's only natural to turn to God when we are at the end of our tether – after all He is our Heavenly Father! Don't we want our children to turn to us when they are in trouble? Remember God understands our motives better than we do and still loves us! David wants us to remember that even in our lowest points God is for us. That's true for you and all God's children. If you know someone going through hard times why not phone them or drop them a text or a letter right now, to remind them that God still loves them even when things look bleak! He is not a fair weather God – He is a God for the storms of life and loves His children to turn to Him for help. Are you feeling low yourself? He is waiting to hear from you!

God Is Worthy Of Our Praises

The Big Picture

Five anonymous Psalms bring this book to a close. 146:3 reminds us to 'not put our trust in princes' – a repeat of the central verse of the whole Bible in Psalm 118:8. The next Psalms urge us to praise God because He is our healer and an 'always present' protector – and because He is the God of creation He is worthy of our praise and adoration. Then we are reminded that God is the God who gets pleasure out of us His people. Lastly a great benediction or doxology to gather up all our praises at the end of a book constantly praising God in all circumstances. 'Praise Him' – is proclaimed 12 times in just 6 verses!

Thinking Step

The Hebrew text includes 'selah' 71 times from Psalm 3:2 to 143:6. Apart from 3 further references in Habakkuk it is found nowhere else in the Bible. Some think it could be a musical term but if so, Habakkuk's use of it is a puzzle. A more acceptable translation is 'to weigh or measure'. Literally – "think about this!"

Action Step

As we bring to an end our reading of the Book of Psalms let us reflect that its writing is spread over 1000 years with three major compilers. David compiling book 1 with Hezekiah or Josiah compiling books 2 & 3 and Ezra or Nehemiah compiling books 4 & 5. David wrote 75 psalms, Asaph 12 and the sons of Korah another 12 (if you include those by Heman and Ethan). Solomon has two Psalms attributed to him with Moses having one. The authors of the remaining 48 are uncertain. 150 songs of Praise, Thanksgiving and Lament – PTL! We began with the thought 'Oh, the joys of those who do not follow the advice of the wicked' and concluded with 'Praise the Lord!' In our everyday lives we hear much advice, some good, some bad, some Godly! May we give pre-eminence to that which is Godly – and follow it – and Praise the Lord! The Book of Psalms encourages us to put God at the centre of our lives and to praise the Lord who is our Saviour. Take time today to re-adjust your priorities to make sure God is central in your life and praise the Lord who continues to equip you to live life to the full. We are now exactly half way through our massive reading project – it's the home straight from this point! We can please God by the way we live – 149:6. Let's please Him today!

Proverbs

Proverbs

You can be forgiven for thinking that this book was written in order to provide pithy sayings for desk calendars! However it is clear from the first few verses that it was written for a more noble cause. The key theme of Proverbs is 'wisdom' or the ability to live life skilfully. As the man who asked God for wisdom and received it – 1 Kings 3:9 – and composed about 3,000 proverbs – 1 Kings 4:32 – King Solomon is an obvious choice to be the author and compiler of much of this book. We know that his first efforts were supplemented during the reign of Hezekiah – Prov. 25:1. Isaiah and Micah ministered at this time and could have been involved too. Parts of the book and in particular the last two chapters were not written by Solomon but are included as wise sayings by other wise men.

Below is an acrostic which summarises each chapter of the book.

1. Usefulness of God's wisdom
2. Nature of loose women
3. Discipline results in wisdom
4. Exhortation to get wisdom
5. Results of human lust
6. Sluggard, ant, strange women
7. Temptation by seductive women
8. Appeal to God's wisdom
9. Necessity of God's wisdom
10. Diligence compared to slothfulness
11. Instructions for the righteous
12. Nature of the righteous
13. Good understanding produces favour

14. Advise for the wise
15. New use of tongue
16. Destruction of the proud

17. Unity of good friends
18. Safety through God's wisdom
19. Insights into personal priorities
20. Nobility of trusting God
21. Goals of Godly men

22. Guide for wise living
23. Outcome of wise living
24. Destruction of the fool
25. Solomon's proverbs on humility

26. Ways of the lord
27. Illusion of man's wisdom
28. Safety of seeking wisdom
29. Delights of Godly wisdom
30. Oracles given by Agur
31. Mission of Godly women

Day 182
Proverbs 1-4
1st July

1 - Wisdom In The Home
2 - Wisdom In The World
3 - Wisdom Is Beneficial
4 - Wisdom Is Personal

Wisdom Is A Great Foundation For Life

The Big Picture

The reasons for writing this book are clearly stated at the very beginning, to provide a resource for wisdom in daily living. We should benefit from those who have undergone some of life's experiences and from the lessons they learned. Practical advice is to be found in abundance. Obey parents and avoid those who would lead you astray, are the two key instructions of chapter one closely followed by the imperative to seek wisdom, which continues into the following chapters. The basic family unit of parents and children is assumed as the norm. It is not without significance in the twenty first century, that this needs to be stressed once again as the best starting point for wise living.

Thinking Step

Until the middle of the twentieth century many scholars believed Proverbs was too Persian or Greek to be Solomonic. However work on the writings of Pharaoh Amenemope, a contemporary of Solomon, reveals so many similarities with much of Proverbs that it seems very probable that both writings are a similar age. Both originating around 1,000 BC which is when Solomon reigned.

Action Step

1:8 – 'My child, listen when your father corrects you. Don't neglect your mother's instruction.' As an officer in the Boys' Brigade many years ago I was always struck by the beauty and Biblical truth of the 'Object' of that organisation for boys – 'The promotion of obedience, reverence, discipline, self-respect and all that tends towards a true Christian manliness.' Proverbs goes on to say that what mothers teach is just as important as correction by their fathers. I believe children should learn from both parents. So many children today can't use a knife and fork properly, cook, sew, replace a fuse or be well mannered because they were never taught. So what other even more important things are being neglected? The 'BB Object' reminds us very clearly. Proverbs begins in the home which is where proper child development should be nurtured. It is not the responsibility of schools or churches to bring up children it is the responsibility of the parents who are blessed by God with children. When your children or grandchildren or friend's children try your patience, remember you only have so long to establish them on a firm foundation for life after that it could be too late, or at least really difficult! So now is the time to help form their personalities for good.

5 - Faithfulness In Marriage
6 - Don't Be Lazy Or Commit Adultery
7 - Remember What You Know Is Good
8 - Wisdom Really Makes Sense
9 - Respect For God Is A Great Beginning

Day 183
Proverbs 5-9
2nd July

Wisdom In Life And Marriage Is Essential

The Big Picture

Very practical teaching on not committing adultery and being faithful to your wife gets this section off to a vital start. We have some hard hitting picturesque advice which is both graphic and clear. The importance of being wise in the realms of guaranteeing loans is explained next, then instruction on why you should not be a lazy person! An interesting check list of the six things most hated by God is followed by further warnings about committing adultery. Wisdom is extolled as something that should be sought after in order to live a full and contented life. The last few verses of our reading today reminds us that fear of the Lord is the beginning of wisdom.

Thinking Step

Do you remember the phrase in 'Monty Python' from a 'conman' character "Nudge, nudge, wink, wink, say no more!" 6:12-14 could have been the inspiration for this sketch! In Biblical days transparent motives were admired. No misleading behaviour when negotiating. No winking to others to give false impressions.

Action Step

6:6 – 'Take a lesson from the ants you lazybones. Learn from their ways and become wise!' seems to confirm this idea that we have much to learn from simply looking around us. I remember watching some swans dozily drifting on a river not far from our home. The current of the river was carrying them downstream but they wanted to go upstream. As long as they were focused and active they had little trouble making progress. However it was getting towards the end of the day and one swan in particular seemed more tired than the others. He needed to take rests and as he rested, he drifted down stream. As soon as he realised, he made a strenuous effort to swim upstream but he soon got tired again – nodded off – and slipped back. An unforgettable sermon in picture form. If we are not making steady progress we are probably backsliding! The Christian life is very difficult to experience and at the same time remain static because we need to keep on following Christ. Are you slipping occasionally, if so what's causing it? As soon as you know you are well on the way to a remedy. So why are you drifting?

Day 184
Proverbs 10-13
3rd July

10 - Solomon's Proverbs Begin
11 - Evil Doers Will Be Punished
12 - Always Do Good In God's Sight
13 - Wisdom And Godliness Go Together

Godly Lives Are So Different To Ungodly Ones!

The Big Picture

The first verse in our reading today tells us that this passage is covering the proverbs of Solomon. A contrast between the Godly and the wicked is the main theme of all the proverbs in these four chapters. Like today, in Solomon's time there were many who did not follow the way of the Lord and Solomon has much to say about the two sides as he compares one with the other. There are some reminders of Job when he and his friends were confused by the way God seemed to treat the Godly and the ungodly alike and protested "Surely this cannot be so!" Solomon explores the evidence further.

Thinking Step

1:1 tells us that this book is 'The proverbs of Solomon, son of David, King of Israel.' Probably an official compilation made by Solomon, from his own and other wisdom writings of the day. It seems from 10:1 to 29:27 however, Solomon was probably the writer rather than just the collector.

Action Step

Simply looking after self rarely brings satisfaction. I remember leaving secular employment for the last time and entering the ministry in 1983. The men and women I worked with in that construction company in Newcastle-on-Tyne couldn't grasp how going to do a job which paid only half what I was then earning could be seen as anything other than a real sacrifice. It was no sacrifice! Giving time and money to the work of the Gospel is no sacrifice – it's very fulfilling and dare I say it, great value for money! Giving money away is a terrific act that benefits the giver every bit as much as the receiver. Giving time to worthwhile Godly ventures is the best way to live! A dear friend who was told he had a terminal illness, took the step of giving much of his inheritance to his family whilst he was still able to enjoy seeing what they did with it. He said it was one of the best things he ever did. Leaving money in your will is a great thing to do but giving whilst you are still alive is far more satisfying. Doing things with God is the best way to live. So what are you going to do and/or give this week? You'll be amazed how satisfying it will be. 11:25 – 'The generous will prosper, those who refresh others will themselves be refreshed.'

Solomon Continues To Make So Much Sense

The Big Picture

This rich vein of wisdom from Solomon continues in our reading today. He lifts up a Godly standard that can only be attained with God's help. Meanwhile the wicked are doing everything the best they can in their own strength. On the other hand because they are following the example of Solomon and asking God for help, the Godly continue to be given guidance from God Himself. We are reminded that many of our shortcomings are not because we belligerently go our own way but because we genuinely believe we are right and the steps we are taking are for our benefit as well as our neighbours. How wrong can you be!

Thinking Step

14:14 – 'Backsliders get what they deserve, good people receive their reward.' Consider the lives of 2 Sauls. King Saul – 1 Sam 26:21b – "Then Saul confessed ...I have been a fool and very, very wrong." Saul of Tarsus – 2 Tim 4:7 – "I have fought the good fight, I have finished the race and I have remained faithful."

Action Step

If there is a word that sums up many in the twenty first century it is 'attitude.' A strident forceful approach which seems to have at its core "If I shout loudest and get in first then I win!" Solomon's advice is quite the opposite, 15:1 – 'A gentle answer deflects anger but harsh words make tempers flare.' How to live like this is what all Christians should be searching for. When Jesus is described as meek and mild by many people today it's usually far from complimentary. The Lord is seen by many as a weak emaciated man who is soft and spineless. This is far from the truth and is equally inaccurate when used to describe His followers. In my experience the more pushy people are the less they are confident of what they are saying. You know what they say to new preachers "If you are unsure say it loud and thump the pulpit!" As one who tends to jump in quite forcefully, if I am not careful, let me share some advice my wife gave me years ago when I was rather tense and heading for what could have been a difficult elders' meeting. "Count to ten before you say anything." I did and the meeting flowed very well and all I had hoped for was approved! Try stepping back sometimes instead of pushing forward – it can give the Holy Spirit a chance to do His work!

Day 186
Proverbs 18-21
5th July

18 - No Man Is An Island
19 - Lying Is So Unhelpful
20 - Wait On The Lord
21 - A Wise Man Lives Well

Society Benefits From Wise Men

The Big Picture

Four more chapters of great pearls of wisdom from Solomon. Lots of advice on relationships with both fellow man and woman and also with God. 18:22 makes a beautiful observation 'The man who finds a wife finds a treasure and he receives favour from the Lord.' Of course Solomon has other less complimentary things to say about women but this one outweighs them all in my opinion and experience. As we approach the end of Solomon's own proverbs (with more to come from Hezekiah later) there is no sign yet of what a mess Solomon is to make of his life after such a great start and receiving so much wisdom from God.

Thinking Step

In Judaism repeating things is a way of stressing how important they are. In our reading today Solomon 'repeats' something from last time – so it must be important!

21:2 – 'People may be right in their own eyes but the Lord examines their heart.'

16:2 – 'People may be pure in their own eyes but the Lord examines their motives.'

Action Step

18:24 – 'There are "friends" who destroy each other but a real friend sticks closer than a brother.' Solomon shows a sarcastic side to his character when he describes as friends, people who were far from it. I don't know about you but when I read the second part of this verse it put me in mind of Jesus Himself. Closer than a brother and never a disappointment. Of course friendship is a two way street and for it to exist there has to be a minimum of two people who respect and trust each other. Being let down by a close friend is hard to bear but surely the challenge here is to make sure that you are not the one who is betraying a friendship. We have no power over whether a friend will let us down but we do have a say in whether we will let someone else down. I think we could double the size of most congregations if those who had been let down and hurt, came back to the church family who had hurt them! Can you think of an instance when you were the failing side of a relationship? Ask God afresh for forgiveness and if possible put it right before the week is out. Resolve anew to always be the friend who can be trusted.

22 - Solomon Looks To The Next Generation
23 - Other Wise Men Have Something To Add
24 - Wisdom Is A Vital Ingredient For Life

Day 187
Proverbs 22-24
6th July

Wisdom Needs To Be
Passed To The Next Generation

The Big Picture

Solomon gets back to where it all started – the family unit – where the training of the next generation takes place. He closes his personal proverbs with advice on dealing well with both rich and poor in society. From 22:17 Solomon includes the wisdom he admires from other wise men of his day. Their names are not given but their wisdom is nevertheless powerfully endorsed by the wisest King Israel ever had. A heavy emphasis on truth is the first thing that Solomon includes in this section. The remaining verses have much to say about how to deal with people of all kinds in the correct and best ways – with wisdom!

Thinking Step

Real wisdom is always 'God centred.' 'Babylonian Job' who pre-dated Judges said "I wish I knew that these things were pleasing to one's god." Solomon with wisdom from God said "The Lord will not let the Godly go hungry" – 10:3. Solomon also said "The blessing of the Lord makes a person rich" – 10:22.

Action Step

22:6 – 'Direct your children onto the right path and when they are older they will not leave it.' This is not the first advice that Solomon gives in Proverbs about rearing children but it sums up the very essence of good parenting. St. Francis Xavier said "Give me the child until he is seven and I'll give you the man." I am convinced this was probably made with Proverbs 22:6 in mind. Some would say that this presents us with heavy responsibilities, whilst others would say it presents us with terrific opportunities – to be instrumental in helping to form another character. Our eldest son has three children and whenever he has time with them he always tries to teach them something good. Something that will help them in future years. He also makes sure that he has lots of fun with them! Parenting is not something you do whilst you wait to get a proper job. Parenting is the most important task in any family. Too many parents today see their job as keeping their children happy. Whereas their real job is to rear them to be a God fearing generation – which will make them very contented and happy! Of course we don't all have children but we all have contact with them and can do our best to form their character into a Godly one. Which children are you going to influence for good today?

Day 188
Proverbs 25-28
7th July

25 - Proverbs Fit For A King And Your Neighbour
26 - Proverbs For Fools, Sluggards And Gossips
27 - Be Wise In All You Do
28 - Being Wicked Has Consequences

Wisdom For All Occasions

The Big Picture

Hezekiah, one of Judah's Godly Kings, decides to compile many of Solomon's proverbs and most of them are to be found in these chapters. It is not without significance that dealing with Kings is the first subject covered by King Hezekiah! It soon broadens out to cover neighbours, enemies and self. Then how to treat fools, 'lazy-bones' and gossips makes interesting reading. This all reminds us that people are people, whether today or three thousand years ago in the days of Solomon or Hezekiah. We are warned not to boast about tomorrow because we don't know what that will bring. Over-planning can ruin lives and destroy today as we make plans for a tomorrow that never arrives!

Thinking Step

Much that Jesus says and does is rooted in the Old Testament! 25:7a – 'It's better to wait for an invitation to the head table than to be sent away in public disgrace.' Look at Jesus' teaching in Luke 14:8-9 – "When you are invited to a wedding feast don't sit in the seat of honour ...(or you may be) embarrassed..."

Action Step

27:2 – 'Let someone else praise you not your own mouth – a stranger, not your own lips.' I am always suspicious of a new acquaintance who tells me how good they are at particular things. "Oh I can do that no problem!" brings my antennae up very quickly! In church life I believe our talents or gifts should be recognised by others rather than by us. I remember being in a church and being asked to stand as a deacon in the forthcoming elections. My immediate reaction was that I was sure there were better equipped people than me. I was told that I had been observed and I was acting as a deacon already, therefore my gifting should be confirmed by the church! I have to say that volunteers are usually not the best for jobs! When we started Walk Through the Bible we asked for volunteer workers but the people who could do what we wanted rarely came forward. We had to go to them and ask them – to confirm their suitability in their own eyes. Remember Jesus chose His own apostles from His volunteer disciples. He chose them for what they were and not on the basis of them telling Him that they could do what He needed. If it's only you that thinks you can do something and others don't – the majority is usually right!

29 - Some Final Thoughts From Solomon
30 - Wise Man Agur Speaks Out
31 - King Lemuel's Wisdom And The Wise Woman

Day 189
Proverbs 29-31
8th July

Wise Men Of Old Share Their Wisdom

The Big Picture

Chapter 29 contains the last proverbs from Solomon and includes one of his most popular verses for inspiring congregations to follow a programme of evangelism or fundraising and it's usually quoted in the KJV – 29:18 – 'Where there is no vision, the people perish.' A compilation of wisdom from Agur and King Lemuel – wise writings recognised at that time brings us close to the end of the Book of Proverbs. The last 22 verses of this book form an acrostic with each letter of the Hebrew alphabet being used to describe a lady of 'wifely excellence.' It is thought that before this passage was added to Proverbs it was a short separate document in its own right.

Thinking Step

Agur and Lemuel are not found elsewhere in the Bible and there is considerable doubt over their identities. Most sources yield nothing but according to the Babylonian Talmud, Solomon had six names – Solomon, Jedidiah, Qoheleth, Ben Iokoh, Agur and Lemuel. Therefore the ancient rabbinical scholars identified Agur and Lemuel with Solomon. If this is accurate Lemuel's mother in 31:2 was Bathsheba.

Action Step

How many times have you heard 29:18 and misunderstood it thinking that it meant 'unless we have a clear plan or vision people will perish?' The meaning is so much clearer in modern translations – 'When people do not accept divine guidance, they run wild but whoever obeys the law is joyful.' In other words if we are not guided by God's written revelation, i.e. the Bible, then we don't know which way is right. In Exodus 32:4 when Aaron foolishly made a golden calf, we learn that the people go wild. This is what it means when in Proverbs we read that the people perish or run wild. We all need a divine compass and that is why I have spent most of my adult life urging as many as I could to get into their Bible and be guided by what the Holy Spirit teaches as they read it. We have read many wise sayings over the past few days and some have made us scratch our head I am sure and many will have brought a smile to our face too! The whole Bible is like that! Some of it is hard to understand and some of it is so refreshing that it makes us smile. Don't linger too long on the passages you don't understand – just revel in what God is teaching you and remember – 'Whoever obeys the law is joyful.'

Ecclesiastes

Ecclesiastes

The key idea of this book is that all is vanity or emptiness when you try to live your life to the full without God. The author is generally recognised as Solomon even though he only describes himself in 1:1 as the teacher or preacher, the son of David, King in Jerusalem. Some believe Hezekiah and his scribes could have been involved in some editing – as Prov. 25:1 records that Hezekiah's men were involved in similar work with Proverbs. Assuming Solomon did write it then it was probably late in his reign as he looks back at how well it all started and how it quickly deteriorated. He had it all, everything under the sun but it brought no satisfaction. Only God can truly satisfy – everything else is of no substance. Towards the end Solomon declares that you should remember your creator in your youth and fear God and obey His commandments throughout your life.

Below is an acrostic which summarises each chapter of the book.

1. Emptiness of accumulating wealth
2. Conclusion to seeking pleasure
3. Completeness of God's timing
4. Labour is also vanity
5. Exhortations on hoarding wealth
6. Sin is never satisfying
7. Inadequacy of being affluent
8. Abuse of God's authority
9. Same end for all
10. Temporary wisdom of man
11. Emptiness of godless living
12. Serving God brings satisfaction

Everything In Life Is Meaningless

The Big Picture

'Vanity, vanity, all is vanity' – some of the most thought provoking words in the Bible are at the beginning of our reading today, (when read in the King James Bible). So many avenues to explore and they all end up producing vanity. These are the conclusions of the teacher, literally 'Qoheleth' which, according to the Babylonian Talmud is one of Solomon's names. Of all men Solomon had the best opportunities to look for satisfaction in life but concludes that they are all futile. Nevertheless there is a time for everything under heaven and God is always in control. Ultimately nothing gives satisfaction, God is the only solution.

Thinking Step

5:6 – 'Don't let your mouth make you sin and don't defend yourself by telling the Temple messenger that the promise you made was a mistake.' Who was this Temple messenger we are to be honest with? The Hebrew word 'malak' may be translated angel or messenger. There is no difference between an earthly or heavenly messenger in Hebrew!

Action Step

1:9 – 'History merely repeats itself. It has all been done before. Nothing under the sun is truly new.' I once heard a preacher addressing a family congregation saying that he had in his pocket something that no one else in all the world had ever seen before. In fact he hadn't even seen it himself but he would be happy to let the congregation see it at the same time as he viewed it – for the first time. Can you guess what it was? A peeled banana! When we read 1:9 the preacher in Ecclesiastes is referring to more than a peeled banana! Nothing is unseen by God – even if it surprises us. He is always in control. In the book of Ruth, Boaz was second choice to be her 'kinsman redeemer'. On a human level Boaz only married Ruth because her closest relative refused to do so – Ruth 4:6. God worked out His purposes despite the disobedience of this unnamed closest relative. I believe God often has to do things like this because His 'first choice' failed to be obedient... What are you pondering over today? Stop procrastinating and obey Him without delay. You know it makes sense and what a privilege to be chosen by God!

A Life Lived Wisely
Is A Life Enjoyed To The Full

The Big Picture

Having proclaimed all is emptiness and vanity, Solomon now continues to urge his readers to take God more seriously and revere Him every day. He begins with some sayings that could lead you to believe you have slipped into the Book of Proverbs again but you haven't! In the middle of them all is that sobering reminder that 'there is not a single person in all the earth who is always good and never sins' – 7:20. Wisdom is the key to a fulfilled life. Life without God is folly and people constantly make the wrong decisions. The best advice Solomon can give is to remember God whilst you are still young and continue for the rest of your life.

Thinking Step

My Mum would often tell me she knew because 'a little bird told her.' I never knew she was quoting the Bible! 10:20 – 'Never make light of the King even in your thoughts and don't make fun of the powerful even in your own bedroom. For a little bird might deliver your message and tell them what you said.'

Action Step

We live in an instant world today don't we? So what happened to instant obedience to what God is saying to us? In 12:1 Solomon tells us 'Don't let the excitement of youth cause you to forget your Creator. Honour Him in your youth before you grow old and say "Life is not pleasant anymore."' Too many Christians have one set of rules for their secular or professional life and another set for their spiritual life. This is both hypocritical and unbiblical. Deferring what God has for you until another day is foolishness. Conversion is only the start – we need to respond to His guidance in our lives everyday. My mother always used to tell me that she didn't know where the years had gone. All of a sudden she was old and it only seemed like yesterday that she was young. I used to laugh but now I am saying it too! Responding to Christ was the best thing I ever did and daily responding to His guidance is the best way of life I have ever heard of. Is there a sense in which you have accepted His gift of eternal life but are now getting on with your own life without Him? Whatever the Holy Spirit says to you when you are reading this – respond today. Do it, give it, say it – don't just sit there!

Song of Songs

Song of Songs

This book is often referred to as The Song of Solomon because of the clear claim to his authorship in 1:1. It is usually interpreted as an account concerning two lovers – or allegorically as an image of Christ and His bride the Church. It is possible to accept it as either historical or fictional and still appreciate it as an allegory of Christ and His Church. There are strong indications that Solomon is the writer in 6:4 when the cities mentioned are clearly before the Kingdom divided after Solomon's death. The sexual and physical references throughout the book mean that Jewish children are usually forbidden from reading it until they are thirteen years old – which guarantees every child reads it before their thirteenth birthday! The storyline follows what many believe to have been the only true love that Solomon ever experienced despite having 700 wives and 300 concubines.

Below is an acrostic which summarises each chapter of the book.

1. **T**estimony of bride's love
2. **H**eart yearnings of bride
3. **E**xpectations of the bride

4. **B**ridegroom expresses his love
5. **R**esponse of the bride
6. **I**mage of love divine
7. **D**esire expressed for intimacy
8. **E**xpectations of the bride

Day 192
Song Of Songs 1-4
11th July

1 - Love Is Expressed For Each Other
2 - The King Visits The Bride's Home
3 - Fearful Dream But Wedding Procession Arrives
4 - Bride's Beauty Is Praised And Wedding Follows

Courtship Results In Beautiful Wedding

The Big Picture

We begin with a conversation between a young woman and a young man. They are obviously in love but long to deepen their relationship. The young woman longs for affection but is worried she may be rejected because she is not like other women. The young man tries to reassure her that he loves her deeply. The young woman relates a dream when she thought she had lost her lover for ever then suddenly she is made aware of the pending arrival of Solomon's carriage – in a wedding procession. The young bridegroom addresses his bride who is now wearing a veil. The bride's beauty is praised and the marriage takes place.

Thinking Step

The Song of Songs was a late addition to the Hebrew Scriptures. Even after the time of Jesus around 90 AD, the rabbis were debating whether or not it should retain its canonical status. Nevertheless after it was read, as with other holy writings the reader's hands always had to be washed to prevent holiness being transmitted to unholy things.

Action Step

The courtship and marriage are both natural and beautiful. Many would interpret the bride as the Church and the bridegroom as Christ. The beauty of that first meeting with Jesus and hearing His call has no equal! The thought that He, the creator of the universe is interested in someone like me! In our weaker moments it seems too good to be true and the dream of losing her beloved in chapter three, reminds us how futile our life would be without Christ. The consummation of the marriage could be seen as our re-birth or our rapture when Jesus returns to take the whole church to be with Him for eternity. As the young woman in today's reading can hardly believe this marriage will include her – so it is for many of us. We talk of the second coming when Christ will claim His Church but there are many times when it seems like a dream. Be assured from our reading today and from the confirmation of the Holy Spirit that Jesus will come again and claim you along with all the others who have responded to His gift of salvation. Make sure you are included there is no need to miss out! Day 21 in this book will remind you of the simple A B C steps of accepting Jesus as Lord and Saviour. Why not refer back to it to confirm your own salvation today?

5 - Bride Again Fears Separation
6 - Bride's Beauty Is Praised Once More
7 - Bride Longs To Visit Her Home
8 - Journey Home And Welcome

Day 193
Song Of Songs 5-8
12th July

They All Live Happy Ever After

The Big Picture

As this Song of Songs continues, the bride now confirmed as a maid of Shulam – 6:13 – once more has fears that she may lose her husband. She dreams again of losing him and then describes her beloved bridegroom in glowing terms as she recalls how lovely he is and how much she loves him. Once again he thinks longingly of his bride and indulges himself in her beauty as he remembers her unmatched features. When we recognise the bride as the Church and the Bridegroom as Christ we are reminded in this passage of just how much Jesus loves the Church – that He was willing to die for us.

Thinking Step

Abishag, who nursed King David in his old age – 1 Kings 1:1-4 was from the city of Shunem. Solomon's wife in The Song of Solomon is from the city of Shulam. Both names describe the same city in Hebrew and Arabic respectively. It is therefore possible that it was beautiful Abishag who became the wife of King Solomon.

Action Step

In these days of temporary and short term relationships I am reminded of a trip to the Ukraine some years ago when I was introduced as a family man who had been married for the past thirty years. You wouldn't believe how many folk asked me afterwards "How many wives have you had during those thirty years?" When I said it was with the same woman, I don't think they all believed me! The two lovely refrains in Song of Songs 'My beloved is mine and I am his' – 2:16 and 'I am my beloveds and my beloved is mine' – 6:3 are statements of the young couple in the song which may also be taken allegorically as the relationship of Christ and His Church. I would like to take it as a statement for Biblical marriage too. I realise some are not called to marriage and for some, marriage is not a success but for me it has been and I regularly praise God for that. Without my wife I am convinced my ministry would be incomplete. On a wider canvas why not thank God for the special relationships He has given you? They don't have to be marriages they can be friendships. For me it is marriage and I thank God for providing me with such a loyal, loving, lovely and lasting partner.

Isaiah

Prophets In Perspective

MAJOR PROPHETS	ISAIAH	DIVIDED KINGDOM	MONARCHY
	JEREMIAH		
	LAMENTATIONS		
	EZEKIEL	BABYLON	EXILE
	DANIEL		
MINOR PROPHETS	HOSEA	ISRAEL	
	AMOS		
	JOEL		
	MICAH		
	HABAKKUK	JUDAH	PRE-EXILE
	ZEPHANIAH		
	OBADIAH		
	JONAH	NINEVEH	
	NAHUM		
	HAGGAI		
	ZECHARIAH	JUDAH	POST-EXILE
	MALACHI		

Isaiah

The basic theme of this book is revealed in Isaiah's name which means 'Salvation is of the Lord.' It has been called the miniature Bible as there are 66 chapters which neatly split into 39 and 27 – just like the books of the Bible! The first 39 filled with judgement like much of the Old Testament and the last 27 full of hope and glory just like the New Testament. Isaiah prophesied to the southern Kingdom at the same time as Micah, while Hosea ministered in the north. About half way through his ministry he witnessed the northern Kingdom being scattered by the invading Assyrians leaving only two southern tribes, Judah and Benjamin. Assyria tries to defeat Judah too but God intervenes. Isaiah's ministry spanned four Kings of Judah from Uzziah to Hezekiah. His writings about the coming Messiah are amongst the clearest prophetic statements in the Old Testament.

Below is an acrostic which summarises each chapter of the book.

1. **T**ruth of Israel's corruption
2. **H**opelessness of Israel's pride
3. **E**xecution of Judah's leaders

4. **P**urging sin from Jerusalem
5. **R**emoval of God's vineyard
6. **O**pening of Isaiah's lips
7. **P**rophecy of virgin's child
8. **H**orror of Assyrian invasion
9. **E**stablishing of Messiah's kingdom
10. **C**allousness of Assyrian army
11. **I**ntervention of Jesse's branch
12. **E**xalting the Lord's salvation
13. **S**ure destruction of Babylon

14. **O**verthrow of proud Lucifer
15. **F**ailure of Moab predicted

16. **T**riumph of righteous king
17. **H**opeless future of Assyria
18. **E**nd of Edom predicted

19. **J**oyful shouting in Zion
20. **U**psetting news for Hezekiah
21. **D**oom comes to Sennacherib
22. **G**od grants Hezekiah's prayer
23. **M**essengers arrive from Babylon
24. **E**ternal comfort from God
25. **N**ature of God's power
26. **T**riumph of God's Servant

27. **A**ssurance of Israel's forgiveness
28. **N**onsense of serving idols
29. **D**eliverance by King Cyrus

Day 194
Isaiah 1-3
13th July

1 - You Need To Change Your Ways Judah
2 - The Day Of The Lord Is Coming
3 - Judgement Is Coming To Judah

Judgement On Judah Is Unavoidable

The Big Picture

Isaiah shares his message with God's people for about half a century! He tells them that God does not understand why His people have turned against their God. He tells them there is little difference between Israel and the sinful nations around. He reminds them that their sacrifices are not enough – God wants their allegiance. Graciously God tells them that He wants to talk this through with them even though their sins are as red as crimson He wants them to be as white as snow – 1:18. Isaiah tells them that in the last days, the Temple in Jerusalem will be visited by many nations and all wars will cease. Judgement is coming for sinful men, women and children alike.

Thinking Step

Talmudic tradition records the fate of one of the greatest prophets that Israel has ever seen and who had served his God so faithfully for a whole lifetime. It records that he was one of a group of prophets who was sawn in two. The New Testament records this event without specific names in Heb. 11:37.

Action Step

1:18 – "Come now, let's settle this," says the Lord. "Though your sins are like scarlet, I will make them as white as snow. Though they are red like crimson, I will make them as white as wool." What a gracious God we have. He begins with such a reconciliatory statement, the beginning of which literally means 'Come now and let us reason together.' A reasoning God! We need to hold on to this fact when folk ask "So where was your God when a particular disaster happened?" The answer is that He was there with those suffering. Little logical thought is given to what it would be like to have a God who removed all free will so that nothing could go wrong. It would be hell on earth, we would be little more than clockwork soldiers or remote controlled robots. We have a God who longs to reason with a fallen world and help us see what His will is in particular situations. However He will not force His will upon us but He wants us to be aware of how much He loves the world in general and you and me in particular. Is there a particular thorny issue you are trying to resolve at the moment? Then reason with God about it but remember He is God and always knows best but He would like to discuss it with you! Why not now – no appointment necessary!

4 - The Day Of The Lord Continued   Day 195
5 - Parable Of The Vineyard   Isaiah 4-7
6 - Isaiah Is Commissioned   14th July
7 - A Virgin Will Conceive And Bare A Son

Isaiah Is Commissioned
And Immanuel Is Promised

The Big Picture

Isaiah concludes his declaration of The Day of The Lord. God's people are then taught very clearly in the parable of the vineyard, that the Lord required so much more from them. He expected justice and righteousness but found neither. The classic chapter of God's call to Isaiah and his beautiful reply "Lord, I'll go, send me!" This is followed in the darkness of the threat from Assyria and a new untried King called Jotham, by God giving an earth shattering promise to the world in 7:14 – '...Look! The virgin will conceive a child! She will give birth to a son and will call him Immanuel (which means 'God is with us').'

Thinking Step

6:2 – '...mighty seraphim, each having six wings. With two wings they covered their faces, with two they covered their feet, and with two they flew.' They covered their faces so as not to look on a Holy God. They kept their feet covered to remind them not to follow their own pathways. They flew with immediate readiness for God.

Action Step

7:14 contains the first of many clear statements from Isaiah that God is about to act for our benefit! Messiah is promised and God always keeps His word. In the New Testament Dr. Luke picks up this thread of virgin birth and of all people chosen to substantiate the virgin birth – God chose a medical man who knew it was impossible! All his training and experience denied it. I believe God wants us to use our intellect as we follow Him but sometimes we just have to follow by faith. The biggest mistake we can make is to only follow God to the limit of our knowledge or experience. I remember a believer who was amazingly confronted by God in a miraculous way and found himself telling God that this can't be happening because his theology didn't allow it! He said that God immediately told him that his theology had to grow! Is there an issue in your life at the moment that you just can't get your head around? Just like Dr. Luke must have felt about the virgin birth! You have only two options. Stop where you are and rob yourself of a wonderful experience as you obey God or obey Him and then get ready for more stretching of your theology in the not too distant future as you continue to develop into the person God wants you to be.

Day 196
Isaiah 8-10
15th July

8 - Assyria's Invasion Prophesied
9 - Messiah's Birth Prophesied
10 - Assyria's Destruction Is Certain

God Knows The Future Is Secure

The Big Picture

Isaiah's wife gives birth to a son and he is named – Maher Shalal Hash Baz meaning 'swift to plunder and quick to spoil.' The Assyrians are coming and that's certain. First the north will fall and then later the south will be threatened but God will intervene for Judah. Here we have more details about the promised Messiah. He will be a light for those walking in darkness and will even minister to the Gentiles in Galilee. However Galilee in the north, the land of Zebulun and Naphtali will be amongst the first casualties to fall to the Assyrian invaders. Nevertheless they will be the primary witnesses of Messiah as He grows up and lives there.

Thinking Step

9:6 – '...He will be called: Wonderful Counsellor, Mighty God, Everlasting Father, Prince of Peace.' In the Hebrew language 'Wonderful' and 'Counsellor' are two separate names. However in view of the other names being in pairs it is assumed they form a pair also. He is 'Wonderful' and He is a 'Counsellor' and He is 'a Wonder of a Counsellor.'

Action Step

9:2 – 'The people who walk in darkness will see a great light' is the source for Luke as he records the prophecy of Zechariah concerning John the Baptist in Luke 1:79 – 'to give light to those who sit in darkness and in the shadow of death.' What an honour to be God's mouthpiece as John the Baptist was. He enters with a bang closing the 400 years of silence since Malachi – with that mighty declaration as he urged the people to repent for the Kingdom of Heaven was imminent. However the gospel of John goes on to tell us in 1:18 – 'John himself was not the light; he was only a witness to the light.' It was his job to point to Jesus and he goes on to say that Jesus must increase and he John, must decrease. I clearly remember being an associate minister in a church when the senior minister resigned (not due to me I hasten to add). People asked me why I was not 'going for the top job' and questioned whether or not I had any ambition! There is room for ambition in life but not in the church. We need to be content with the calling that God gives us and not be constantly dreaming of climbing to the top. John was happy to be number two and we ought to be too.

11 - Restoration Of Messiah's Kingdom   Day 197
12 - Thanksgiving For Messiah's Kingdom   Isaiah 11-13
13 - Prophecies Against Babylon   16th July

Messiah's Kingdom Is Assured

The Big Picture

In the midst of uncertainty in Israel Isaiah declares that the Messiah's Kingdom will be so peaceful that the wolf will dwell with the lamb and children will be safe even when crawling amongst poisonous snakes. What a glorious image God gives to Isaiah as more is revealed of what the Messiah will produce. I am sure many of Isaiah's hearers would have accused him of wishful thinking but where God is concerned, nothing is impossible. Isaiah goes on to prophecy to the surrounding nations as he tells them of the judgement of God for the way they have lived and the way they have mistreated God and His people Israel.

Thinking Step

11:1 – 'Out of the stump of David's family will grow a shoot – yes, a new branch bearing fruit from the old.'
Many of the olive trees in today's Garden of Gethsemane in Jerusalem date back hundreds of years. Despite being hacked back over history their roots remained viable and some probably go back to the time of Jesus.

Action Step

11:6-8 – 'In that day the wolf and the lamb will live together; the leopard will lie down with the baby goat. The calf and the yearling will be safe with the lion and a little child will lead them all. The cow will graze near the bear. The cub and the calf will lie down together. The lion will eat hay like a cow. The baby will play safely near the hole of a cobra. Yes, a little child will put its hand in a nest of deadly snakes without harm.' In these days of equality and health & safety it seems to me that we are trying to achieve this utopian society in the UK by trying to reduce risk to such an extent that nothing can go wrong. We want all that Christianity and the Bible has to offer as long as we don't have to bring God into it! Don't be misled into thinking that increasingly restrictive legislation will ultimately produce a wonderful law abiding peaceful society like Isaiah is talking about in our reading today. Only individual life change from within can do that. We need to concentrate on changing individuals and it's a slow process but it does work! Don't settle for converts in your church. Remember we have to make disciples otherwise we will be surrounded by ill disciplined babies in our churches! So are you just a convert or a disciple?

Day 198   14 - Prophecies For The Assyrians And Philistines
Isaiah 14-17   15 - Prophecies For The Moabites
17th July   16 - Judgement On The Moabites
17 - Prophecies For Damascus And The Samaritans

Surrounding Nations Are Warned

The Big Picture

A timely reminder that God will have mercy on the descendants of Jacob. They will get to settle in the land that was promised to them by God so long ago. Babylonia will come and go but Israel will remain for ever! The Philistines who have been Israel's enemies for what seems like forever, are ultimately doomed to be defeated. Moab is doomed too. What was once a fertile land on the east side of the Jordan river will soon be no more – the future is equally bleak for these people. The coming years are no better for Damascus where useless idols have flourished for generations. They will be found wanting and totally inferior to the living God.

Thinking Step

15:1-2 – 'This message came to me concerning Moab: ...they will wail for the fate of Nebo and Madaba ...' Nebo the 'Israel viewing point' used by Moses and Madaba the traditional birthplace of Ruth, an ancestor of Jesus. This is the area where many of the first churches were established – outside Israel but still able to view it!

Action Step

16:1 – 'Send lambs from Sela as tribute to the ruler of the land. Send them through the desert to the mountain of beautiful Zion.' These lambs were often referred to as 'tribute lambs' and were the currency by which Moab paid tribute to Israel. 2 Kings 3:4 – 'King Mesha of Moab was a sheep breeder. He used to pay the King of Israel (Ahab) an annual tribute of 100,000 lambs and the wool of 100,000 rams.' Thousands of sheep were donated by Moab every year in order to placate Israel. Later in his book Isaiah talks about a very special being, the Lamb of God in 53:7 – '...He was led like a lamb to the slaughter and as a sheep is silent before the shearers, He did not open his mouth.' In the ancient world thousands of sheep were required to pay your debt but Isaiah had a vision of the day when one would be all sufficient. What an idea, something so small but all encompassing. Something that seems so limited and yet is limitless. That's what the sacrifice of Jesus means for all believers and it's a reminder that it is all that is necessary. If you are trying to add to it – then stop it! Christ is all sufficient and can be the power by which you are saved – today. Why not turn to day 21 on page 40 for the **A B C** steps of salvation?

18 - Prophecies Against Ethiopia
19 - Prophecies Against Egypt
20 - Isaiah Bares All!
21 - Prophecies Against Babylon, Edom And Arabia

Day 199
Isaiah 18-21
18th July

Time Is Running Out For Neighbouring Nations

The Big Picture

Ethiopia is doomed but there will come a day when they will bring gifts to The Lord Almighty in Jerusalem. Egypt on the other hand will see many turning to the God of Israel as turmoil engulfs the whole nation. Many Egyptians will even speak Hebrew, the language of Israel. Isaiah becomes a striking visual aid and unforgettable sign as he lives his life as a nudist for three years. All of this to convey what will eventually happen to Egypt and Ethiopia as they are conquered by the Assyrians and taken naked into slavery in total degradation. Time is also running out for Edom and Arabia.

Thinking Step

When conquering the Promised Land Joshua referred to 5 Kings in Josh. 10:22 – 'Remove the rocks covering the opening of the cave and bring the five Kings to me.' When Isaiah foretells the defeat of Egypt he uses 5 again, in 19:17-18 – 'In that day five of Egypt's cities will follow the Lord of Heaven's Armies. Both FIVES signifying absolute defeat.

Action Step

A pastor friend of mine had a call from a local public house telling him that a member of his church, who was a notorious alcoholic in the town was asking for help. Without delay my friend rang another leader from his church and the pair of them met up outside the public house. They soon found their errant church member who was almost unconscious by now because of the amount of alcohol he had consumed. They got him to his feet and one on each side of him started to leave the building. As they hit the cold night air they were all swaying to the rhythm of the central one as they crossed the car park. As they approached the pastor's car, just across the road they saw a couple of very conservative ladies from a neighbouring fellowship. From their reaction it was obvious that they recognised the pastor and thought the whole group was swaying because they had just enjoyed a 'good time' in the pub! There was no time for explanations, the two 'good Samaritans' just had to risk being misunderstood and continued to the car. It's the same with Isaiah in – 20:2-3. Just imagine your minister 'doing an Isaiah' and explaining what God had asked him to do for the next three years! Are you holding back on being obedient because you could be misunderstood? Risk it – for the Kingdom!

Day 200
Isaiah 22-25
19th July

22 - Prophesies Against Jerusalem
23 - Prophesies Against Tyre
24 - Tribulation Explained
25 - Praises For Kingdom Blessings

The Day Of The Lord Is Coming!

The Big Picture

It may be hard to accept and understand but chaos will come to the city of Jerusalem. Invaders will attack and succeed against you because you are not relying on your God. You take little notice of Him and don't ask for His help when you need it! Disaster will come to the harbour of Tyre – the very facility that gives it its importance and power. During the time of tribulation which God will send, the vital grape harvest will fail and there will be no more wine. However this will not last forever because God is so good. He will protect the poor and will ultimately reign in Jerusalem.

Thinking Step

Fools' words are always foolish!
22:13 – '...instead, you dance and play...you feast on meat and drink wine... you say, "Let's feast and drink, for tomorrow we die!"'
Luke 12:19-20 – '...Now take it easy! Eat, drink and be merry!... but God said to him "You fool! You will die this very night..."'

Action Step

How many times have you had a discussion at church which was brought to a close with the comment "Surely we can do it cheaper than that, it seems a lot of money to me!" Christians really can seem to be followers of Ebenezer Scrooge sometimes! We regularly need to remind each other that God wants the best for all of us! 25:6 tells us – 'In Jerusalem, the Lord of Heaven's Armies will spread a wonderful feast for all the people of the world. It will be a delicious banquet with clear well-aged wine and choice meat.' Not any old cloudy wine but beautiful vintage! – not any chunk of gristly beef but choice meat. The best! I have lost count of the number of times that I have been asked why Walk Through the Bible uses such good quality manuals when they could be photocopied far cheaper! Actually that's not economically accurate and it's not the best God honouring option anyway! I'm glad God organised the first visual aid in the world because we would have ruined it totally. After the flood He went for a multi-coloured rainbow. Many of us would have gone for a black and white one! Don't penny pinch for God! Use the best to His glory! After all, in the words of the well known shampoo advert "You're worth it" and so is He!

God Is Always Worth Worshipping

The Big Picture

Our reading today starts where everyday should start – worshipping our God who protects us and supplies our every need. Israel is likened to a vineyard which will be protected from the thorns and briars which surround it. On the other hand the end is near for Samaria. Assyria will come and scatter them and they will be no more! Nevertheless Israel is still acting like a load of children and their leaders continue to act like drunken men and are leading very badly. In fact they are showing that without God they are incapable of leading God's people and things will go from bad to worse until God intervenes.

Thinking Step

28:20 – 'The bed you have made is too short to lie on. The blankets are too narrow to cover you.' In other words, you've made your own bed – now lie on it! In short, you could use better protection just like Ruth when she approached Boaz – Ruth 3:9. Ruth asked Boaz and received but Ephraim didn't ask God!

Action Step

Take a glass and fill it to the top with water – if you are very careful you can move it slowly without spilling much. However, if you are jostled or other difficulties come your way then you will spill much of what is in the glass. In 28:7 it is very obvious from the 'overspill' that the spiritual leadership of Ephraim is filled with very unhelpful influences. The Apostle Paul pleads with believers in Ephesus – 'Don't be drunk with wine because that will ruin your life. Instead be filled with the Holy Spirit' – Eph 5:18. Whatever you are filled with will spill over into your daily life. If you are filled with bitterness then you will reveal much bitterness, if you are filled with envy you will show much envy and so on. A good question to ask yourself is "What single word would describe me?" Be careful! Don't answer what you would like folk to think of you but try to be honest and evaluate yourself accurately. Thankfully as believers this is just the beginning. To help you, a good check list may be found in Gal. 5:22-23. If you aspire to be filled with 'love, joy, peace, patience, kindness, goodness, faithfulness, gentleness and self-control' then with God's help these will overflow from your life in good times and bad. Being filled with the spirit is not a doctrinal nicety – it's a way of life!

Day 202
Isaiah 29-31
21st July

29 - Trouble For Jerusalem
30 - Beware Of Egypt
31 - Don't Trust Egypt

Trust In God Alone

The Big Picture

Jerusalem is challenged by Isaiah as he calls it Ariel and declares that judgement is coming. This is the only place in the Bible where Jerusalem is given this name. Many misunderstand what will happen and find it hard to believe that God will rescue the city which is His pride and joy. Isaiah tells the Israelites straight that whilst Egypt is a very powerful nation it is not powerful enough to protect them from God's judgement. Making an alliance with such Godless neighbours will result in disappointment and failure. Israel tried this plan with several nations over its history but always found that God was their best protector and provider and the only one who was absolutely trustworthy.

Thinking Step

Isaiah calls Jerusalem 'Ariel', five times in chapter 29. It means 'lion of God.' 'Ari' = lion and 'iel' = of God. The name was used to remind Jerusalem that it was to be a strong and brave beacon for God. During Isaiah's lifetime it never was. Since then 'Jerusalem' has rarely lived up to its name which means 'possession of peace.'

Action Step

Have you noticed whenever an election looms, politicians are tempted more than ever, to tell the people what they want to hear rather than the truth? Isaiah sums it up beautifully in 30:10 – '..."Don't tell us what is right. Tell us nice things. Tell us lies."' I remember having an interview at head office after I had worked in my first job for several months. The idea was to gauge my progress. I was sixteen years old and the advice I was given was to tell them what I thought they wanted to hear. Even to exaggerate to give the 'best' impression. After the interview I compared notes with a colleague who said he had simply told the truth. I had to admit I had lied through my teeth! A few weeks later we were called into the manager's office. My position was made permanent but my colleague was dismissed! I was unaware then that God could have helped me tell the truth at my interview if I had thought to ask but as an unbeliever it never entered my head. One of the things I love about the Bible is that it always tells the truth warts and all. Take this as a reminder that God loves us warts and all and wants us to declare the truth in all situations. Do you need His help to do that today? If so why not ask Him NOW?

God's Protection Of Jerusalem Is Supreme

The Big Picture

A timely reminder is made by Isaiah as we begin today's reading. The King is on His way. Messiah is coming. Assyria will invade Jerusalem but unlike in the north they are destined to fail. They will not succeed and overcome Jerusalem but they will come very close and only God is able to stop them. Nations will be judged and Edom will become a wilderness area inhabited by many of God's creatures. Even here the glory of God will shine through as the Coming Kingdom is established. All is not lost – God will redeem His people and ultimately the whole world will witness what God is doing when Messiah reigns.

Thinking Step

In chapter 34 Isaiah focuses in on the nation of Edom. Ancient enemies of Israel from the days of their forefathers, Esau and Jacob. Isaiah uses Edom to represent all wicked nations. The Edomites were only ever truly subdued by King David and Isaiah is now looking to the rule of Jesus Christ, Son of David.

Action Step

Over these recent years things that seemed absolutely permanent have failed and collapsed. Large companies and banks have been unable to carry on due to unforeseen events. In Isaiah's day the only thing that was certain was the sheer uncertainty of life. Rainfall was not guaranteed, crops could fail. Life was so much cheaper than today and could be snuffed out by any passing invading army who took a liking to your land. In the midst of all this insecurity Isaiah wrote words of certainty as he anticipated the Kingdom of God coming soon – 35:4 'Say to those with fearful hearts "Be strong and do not fear, for your God is coming to destroy your enemies. He is coming to save you."' Everyone knew that the Assyrians could attack whenever they wanted. There is something to be said for having nothing to rely on except God. Today we have so many phony crutches to lean on and we tend to try them all before turning to God. So what about you – are you totally relying on God or is He your last resort? Can you think of anything that would cause your life to collapse if it was taken away? If so hand it over to God now and rely on Him instead. Let go of the unreliable and hold on to the reliable. Everything else could fail but our Father in Heaven won't.

Day 204
Isaiah 36-39
23rd July

36 - Assyria Invades
37 - Assyria Repelled
38 - Hezekiah's Life Threatened
39 - Hezekiah's Foolish Actions

Hezekiah Withstands Assyrian Assault

The Big Picture

The historical account from 2 Kings 18 and its parallel Godly commentary in 2 Chron. 32 are covered in this short section of Isaiah. It covers the failure of Sennacherib's army and Hezekiah's reaction to hearing he is about to die – then his reprieve as Isaiah intervenes. The majority of Isaiah's first 39 chapters are dominated by judgements on the surrounding nations but these four chapters are dedicated to their miraculous deliverance from the Assyrian invasion which should have been impossible considering how big and powerful the Assyrian army was compared to Israel's. This short section provides an interlude between the judgements and prophecies against Israel's enemies and the remaining majestic chapters foretelling the coming Messiah.

Thinking Step

It was the Assyrian army that created the first 'middle east empire' known to the world. What they achieved was later ruled by the Babylonians, then the Persians followed by the Greeks. They welded together many ethnic groupings so that the term 'middle east' still covers their original empire today. Throughout all this God protected His people and their land.

Action Step

Walk Through the Bible had only been in existence in the UK less than ten years when it became obvious that our finances would not sustain this ministry for more than a few years more. We could have surrendered and allowed this innovative Bible teaching ministry to slip into oblivion. On the other hand we could have simply carried on trusting that when God chose to bring it to a close then it would close no matter what. We chose the latter with the thought at the back of our minds that we would be saddened by Walk Through's demise but we would accept that God knew best. Hezekiah and Isaiah really wanted Sennacherib to fail and he did! I often wonder how they would have reacted if Sennacherib had conquered them! Sometimes it doesn't work out like we want and what we dread does come to be. Are you struggling with something in your life today? I believe the way to stop you ever becoming bitter and twisted is to sincerely ask God for what you genuinely want but accept joyfully what God actually does. Is today the day to accept that what you were hoping for is not what is in God's mind? Don't let a disappointment ruin the rest of your life and witness!

40 - God's Character Brings Comfort
41 - God's Greatness Brings Comfort
42 - God's Servant Brings Comfort

Day 205
Isaiah 40-42
24th July

Our God Is A Comforting God

The Big Picture

From chapter 40 onwards the tone changes from prophecies of condemnation to prophecies of comfort. Some of the prose to come is the reason that Isaiah has been called the 'Shakespeare of prophets.' The loving comforting side of God is constantly revealed by Him through His prophet Isaiah. Messiah will come to fulfil the promise of ultimate comfort for God's people. Judgement which will be delivered through the Babylonians will inevitably come but God will save His people from total destruction. He protects them from the Assyrians because they would have scattered them as they did the northern tribes. Instead He chooses the Babylonians as His instrument because He knows Israel will be taken into exile and kept intact.

Thinking Step

In the Dead Sea Scroll of Isaiah (with no chapters or verses) the 'doom verses' of 39:5-7 and the 'comfort verse' of 40:1 lie side by side in the scroll. More than that the doom pronounced by Isaiah is a singular voice whereas the comfort comes from God Himself and is plural in the following verses 3, 6 and 9!

Action Step

40:31 – 'Those who trust in the Lord will find new strength. They will soar high on wings like eagles. They will run and not grow weary. They will walk and not faint.'
What a truly awe inspiring verse. Four things are promised in it.

1. Daily strength will be given new every morning. Not our strength but strength from God.
2. We will be lifted high as only God can lift. Life in all its fullness as only God can provide.
3. When we need something extra in particularly trying times, God will meet our need fully and help us run.
4. In the humdrum walk of daily life where we spend most of our time, God will be with us to encourage.

The order is interesting. God begins with strength for flying then running and finally walking. This reminds us that whilst we spend most of our time walking our daily walk God has so much more for us. He wants us to regularly experience flying and running times when God uses us in special ways. Why not thank God now for His faithfulness in your daily life and then ask Him for a flying or running experience today when you can be particularly useful to Him and be specifically blessed yourself!

Day 206
Isaiah 43-44
25th July

43 - God Will Continue To Be Faithful
44 - God Plans Way Ahead!

Our God Is Not Limited By Time!

The Big Picture

The mighty all-powerful nature of God continues to be declared. Unlike other false gods which are made by men, Israel's God is the true God who made men! Looking back you will see that He rescued His people from Egypt and can be relied upon when the Babylonians decide to attack. Wooden gods are useless especially when compared to the Living God who made the heavens and the earth and everything else. He has already planned the rescue from exile in Babylonia before His people are taken away! He has already chosen who He will use to fulfil His plan even though he has not even been born yet!

Thinking Step

Around 150 years before Solomon's Temple was rebuilt by Zerubbabel, Isaiah confirms it in – 44:28 (it wasn't destroyed yet!) and we are told Cyrus will command it (he wasn't born yet!). Some say this detail is impossible unless it was added after Cyrus became King. Personally I think God could have told Isaiah – if He had chosen to!

Action Step

43:25 – "I – yes, I alone – will blot out your sins for my own sake and will never think of them again." When I think of how many times I have heard the Gospel preached by others and by me, I have never realised previously that God wants to forgive our sins and never think of them again – for Himself! The emphasis is always on the one who needs forgiveness rather than the One who will do the forgiving! That must be why the Bible tells us that there will be "... more joy in heaven over one lost sinner who repents and returns to God than over ninety-nine others who are righteous and haven't strayed away!" – Luke 15:7. At a recent birthday party for one of our grandchildren we couldn't help but smile as our grandson opened his presents and was totally captivated by them. We were so glad we had played our part in this moment of sheer ecstasy. This is surely a very pale imitation of what Jesus meant when He referred to joy in Heaven. However, reflect on this for a moment. Our actions can cause God to be joyful! As you live out today bear this in mind and do all you can to cause joy in Heaven. Seemingly unimportant things will take on a whole new dimension as you play your part in giving joy to your Father in Heaven.

Babylonia Will Play Its Part

The Big Picture

We begin with more information on Cyrus who will be used by God to facilitate the return of Israel to the Promised Land after the exile which has not happened yet! He foresees Cyrus and his Persian army overcoming Babylonia even before Babylonia takes Israel off into exile! They have been used by God to judge His people but they will not last for ever no matter how powerful they may think they are! God constantly tells His people through the prophets what will happen. This is to show that He is truly God and that the handmade idols of the Babylonians and many others nations are of no value whatsoever.

Thinking Step

Before Assyria ultimately fell to Babylonia, historians tell us that Sennacherib attacked Babylon in 703 BC. The King of Babylonia at that time Merodach-Baladan, organised evacuation of their gods on ox carts! This is exactly what Isaiah prophesied would happen again when Babylonia fell to Cyrus, King of Persia many years after Isaiah's time – 46:1-2.

Action Step

We constantly hear of unique events or unique things. Particularly on TV and even more specifically during the adverts! So much so that we can tend to forget that few things are truly unique but our reading today confirms to us that 'There is no other like me!' – 46:9, 47:8, 10. Isaiah tells us that our God is unique unlike the false gods of his neighbours whose idols could be duplicated if the originals were damaged or lost! In our multicultural and multiracial society today we need to remember that Jesus is unique and said so "I am the way, the truth and the life. No one can come to the Father except through me." – John 14:6. This was a truly blasphemous claim if Jesus was just a man but He links Himself to God the Father in such a way that there is no doubt what He meant – John 14:11 – "...I am in the Father and the Father is in me." Jesus claimed He and the Father are one – He is God! This truth does not give us the right to denounce people of other faiths or beliefs but it does give us a responsibility to live appropriately in our daily lives. Have you already failed to do this today? Resolve now with His help to declare that Jesus is the way, the truth and the life as you live your life today.

Day 208
Isaiah 49-52
27th July

49 - You Need To Be God's Light
50 - You Need To Live In God's Light
51 - God Gives His Salvation
52 - God Brings His People Back

God's Light Will Never Be Extinguished

The Big Picture

After hearing about Cyrus being a saviour who gets the people back from exile – now get ready for the real Saviour and Messiah of the whole world! Israel has always been called to be God's light to the world. Even before the exile period God reassures His people that many will safely return – 49:20. "You deserve to go into exile but God will bring you back. When that happens you need to live in God's light not your own small fires. Over the years God has rescued you many times and has never let you down. You can be certain that you will return from exile."

Thinking Step

As Hosea's ministry in the north finishes, closely followed by that of Micah in the south, Isaiah's days are numbered too. The Godless reign of Manasseh begins and stifles the prophetic word for the next fifty years. Nevertheless all that God proclaims through Isaiah will be fulfilled and Messiah will come but not for another 700 years!

Action Step

52:7 – 'How beautiful on the mountains are the feet of the messenger who brings good news, the good news of peace and salvation, the news that the God of Israel reigns!' In Biblical times, as today, our feet are rarely the most beautiful parts of our bodies! However even the feet of a runner who brings news are described as beautiful. In this instance the response to good news was not negatively influenced by anything to do with the messenger. Oh that this was true every Sunday in churches up and down our country. We are all so easily distracted by a preacher's mannerisms or their doctrinal stance or by something they did or said years ago. It's not their feet that's the problem – its our ears! We can't hear them or more importantly what God is saying through them because we are not listening. Surely this is one of the main tools that the devil uses when he wants us to stagnate. I think it's acceptable to switch off your radio or TV if you don't like the announcer or presenter at the time – at least I hope so because I do it more and more as I grow older! You are not however, permitted to do the same with the preacher because God may have something to say to you and you really need to hear it!

53 - The Suffering Servant
54 - Messiah Will Take Our Punishment
55 - Everlasting Covenant For You
56 - God Loves Jews And Gentiles

Day 209
Isaiah 53-56
28th July

Suffering Messiah For Needy World

The Big Picture

Chapter 53 describes Jesus so well it's hard to believe it was written so many centuries before He was born in Bethlehem. In the days of Jesus the Jews were expecting a conquering Messiah who would defeat the Romans who were crushing them into submission. Instead they were given a helpless baby. Whilst He was still a young man He was crucified by the dominating Romans, in collusion with the Jewish authorities. His resurrection provides the final declaration of the Father's love for us and of His mighty power to reign. In Isaiah, Messiah is promised as the ultimate sacrifice for mankind. This final covenant in blood is eternal and is for both Jews and Gentiles.

Thinking Step

The last 27 chapters of Isaiah are tingling with Messianic promises. The central verse of these chapters, which sums up what Messiah will offer to the whole world is 53:6 – 'All of us, like sheep, have strayed away. We have left God's paths to follow our own. Yet the Lord laid on him the sins of us all.'

Action Step

In the first three verses of chapter 55, Isaiah repeats the word 'come' several times. It is used four times in all. Each one reminds me of hearing an ex communist giving his testimony and saying that he listened to the claims of Jesus because it was not forceful, He was very 'human'. He said that he felt he had a choice, that Jesus was a gentleman and that he could trust someone who was not trying to force him into obedience. I never forgot that. In these few verses the invitation to come is firstly addressed to those who are thirsty. In other words everyone! To those who are hungry – that's all of us again. To those who want to enjoy life, that's everyone again. To those who want to live life to the full – all of us again. What Jesus has is for everyone not just those who are 'religious.' I remember telling a work colleague that I was moving to take up an appointment as a church minister. He hesitated and then said "I never realised you had a religious bent!" I asked him "A religious bent what?" and we both laughed out loud in his office! He thought I was too normal to be religious. I took it as a compliment. However, take this as a reminder, unless we appear 'normal' we may appear so heavenly minded that we are no earthly use!

Day 210
Isaiah 57-60
29th July

57 - God Loves Us Even When We Sin
58 - God Wants Genuine Followers
59 - God Is Sending Messiah For Such As You
60 - God's Light Will Shine Throughout The World

God Will Shine Through A Sincere Believer

The Big Picture

Idolatry continues to be a real problem in Isaiah's day. People persist in worshipping idols and ignoring the Living God. God is not impressed by people who come to Him trying to make a good impression. He wants His followers to act sincerely rather than bring big offerings. Isaiah reminds the people that their sins have created a barrier which cuts them off from God but it is for such people that God is sending His Messiah! He wants Jerusalem to be the beacon He always planned it would be. As the exile finishes (and remember it has not started yet!) many will return and claim God as their everlasting light.

Thinking Step

57:21 – '"There is no peace for the wicked" says my God.'
48:22 – '"But there is no peace for the wicked" says the Lord.'
God's standards remain the same whether its for those who are in inner turmoil like those in 57:21 or returning from Babylonian exile as in 48:22. It's worth repeating – wickedness never produces peace.

Action Step

59:21 – "...and this is my covenant with them" says the Lord. "My Spirit will not leave them and neither will these words I have given you. They will be on your lips and on the lips of your children and your children's children forever. I, the Lord, have spoken!" This lovely word from Isaiah about the faithfulness of God being passed on from one generation to the next warms our hearts and when we look around and see how far we are from this ideal it's like a bucket of cold water being poured over us! God is faithful but we have let Him down. We have no one to blame but ourselves. In schools we have on average one pupil per class who attends church and they tend to come from Christian families. So how do we redress the balance? It's quite simply really – we have to take the Bible and its teachings to school children where they are – in school! We have to enthuse kids with what the Bible says. Since the mid 1990's Walk Through the Bible has trained hundreds of adults to teach hundreds of thousands of primary school children all about the whole Bible, in exciting and thought provoking ways. All in line with their locally agreed syllabus on RE. You can get more information about supporting and/or joining our Bible Explorer team on our website www.Bible.org.uk

61 - God Loves Justice And Hates Wrongdoings   Day 211
62 - God Will Never Give Up On Jerusalem   Isaiah 61-63
63 - God Is Always Faithful   30th July

God Is Our Reliable Heavenly Father!

The Big Picture

The opening words from chapter 61 are those which Jesus read many centuries later on a visit to the synagogue in Nazareth – Luke 4:18-19. They underline the fact that God is a just God and will not put up with injustice without taking action. Nor will He will ever give up on Jerusalem. Isaiah and his hearers would not witness the Babylonians ransacking Jerusalem in about 100 years time but he wants them to know that God will safeguard His favourite city before, during and after Israel is judged for its wickedness as God uses the Babylonians to work out His purposes. Even though His people have failed Him many times God will continue to be a faithful God.

Thinking Step

Is 61:1 -"...He has sent me to comfort the broken-hearted and to proclaim that captives will be released and prisoners will be freed." What significant words to a people who were to be carried away into Babylonian exile. The same words were then spoken by Jesus to a people who were 'imprisoned' in their own country by the Romans!

Action Step

63:17 – 'Lord, why have you allowed us to turn from your path? Why have you given us stubborn hearts so we no longer fear you? Return and help us, for we are your servants ...' When Isaiah was thinking of stubborn hearts it makes me think of the many times we are stubborn. We paint ourselves into a tight corner from which there is no escape except by the 'bridge of apology!' 63:17 implies it is all God's fault and none of it is ours. Of course it is usually the exact opposite. Having said that it doesn't stop us blaming everyone else rather than taking the blame ourselves. I know a man who when he was a child picked up a paint brush that his Dad had been using and painted part of the kitchen door. When his parents saw what had happened they challenged him about his misdemeanour. "It wasn't me, it was the cat!" was his reply – and he still sticks by that with a wry smile even though he recently became old enough to retire from work! Stubbornness can be a barrier in many relationships – human and Godly. Has the Holy Spirit just brought a specific to mind as you read this? If so why not build a 'bridge of apology' and start walking across it. Hardly anyone will refuse a genuine apology and God never does, so you have a good chance of making progress.

Day 212
Isaiah 64-66
31st July

64 - We Need Your Help Now
65 - We Need To Be Obedient People
66 - Believers Have Eternal Security

Only God Can Offer Real Security

The Big Picture

As we approach the end of this longest prophetical book in the Bible there is a sense of urgency as Isaiah pleads with the Israelites on God's behalf. He reminds them that God is the potter and they are only the clay. He reminds them that God is available to them and is waiting for them to turn to Him. The next move is theirs. All God demands is obedience and in return He offers security and protection. Deliberate sinners will be rejected but genuine believers will always be taken in by a God who loves them despite all their history of rebellion and their continued determination to go their own sinful way.

Thinking Step

66:3 – It's the thought that counts...
'When such people sacrifice a bull, it is no more acceptable than a human sacrifice. When they sacrifice a lamb, it's as though they had sacrificed a dog! When they bring an offering of grain, they might as well offer the blood of a pig. When they burn frankincense, it's as if they had blessed an idol.'

Action Step

By this time the northern tribes have been scattered by the invading Assyrians and the future looks bleak. Isaiah has prophesied clearly that Messiah will be sent by God and all believers will be safe but in the meantime their threatening powerful neighbours the Babylonians, will one day invade and take them away into exile. For the majority there will be no return. Only the remnant will come back. I wonder how many times the Israelites asked Isaiah "Why doesn't God do something now?" 64:12 – 'After all this Lord, must you still refuse to help us? Will you continue to be silent and punish us?' So often from our narrow viewpoint God does seem very slow to act. When we read the Bible there is a sense in which we get a glimpse of a Godly perspective as we see the beginning and the end and thereby begin to understand something of God's timetable. Isaiah had been told clearly by God that the Babylonians would take the Israelites into exile. Surely God owed them more than this! He didn't and He is not indebted to us either! Just be grateful that we have a loving Heavenly Father. Our God doesn't limit us to what we have earned or deserve but that would be justice. I'm glad He gives us what we haven't earned and what we don't deserve – that's grace!

Jeremiah

Jeremiah

The ministry of Jeremiah lasts about forty years beginning mid way through Josiah's reign. His prophetic role coincides with those of Zephaniah and Habakkuk. A little earlier Nahum has condemned the Assyrians years after their amazing revival under Jonah. Jeremiah prophesies when Daniel and Ezekiel are in Babylonia. He is commanded by God not to marry and undergoes many testings which see him tried in Jerusalem put in stocks and thrown into a cistern. The first half of his book consists of twelve sermons condemning Judah. It is his final sermon that confirms the exact length of the exile as 70 years – 25:11. His whole ministry can be split into three sections. His initial years of prophecy when Israel was threatened by Assyria and Egypt. His faithfulness to Judah when Babylonia attacks. Finally his loyalty to God's call right to the end as he ministered in Jerusalem after its downfall.

Below is an acrostic which summarises each chapter of the book.

1. **P**rophet Jeremiah is called
2. **R**eview of Jerusalem's apostasy
3. **O**ffer of God's pardon
4. **P**rediction of Judah's ruin
5. **H**orror of Judah's punishment
6. **E**nemy conquers from north
7. **C**ounterfeit worship of God
8. **I**nsensitivity toward Judah's sin
9. **E**xile and ruin foretold
10. **S**enselessness of idol worship

11. **O**utcome of Judah's disobedience
12. **F**airness of judgements questioned

13. **J**eremiah hides linen girdle
14. **E**xhortation about coming drought
15. **R**emnant is given instructions
16. **E**xile and return predicted
17. **M**isdirection of man's heart
18. **I**llustration from potter's house
19. **A**nnihilation of potter's vessel
20. **H**opelessness felt by Jeremiah

21. **O**verthrow of Jerusalem imminent
22. **N**ation of Judah warned

Day 213
Jeremiah 1-3
1st August

1 - Jeremiah's Call From God
2 - First Sermon Condemns Judah
3 - Second Sermon Promises Judgement

Jeremiah Is Called To Warn Judah

The Big Picture

Prophesying under five Kings of Judah, Jeremiah was called as a young man but warned by God to minister with confidence, to trust God and speak boldly. God shows him an almond tree to remind him that God is watching (both 'almond tree' and 'watching' sound very similar in Hebrew). God then shows him a pot of boiling water to warn him that armies from the north would boil over into Judah. Jeremiah also warns the people that they must turn from dead idols back to the Living God. God was saddened by Israel turning against Him and they paid the price as the Assyrians invaded. He implores Judah not to do the same thing but to return to Him.

Thinking Step

3:16 – '...you will no longer wish for 'the good old days' when you possessed the Ark of the Lord's Covenant...' No one knows what happened to the Ark but some believe it was smuggled away by priests when godless Manasseh was King. There is a theory that it could have been taken as far away as Ethiopia!

Action Step

1:6 – "O Sovereign Lord" I said "I can't speak for you! I'm too young!" Being young is acceptable to God! You don't have to wait until your hair goes grey or even until it just goes...! When you are chosen by God you are old enough. It is said of some young footballers "If they are good enough then they are old enough!" It doesn't seem so long ago that all children were expected to be 'seen and not heard' – how things have changed! Nowadays there is a brashness in some youth and I emphasise 'some' that is not attractive. Sadly much of it is encouraged by parents as they urge their offspring to be young adults rather than children. If I had my way all stickers in the backs of cars that declare 'small person on board' would be replaced with ones saying 'child on board'. The Bible has many instances of young people being called by God. Samuel and David to mention but two. This is not the same as pushing your children to be adults before they have been children. God does choose youngsters to do His work and we older ones must accept that. However this doesn't mean all children should be squeezed into adulthood before they have had the joy of being innocent children. As with so much in life, balance is required and should be encouraged.

Change While There Is Still Time!

The Big Picture

Everyone knows what is going to happen but Judah is acting like a load of children and pretending the worst will not come to be! God challenges the people through Jeremiah to find a just and honest person, and then He will cancel His destruction plans! Then He adds "I know you can't, all are liars and the leaders who should know better are just as bad as the people." Foreigners will overcome you because you have turned to foreign gods. Time has almost run out. It's too late to offer last minute sweet sacrifices. They are repugnant to God because they are coming from a people who are happy to be sinners and liars.

Thinking Step

6:23 – 'They are armed with bows and spears ...They sound like a roaring sea as they ride forward on horses. They are coming in battle formation, planning to destroy you beautiful Jerusalem.' Plenty of warning in those days! Firstly road repairers for the chariots then the troops who came to surround the city. Plenty of time to repent but they wouldn't!

Action Step

6:16 – 'This is what the Lord says "Stop at the crossroads and look around. Ask for the old Godly way and walk in it. Travel its path and you will find rest for your souls" but you reply "No that's not the road we want!"' I have a friend who regularly worked as an open air speaker. Over the years he has visited the same venues many times. On one occasion he was interrupted by a voice shouting "You said that last time don't you have anything new?" My friend responded by asking "If last time, I told you what I am convinced is true and then came this time and said I had changed my mind would you believe me, would I have credibility with you?" The man smiled as he conceded the point. Not that many years ago church services didn't change at all, the same choruses/hymns/organ and King James Bible! Nowadays I sometimes suspect that there are folk who think if it isn't new then it isn't relevant! I know a lady who was speaking in a school and was using what used to be called 'Flannelgraph' I think it has a more with-it name now! The kids were fascinated and the story she told made a great impact. There's nothing really new under the sun is there? So keep telling me the 'old, old story' but maybe in a new way occasionally!

Day 215
Jeremiah 7-10
3rd August

7 - The Temple Won't Save You
8 - The People Are Heading In The Wrong Direction
9 - Punishment Is Inevitable
10 - Leaders Have Failed - People Are Scattered

Beyond The Point Of No Return!

The Big Picture

God tells Jeremiah to go to the Temple entrance to give the people their final warning. They need to be reminded that the Temple won't save them just like the Tabernacle failed in Shiloh so long ago. Only listening to God and turning to Him in obedience will save them. The people have no idea what God expects from them because they constantly head in the wrong direction. God says that the people have ignored the law for so long their future is bound to be troublesome. They still hanker after the pagan practices of their neighbours. The shepherds of Israel have lost their senses too and their flock is scattered.

Thinking Step

Some traditions are hard to break! 7:31 – 'They have built pagan shrines at Topheth... there they burn their sons and daughters in the fire...'
This is the same general area in Gen. 22:2 – "Take your son, your only son – yes, Isaac, whom you love so much – and go to the land of Moriah. Go and sacrifice him as a burnt offering..."

Action Step

7:4 – '...don't be fooled by those who promise you safety simply because the Lord's Temple is here. They chant "The Lord's Temple is here! The Lord's Temple is here!"' This was a 'good luck chant' that was very acceptable to all Israel's neighbours but the children of the Living God were to be above that. It is however a good opportunity to ask ourselves the question "What are we trusting in today?" I recall visiting an ultra orthodox church in Ukraine where there was a distinct smell of incense and hardly a spare space on the wall that was not covered by an icon. We all stood as the worship was led in a language none of our party understood. As we left a couple of colleagues harshly commented "They need to get that place cleaned up and then they could be saved!" So what were my friends relying on I wonder? Clean, fragrant, unadorned walls and a proclamation in English only or the sacrifice of Jesus at Calvary! Some of us think the less we have in a place of worship the more inspiring it is. Some of us think the exact opposite. Our places of worship are very special to us but they do not save us. If we rely on the blood of Jesus then what is around us can hinder or aid our worship but will never save us – only Jesus can do that.

A Forgiving God And An Unrepentant People

The Big Picture

Sermon 4 tells us of plots against Jeremiah as he continues to declare the word of God. God confirms that He is a forgiving God and will even forgive the heathen nations around Israel if only they will repent and turn to Him. God teaches Jeremiah by using a new linen belt which Jeremiah wears and then hides by the river side. When he uncovers his belt later he finds it is rotten and God tells him that as the belt is rotting away, so must the pride of Judah. Other prophets try to moderate Jeremiah's message and dilute its impact but God confirms again that judgement is coming and nothing will stop it because Israel will not bend its knee.

Thinking Step

Chapter 13 tells us of the linen belt or sash that Jeremiah wears. It was the most intimate of garments worn next to the skin and taking on the shape of the wearer. God wanted His people to be equally close to Him and to 'take on His shape.' Unfortunately Israel had been influenced by pagan deities and reflected them.

Action Step

11:10 – 'They have returned to the sins of their forefathers. They have refused to listen to me and are worshipping other gods. Israel and Judah have both broken the covenant I made with their ancestors.' It came as a shock to me when I entered full time ministry at the age of 39. Of course as I have remarked previously when I say full time I mean paid! We are all full time. I was astounded that promises made by men and women of God were broken as easily as they were made. This approach is what God is condemning through Jeremiah. He is saying in effect "I can't believe a word Judah and Israel say!" Some time ago I was invited to teach at a large pentecostal church in London but a month or so beforehand I received an invitation to attend a large conference in the USA. Was I tempted to cancel my trip to London? I can honestly say "No I wasn't." It never entered my head. I had given my word and that was that. I mentioned my invitation to the USA when I was teaching in London and was amazed and saddened when their leaders told me that similar things happen regularly and usually the speaker cancels when something 'bigger/better' turns up! Are there promises in your life that you have broken? Repent today and resolve it will not happen again.

Day 217
Jeremiah 16-20
5th August

16 - Jeremiah Is To Remain Single
17 - Jeremiah Speaks At The City Gates
18 - Jeremiah Visits The Potter's Workshop
19 - Jeremiah Breaks A Pot As He Preaches
20 - Jeremiah Is Punished For His Faithfulness

Faithful Preacher – Go Away!

The Big Picture

There is so much sadness on its way that God tells Jeremiah not to marry and have children. God challenges Jeremiah to speak at the city gates as people enter and leave. Many of them are breaking the Sabbath and Jeremiah condemns their actions. Jeremiah visits a potter's workshop and buys a pot which he shatters after his next preaching to show the people that they will be shattered too for their wilful disobedience to God's law. Pashhur the priest in charge at the Temple has Jeremiah arrested and beaten. Upon his release Pashhur is renamed and told that when the Babylonians come he and his family will be removed to Babylonia and none of them will return.

Thinking Step

Magor-missabib – Of the seven occasions it's used in the Bible six of them are by Jeremiah. 20:3 and 20:10 are the instances where it's a proper name. The other times it is simply an expression that Jeremiah obviously likes. 6:25 – 20:3 – 46:5 – 49:29 and Lam. 2:22 (Ps.31:13 is the seventh!).

Action Step

We all have 'crosses to bear' but for some of us they are more public than for others. In the days of Jeremiah it was the norm for a man to have a wife and children. God makes it very clear that Jeremiah would have neither 16:1-2 – 'The Lord gave me another message. He said "Do not get married or have children in this place."' As Jeremiah was a young man Jer. 1:6, this was a big demand on him. I don't believe this is for everyone but Jeremiah knew it was specifically for him and he obeyed without question. Most of us have a 'thorn in the flesh' as the Apostle Paul did – 2 Cor.12:7. We are often tempted to ask "Why me?" There is no record of Jeremiah asking and as for the Apostle Paul, he knew why! A friend of mine was left deaf in one ear after a severe infection. I was trying to console him when he said "It could be worse, it could be the other one!" Of course I asked the obvious question and he relished in the reply. "My good one is the one I normally lie on so when my wife insists on talking instead of sleeping I don't hear her!" How are you dealing with your 'affliction?' Why not thank God for it and make it positive rather than negative!

Last Desperate Pleas By Judah Fail

The Big Picture

With our reading today we conclude the twelve sermons of Jeremiah addressed to Judah. When it is all too late help is sought from Jeremiah as Nebuchadnezzar attacks. God confirms through His prophet "It is too late!" The Kingdom is in tatters and God tells His people to surrender to Babylonia and go into exile where they will be safe for their seventy year sentence. Many ignore this final plea and are badly cared for by the weak leadership and false prophets of the day. Jeremiah sees a vision of two baskets of figs. One filled with good figs, the other filled with rotting figs. The good have gone into exile and the bad ones are still in Jerusalem!

Thinking Step

Nebuchadnezzar is mentioned in the Bible over 90 times and had a very important role to play. A team of archaeologists was commissioned to restore the city of Babylon and its Hanging Gardens, in present day Iraq. They discovered that such was the ego of Nebuchadnezzar every brick had been inscribed with his name.

Action Step

23:29 – "Does not my word burn like fire?" says the Lord. "Is it not like a mighty hammer that smashes a rock to pieces?" When you consider how much criticism has been levelled at the Bible over the past centuries, particularly the last couple, it is truly astounding that it is still seen by millions around the world as the true living word of God Himself! Our reading today reminds us that the Scriptures are both powerful and all-conquering. Of course lots of criticism seems to come from a lack of evidence. In other words if archaeologists don't find evidence to corroborate the Bible then the Bible is inaccurate! We seem to have different criteria when history is being tested. I was listening to the radio recently, to a programme about that great Queen of the Iceni, Boudicca. I was astounded to hear one of the professors who specialised in Boudicca openly admit that there is no hard evidence that she ever lived! The presenter of the programme was as shocked as me and asked for confirmation of what had just been said. He was happy to confirm it and add to the confusion by saying that no accurate site of her famous last battle with the Romans has ever been confirmed! Nevertheless we all accept that there was such a Queen! Our Bible is far more reliable. Thank God for it, read it, believe it and live it!

Day 219
Jeremiah 26-29
7th August

26 - Jeremiah's Life In Danger
27 - Jeremiah Wears A Yoke
28 - Jeremiah's Yoke Is Broken
29 - Jeremiah Writes To All Exiles

Jeremiah's Final Warnings

The Big Picture

God tells Jeremiah to speak again right next to the Temple. The crowd revolts but Jeremiah simply confirms that what he is saying is what God has told him to say. As a visual aid Jeremiah wears a wooden yoke to signify that Judah will wear the yoke of Babylonia and they had better get used to the idea. Hananiah tells the people that they will be free within two years and breaks the yoke that Jeremiah is wearing. Jeremiah challenges what this opposing prophet is declaring and is proved right as Hananiah pays for his false prophecy with his life! Jeremiah sends a letter to all the exiles telling them to settle in exile and be fruitful.

Thinking Step

There are 14 Hananiah's in the Bible. It means 'Yahweh has been gracious.' Sadly they didn't all live up to the name. The Hananiah in chapter 28 failed to honour his name but there was to be one who was a shining example – he's in Dan. 1:7 and better known as Shadrach with his friends Meshach and Abed-nego.

Action Step

29:11 – "For I know the plans I have for you" says the Lord. "They are plans for good and not for disaster, to give you a future and a hope." Of course these plans were specifically for those exiled in Babylonia but I believe may be taken as general confirmation from God that He always has positive plans like this for His people and that includes you and me. Have you ever been to a meeting where a testimony is being given and it goes something like this "I told God I would go anywhere for Him but I pleaded, please not a cold place I would prefer a beach mission in Hawaii and He sent me as a 'street evangelist' in Siberia!" Of course I made this up but I have heard very similar ones! I don't believe God works like that. I believe we should enjoy what we do for Him. So are you up or down at the moment? If you're up then enjoy! If you are down look forward to being up later! Remember that Jesus came to give us life in all its fullness so there will be ups and downs but if you are not enjoying life at the moment ask God why. If it's your fault then take the necessary action. If it's not then ask God what you are to learn from this experience then be obedient and proceed upwards!

30 - God's Written Return Guarantee   Day 220
31 - God's Promise Of A New Covenant   Jeremiah 30-32
32 - Jeremiah's Faith In The Return   8th August

God's New Covenant Is Promised

The Big Picture

God told Jeremiah to write down what He was going to tell him. "This exile has to be endured but you will survive." God added "I don't enjoy what is happening to My people now but they brought it all on themselves through disobedience!" God then tells Jeremiah to let the people know that He will make a new covenant with them even though their fathers broke the old one. This is a very early glimpse from Jeremiah about the coming Messiah and His new covenant. Towards the end of the reign of Zedekiah, Jeremiah is imprisoned but even as a captive he buys a plot of land to show his faith in God's promise that the people will return.

Thinking Step

32:9 – Jeremiah buys a plot of land from a relative in Anathoth (his home town – 1:1). All in accordance with Lev. 25:25. In Ezra 2:23 we learn that 128 men returned to Anathoth when the exile ended and Zerubbabel led the first group of returnees back to the Promised Land – just as God had promised Jeremiah.

Action Step

Did it ever irritate you when your parents told you that you would understand when you were older? As adults of course we understand that some things can't be understood by children and explanations are sometimes not possible. However in 30:24 God treats the Children of Israel as adults! We read what Jeremiah said would happen after the exile – 'The fierce anger of the Lord will not diminish until it has finished all He has planned. In the days to come you will understand all this.' I have often been told that prayer changes things but in this case it wouldn't! Israel had to experience God's judgement and then in the end they would understand why and they did! Often when we pray we should pray not for things to change but for us to change. Whatever you are going through now, when you pray ask God to help you understand – rather than asking God to change His plans. In the days of Jeremiah he was certain that when God promised a return from exile that is exactly what would happen. He didn't see it himself but nevertheless God honoured His promise and He will do the same for you. Our Father doesn't make promises to break He only makes them to keep! Just like Jeremiah you need to believe this for your own good.

Day 221
Jeremiah 33-36
9th August

33 - Jeremiah Confirms His Prophecy From Prison
34 - Freed Slaves Are Enslaved Again
35 - Recabites Are Fine Examples
36 - Jehoiakim Destroys Scroll Of Jeremiah

Don't Ever Say You Weren't Warned!

The Big Picture

Whilst still in prison Jeremiah affirms the truth of all he has prophesied. He warns Zedekiah that he will be taken by the Babylonians and that God is disgusted by the way slaves who have been given freedom are now being enslaved again even though the city is surrounded by the enemy. Jeremiah thinks back to when Jehoiakim was King and how the Recabites were so faithful to the commandments of their ancestors whilst Israel made no effort to be faithful to God. Baruch takes a freshly written scroll from Jeremiah and reads it to the leaders and to the King himself who destroys it. A new one is prepared but this time it is even longer!

Thinking Step

I recently read about an archaeological dig when fifty clay document seals were discovered. They had been baked in the fierce heat of a fire which the Babylonians had created in Jerusalem in Jeremiah's time. One of them bears the name of 'Gemariah son of Shaphan' – unquestionably the same one who heard Baruch read Jeremiah's scroll – 36:11-15.

Action Step

If at first you don't succeed, try again! This is a saying that I have heard many times from my childhood right through to today. We see a graphic example of this resolve in today's reading 36:32 – 'So Jeremiah took another scroll and dictated again to his secretary Baruch. He wrote everything that had been on the scroll King Jehoiakim had burned in the fire. Only this time he added much more!' How many times have you heard it said especially in churches "We tried that before and it didn't work!" This response is usually an excuse for inactivity. Did you notice in the reading that Jeremiah did a more thorough job the second time? Does that mean practice makes perfect? No, otherwise I would have been the best snooker player in the world when I was eighteen! Practice can however, improve performance! Is there something in your life today that you failed with some time ago and then resolved not to waste time on anymore? Maybe the Holy Spirit wants you to try again. It was Thomas Edison who said "I have not failed. I've just found 10,000 ways that won't work." So no more excuses. If God is asking you to try again with your marriage, your ministry, your family or anything else, then try again but this time with the Holy Spirit's help – it could be so much better than last time!

37 - Jeremiah Thrown Into Prison
38 - Jeremiah Thrown Into A Cistern
39 - Jeremiah Is A Free Man

Day 222
Jeremiah 37-39
10th August

In And Out Of Prisons,
Then Freedom For Jeremiah

The Big Picture

Jeremiah looks back to a brief period of respite as the Babylonians temporarily retreat and he tries to visit his recently purchased land in Anathoth. Suspecting he could be defecting to Babylonia he was arrested and imprisoned but then transferred to the palace prison at the request of Zedekiah. After escaping a possible death sentence and a brief episode in an empty cistern Jeremiah is returned to prison where he remains until Jerusalem falls. In the chaos caused as the Babylonians enter the city, Zedekiah tries to escape but is captured and forced to witness the murder of his sons before being blinded and taken away to Babylon. The invading Babylonians respect Jeremiah and planned to look after him well.

Thinking Step

38:7-13 – Ebed-melech risks all as he trusts a prophet of the God of Israel. In Isaiah's prophecy about 100 years earlier the prophet spoke out in favour of eunuchs in chapter 56, despite them being outlawed in Deut. 23:1. Years later in Acts 8 we find another Ethiopian eunuch. He trusts the Messiah of the God of Israel.

Action Step

Zedekiah is like a lot of people in the Bible and in the world today, they turn to God when they are in trouble but then turn away from Him when the trouble goes away. It has been said that there are very few atheists in a crashing aeroplane! Most people would say that it's always worth saying a prayer just in case! I had a good friend who was given the gift of healing and exercised it with great empathy and wisdom. He told me that he had a regular visitor to see him over several years. She was a professional singer who suffered from a throat disorder which her doctor couldn't cure. Each time she came to see my friend he prayed with her and she was healed only to come back when the problem re-appeared later. "Could it just be that God is not healing you permanently because you are not taking Him seriously" she was asked. Her response was that she didn't want to take God too seriously because of the demands He might make on her. So she preferred to keep Him at arms length, so to speak. I am sure there was something of this with Zedekiah – but what about you? Don't keep God at arms length welcome Him into your heart. He ALWAYS has the best for you. If you need more information on where to start please check Day 21 reading.

Day 223
Jeremiah 40-45
11th August

40 - Jeremiah Remains Faithful To His Call
41 - Governor Gedaliah Is Assassinated
42 - Judah's Remnant Advised To Stay
43 - Judah's Remnant Goes To Egypt
44 - You're Not Safe In Egypt!
45 - Comfort For Baruch

Jeremiah Is Faithful To The End

The Big Picture

Gedaliah is appointed Governor and Jeremiah remains in Judah. Civil war erupts as Gedaliah and his officials are assassinated by Ishmael who in turn is replaced by Johanan. Both of these last two men were originally part of the group who met with Gedaliah soon after he was appointed Governor – 40:8. Johanan approaches Jeremiah asking him to consult God on the people's behalf and assured him that they would do whatever God said. Jeremiah tells them that God said they are to remain in Judah. They subsequently leave for Egypt! Jeremiah continues with them and ministers in Egypt but they are adamant that they know best and will not turn back to the God of their fathers.

Thinking Step

'Queen of Heaven' is found five times in Jeremiah – all in chapter 44. Centuries later we find another pagan goddess with the same title when the Apostle Paul confronts worshippers of Artemis in Acts 19. The Greek Artemis was replaced by the Roman Diana but the title remained 'Queen of Heaven.' Later the virgin Mary inherited the title.

Action Step

44:16-17 – "We will not listen to your messages from the Lord! We will do whatever we want... For in those days (previously) we had plenty to eat and we were well off and had no troubles!" Many people today are convinced that religion is the root of all the world's troubles and if we lived in a truly secular society then all would be well! Well the people of Judah weren't exactly saying "Lets reject God for no-god" but they were saying they preferred 'false-god.' They wanted to do their own thing and not be dictated to. I once talked to a lady at Church and she said that she enjoyed attending meetings but did not appreciate the preacher telling her how to live her life! I wonder if you are harking back to the good old days. If you are then stop it! You are where you are and God still loves you and wants you to get the most out of your life. Rather than looking back through 'rose tinted' specs why not look forward through 'blood covered' specs and trust that the sacrifice of Jesus was not only all you need but is the best option by far!

46 - Judgement Is Coming, Egypt
47 - Judgement Is Coming, Philistia
48 - Judgement Is Coming, Moab
49 - Judgement Is Coming, Ammon

Day 224
Jeremiah 46-49
12th August

God Hasn't Finished With Any Of You Yet!

The Big Picture

This current section of Jeremiah is addressed to the majority of gentile neighbouring nations who are well aware of the threat that Nebuchadnezzar poses to them all. Jeremiah warns all of them that they are helpless against the mighty armies of Babylonia. He warns Egypt which is a powerful nation in its own right, that they will fall to Babylonia too. The same fate will overcome the Philistines, the Moabites, the Ammonites, the Edomites and the inhabitants of that ancient city of Damascus. Kedar, Hazor and Elam are also doomed because God is allowing the armies of Nebuchadnezzar to be His instrument as He judges the nations.

Thinking Step

What a geography lesson! Ammon and Moab on the east bank of the Jordan river, Hazor north of the Sea of Galilee, Egypt in north Africa, Kedar (Jordan, Syria and Iraq) and Elam (Iran). At the centre is a strip of land called Israel linking these nations together in history and still at the centre of the world stage today.

Action Step

Do you ever feel as though you are the only believer in your neighbourhood or office or even family? When you read today's chapters with all those foreign lands surrounding that small family of God's people, could you empathise with them? I was in hospital recently and my wife stayed with me for most of the time as I was 'wired up' following a heart attack that required a stent procedure. When I was left on my own I wondered where the next believer was or even if there was another one in the hospital. I took the opportunity to read more than usual and was reading the Bible and referring to a commentary on a particular passage when in came someone who wanted to scan my heart with one of those clever laptop gizmo's that make you wonder what we did before computers. "Oh I am sorry to disturb you when you are studying the Scriptures" she said. Unbelievers don't use language like that do they and sure enough she was a real believer. We discussed the pros and cons of particular churches as she had just moved house and was settling into a new fellowship. We even found time to talk about my stent! Then we prayed and she left. I think we encouraged each other that afternoon. Who do you think you will be able to encourage today? Keep on the look out – you are not alone!

Day 225
Jeremiah 50-52
13th August

50 - Jeremiah Thrown Into Prison
51 - Jeremiah Thrown Into A Cistern
52 - Jeremiah Is A Free Man

Jerusalem Falls But Babylonia Will Be Judged

The Big Picture

Finally a word for the all-conquering Babylonians who actually only dominated their part of the world for a little over seventy years. God declared that they would fall and His people would return. Jeremiah prophesies the coming of the Medes from the north, who along with the Persians in the south would eventually set the Jews free to return. Jeremiah's message was written on a scroll tied to a stone and then thrown into the Euphrates river to sink – just as Babylon would. The final chapter of this book summarises one of the saddest events in Jewish history, it covers the account of the fall of Jerusalem and the destruction of the Temple (chapter 38 parallels much of this).

Thinking Step

After the death of Nebuchadnezzar his empire lasted just 23 years more before falling to Persia's Cyrus. Nebuchadnezzar's immediate successor was his son Amel-Marduk who was nicknamed 'Evil-merodach' in 52:31. Nevertheless he was praised for his treatment of Jehoiachin in exile. His benevolence was recorded on a tablet recently recovered from the Ishtar Gate excavations in Babylon.

Action Step

Have you ever heard people say "How much easier it would have been to believe if I could have been in contact with some of the greats of the Bible, if I could have experienced a miracle or heard the actual words spoken, then my faith would have been so much stronger!" Yes I have heard that too but frankly I don't believe it for a minute. You can scour the Bible and read of people who rubbed shoulders with the greatest Bible characters but were still not convinced. What about Zedekiah for instance? During his lifetime Ezekiel and Daniel were ministering in exile to the people of Judah and nearer home, Jeremiah constantly spoke God's words in Jerusalem, often directly to Zedekiah himself. So why wasn't he persuaded? I believe it's usually not an emotional or intellectual issue it's a matter of the will. We need the work of the Holy Spirit in our lives of course but we also need to 'bow the knee.' When I hear folk say that they have intellectual problems with some Biblical matters I have to say that I often substitute 'obedience' for the word 'intellectual.' Of course that's not always the case but I am convinced that 'obedience issues' far outnumber the 'intellectual ones'! Do you have a sticky problem? Try asking God to help you make sense of it then determine that you WILL be persuaded!

Lamentations

Lamentations

Probably written by Jeremiah, some even refer to it as 2nd Jeremiah! Obviously written by an eye witness to the tragedy and Jeremiah was there when the city fell. It is in memory of a once great city Jerusalem, which has just died. It is written as a series of acrostics for easier memorising. Chapters 1,2,4 and 5 each has 22 verses one for each letter of the Hebrew alphabet. Chapter 3 has three times as many verses with three for each Hebrew letter. The major themes are firstly mourning over a desolate city, then acknowledgement that God was right and finally hope for the future which is in the hands of a faithful God. Jeremiah was often called the weeping prophet and that part of his character is clearly seen in these poems and was reflected in Jesus Christ as He looked over the same city centuries later.

Below is an acrostic which summarises each chapter of the book.

1. **D**esolation of Jerusalem announced
2. **I**srael's misery is lamented
3. **R**eminder of God's mercy
4. **G**rimness of Israel's sin
5. **E**xiles pray for mercy

1 - Jerusalem Is Justly Destroyed
2 - God Is Rightly Angered
3 - Mercy Is Sought From God
4 - Jerusalem Under Siege
5 - The People Seek God's Mercy

Day 226
Lamentations 1-5
14th August

O Jerusalem, Jerusalem, Why?

The Big Picture

It all begins with an eye witness account of what the city looked like after Nebuchadnezzar had finished with it! It's not as if God didn't warn them! He warned them and offered them many opportunities to repent. The people brought this on themselves. At the centre of the book we have 3:22-24 – 'The faithful love of the Lord never ends! His mercies never cease. Great is His faithfulness, His mercies begin afresh each morning... I will hope in Him!' The siege brought the worst out of the people and they sank low but finally triumphantly 5:21 – 'Restore us O Lord and bring us back to you again! Give us back the joys we once had!'

Thinking Step

In synagogues, 5:v21 is often repeated for a positive finish!
v21 – 'Restore us O Lord and bring us back to you again!
        Give us back the joys we once had!'
v22 – 'Or have you utterly rejected us? Are you angry with us still?'
v21 – 'Restore us O Lord and bring us back to you again!
        Give us back the joys we once had!'

Action Step

Crying, or more accurately weeping, is a very beneficial thing. In our society today shedding tears over sport or dramatic songs is acceptable but in church it is often seen as emotionalism rather than emotion! The ancient Jews used tear cups to collect tears and on the Mount of Olives there is a church built to commemorate Jesus weeping over the city of Jerusalem. It was designed in the shape of a teardrop and is called the 'Dominus Flevit' – literally 'the cry of the Lord.' So many times we see tears as signs of weakness but they are often signs of strength. When Jeremiah was weeping for Jerusalem it was out of love and frustration, it was not because he was a weak man. Scientists tell us that tears of sadness remove toxins from the body. In ancient days funerals always had a group of professional wailers to lead the weeping. The act of weeping helped the bereaved to recover quickly and more effectively. How long is it since you really wept? Perhaps the Holy Spirit is convicting you even now to repent of something in your life. If it results in you weeping – all the better. If it doesn't perhaps it should have done.

Ezekiel

Ezekiel

Ezekiel is a special name which means 'God strengthens' and this is probably why it is never changed to a Babylonian one as happened with many others. His name is unique and is found nowhere else in the Bible. His ministry ran parallel with Daniel who started a little earlier and finished a little later. Ezekiel was probably part of the deportation to Babylon in 2 Kings 24:14 when he was still a young man. His book opens with his call and his preparation by God. God gives him signs of the impending judgement on Judah. This dominates the first half of the book. Ezekiel then pronounces judgement on the Gentile nations who had been condemned earlier in Jeremiah's prophecies. In an amazing visual way Ezekiel then reveals the restoration of Israel with the famous 'dry bones' vision. He foretells that God's people will return to the Promised Land.

Below is an acrostic which summarises each chapter of the book.

1. **T**hrone vision of Ezekiel
2. **H**earing of God's call
3. **E**ndowment of God's Spirit

4. **P**ortrayal of Jerusalem's judgement
5. **R**easons for God's judgement
6. **O**bliteration of high places
7. **P**owerless Israel against God
8. **H**orror in Israel's temple
9. **E**xecution of Jerusalem's idolaters
10. **C**herubim seen leaving temple
11. **I**dolatrous leaders are judged
12. **E**nactment of Israel's captivity
13. **S**tatement against false prophets

14. **O**rder to forsake idols
15. **F**ire to consume Jerusalem

16. **E**xamples of spiritual prostitution
17. **Z**edekiah rebels against Babylon
18. **E**ach person held responsible
19. **K**ingdom lies in captivity
20. **I**srael's history of rebellion
21. **E**xecutioner's sword over Jerusalem
22. **L**egal case against Jerusalem

23. Assyrians and Babylonians coming
24. Boiling pot pictures judgement
25. Other surrounding nations judged
26. Utter destruction of Tyre
27. Tyre lamented for desolation

28. Judgement of Tyre's King
29. Egypt will become desolate
30. Ruthless Babylon destroys Egypt
31. Undoing of Pharaoh's kingdom
32. Slaying of Pharaoh's army
33. Admonition not to sin
34. Lessons for the shepherds
35. Exaltation over Edom's desolation
36. Miraculous restoration of Israel

37. Announcement of Israel's return
38. Nations allied with Gog
39. Destruction of Gog predicted

40. Temple vision of Ezekiel
41. Holy place is measured
42. Expanse of the temple

43. Temple filled with glory
44. Excluding some from temple
45. Mandates regarding the prince
46. Preparation of the offerings
47. Land boundaries of Israel
48. Endowment of Israel's land

1 - Ezekiel's Call With Visions

2 - Ezekiel Commissioned

3 - Ezekiel Consumes The Word Of God

4 - Ezekiel's Left-Side And Right-Side

5 - The People Will Be Scattered

6 - The High Places Will Be Scattered

Day 227

Ezekiel 1-6

15th August

God Calls And Equips Ezekiel

The Big Picture

Ezekiel is in exile with many of the Israelites when God appears to him and shows him visions of strange creatures which move around on wheels which are hard to visualise. Ezekiel is told to prophesy to the Israelites and given a special scroll which he has to eat! God next tells Ezekiel to lie on his left side for 390 days! Then to turn over to his right side for 40 days. What an amazing visual impact this must have had! Ezekiel is to have a haircut and shave next and use the hair to show what will happen to Jerusalem. What great visual aids – so memorable. Lastly all worship at High Places must stop immediately!

Thinking Step

The figures in 4:4-6 could refer to the 390 years since the Divided Kingdom when Israel split away from Judah and 40 years since Judah rejected the words of God through Jeremiah. Their total of 430 years also coincides with the years spent in Egypt – Ex.12:40. During both periods God was rejected or forgotten by His people.

Action Step

3:11 – 'Then go to your people in exile and say to them "This is what the Sovereign Lord says!" Do this whether they listen to you or not.' We've all been in church when the only one who seems to be listening to the preacher is the preacher, haven't we? Well this is not a license for such behaviour to continue! As speakers or preachers we have a duty to be as interesting as possible and to engage our listeners until they are hearers and doers of the Word. I believe God was reminding Ezekiel and all of us today that there are sometimes things we don't want to hear but we need to hear them for our own benefit. Politicians are often criticised for not telling us the truth but when they do we are tempted to vote the other way. Preachers are encouraged to be open and honest but only if it doesn't offend us! I know pastors who rely on itinerant preachers to come and speak on tithing and church discipline because they fear what will happen if they do it themselves! Of course this does not mean we can say what we like without thought or tact. Balance is something we need to seek everyday. Nevertheless Ezekiel was told to tell the truth no matter what. Dare we do any less today?

Day 228
Ezekiel 7-11
16th August

7 - The End Is Here For Judah
8 - Visionary Journey To Jerusalem
9 - Jerusalem - City Of Rebellion
10 - Cherubim In The Temple
11 - Jerusalem Is Unsafe For Now

Jerusalem In A Vision

The Big Picture

Already some have been taken away into exile and more will follow soon. The year after his first vision Ezekiel has another but this time he is taken away from Babylonia to visit the Temple in Jerusalem. He sees an idol in the Temple and many people worshipping idols including some who are worshipping the sun. He experiences similar beings to those he saw in his first vision. Ezekiel reminds the leaders in the Temple that Jerusalem is not a safe city now but in time all of them will be reunited and returned to Jerusalem as God has always promised.

Thinking Step

10:14 – 'Each of the four cherubim had four faces, the first was the face of an ox the second was a human face the third was the face of a lion and the fourth was the face of an eagle.' These were previously seen in 1:10. Similar beings are in Rev 4:7 when the Apostle John sees the judgement throne.

Action Step

11:19-20 – "...I will give them singleness of heart and put a new spirit within them. I will take away their stony stubborn heart and give them a tender responsive heart so they will obey my decrees and regulations. Then they will truly be my people and I will be their God." What a wonderful reminder of the love of God. This was directly for those who would return after the exile but is equally appropriate for us today. The order of events is so significant:-

1. God gives us one heart.
2. God puts a new Spirit within us.
3. God takes away our stony stubborn heart.
4. God gives us a tender responsive heart.
5. We are obedient.
6. God recognises us as His people.

We only have number 5 to do for our heavenly Father! He does all the others. How significant it's number 5 as that's the commandment to honour our earthly parents in the 10 commandments and the only one that includes a promise! The God of Ezekiel makes His promise to each of us today. What a great chance now to ask God to give us a tender responsive heart. This is more than a wise action it is an act of obedience so that you can deal with a special someone today better than you did yesterday and only you and God knows who it is!

Exile Is Coming – You Better Believe It!

The Big Picture

Further messages come from God and Ezekiel is told to pack his belongings as if he was about to go into exile and then leave it in full view of all passers by. He was then to pick up his belongings and break through a wall as a sign of leaving the city for another country. This would be exactly what would happen to Judah and its King Zedekiah. False prophets are once again condemned as they declare peace when it isn't going to happen! The leaders are told that it is the end of the road for all of them and even the righteousness of Noah, Daniel and Job can not save them from their deserved fate.

Thinking Step

14:14 – 'Even if Noah, Daniel and Job were there, their righteousness would save no one but themselves, says the Sovereign Lord.' Noah a non Jewish righteous man – Gen. 6:9, Daniel, so Jewish he would not accept his Babylonian name – Dan 1:7 and non Jewish Job of whom God said "...he is blameless and upright" – Job 1:8!

Action Step

In chapter 13 of Ezekiel we have a rare usage of the word translated 'whitewash' and he uses it 5 times! There is one record of it being used in the NT and that is in Matt. 23:27 – "What sorrow awaits you teachers of religious law and you Pharisees. Hypocrites! For you are like whitewashed tombs – beautiful on the outside but filled on the inside with dead people's bones and all sorts of impurity." Both Ezekiel and Jesus disliked whitewash because it only covered bad things up rather than repair or replace them permanently. We can turn over as many new leaves as we like, we can make as many vows and promises to change as we dare but unless we are changed inside all the 'whitewash in the world' won't do the job. One of the main criticisms of the church today which is regularly quoted by those who don't attend, is that it is full of hypocrites. Whenever I hear this I have to admit I am tempted to say "That's fine because it means there is room for another one – you!" There is the 'hypocrite' in all of us and we need to be aware of it. Has something just sprung to mind in your life? Ask God to forgive you for that bit of hypocrisy in you and also to give you the grace to understand it in others this week.

Day 230
Ezekiel 16-19
18th August

16 - God Is Like A Parent And A Husband
17 - God Condemns Covenant Breaking
18 - Each Person Is Responsible To God
19 - A Funeral Song To Sing As The Funeral Begins

We're All Personally Responsible

The Big Picture

Another message came to Ezekiel when God told him to remind the people that it was God who gave them birth as a nation and as an individual. God has been like a parent and a husband to them but they still insist on prostituting themselves. God condemns them for making a covenant with Babylonia and at the first opportunity turning to Egypt in the hope that they would help them break it. God confirms that every individual is responsible for their own sins. If a righteous man has a wicked son and then a righteous grandson – each will be judged according to his deeds. God stressed that He wants ALL to repent and live.

Thinking Step

Sin is personal but cannot be limited to a single person's lifetime!
18:20 – 'The one who sins is the one who dies ...' but the consequences of sin can take generations to disappear – Ex 34:7 – '...the entire family is affected – even children in the third and fourth generations.'

Action Step

Have you ever heard people say "What sort of a God is it who sends people to hell?" Well look at 18:32 – "I don't want you to die, says the Sovereign Lord. Turn back and live!" Let's be accurate on this, it is never God who sends people to hell it is the individual person who decides not to accept God's offer of salvation! The opposite side of this argument is expressed by those who wonder why a loving God will only let some people into heaven. Surely He would let everyone in if He loved us so much! The major point to meet both sides of this debate is ultimately 'who decides?' There are those who put the onus onto God Himself but I don't believe He limits the number, if John 3:16 is to be believed when we read that 'God so loved the WORLD...i.e. everyone. I believe mankind limits how many will get into Heaven. It's all a matter of grace and accepting what is on offer. Ezekiel tells the people who are about to be judged very severely and taken into exile, that God doesn't want any to die – He wants all to turn back (repent) and live. Just like in the past, today the choice is yours. Remember YOU choose. For more help take a look at reading 21 which we covered on Jan. 21st. Choose wisely your whole future depends on it.

318

20 - Look Back At God's Faithfulness
21 - The Exile Is Inevitable
22 - God Will Consume All The Slag

Day 231
Ezekiel 20-22
19th August

God Is Reliable – Just As He Was In The Past

The Big Picture

Once again some of the leaders come to see Ezekiel to ask him to consult God on their behalf. The response from God is very abrupt "How dare you come to ask for help?" The rest of the chapter is then a brief Walk Through of God's provision beginning in Egypt but the leaders have trouble understanding the point God is trying to make when Ezekiel uses prophetic language! Despite their covenant with Babylonia God tells them that Jerusalem will be attacked because they previously didn't keep their word and went instead to Egypt for help. Within the city of Jerusalem God's laws continue to be flouted and the leaders are amongst the greatest offenders.

Thinking Step

In 22:18-22 the emphasis is on the worthless slag that remains (in Judah) rather than the precious metal (those who will return from exile). This agrees with the earlier parable of the figs in Jer. 24 which also proclaimed blessings for the returners and not those who disobeyed and remained in Judah. More accurate prophecy from Jeremiah.

Action Step

22:30 – "I looked for someone who might rebuild the wall of righteousness that guards the land. I searched for someone to stand in the gap in the wall so I wouldn't have to destroy the land but I found no one." I would be a wealthy man if I had a £1 for every sermon I have heard using this text in order to recruit another Sunday School teacher or someone to help with the coffee rota! We need to be reminded that we serve a victorious God and that it is both a privilege to serve Him and the best way to live. Too often we are in 'maintenance mode' trying to keep things going, trying to get someone who will 'fill the gap.' I believe we have trouble getting people to operate within the church of God because too often the programme we are following is ours and not God's. If God doesn't supply the labour or the materials then it could be that He wants us to do something else instead! I am not advocating sitting back and waiting for everything to fall into our lap but I am suggesting we make sure God is at the very centre of our plans and then trusting Him to supply all we need to achieve it, with the help of the Holy Spirit and then getting on with it victoriously.

Day 232
Ezekiel 23-26
20th August

23 - God Likens Samaria And Jerusalem To Prostitutes
24 - Ezekiel's Wife Dies But There Is No Mourning
25 - Judgement On Ammon, Moab, Edom And Philistia
26 - Tyre Punished When Jerusalem Falls

Justified Punishment For Many Nations

The Big Picture

God discusses his two brides Oholah and Oholibah or Samaria and Jerusalem as we normally call them. He describes them as wanton prostitutes and tells Ezekiel to accuse them both of unfaithfulness with Oholibah being the worst. Ezekiel is then told to boil some meat in a pot and include all the bones. He then empties the pot and destroys the meat, bones and eventually the pot itself. All indicating what will happen when the Babylonian army will invade. Then Ezekiel's wife dies. We don't know her name and we learn that God tells Ezekiel that there will be no mourning and this will be the norm for all when tragedy hits as the Babylonians invade.

Thinking Step

23:4 – 'The older girl was named Oholah and her sister was Oholibah...' "Oholah represented the 10-tribe Kingdom with its capital at Samaria. Her name can be rendered 'Her Tent' because she rejected Jehovah's law and authority. "Oholibah" means "My Tent Is In Her" indicating God's true people were included in Jerusalem and the 2-tribes of the south.

Action Step

Some of the prophets had very difficult times in their lives and this one is amongst the hardest. 24:16-18 – '"Son of man, with one blow I will take away your dearest treasure. Yet you must not show any sorrow at her death. Do not weep, let there be no tears. Groan silently but let there be no wailing at her grave. Do not uncover your head or take off your sandals. Do not perform the usual rituals of mourning or accept any food brought to you by consoling friends." So I proclaimed this to the people the next morning and in the evening my wife died. The next morning I did everything I had been told to do.' To lose your wife is a tragedy but not to be allowed to mourn would be extremely hard to bear. Of course the Bible tells us more about why Ezekiel went through this trauma if we read further into the chapter. In our lives too we have very sad and trying times to experience and I have heard it said that as Christians we should be joyful at funerals when the world around us is mourning. I don't agree. Jesus wept over Lazarus and we may too. I think we Brits take the stiff upper lip a little too far sometimes! I believe Ezekiel was a special case and not the norm. We are allowed to be upset sometimes!

27 - Funeral Song For Tyre
28 - King Of Tyre Put In His Place
29 - King Of Egypt Put In His Place
30 - Cities Of Egypt Ransacked

Day 233
Ezekiel 27-30
21st August

Then They Will Know That I Am The Lord

The Big Picture

God tells Ezekiel to mourn for the city of Tyre and sing a funeral song in her honour. There is also a message for the King of Tyre who is told to remember who he is. He is not as wise as Daniel and he is most certainly not God! The neighbouring city of Sidon is also warned of God's coming judgement. Egypt is condemned for not helping Israel in the past when God's people were in need of some support. Pharaoh is told that many of Egypt's magnificent cities will be much the worse for wear after Nebuchadnezzar and his armies have attacked and ransacked them.

Thinking Step

Have you noticed how many times Ezekiel quotes God saying "Then they will know that I am the Lord." In the NLT version of the Bible which we are primarily using in this book there are 44 instances with 36 of them in Ezekiel! Ezekiel really wanted everyone to see God for who He is and then to acknowledge Him.

Action Step

It's amazing how many times 'mother nature' is credited with praise when it should have been God's! So many people look at the creation and worship it rather than worshipping its creator. There is a multitude of signs and indications of God but there are also very many individuals who are so blind that they do not see! If we constantly look for the creator in our lives we will see Him often. If we ignore Him but just look at what He has made then we will be amazed how powerful and full of variety 'mother nature' can be!!! Are you very observant? I'm not but if I 'look' I tend to see more. I read recently that very few people see above first floor level because they never raise their heads. Make a special effort to seek our God today and you will be surprised at how many things you will see that cannot be explained without a creator. There are so many signs of a designer in our wonderful world that I am shocked more people don't see them. Ezekiel reminded his hearers in exile and all those still in Judah that there is much evidence for God if only we will look. God repeated Himself many times through Ezekiel – "Then they will know that I am the Lord." Look out for signs today and then you will know!

Day 234
Ezekiel 31-33
22nd August

31 - Egypt is Heading for Failure Just like Assyria
32 - Egypt is Not the Giant She Thinks She Is
33 - Ezekiel is The Watchman for Israel as Jerusalem Falls

Don't Fail To Tell Them Everything Ezekiel

The Big Picture

Assyria was a great powerful nation for a while. God brought it down. Egypt thinks it's an even more powerful nation but they will fall just the same, they are not impregnable. Their conquerors Babylonia, will do as God commands and invade and conquer Egypt because they simply won't listen. God warns Jerusalem that they need to keep a constant watch for invaders and a ready ear to what is being said. Ezekiel is appointed by God to tell the people what action they must take if a catastrophe is to be averted. Then word comes that Jerusalem has fallen. God warns Ezekiel that he must tell the people everything that God commands otherwise he will be responsible for their continued sinning!

Thinking Step

In chapter 31 there are three references to Sheol (place of the dead) which are rendered 'grave.' Sheol is a word used throughout the Old Testament. It comes from a Hebrew word meaning 'to ask' – as Saul asked for help from Samuel in 1 Sam. 28. It seems in ancient times seeking advice from the dead was a regular event.

Action Step

If you believed some people you would think that God gets pleasure out of His people suffering. He enjoys them searching for Him but not being able to find Him. He sets the standards so high so that they are guaranteed to fail and God will get much pleasure..."Somebody up there has it in for me!" is the almost blasphemous claim I hear all too often. Let's look at a beautiful text from our reading today – in 33:11 – 'As surely as I live says the Sovereign Lord, I take no pleasure in the death of wicked people. I only want them to turn from their wicked ways so they can live. Turn! Turn from your wickedness – O people of Israel! Why should you die?' God really doesn't want even wicked people to die – let alone good people! I believe this Living God and His ancient standards have not changed at all. He still wants everyone to escape judgement and be re-united with Him. After all if He had simply wanted to see us fail and then destroy us – what was the point of the cross? In the humdrum of daily living we can sometimes forget that God wants us to LIVE. Rekindle the joy that was there when you first understood that Jesus died for you and enjoy this week in the light of that knowledge. Are you smiling yet?

34 - My Shepherds Are Rubbish!
35 - Judgement On The Edomites
36 - Israel Will Thrive Once Again

Day 235
Ezekiel 34-36
23rd August

Leadership Has Failed So Badly

The Big Picture

A message for the leaders of Israel comes from God. He denounces them as both inadequate and wicked. So bad in fact that God says He will have to take over the leadership role and look after His badly neglected sheep. God condemns the very hills and mountains of Israel for allowing the enemy to gain access to the Promised Land! When Israel finally settles back into the land of their fathers God will start again with them. He will cleanse them and aid their growth into the people He always wanted them to be – with the help of David who will be a Prince among them. A clear proclamation of the coming Messiah, the Good Shepherd!

Thinking Step

Many historic Kings and leaders described themselves as shepherds. King Hammurabi of ancient Babylon called himself 'shepherd of men' and 'supplier of pasture and water.' Merodach Baladan a later ruler of Babylon compared himself to a shepherd whose duty it is to collect the sheep that are scattered. Even the mighty Egyptian Pharaohs symbolically carried a shepherd's crook.

Action Step

When you read chapter 36 did you notice the repeated statement by God? Verses 22 and 32 contain this gem – 'I am not doing this because you deserve it.' I am constantly grateful that God does not give us what we deserve! Throughout the Bible it is very clear that God chose His own people and constantly cares for them. As our Heavenly Father, He does the same for us even though we don't deserve it! So, is that how you treat other people? I was watching a drama on TV recently when a wise piece of advice was given to one of the characters who was so bitter that she couldn't bring herself to do the right thing. She was told that doing the right thing was the best response she could make and would raise her above the level to which her relationship had fallen. In Psalm 23 there is a line in the KJV that has challenged me many times, it's verse 6 – 'Surely goodness and mercy shall follow me all the days of my life and I will dwell in the house of the LORD for ever.' I cannot read the words 'shall follow me' without thinking of what impression is left with other people as I move on? As you live today try to leave the sweet fragrance of goodness and mercy wherever you go especially when they don't deserve it!

Day 236
Ezekiel 37-39
24th August

37 - Valley Of Dry Bones
38 - A Message For Gog!
39 - A Reminder For Gog!

Life In The Presence Of Death

The Big Picture

Ezekiel is whisked away in the Spirit by God – where he sees a valley which is filled with dry bones. God challenges Ezekiel to speak to the bones so that they may live! Obediently Ezekiel does and the bones begin to live! God tells him that these bones represent Israel because God's people have become dry and lifeless. Ezekiel is told to mark two sticks, one representing Israel and the other Judah. He is to use them to show the people that they will be united once more – under 'Shepherd David!' God also gives a warning to Gog of the land of Magog to forget any plans he may have to invade Israel at this time when it is vulnerable.

Thinking Step

Chapters 38 and 39 condemn Gog and Magog but we are unsure who or where they are! There is no obvious link with the same names in Rev. 20:7. However it could be that Gog and Magog are ways of describing real evil, as we would occasionally refer to a very wicked person as 'the devil himself.'

Action Step

37:11 – 'Then he said to me "Son of man these bones represent the people of Israel. They are saying, we have become old, dry bones – all hope is gone. Our nation is finished."' What a sobering verse from this very inspiring vision of bones coming back to life. It always saddens me when the notices are given at Church if the phrase "Next week we will have the usual services" is used. I don't know about you but I yearn for services that are 'extra usual' – not just the usual! You may have already heard this story but it stands repeating. It's about the little boy who is being shown around an old country church and sees plaques of military names on the walls. He asks who all these people are and is told they are people who died in the services. "I am not surprised, some of the services at our church are pretty boring too!" So have you become 'old, dry bones'? Services need to be stimulating as well as relevant for the people who gather each Sunday. What can you do to make them extra-ordinary? I suggest you begin with prayer, asking God what He would suggest! The important thing is that we are not all dried up but that we are supple in the Spirit. Why not pray for those leading your services next week and do what you can to encourage them afterwards!

40 - A Temple To Be Measured
41 - Holy Of Holies To Be Measured
42 - Priestly Rooms To Be Measured

Day 237
Ezekiel 40-42
25th August

A Spectacular New Temple Complex

The Big Picture

Fourteen years have passed by since the Temple in Jerusalem was destroyed by Nebuchadnezzar. Ezekiel is now taken up in the Spirit to get a glimpse of a new Temple. Everything is as precise as you would expect when you reflect on some of God's detailed instructions we have already read in the Old Testament. Today we have a man who measured accurately, beginning with the very substantial outer wall and working inwards to the Holy of Holies and the priestly rooms which are to be used by the priests on duty in the Temple. This whole spectacular vision is shown to Ezekiel so that he can then share it with his fellow countrymen and lift them from their present despair.

Thinking Step

It gets bigger and bigger!
Solomon's Temple was so small, sixteen of them could have been built on one acre of land. The Temple in Ezekiel's vision was substantially larger and covered almost 13 acres! Herod's Temple was the same size as Solomon's but stood on a spectacular Temple Mount of over 35 acres!

Action Step

When I was a child we were often told that 'church' was the 'house of God' and were led to believe that He actually lived there! I don't believe those who told us this actually believed it literally but it was a way of emphasising the special place that church is. We were also regularly greeted with words like "As we come into His presence" once again – as though He lived there. These thoughts were a great influence on the way we dressed for church as we had 'Sunday best' clothes which we wore as a mark of respect as we gathered to worship God. All this came back to me as I read our reading today especially 42:14 – 'When the priests leave the sanctuary they must not go directly to the outer courtyard. They must first take off the clothes they wore while ministering because these clothes are holy. They must put on other clothes before entering the parts of the building complex open to the public.' In today's ultra informal world where I have been told in some churches, not to wear a tie so as not to 'alienate the congregation' – I fear we may have lost some of our reverence for God Himself. Of course God looks on the inside at our hearts but sometimes our appearance can reflect a sloppiness in our approach to Almighty God. Check your attitude next Sunday when you meet to worship!

Day 238
Ezekiel 43-45
26th August

43 - Ezekiel Hears God's Voice In The Temple
44 - The East Gate Is To Remain Closed
45 - Re-Establish The Feasts

God's Plans Are Falling Into Place Now

The Big Picture

The tour of the Temple continues at the east side where Ezekiel hears God's voice telling him that sacrifices are to be re-established and done according to the law. On this east side the city gate is to remain closed because the King of Glory has already entered that way. What a word of prophecy about Jesus entering on Palm Sunday! The priests are to be all that they should have been in the past and teach and correct the people. When the land is re-settled God's people are to be known as honest people who are a pleasure to to deal with. In addition the main festivals are to be celebrated faithfully every year according to the law.

Thinking Step

Looking across the Kidron Valley from the Mount of Olives there is the Golden Gate or sealed gate of 44:2. This is the area where Jesus' triumphal entry takes place on Palm Sunday. The sealed gate is part of the wall built by Suleiman the Magnificent, ruler of the Islamic Ottoman Empire in 1540 AD! Hard evidence of fulfilled prophecy!

Action Step

45:9-11 – '..."Stop your violence and oppression and do what is just and right. Quit robbing and cheating my people out of their land. Stop expelling them from their homes" says the Sovereign Lord. "Use only honest weights and scales and honest measures, both dry and liquid..."' Of course these words were applicable to most people in the days of Ezekiel but are equally relevant today! As for me and maybe you they are not needed are they? We are as honest as the day is long! Wake up and look at yourself! I have a friend who for many years was a car dealer as well as a truly good Christian man. He said that the public were so devious and dishonest and yet it was car dealers who got the bad reputation! Hard statements like we have just read in Ezekiel 45 are difficult to acknowledge for our own lives aren't they? When we are 'off duty' and in situations where no one knows us we are often tempted to take short cuts! Take this as a reminder of God's perfect standards in OT times, in NT times and today. Whatever transactions you are involved in this week let them be truly honest. Even when no one else finds out just how honest you have been your Father in Heaven knows and He is truly pleased with you and that's a great reward to enjoy.

46 - Offerings In The Temple
47 - River In The Temple
48 - Land Allocations For The Tribes

Day 239
Ezekiel 46-48
27th August

Jerusalem Complete – Ezekiel's Final Vision

The Big Picture

Leaders are to offer sacrifices and the people are to follow their example. Ezekiel is given a comprehensive tour of the rest of the Temple including the kitchens! He then witnesses a river running through the Temple all the way down to the Dead Sea. He is challenged by his guide to walk into the river where he paddles, wades and finally has to swim as the river intensifies. The Dead Sea is cleansed by this river and Ezekiel sees fish and fishermen throughout the Dead Sea! Land allocations for the twelve tribes are detailed with Joseph receiving a double portion. Finally we are given a glorious view of the new city with twelve gates named after the twelve tribes.

Thinking Step

Ezekiel's vision has much emphasis on a new temple but after Jesus came, who is 'a sacrifice, once for all time' – Heb. 10:10 John's vision has a different priority in Rev 21:21-22 – 'The twelve gates were made of pearls ...I saw no temple in the city, for the Lord God Almighty and the Lamb are its temple.'

Action Step

Ezekiel's book closes on a high! 'The Lord is there!' After years of faithful and often controversial ministry we don't get to hear about the end of his life but we don't need to really. I am so sure that he remained faithful to his God to the very end. When I was a pastor in a church we had lots of retired folk settle in our town. I remember preaching at a special evangelistic event in a local community centre and was warmly praised afterwards by an elderly man. He was so encouraging and positive. I found out later that he was a real 'star' who had enjoyed a very fruitful radio ministry for many years in the 1950/60s but was now retired from public ministry but continued to minister! Of course we don't know if Ezekiel was like this but I can't believe he wasn't! No matter where you are on life's road there is always something to do for God and remember Christians don't retire, they just go on witnessing. 'The Lord is there' wherever you are and wants to use you throughout the rest of your life. Whether you have been a 'star' like Ezekiel or are one of the anonymous saints like the majority of us, God still has much for you to do. On Sunday take special notice of the announcements. God could have something in them for you to do this week!

Daniel

Daniel

Daniel is one of the best known characters in the Bible and his encounter in the lions' den is one of its most loved historical stories. Daniel prophesied in Babylon as a contemporary of Ezekiel and while Jeremiah was ministering in Judah. Daniel is a well named prophet for the exile and ministers throughout its whole 70 years using his Hebrew name which means 'God is my judge.' The exile was God's judgement. Some scholars doubt Daniel's authorship as his prophecies always worked out so they assume it must have been written after the events; possibly in the time of Antiochus Epiphanes 175 – 163 BC. Of course it could be that God simply told him what was to happen and Daniel wrote it down!! The first chapter overviews his early life whilst the rest of the book is dominated by dreams initially relating to the Gentiles and then Israel.

Below is an acrostic which summarises each chapter of the book.

1. **D**aniel favoured by Nebuchadnezzar
2. **A**nswer to king's dream
3. **N**ebuchadnezzar's furnace of fire
4. **I**nterpretation of tree vision
5. **E**vents at Belshazzar's feast
6. **L**ion's den of Darius
7. **S**cenes of coming kingdoms

8. **F**eatures of four beasts
9. **A**ppointing the seventy weeks
10. **I**nterpreting the final vision
11. **T**error of the king
12. **H**orror of end times

Day 240
Daniel 1-3
28th August

1 - Daniel Is Deported To Babylon
2 - Daniel Interprets Nebuchadnezzar's Dream
3 - Daniel's Friends Thrown Into A Furnace

Daniel – A Giant Amongst Advisers

The Big Picture

We begin with the details of the deportation into exile in Babylon. Then we are told of the early years of Daniel's ministry and his encounter with Nebuchadnezzar who wants his dream interpreting but no one seems to be competent to do it. With God's help Daniel is able to tell the King exactly what the dream means. The idea of the statue in his dream seems to inspire Nebuchadnezzar to build one of solid gold! He insists that everyone bows down to the statue as an act of worship. Notable defectors are the three friends of Daniel and they are thrown into a furnace. Shadrach, Meshach and Abed-nego survive the ordeal and their God is greatly honoured.

Thinking Step

3:1 – 'King Nebuchadnezzar made a gold statue ninety feet tall and nine feet wide and set it up on the plain of Dura in the province of Babylon.' In Iraq today on the plains of Dura there is a mound about twenty feet high an exact square of about forty-six feet at the base, resembling the pedestal of a colossal statue.

Action Step

3:18 – '...even if He doesn't, we want to make it clear to you Your Majesty, that we will never serve your gods or worship the gold statue you have set up.' Here we have the account of three young men taking a stand for God. They were far from perfect as they have already accepted Babylonian names glorifying pagan gods. Unlike Daniel they seem willing to drop their beautiful Hebrew names. So it seems you don't have to be perfect to take a stand! When was the last time you took a stand for God and for what is right? These three men certainly had faith but were not blind to the possibility that God's answer to their predicament may not have been the same as theirs. 3:17-18 – 'If we are thrown into the blazing furnace, the God whom we serve is able to save us. He will rescue us from your power Your Majesty but even if He doesn't...' This is the crux of this wonderful account. Even when God doesn't do what we want we will still obey Him. I have lost count of the number of people I have spoken to over the years who have said something like "When God let that happen, I lost my faith in Him." Explore your own memory and ask God for forgiveness for the times you have rebelled when His will was not the same as yours!!

Daniel Serves Four Kings

The Big Picture

Nebuchadnezzar tells everyone "How great is the God of Daniel." Then he has a dream and Daniel tells him that he would prefer this to be a dream for the King's enemies rather than the King himself! The dream is basically telling Nebuchadnezzar that like a tree he will be 'cut down to size' by God and will live like a beast. Years later Belshazzar is King and terrified by a message mysteriously written by a human hand on a palace wall. That night Belshazzar was killed and Darius the Mede took the throne. He admires Daniel but is tricked into sending him to the den of lions. Daniel is protected by God and goes on serving Darius and later Cyrus.

Thinking Step

In Genesis the Pharaoh offers Joseph the number two position – Gen. 41:41-44. Yet Daniel is only promised third place in today's reading – 5:16! The last King to reign before the Babylonian Empire fell to Cyrus was Nabonidus. He appointed Belshazzar his son, as co-regent to rule Babylon. With 'two Kings' the best position available was third place!

Action Step

5:29 – 'Then at Belshazzar's command Daniel was dressed in purple robes, a gold chain was hung around his neck and he was proclaimed the third highest ruler in the Kingdom.' 6:28 – 'So Daniel prospered during the reign of Darius and the reign of Cyrus the Persian.' It seems you don't have to be financially squeezed to serve God! It's not how much money or wealth you have but how you use it. I knew a man in the USA who had a ministry amongst very wealthy Christians who wanted to support God's work financially and sought his advice about the best ways to do it. He said he had real problems persuading some of them not to give everything away but to keep much of it well invested and give the produce away every year. "Give it away and it's gone!" – "Invest it and you can give it away over and over again!" Jesus didn't say it was impossible for a rich man to get into the Kingdom He just said it was very hard – Matt 19:23-24. No matter what your financial situation is remember that the money you now have is only yours on loan! Use it wisely as a good steward. Remember the recollection of Jesus' words by the Apostle Paul in Acts 20:35 – "It is more blessed to give than to receive." Want to be blessed? Well you know what to do now!

Day 242
Daniel 7-9
30th August

7 - Vision Of The Four Beasts
8 - Vision Of The Ram, Goat And Little Horn
9 - Vision And Big Numbers For Daniel

Graphic Visions Of World Powers

The Big Picture

Daniel steps back a few years to the beginning of the reign of Belshazzar when he had a vision of four beasts with one being particularly powerful and all conquering until the 'Ancient One' (Father God) intervenes and then empowers a 'son of man' who reminds us particularly of Jesus. This is a great reminder that the world powers may be powerful but God is so much more powerful. Two years later Daniel has another vision, this time of a ram and a goat. The references to horns are all symbolic of power in the dominating nations of the day. Many believe the small horn was Antiochus Epiphanes who was trying to subdue the Jews' rebellion led by the Maccabees.

Thinking Step

Josephus records Alexander the Great's visit to Jerusalem – 332 BC. He describes how the prophecies of Daniel specifically 8:5-8, 20-22 and 11:3-4 made such an impact that Alexander granted the Jews the right to live in 'full enjoyment of the laws of their forefathers.' A major step in preserving God's people and the Bible.

Action Step

Some of Daniel's writings can be very confusing, even to him! – 8:27. However the major events described in Daniel's prophecy were all fulfilled just as predicted :-

- That there would be a decree to rebuild Jerusalem.
- Then Jerusalem and the Temple would be rebuilt.
- Then an anointed one (Messiah) would make an appearance and then be "cut off."
- Then Jerusalem and the Temple would be destroyed again.

All of this was very encouraging for God's chosen people at a time in history when being totally wiped out was more than a possibility. People going back to their homeland was something that just didn't happen. What usually happened was that they lost their identity and were swallowed up by the conquering nation. Daniel however, confirms to us that we have a God who is very trustworthy and knows the beginning from the end. Did Daniel and the Jews of his day understand everything that God was saying? No! In fact there is much controversy over lots of what was said, even today! However God proved true to His word then and many times since and will continue throughout your lifetime too. Thankfully we don't need to understand everything! Any more than we need to understand computers so that they can impact our lives. Ultimately all we have to do is trust God and encourage others to do the same. Starting today!

Detailed Prophecies About Israel's Future

The Big Picture

This is the last vision recorded by Daniel and takes place when Cyrus is ruling. Graphic descriptions of spiritual warfare are described in his vision and whilst we may not use the same expressions, the concepts of evil versus good are part of daily life for believers today. Many details about Alexander the Great's Empire and what happens after his death are given in this vision. It seems very likely that the northern Kingdom is that of the Seleucids whilst the southern one is the Ptolemies – two of the smaller factions that followed the split of the massive Greek Empire. Daniel is encouraged to trust even when he cannot understand.

Thinking Step

11:36 – 'The King will do as he pleases, exalting himself and claiming to be greater than every god even blaspheming the God of gods...' If as many believe, these verses are words of prophecy about a future Seleucid King then they are very appropriate. He was Mithradates but he changed it to Antiochus Epiphanes which means 'Antiochus, manifestation of God.'

Action Step

10:7 – 'Only I Daniel, saw this vision. The men with me saw nothing but they were suddenly terrified and ran away to hide.' There are some similarities with Acts 9:7 – 'The men with Saul stood speechless for they heard the sound of someone's voice but saw no one!' In both cases something miraculous happened but it was not fully experienced by all who were present. God doesn't treat us all alike because we are different! If like me you have many faults and weaknesses, please don't question God's choices when He made you! Of course this does not mean we are not to change, as God moulds us into a more accurate likeness of His Son Jesus. We are always to be involved in the process of becoming. We sometimes forget that God sees us as we are and also as we will be, in Jesus and loves us anyway. It won't be long before we are reading the Gospels together. Four independent accounts written by four individuals who are inspired by God to put 'pen to paper.' I am constantly amused that critics doubt the Gospels because they make differing observations. I would be more inclined to doubt them if they agreed on every point, after all remember, different people see different things. Thank God for your individuality then ask Him what needs to be adjusted to make you more like that perfect individual Jesus.

Hosea

Hosea

Today we begin to look at the twelve minor prophets which are all on one scroll in the Hebrew Bible. Hosea's name has the same basic root as Joshua and Jesus and is usually rendered 'salvation.' Hosea is already an established prophet when Isaiah comes onto the scene. He ministers in the north (sometimes referred to as Ephraim, after its largest tribe) in the period leading up to the Assyrian invasion and the subsequent scattering of the northern tribes. He follows the faithful northern ministry of Amos and is as poorly received!! Indeed both are rejected and laughed at. Hosea and Amos – HA! Hosea's writings reflect a one sided love story – with God being constantly faithful and His people always being unfaithful. The first three chapters concentrate on a personal picture of Hosea with the remaining ten chapters addressed to Israel in a final and ultimately futile appeal to repent.

Below is an acrostic which summarises each chapter of the book.

1. **G**omer's lifestyle and children
2. **O**bstinate wife is restored
3. **M**essage of second marriage
4. **E**rror of Israel's ways
5. **R**ebuke of Israel's leaders

6. **T**estimony of God's love
7. **H**opelessness of Israel's desertion
8. **E**xile unavoidable for Israel

9. **H**arlotry will be punished
10. **A**ssyria will enslave Israel
11. **R**ebellion against God's love
12. **L**egal case against Israel
13. **O**verthrow of Ephraim certain
14. **T**ransformation if Israel repents

Day 244
Hosea 1-3
1st September

1 - Hosea Marries Unfaithful Gomer
2 - Israel Is Unfaithful Like Gomer
3 - Hosea Redeems Gomer

Israel Is Unfaithful – Just Like Gomer

The Big Picture

In the final thirty years or so before the northern tribes are scattered by the Assyrians, Hosea who is ministering in the north is instructed by God to marry a prostitute. Some people seem to be asked to do really difficult things for God and Hosea is certainly one of them. Gomer gives Hosea a son quickly followed by a daughter and then another son. God pleads with His unfaithful people through an obedient prophet who can empathise with God as he has an unfaithful wife. Gomer slides back into prostitution and God tells Hosea to buy her back again – just as He will rescue His people and keep them safe in exile.

Thinking Step

Gomer has three children in the space of seven verses in chapter one. Hosea only has one!

1:3 – 'So Hosea married Gomer... and she became pregnant and <u>gave Hosea a son</u>.'

1:6 – 'Soon Gomer became pregnant again and <u>gave birth to</u> a daughter.'

1:8 – '...Gomer ... again became pregnant and <u>gave birth to</u> a second son.'

Action Step

When we are faithful we can be described as having trust or confidence in another person. So much so that it then influences and shows itself in our daily life. In the case of God, in our narrative today He is faithful to Israel and never discards them to choose another more faithful people. In return the Israelites have a history of many generations of fickleness, turning from one idol to another and breaking God's heart. Hosea is asked to take a life changing action and marry a prostitute! It would be bad enough in the 21st century but in Old Testament times it was totally shameful. Gomer should have been so grateful to Hosea for his redeeming action that she would never have been unfaithful again! That's how we should live but sometimes the price that Jesus paid for you and me simply fades into the background and we take God for granted. Knowing He will forgive us when we fail again. In a fundamental way God wants us to take Him for granted – He doesn't want us to live our lives doubting Him! However He wants us to be aware of all He continues to do for us and live our lives accordingly. The Israelites only missed Him when they 'lost Him' and went into exile. Don't wait for something to happen to turn you back to God – turn to Him now even if the going is good!

Rebellious Leaders Need To Lead The People Back

The Big Picture

There is such a lack of good Godly standards because Israel has turned its back on God and it's the leaders' fault! The ordinary people need a better standard to be set by those who are supposed to be their moral and spiritual leaders. The leaders are going the wrong way and the people who don't know any better are simply following them. Offering sacrifices simply feeds the wicked priests who benefit from a population who need to go on repenting but fail to change. Regular attendance at the Temple is 'good for business' but God hates the whole ritualistic sham. God wants His people to turn back to Him and then they can get to know Him again.

Thinking Step

Have you noticed the references to southern Judah from this northern prophet? In today's reading alone – 4:15, 5:5,10,12-14, 6:4,11. It seems probable that devoted Jews migrated south as the north became less Godly whilst the south occasionally had Godly Kings. By the time of the exile, the south included Jews from all twelve tribes of Israel.

Action Step

4:1 – 'Hear the word of the Lord, O people of Israel! The Lord has brought charges against you saying "There is no faithfulness, no kindness, <u>no knowledge of God</u> in your land."' 4:6 – 'My people are being destroyed because they don't know me. Since you priests refuse to know me I refuse to recognize you as my priests. Since you have <u>forgotten the laws of your God</u> I will forget to bless your children.' No knowledge of God and a discarding of God's laws – just about sums it up. Years ago an accurate statement by Billy Graham was totally misunderstood as it crossed the Atlantic. He said "Britain is a Godless country." However journalists heard him say "Britain is a wicked country" and took him to task for saying we were bad when the USA was much worse! The USA may be a wicked country, who am I to judge but you can still mention God in your daily life without appearing to be totally out of touch or something worse. The concept of God is still real in much of America but He has been de-throned in the UK, so much so that politicians rarely mention God or prayer in their public pronouncements. We need to re-enthrone God in our nation if we are to benefit from His standards in society. This process needs to start with you and me and it needs to start today.

Only God Can Truly Satisfy

The Big Picture

In what a human would describe as despair, God makes a final attempt to shake Israel into repentance but all to no avail. Their sins are too great and so much part of their lives. The problem is far bigger than they think. Mixing with so many Godless people has changed their approach to life but it does doesn't it? Like fluttering birds they go from one thing to another but it doesn't matter which idol they choose – they are all equally useless. They don't seem to be able to grasp the logic of approaching the creator God rather than bits and pieces made by other men!

Thinking Step

7:8 prompted George Adam Smith to say "How better to describe a half-fed people, a half-cultured society, a half-lived religion, a half-hearted policy, than by a half-baked scone?" How beautifully summed up! In reality God's people were neither a light to the Gentiles nor a good advert for paganism.

Action Step

Isn't it odd that we sometimes never seem to learn! 8:5 tells us that God said "O Samaria I reject this calf – this idol you have made. My fury burns against you. How long will you be incapable of innocence?" It's not that God had ever been vague about His attitude to the calf. From its first appearance with Aaron in the book of Exodus, God has denounced it as unacceptable but the Children of Israel thought it was worth another try! It's a bit like a man dropping coins into a pond in the hope that one time the coin would stay on the surface rather than sink! It isn't going to happen. God does not change His mind like mere mortals. There are many issues in our modern world that God has made clear from His word that He will not accept but we often think if we have enough people protesting God might just change His mind! He won't! It saddens me when I see folk refusing to see what is clearly written in the Bible as God's unchanging Word. They think if enough scholars throw doubt on the text then God will have to agree with them! He won't! So rather than waiting for God to change His mind over an issue in your life, just accept that He won't – that the Bible is clear and get on with life. Don't waste any more time arguing.

9 - You'll Regret Going Into Exile   Day 247
10 - Your Golden Calf Won't Save You   Hosea 9-11
11 - Israel Is Doomed But Judah Is Safe   4th September

Exile Will Be Really Tough!

The Big Picture

God reminds the people through Hosea, that exile will be harder to bear than they think. He tells them that so much of daily life within Judaism and all its rituals will disappear. God reminds them that they have prospered so much over the years but much of their wealth has been wasted on pagan worship and idols. Wealth that God has made possible has been given to His enemies! Hosea reminds the people that God, so long ago rescued them from slavery in Egypt but they are heading back into captivity now and there will be no escape. In reality the northern tribes disappear when the Assyrians invade and are never again heard of as individual tribes.

Thinking Step

11:8 – "...How can I destroy you like Admah or demolish you like Zeboiim? ..." These two cities are usually linked with the cities which are the epitome of wickedness, Sodom and Gomorrah – Deut. 29:23. In order to grab Israel's attention and make a more memorable point God uniquely chooses the less obvious cities this time.

Action Step

Have you ever been looked at rather strangely when you defend God or the Bible? If you have you are in good company and should have been encouraged when you read 9:7 – '...because of your great sin and hostility, you say, "The prophets are crazy and the inspired men are fools!"' Isn't it great to be inked with some of the prophets in the Bible? Or what about when a similar accusation was made in Acts 26:24 – 'Suddenly Festus shouted "Paul you are insane. Too much study has made you crazy!"' Being linked with Paul is something of a compliment too, don't you think? On the other hand do you find it hard to stand firm and much easier to fade into the background when a simple affirming word would be a great witness. Don't ever be afraid to appear crazy for God! In my experience a word of witness gently offered and without a challenge for an argument can be something the Holy Spirit can use even if there seems to be no response at the time. I remember a well known left wing politician being told by an interviewer that he would never get into power until he changed his extreme policies. He had a great answer "It is more important to be true to my beliefs than to get on in life." Why not ask God to make you 'gently' bold for Him today?

Day 248
Hosea 12-14
5th September

12 - Follow The Good Example You Were Shown
13 - Be A Better Example Yourselves
14 - Unfaithful Israel Has A Faithful God

Israel Ignored The Right Way For Too Long

The Big Picture

God declares that Israel is just plain untrustworthy! He urges them through Hosea, to return to the principles of their father Jacob who, after wrestling with God finally succumbed to His will. He tells Israel that at one time they were a good example and one worth following. However now they are going their own way and it is a pathway doomed to failure. He reminds them that they have sought help from surrounding nations and have been let down by all of them. Only their God is reliable. God tells them to repent now and be healed. Ultimately He will keep His promise to Israel and they will return after the exile.

Thinking Step

13:10a – 'Now where is your King? Let him save you!' Israel asked for Kings during the period of Judges ignoring the fact that God was their King! Hosea prophesied to the last Kings of northern Israel. What an unholy mess! Zechariah murdered by Shallum, Shallum murdered by Menahem, Pekahiah murdered by Pekah and Pekah murdered by Hoshea!

Action Step

12:6 – 'So now come back to your God. Act with love and justice and always depend on Him.' This just about sums up the message of Hosea and accurately reflects the essence of the whole Gospel. Like all good texts it falls into three parts! 1st – 'Come back to God.' No matter how many times God calls us we have to make the all important move towards Him. For most people it is a return. Rarely does a move to God come 'out of the blue' it is usually a returning to the God we sought previously. I have spoken to people over the years and it constantly amazes me how many heard God calling several times before they fully responded themselves.

2nd – 'Act with love and justice.' In other words, live out your faith in everyday life. I am sure you have heard this many times but until you do it, you actually haven't heard it you have simply been there when it was said!

3rd – 'Always depend on Him.' This is where too many of us fall down on a regular basis. We begin with God and as soon as things are going well we are like a child learning to ride a bike and telling our helper and guide to let us loose as we don't need them anymore and then falling! Today – may we turn back to God, live with God and depend on God.

Joel

Joel

What a beautiful name! Literally, Yahweh is God. Joel is probably a very early prophet to Judah. He could have been a contemporary of Elisha who spoke to the north. This would make him a prophet to Joash one of the eight Godly Kings of Judah. Some scholars however see Joel as very late after the exile and therefore after the period of Kings. He uses a natural disaster to proclaim God's message to a reeling people who have just been hit by the unexpected. He tells them that God's judgement will come and for many will be just as unexpected. The 'Day of the Lord' will take many by surprise. This is a warning to Israel to mend their ways and turn back to the God of their fathers. Locusts are naturally inevitable but God wants His judgement to be deferred as the people turn back to Him..

Below is an acrostic which summarises each chapter of the book.

1. **C**ry to avoid judgement
2. **R**eturn to God's blessing
3. **Y**ield to God's sovereignty

1 - The Locusts Come And Devour Everything   Day 249
2 - The Day Of The Lord Is Coming   Joel 1-3
3 - Judgement Is Coming For All Israel's Enemies   6th September

Natural Disaster Forewarns Israel Of Judgement

The Big Picture

A massive locust invasion takes the whole nation by surprise. It affects everyone from priests to farmers. With it still clearly in their memory Joel tells the people that the 'Day of the Lord' will be even more breathtaking and full of impact. God challenges them through His prophet Joel, to consider how they will cope with the 'Day of the Lord' after this 'taster experience' of the devastating locust invasion! God lets His people know that He will ultimately 'pour out His Spirit on all people' and centuries later He does, on the Day of Pentecost in Acts 2:17. Significantly this celebration was the equivalent of our Harvest Festival which would be all the better for no locusts!

Thinking Step

3:10 – 'Hammer your ploughshares into swords and your pruning hooks into spears.' The exact opposite of Isa. 2:4 – 'They will hammer their swords into ploughshares and their spears into pruning hooks.' Thus fulfilling Ecclesiastes 3:8 – 'A time to love and a time to hate. A time for war and a time for peace.'

Action Step

2:25 – 'The Lord says "I will give you back what you lost to the swarming locusts, the hopping locusts, the stripping locusts and the cutting locusts. It was I who sent this great destroying army against you."' Scholars are unsure about these four kinds of locusts and so are many commentators! What is abundantly clear is that God wants to give us back wasted years. The word translated 'give back' is actually a very substantial word with legal connotations. It means to restore or repay and God is willing to do that for you and for me. The four types of locusts remind me of four types of time and resource wasting:-

> Swarming Locusts – when we are completely surrounded by difficulties and see no way out.
>
> Hopping Locusts – when we fail to concentrate on what God has for us and jump from project to project.
>
> Stripping Locusts – when we need to remove barriers in our lives in order to get on with our God given tasks.
>
> Cutting Locusts – when we are hurt and unable to continue. We want to but are unable to get over the hurt.

Do any of these remind you of times in your life? Well the Lord is able to 'give you back what you lost.' To give you a second chance. Why not ask Him now?

Amos

Amos

Amos whose name means 'burden bearer' preceded Hosea in prophesying to the north. These two were the only ones from the twelve minor prophets to be called to Israel in the north. Amos came from Tekoa twelve miles south of Jerusalem where he was a shepherd. He had a clear message for the northern tribes being ruled by Jeroboam II, who had another famous prophet advising him called Jonah. His message was that judgement was coming from a Holy God who condemned the sinfulness of His covenant people. This book breaks into four parts beginning with prophecies, then sermons, then visions and finally promises. It was only twenty years or so since Jonah had preached in the Assyrian capital Nineveh and witnessed repentance from everyone – 120,000 in all! Consequently at that time there was little perceived threat from their northerly Assyrian neighbours so it was easy to ignore Amos and they did!

Below is an acrostic which summarises each chapter of the book.

1. Judgement on Judah's neighbours
2. Ungodliness of Israel explained
3. Destruction of Israel coming
4. God's reproofs went unnoticed
5. Making plea for repentance
6. Extravagance will be judged
7. Nature of God's judgements
8. Time ripe for judgement
9. Scattering and Israel's restoration

Judgement For Both Sides

The Big Picture

With very broad brush strokes Amos sweeps around the surrounding nations, condemning them all and promising God would judge them for all they were doing and for the way they were living. Just as his Jewish relatives were swelling their chests with pride, he then condemns his fellow southerners in Judah as being no better that these Gentile nations. Before they could take a breath the northerners of Israel were told that their lifestyle was totally unacceptable too. Having been brought out of Egypt so long ago and settled in a prosperous land given to them by the God of their fathers, they had quickly become indistinguishable from their pagan neighbours. Judgement time is imminent!

Thinking Step

Following the division of the United Kingdom after Solomon's reign there was constant rivalry and animosity between north and south. This lasted until the days of Jesus when a pronounced north-south divide pervaded the whole of His ministry. So imagine a southern layman, a shepherd called Amos going north and telling the northerners how to live their lives! What a challenge!

Action Step

'It ain't what you do it's the way that you do it. That's what gets results!' So goes that great old song of many years ago and which has seen several revivals over the years. Some of the things that Amos said would automatically get a negative response because of who said it. After all what did he a southerner know, that would help a northerner! Sometimes an argument is lost before a word is said. I wonder how confrontational Amos was? I wonder how many times he smiled before he pronounced his message? I am convinced that many of the problems in our churches today could be avoided or at least diffused with better approaches from either or both sides. Of course this isn't a reminder for you or me it's something for those other awkward and difficult people who attend our churches and who we see more as sanctification testers rather than brothers and sisters in Christ! Are you smiling? Yes this is a reminder to all of us of course. Why not at the next church meeting or PCC you attend, try to approach others as you would have them approach you? There are times for confrontation but there are many more times for paving the way beforehand and thus producing a better atmosphere before discussion begins. Want results? Well you know the approach to take!

3 - Your Enemy Is Coming Soon
4 - Trying Times Have Failed To Turn You To God
5 - Day Of The Lord Is To Be Feared

Day 251
Amos 3-5
8th September

Stubborn People Will Not Turn Back To God

The Big Picture

Amos has a message from God for both northern Israel and southern Judah. An enemy will attack you and you'll be in serious trouble. "Listen to me" says God to the women of Samaria in particular as He continued telling them that their otherwise good deeds were not pleasing to Him because they were not doing them sincerely. It was all just for show. God pleads with them to come back to Him and live life to the full once more. They are condemned because of the way they are treating the poor. Amos advises them not to hasten the 'Day of the Lord' because it will not be anywhere near as good as they think it will be.

Thinking Step

I remember asking a man called Amos who was once our Jewish guide in Israel, if he acknowledged Jesus as Messiah. After a pause he said "No because He never said He was!" I then asked him if he would have done so if Jesus had made such a claim. Amos responded "No because if Jesus was Messiah He wouldn't have had to say!"

Action Step

The message of God through Amos comes across very clearly in chapter 5. It is so refreshingly positive. Verse 4b – "Come back to me and live!" Verse 6a – 'Come back to the Lord and live!' The Church has done such a poor PR job over the past 2,000 years that the things we hold most dear as believers are for many synonymous with 'boring', 'outdated' and 'for weak people!' Where did we go wrong? By concentrating on the negative at the expense of the positive – that's where! Can you imagine a car dealer, estate agent or computer salesperson allowing the negatives to outnumber the positives about their products? Of course we are not selling products, we are in the realms of spiritual warfare but please stop helping the enemy! There was a concert at a local Church we attended some years ago and due to a mix up with opening the front door a long queue formed before everything was resolved and we were able to gain access. I remember the pastor saying "What a great idea, letting people see that what is going on in the Church is worth queuing for! I think we should keep the doors locked until the last minute every Sunday!" If you have two things to say on Sunday, one is negative and one is positive, try using the positive. It could make the world of difference.

Enjoy It While You Can, Israel!

The Big Picture

Amos challenges the people especially the wealthy ones to look around at the places where God's judgement has already fallen. Then he reminds them that they are no better and therefore they had better expect to be treated in similar ways! He warns that the enemy who will invade, is nearby and ready to pounce very soon. Amos has two visions, one of attack by locusts and one of being destroyed by fire but neither come to be after he pleads with God. Then his most famous vision, the one where a plumb-line is used by God to urge perfectly straight living. This was a reminder that the people were far from straight and were short of God's standard.

Thinking Step

6:10 – '...When the person begins to swear "No, by . . ." he will interrupt and say "Stop! Don't even mention the name of the Lord."' They took the name of the Lord in vain in the days of Amos and paid the price. We constantly hear His name being taken in vain and I wonder what the price will ultimately be!

Action Step

I was 39 years old when I entered the paid ministry by becoming an associate minister in a large Free Church in Essex. I was then an elder in a Baptist Church and had a lot of experience with people but at that time, had done no theological studying. We initially contacted the Church in Essex because we knew the senior minister but hadn't seen him for ages. My wife suggested we 'push the door' and make contact for advice! It was straight from God. It turned out that they had just had a leadership meeting which resolved they would seek out an associate minister who was around 40 years old, married with a family and plenty of worldly experience rather than a theological degree. It described me perfectly except of course I was only 39! I was, like Amos not a professional but the Lord called me anyway. 7:14-15 – '...Amos replied "I'm not a professional prophet and I was never trained to be one. I'm just a shepherd and I take care of sycamore-fig trees but the Lord called me away from my flock and told me, Go and prophesy to my people in Israel."' I strongly suggest you seek the Lord about how He could use you and then go for it. You never know what God has in store until you gently push the door and see what happens. Start pushing today!

Punishment And Restoration Are Both Certain

The Big Picture

Another vision for Amos begins our reading today. He sees a bowl of ripe fruit and God tells him that just as the fruit is ripe, so is Israel ripe for punishment. God is fed up with the way His people constantly cheat each other giving short measures and short change. From their current plenty will come a famine, not a shortage of food but a lack of God's Word! When punishment comes there will be no hiding place for anyone anywhere. God confirms that Israel is very special to Him but He also tells Amos that He has helped other nations too. He doesn't just help Israel! Finally God proclaims the certainty of restoration back to the Promised Land.

Thinking Step

9:11 – "...will restore the fallen house of David..." The word 'house' may also be translated 'booth' the same as used in the Festival of Booths when increasingly, the reigning King took a central role as the middle-man between God and the people; 1 Kings 12:32-33. A prophetic sign of the ultimate middle-man, Jesus Christ Himself.

Action Step

I remember being invited to be one of the speakers at a conference in Norfolk some time ago. I sat in the congregation as the first speaker spoke with great eloquence. He had been everywhere, done everything and was held in high standing and I was due to follow him! After a while I wondered when he was going to get to the main issue as he drifted through story after story trying to make a point that frankly evaded me and those around me too I hasten to add. As his time began to come to an end he suddenly stopped mid sentence and declared "Oh I suppose I had better give you a Bible reference for this." He did then vacated the platform. As I got up to speak there was muttering which included "I hope we will get some Bible this time!" They did, as I have little else of value to say other than what the Bible says! I was reminded of this when I read 8:12 – 'People will stagger from sea to sea and wander from border to border searching for the word of the Lord but they will not find it.' I don't know what your Church is like but make every effort to root all you do personally and as members of the body of Christ, on and in the Word of God. A great sure and certain foundation.

Obadiah

Obadiah

Many prophets are called to the people of Jacob (Israelites) but Obadiah is the only one we have on record who is called to Jacob's brother Esau (Edomites). Obadiah, which means 'servant of Yahweh' possibly lived in Judah and is one of thirteen Obadiahs in the Bible! He was probably ministering in Edom at the same time as Elisha was prophesying in Israel around 100 years before the northern Kingdom of Israel was scattered by the invading Assyrians. Having refused the Israelites permission to pass through their land after they were delivered from Egypt under Moses, the Edomites continued to be antagonistic towards their close relatives – v10. There are several incidents of this in the Old Testament e.g. 2 Chron. 21:8-10. Judgement could have been brought to a head when the Philistines and Arabs invaded Judah – 2 Chron. 21:16-17 when the Edomites apparently offered no support.

Below is an acrostic which summarises each chapter of the book.

1-9   **E**dom's doom is prophesied
10-14   **D**ay of Edom's distress
15-16   **O**ath of God's judgement
17-21   **M**ount Zion is delivered

Don't Think You're Safe Up There!

The Big Picture

A vision is given to Obadiah telling him what is about to happen to the land and people of Edom. The Edomites are condemned for their arrogance and for feeling that they are beyond God's judgement. Living in a physically strong and secure environment is not the same as resting in the safe and secure arms of the living God. They had refused to support their own relatives and continued the feud, started by Jacob and Esau. Obadiah tells them that their demise will come as invaders attack and they will disappear from the earth but Israel will survive. Many years later the Nabataeans push the Edomites out of their land and they are finally destroyed by the Romans.

Thinking Step

The Edomites became known as the Idumeans after they migrated to an area south of Judah. Their most famous son was King Herod the Great. As an 'Edomite', Herod continued the Jacob-Esau feud by trying to kill Jesus! He built the Great Temple in Jerusalem in the hope that the Jews might warm to him, a non-Jew.

Action Step

During one of our visits to Petra the 'Rose-red City' we stopped at the entrance to the city. This is a kilometre long, cool and shaded siq, a long narrow gorge whose steeply rising sides all but obliterate the sun. There we read the whole of a book from the Bible. Not as daunting as it sounds because the book we read was Obadiah! The Edomites to whom Obadiah was writing would have lived in the same vicinity as Petra with its tall rock faces and dry red rocks. We read with extra interest verse 3 – 'You have been deceived by your own pride because you live in a rock fortress and make your home high in the mountains. "Who can ever reach us way up here?" you ask boastfully.' As we walked through the ancient city we constantly caught sight of locals in some of the caves above us – thinking they were safe up there! It seems today that many people live their lives as though God cannot reach them. As though they are beyond God's reach and there is no connection possible between them and God. You and I have the privilege of sharing with them that God loves them and has made a re-connection possible through Jesus Christ. Remember just because people don't seem interested in God it doesn't mean they have rejected Him. Often it's just that they have never been introduced! Over to you!

Jonah

Jonah

You live in Birmingham. God tells you to go to Newcastle and off you go to Dublin! Not even close! Well as close as Jonah got to Nineveh when he decided to take a ship to Tarshish! The four chapters of Jonah tell a unique account of a prophet's life story and of him being swallowed by a big fish. Very little about his prophetic message or ministry! This makes it so different from all the other prophetic books where the message is more important than the prophet. He came from the north and served Jeroboam II, the same King as was later served by Amos. His name means 'dove' a peaceful bird, so it is ironic that he is called to the warmongers called Assyria who had such a massive army that they ultimately dominated the whole area of what today we call the Middle East.

Below is an acrostic which summarises each chapter of the book.

1. **F**light from God's presence
2. **I**ntercession from inside fish
3. **S**ackcloth shows their repentance
4. **H**elp given to Jonah

1 - Oh No, Not Me Lord!
2 - It's Not As Bad As It Could Have Been!

Day 255
Jonah 1-2
12th September

Just Do It – But Don't Expect To Get Away With It!

The Big Picture

Called by God to go to a needy mission field of his day Jonah decides he knows better and takes evasive action! Instead he boards a ship that is scheduled to go west, the full length of the Mediterranean, possibly all the way to the Gibraltar Straits. This is where it is believed Tarshish could have been but there are several opinions on its geographical location. A terrible storm thwarts his voyage and after drawing lots to determine whose fault the storm was, Jonah is thrown overboard and swallowed by a large fish. After three days and nights in the fish's stomach Jonah is vomited up onto dry land safe and well.

Thinking Step

Jonah came from Gath-hepher which is extremely close to Nazareth in Galilee. Jonah had time for Gentiles and so later did Jesus and they came from adjacent villages. Little wonder that Jewish Nathanael from the nearby big city of Cana of Galilee – John 21:2, did incredulously ask "Can anything good come from Nazareth?" – John 1:46.

Action Step

Asked in Sunday school what the moral of the story of Jonah was, a little boy quickly put up his hand. Surprised, the teacher asked him to tell the class the answer "People make whales sick!" he said with pride. Before you shake your head because you know the real moral of the story please consider this point which I believe is a very important aspect of the narrative. Nowhere does it say that Jonah was running away from God. It says that he was running away from the presence of God! Most translations usually describe Jonah's actions as running away from God but the Hebrew language is a little more involved than this and it is the influence or presence of God that Jonah is trying to escape from. In 1:9 Jonah is more than happy to testify to his allegiance to God but he is in his present predicament because he doesn't want to obey God! We don't need to reject God to be disobedient, all we need to do is ignore what God wants. It happens all the time. When God makes something really clear and we respond by doing something else. You don't need to sail the Mediterranean to rebel! What has God said to you lately but it sounds too much like hard work or just plain inconvenient? It took Jonah three days to obey. Why wait that long? You know God always knows best!

Everyone's Happy, Except The Preacher!

The Big Picture

God speaks for a second time and this time Jonah obeys. Revival breaks out in Nineveh and includes the King. Instead of being ecstatic Jonah is furious! Having preached 'hellfire and damnation' these Gentiles repent and God forgives them! Jonah suspected this might happen and now his worst fears have come to be. Imagine any evangelist today taking this stance after seeing a whole city is converted, a city about the size of Cambridge or Rotherham! Unthinkable! However Jonah broods under an isolated shelter. God provides shade for him but then removes it. Jonah is furious again but God reminds him that Nineveh contained 120,000 people who needed to come out of spiritual darkness. Get your priorities right Jonah!

Thinking Step

The repentance of Nineveh probably occurred in the reign of Ashurdan III (773-755 BC). Two plagues (765 and 759 BC) and a solar eclipse (763 BC) may have prepared the people for Jonah's message of judgement. Disasters that they could not explain could have paved the way for listening ears from the King and the people of Nineveh.

Action Step

I am sure that some within the city of Nineveh would have been very secure in their faith whilst others would have had some doubts and voiced some queries. Just like all of us the Ninevites were individuals and each had their own personality traits. It's a thin line between blindly following and always being the odd one out. Sometimes we need to 'go with the flow' rather than swim 'against the tide.' The story is told of a farmer in the north of Scotland who was at the centre of one of the great revivals experienced in that part of the world. He saw what was happening within his family and circle of friends but rebelled from getting involved himself. In fact one day he told God to leave him alone and not approach him again! It is said that this is exactly what God did and he heard nothing more from God from that day. The church is made up of individuals but sometimes we need to be one and support each other in the grand plan of God. There is a time to stand firm despite all others around us but there is also a time to be totally at one and suppress any dissenting thoughts we may have. Let's ask God for wisdom to discern one from the other as we seek His will for our lives today.

Micah

Micah

Micah a contemporary of Isaiah, ministers to Judah primarily but the north is not ignored. Micah a southerner came from a village very close to it's more infamous neighbour Gath – home of Goliath. Along with Isaiah Micah sees the northern tribes scattered by the Assyrians and predicts it in 1:6. Much of Micah's early ministry in the south coincided with Hosea working in the north. He foresees the Babylonian invasion in 4:10 but this must have seemed very unlikely at the time. He speaks out very clearly against the corruption of his day and particularly denounced the way many of the leaders, both secular and religious were oppressing the poorer inhabitants of Jerusalem. Like many of his fellow prophets he declares judgement on the wickedness of the people but assures them that God will intervene after the forthcoming judgement and restore His people back into the Promised Land.

Below is an acrostic which summarises each chapter of the book.

1. **M**essages against Samaria, Jerusalem
2. **E**vils committed by Israel
3. **S**ins of Israel's leaders
4. **S**tarting the future Kingdom
5. **I**nside of Messianic Kingdom
6. **A**ctions of injustice rebuked
7. **H**ope in God's future

Judgement Is Coming And Here's Why!

The Big Picture

Visions were given to Micah regarding Judah and Samaria. These take place before Assyria attacks and may be seen as some of the last pleas from a God who does not want His people to suffer more than necessary. They must be judged of course and that is just around the corner! Sadly there are no signs of repentance from the people and this makes God's judgement unavoidable. The prophet Micah tells the people that their wickedness has given God no alternative but to bring judgement on them. They have only themselves to blame but to date the penny has not dropped amongst God's chosen people that they have done anything wrong!

Thinking Step

1:1 Tells us the names of the Kings of Judah when Micah prophesied but he gives no details of the northern Kings! It seems God had nothing else to say to Pekah and Pekahiah who both murdered their predecessors in order to grab the throne. However God hasn't given up on the people and they are still addressed by Micah.

Action Step

1:6 God describes what He will do to that great city of Samaria. Not only will He destroy it and make it into a pile of rubble but He will plough it up and plant vineyards. When this was done then there would be no trace of the city because God had wiped it out! It must have been difficult to imagine that God was that powerful but He is! Micah is telling both north and south that things have become so bad that only a completely fresh start will succeed. After the scattering of Israel and the exiling of Judah a totally new start was then handed to the Children of Israel. Faithful Jews in Micah's day must have almost given up hope. The society in which they lived was so corrupt that it could never be revived. I believe however that it could have been if the people had repented. There would have been no need for the Assyrians to invade or for the Babylonians to scoop up Judah and take them into exile. It could all have been avoided if there had been changes in lifestyle following personal repentance by enough individuals. This solution will work today too! Only life change in individuals will succeed in making our society all that God wants it to be. Where can you start? With you of course – and with me too. Care to join me?

You Can Rely On Our God!

The Big Picture

God tells His people that a major source of their problems is their leadership. The leaders are acting like animals! They only turn to God when they want something. They listen to false prophets but never listen to God! Micah tells them that the day will come when people from all over the world will flock to the Temple in Jerusalem and all wars will cease. God will gather together all His people and rule in peace forever. However there is the issue of the exile before all that. They will be taken away from this land but God will see to it that they are returned safely when this judgement is over.

Thinking Step

3:12 – '...Mount Zion will be ploughed like an open field, Jerusalem will be reduced to ruins! A thicket will grow on the heights where the Temple now stands.' About 100 years later Jeremiah quotes Micah exactly in Jer. 26:18 The only time in the whole Old Testament where one writer quotes a saying or 'verse' of another, word for word!

Action Step

Micah has some stinging things to say about the corrupt leadership in power when he was a prophet in Judah. The issue of poor leadership was a key reason for God's judgement of the coming exile. Whilst our church leaderships are unlikely to be quite as bad as in Micah's day there are issues in all fellowships that need to be checked in the light of Scripture and with the help of the Holy Spirit. If you are a leader then you are directly responsible to God for the faithful shepherding of all the sheep in your Church. Ruling them rather than serving them is a mistake we all make, occasionally. If you have slipped over this line now is the time to get back onto the serving path. If you are not currently in leadership there is much for you to do too! Remember to constantly pray for your leadership team.

1. Support them as you would like to be supported.
2. Encourage them as you would like to be encouraged.
3. Trust them as you would like to be trusted.

In Micah's day they could easily have looked north to Israel and said "At least we are not as bad as them!" Thankfully Micah made it very clear that the standard to aspire to is not set by other people but by our God in His Word. Got any adjustments to make? The time to make them is now!

Get Ready For Jesus' Coming

The Big Picture

God warns the Israelites to get ready for invasion. The enemy is coming! However ultimately Bethlehem will produce a ruler who is the source of peace – Messiah Himself! Israel will fall to the Assyrians but Judah will be preserved only to fall to the Babylonians more than a century later. God challenges Judah to stand up and make a case for itself as in a court of law with God as the judge! Their immediate reaction is to consider offering more sacrifices but they are reminded that walking humbly before their God is far more appropriate. They must stop following bad role models like Omri and Ahab, wicked Kings of the north in the days of Elijah and Elisha.

Thinking Step

Bethlehem Ephrathah. Its two names may be translated – Bethlehem, (house of bread) and Ephrathah (after its original name Ephrath which means 'fruitfulness' – Gen. 35:19). Specifically named in full by Micah as the birthplace of Messiah, so as not to be confused with Bethlehem of Galilee – Josh. 19:15 a city of the northern tribe of Zebulun.

Action Step

Every time I read the prophecy of Micah about Bethlehem Ephrathah being the place which would produce a ruler who would lead His flock in the Lord's strength and would be the source of our peace – 5:5-8 – Jesus the Messiah, I am constantly amazed that it wasn't a fact that everyone was aware of – Matt 2:4. You would think everyone would have been certain of such an important prophecy especially if you lived nearby and ruled the land as Herod did! Then my mind would pass on to the second coming the timing of which has been written about by many learned men and women over the years, even though Jesus said that no one will know, Matt. 24:36 – "However no one knows the day or hour when these things will happen, not even the angels in heaven or the Son himself. Only the Father knows." So why waste time trying to find out? I am happy enough knowing that Jesus is coming back aren't you? Even though I don't know when I am convinced He will. The Bible gives some details of how and that's enough for me. It will be one of those surprises that will be so much better than we can imagine – and what a surprise! Make sure you are ready by accepting Jesus as Lord and Saviour now without further delay. See Day 21 for more details.

Day 260
Micah 7
17th September

1-7 - The People Deserve All That's Coming To Them!
8-20 - God Won't Stay Angry For Ever!

The People Are Guilty But God Will Forgive

The Big Picture

God the judge expresses His disappointment and says that He is like a fruit-picker who can't find anything to eat just after harvest! No food and nothing but crooked people! In the midst of all this Micah declares that he will trust God to see him through all his trials and tells his hearers to take their punishment on the chin! After all, they deserve it and God will be there to look after them when they return. He joyfully tells the people that God is such a loving God that He can't remain angry for long! He will redeem His people and they will be re-established into the land of their fathers Abraham and Jacob.

Thinking Step

7:5-6 – Just as those waiting for the invading hoards had to stand firm, despite the confusion all around them – so those who turn to Christ have to be similarly focused when being distracted by members of their families who are confused as established relationships are challenged and change – Matt. 10:35-37.

Action Step

Our elder son spends a lot of time on his own as a long distance lorry driver and has many philosophical thoughts! I remember him telling me many years ago that there is no real alternative to believing in God and Jesus coming to be our Saviour. The other options just don't add up! Micah says something very similar particularly to the people of Judah shortly before judgement comes to northern Israel. He warns them that the same will happen to them – and it does! 7:18 – 'Where is another God like you, who pardons the guilt of the remnant, overlooking the sins of his special people? You will not stay angry with your people forever because you delight in showing unfailing love.' These are revolutionary words to a people whose neighbours worshipped gods to whom you simply paid homage. There was little concept of a god that cared or even less got involved with humanity. In a way we have come full circle and are now surrounded by people who tend to think that there may be 'something up there' but it doesn't affect everyday life. How wonderful it is that we have a God who is interested in our day to day activities because He made us and sent Jesus to die for us. Whatever you're doing today, God is interested so why not share it with Him as the day progresses? There is no viable alternative.

Nahum

Nahum

More than 100 years have passed since the amazing revival under Jonah and Nineveh has now reverted to its wicked old ways. After JoNAH we have NAHum. The link in the names give you both of the prophets and the order they prophesied! Several suggestions have been made about where Nahum lived, including Capernaum (city of Nahum) in the north but many scholars would place him in Judah in the south and date him from the Egyptian historical details in 3:8-10 which would imply Manasseh was king of Judah at the time. With walls more than 30 metres high and wide enough for chariots to be ridden three abreast, Nineveh was a city that seemed impregnable when Nahum prophesied its downfall in 1:8. The flood that came was an overflow of the river Tigris creating a breach in the wall for the Babylonians to pour in victoriously.

Below is an acrostic which summarises each chapter of the book.

1. **G**od's character and judgement
2. **O**verthrow of Nineveh imminent
3. **D**etails of Nineveh's judgement

1 - God's Judgement Is Deserved
2 - God's Judgement Is Imminent
3 - God's Judgement Is Unavoidable

Day 261
Nahum 1-3
18th September

God's Powerful Enemies Are Powerless

The Big Picture

A native of Elkosh, Nahum continues the ministry of Jonah but this time it is to declare judgement on back-sliding Nineveh. He tells them that what is about to happen is Godly justice and will happen soon and no matter what they try it's inevitable. They are doomed despite having been the 'super-power' of the world up to that point. Unlike Jonah, Nahum probably doesn't visit in person but tells the Ninevites that they don't know what they are doing if they think they can stand against the powerful living God of Israel. Despite already having recently scattered the northern tribes of Israel, Nahum tells Nineveh that they themselves will soon fall. Significantly he probably lived to see it!

Thinking Step

The Assyrians were known as the 'murderous people' and Nineveh was known as the 'bloody city.' Their Kingdom was built upon violence, murder, warfare, broken promises, extortion, plundering and rape.

Nahum's prophecy was fulfilled exactly as described. Nineveh disappeared from the scene of history until 1842 when French and English archaeologists uncovered the site of the once mighty city.

Action Step

The prophecy of Nahum reminds us that God has a great memory. In 1:3 we read 'The Lord is slow to get angry but His power is great and He never lets the guilty go unpunished.' He is certainly not a vengeful God but when He promises justice it always comes – in His good time. In our 21st century world we see lots of wickedness and flouting of God's Word and Will but justice will ultimately follow. I am very glad that I am not on the judgement throne but that I know who is! That's why I know there will be no hint of unfairness on judgement day. It helps to be reminded that even if I don't see things work out as I would like them to, they will – in the fullness of time. This may sound like 'pie in the sky when you die' but I believe God is a God who gives us 'cake on the plate while we wait!' However there will always be 'rough edges' until that last day. I think your blood pressure and mine, will benefit from this reminder when we see people, 'getting away with murder'. Why not put this verse on your mobile phone or computer. I have it printed on paper over my desk – with other necessary reminders!

'The Lord is slow to get angry but His power is great and He never lets the guilty go unpunished.'

Habakkuk

Habakkuk

Habakkuk was a contemporary of Jeremiah and ministered to Judah in the early part of Jeremiah's ministry. He gives us few clues as to his location or lineage but seems to be a priest, possibly in the Temple. Habakkuk is a rather unusual Hebrew name and probably means 'one who clings or embraces.' This sums up his attitude very well as after many doubts and questions he clings to God with conviction and rejoices in the fact that 'the righteous will live by their faith.' He had many problems understanding God's methods of justice, in particular how could God's chosen people be disciplined by the godless unclean Babylonians who were the lowest of the low! His prophetic writings cover three chapters and fall into two parts. The first two chapters are filled with his doubts and questions and the third chapter resounds with triumph as Habakkuk trusts God anyway!

Below is an acrostic which summarises each chapter of the book.

1. **W**hy is evil unpunished
2. **H**aughty Chaldea will fall
3. **Y**ielding to God's sovereignty

Day 262
Habakkuk 1-3
19th September

1 - God Has A Unique Strategy
2 - Habakkuk Doesn't Like What He Hears
3 - Habakkuk Trusts God And Worships Him

God's Ways Can Be Hard To Understand!

The Big Picture

The opening verses could have been written today in the 21st century. Chaos all around and a God who doesn't care or so it seems. God's response to Habakkuk's plea was to advise. "Watch and be astounded!" Habakkuk does – and is! God using the Babylonians was simply unthinkable. They were the worst people on earth, surely God knew that! Habakkuk retreats to his watchtower hoping either God will change His mind or Habakkuk will finally understand better. It slowly dawns on the prophet that God means what He says and the proud and arrogant of Judah who were misusing their power were going to get some of their own medicine! His response was to trust God and praise Him.

Thinking Step

1:6 '- I am raising up the Babylonians to be a new power on the world scene.' This was rather like God deciding to use some of the extreme terrorist groups of the 21st century. Unthinkable perhaps but action that God could take if He wished! Ps 115:3 – 'Our God is in the heavens and He does as He wishes.'

Action Step

I firmly believe that 'the righteous will live by their faith ...' – 2:4. I'm not the only one either! So did Paul in Rom. 1:17 and Gal. 3:11 as well as the writer to the Hebrews in Heb. 10:38. It is one of those fundamental parts of doctrine that is an essential part of real Biblical or evangelical faith. However sometimes we have trouble putting what we believe into practice don't we? Believing that what we do doesn't save us is the relatively easy bit. It's the daily living by faith that's more complicated. How do we do it? The original Hebrew in this verse may be translated to read, 'the righteous will live by their faithfulness ...' I think this is easier to grasp. We need to live as faithful people and this is a very practical issue. We need to be faithful to our church and earthly families. Part of being faithful is being positive. I cannot see how one can be faithful and negative. Faithfulness goes with positive doesn't it? Believing the best no matter what. Communicating the positive aspect of an issue rather than the negative side. Nurturing the best in our children and grandchildren rather than simply condemning their bad behaviour. I could go on but I trust I have said enough to make this practical outworking easier to understand.

Faithfulness to God shows in daily positive living. Got it? Now live it!

Zephaniah

Zephaniah

Shortly before God speaks through Habakkuk in Judah some messages are given to Zephaniah, a great great grandson of King Hezekiah who was a Godly King of Judah about seventy years earlier. His ministry overlaps that of Nahum to Nineveh and Jeremiah to Judah. He is uniquely a prophet from royal descent and this royal lineage could have been a real 'door-opener' for Zephaniah to have influence in the palace of Josiah who was a Godly King from being a young man. His message is laced with many warnings of the coming 'Day of the Lord.' Most of this prophecy goes into detail about the awesome impact of that day with the latter part of the final chapter covering both the judgement and restoration which will take place. He condemns the leaders of Judah in particular especially for their encouragement to allow the worship of pagan deities.

Below is an acrostic which summarises each chapter of the book.

1. **J**udah's day of judgement
2. **E**nemies of Judah punished
3. **W**rath and coming restoration

1 - The Day Of The Lord Approaches

2 - Moab And Ammon Beware!

3 - Judah's Leaders Beware!

Day 263

Zephaniah 1-3

20th September

Be Ready For The Day Of The Lord

The Big Picture

God tells Zephaniah how sad and angry He is by the pagan worship of the people of Judah. He repeats the warning several times in his writings – 'Beware, the day of the Lord is coming!' He urges the people to act now and get into a better relationship with the living God by begging Him for forgiveness. He also has a word for the Ammonites and the Moabites, that they have acted disgracefully towards the people of Judah and will be punished accordingly. In many ways Jerusalem which should be the best, is the worst. Its leaders are content with pagan worship. The 'Day of the Lord' is truly coming!

Thinking Step

1:8 – "On that day of judgement" says the Lord "I will punish the leaders and Princes of Judah and all those following pagan customs." (NIV – 'all those clad in foreign clothes.') Wearing foreign clothes was a statement of allegiance to foreign gods. Individuals wore special clothing as preparation for offering sacrifices in foreign temples.

Action Step

The key theme of Zephaniah, the 'Day of the Lord' is something to be feared, respected and welcomed according to this prophecy! It is not simply judgement day when God will punish sinful mankind but that is part of it according to 1:8. People today don't like to think of a day of reckoning so they choose to laugh at it hoping it will go away. The book of Revelation tells us in 14:13 – "Happy are the dead who die in the faith of Christ" ...says the Spirit "they may rest from their labours for they take with them the record of their deeds!" Every time I conduct a funeral service and read these words this hits me with great force and I am so glad that all my deeds, good and bad are covered by the blood of Jesus! Zeph. 3:16 tells us not to be afraid on that day. There is so much silly talk about heaven and hell today and what they will be like. Such talk is deliberately infantile otherwise it may be convicting! So for believers the 'Day of the Lord' is a day to be welcomed. Remember we will all have to experience such a day so it makes sense to think about it and make plans beforehand rather than leave everything to the last minute. If you need more guidance about being covered by Jesus please turn to day 21.

Haggai

Haggai

The last three prophets are the last three prophets! They are called the post exilic prophets because they ministered after the exile. They are in chronological order and Haggai is the first one. His ministry is to encourage those who have returned to the Promised Land under Zerubbabel to get on and complete the rebuilding of the Temple which was started earlier but remained unfinished. Haggai worked alongside the prophet Zechariah. We have very specific dates throughout this short prophecy and there is little doubt about the accuracy and authenticity of the whole book. This rebuilt temple was never fully appreciated and consequently the next temple built by Herod the Great is usually referred to as the second temple. The Talmud teaches that the Ark of the Covenant, the Shekinah Glory and the Urim and Thummim were not in the rebuilt temple all of which weakened its credibility.

Below is an acrostic which summarises each chapter of the book.

1. **G**od's temple needs building
2. **O**lder temple less glorious

Day 264
Haggai 1-2
21st September

1 - The Temple is Not Finished!
2 - The Foundation is Completed!

Temple Project Must Be Completed For God

The Big Picture

Haggai the prophet is given a word from the Lord for Zerubbabel and the people settling in the Promised Land after the return from exile. He tells them that their priorities are wrong. They are carefully building fancy panelled houses and yet the Temple of the Lord is still a ruin. If they are to prosper they must get on with rebuilding God's Temple. The question is asked about how it compares to Solomon's original. The older folk who remembered the original didn't rate it very highly! Haggai tells the people that their progress is slow because they have not yet fully returned to God. They have returned to their land but not to their God!

Thinking Step

Religions in general demand obedience from adherents. Bible believers on the other hand are constantly urged to use their reasoning powers. Haggai, over 2,500 years ago, encourages his hearers to think rather than simply obey. His promptings in 1:5, 1:7, 2:15, 2:18 may be summed up as "Consider this." Truly reflecting a 'thinking person's religion!'

Action Step

When we first moved to the small coastal town of Frinton-on-Sea in Essex, we lived very near its centre and tended to walk everywhere. Banking, post office, Church and shopping were all attended to on foot. This was great until people began stopping me in the street with the latest news on fellowship members who were ill or having difficulties or simply to have a chat. I would regularly set of to the bank and return an hour later having had some beneficial conversations but still clutching the banking in my hand! It was the same with posting letters that were too often not posted but I am sure enjoyed accompanying me on a walk by the seaside! In our reading today we learn of an interesting episode in the history of the Jewish people. An incident where they were deflected from the primary aim to concentrate on other benign projects but which caused them to ignore their No.1 calling. Jesus was often side-tracked as He ministered in Galilee and Judea but He never lost His direction. It's a very worthwhile exercise to occasionally look at our personal workload. It's usually good things that detract us from the best. Playing golf rather than attending Church or watching TV rather than attending housegroup. We need to be constantly vigilant to keep our priorities God's priorities. Time for a check up today maybe?

Zechariah

Zechariah

Zechariah's ministry begins about the same time as that of Haggai but lasts longer as he is generally thought to be the younger of the two. As minor prophets go Zechariah is one of the longer ones alongside Hosea both having fourteen chapters. Whilst he prophesies at the same time as Haggai his approach is quite different. Haggai tends to urge action on the Temple and scolds inaction. On the other hand Zechariah seeks to be encouraging by emphasising the benefits and blessings that will come with a completed Temple which will be graced by Messiah. As with Haggai there is little doubt about this writing being the work of the person whose name it bears. The first eight chapters encourage the people to rebuild the Temple whilst the last six chapters seem to be after this task was completed and concentrate on Zechariah's two burdens – the rejection and reign of Messiah.

Below is an acrostic which summarises each chapter of the book.

1. **M**eaning of Zechariah's vision
2. **E**xamination with measuring line
3. **S**atan and the Branch
4. **S**even lampshades of gold
5. **I**nterpreting the flying scroll
6. **A**ct of crowning Joshua
7. **H**earts become like flint
8. **S**ecurity comes to Jerusalem

9. **R**eturn of the Messiah
10. **E**phraim and Judah restored
11. **T**eaching about wicked shepherds
12. **U**nderstanding whom they pierced
13. **R**efining of God's remnant
14. **N**ew kingdom ushered in

Zechariah's First Visions

The Big Picture

Zechariah has a word from the Lord for Judah. He reminds the people that their forefathers rejected the words of the prophets of old. Now He tells them that they all know that what God promised and prophesied through His prophets was true and duly came to be. It happens like that every time! Three months later Zechariah receives a vision from God, a vision of horses and angels. The horses carried men who patrolled the earth and the angels were in charge and received reports from the riders. God declared that He was angered by the way other nations had mistreated His people and they would pay the price!

Thinking Step

Zechariah is 1 of 30 men who bear this name in the Old Testament. It means 'God remembers' and was naturally a very popular name amongst the Israelites. Like the apostle John who sometimes referred to himself as 'the disciple Jesus loved' Zechariah simply refers to himself in 2:4 as a young man.

Action Step

When you study history one of the big things that hits you is the way mankind makes the same mistakes over and over again. It's even more obvious when you study Church history. The same imbalances, over-reactions and stiff-necked people keep showing up. On the other hand God is the exact opposite. He is totally dependable and unchanging. Zechariah speaks on behalf of God and reminds the people that history is very clear where God is concerned. He always means what He says. 1:6 – "...everything I said through my servants the prophets happened to your ancestors, just as I said..." So why would it be any different now is the essence of what Zechariah is saying. Sometimes we are so used to being let down by people that we expect similar treatment from God. It will never be so! Stop making things unnecessarily complicated. Is there something you need to be reassured about? Ask God today to confirm to you that this is part of His will for you then get on with your life trusting Him. If there is no confirmation then you need to go back a step and ask if this is part of His plan for you. Of course it is easier said than done but it is the narrow pathway we need to walk. This simple approach can save many future heartbreaks. Try being simple and childlike for a refreshing change!

Visions Of Priests, Lampstand And Olive Trees

The Big Picture

Zechariah has a further two visions. Firstly he sees the Angel of the Lord and Satan side by side with the High Priest before them. The High Priest is defended by the Lord and then has his dirty clothes symbolically replaced with clean fresh ones signifying his sins have been forgiven. Then at the request of Zechariah the High Priest's turban is also replaced. The Lord promises all the priests as well as the High Priest complete freedom within the Temple area. Zechariah's next vision is of a golden lampstand with olive trees. He is then told that Zerubbabel's work will be successful and the Temple will be completed by him.

Thinking Step

Essential wear! 3:5 – 'Then I said "They should also place a clean turban on his head." In accordance with Ex. 28:37-38 – 'Attach the medallion with a blue cord to the front of Aaron's turban where it must remain. Aaron must wear it on his forehead so he may take on himself any guilt of the people of Israel ...'

Action Step

4:6 – 'Then he said to me "This is what the Lord says to Zerubbabel: It is not by force nor by strength but by my Spirit, says the Lord of Heaven's Armies."' This is a specific word for Zerubbabel who was completing the rebuilding of the Temple for God. However I believe it can equally be applied to you and me today because it is such a fundamental principle. When the text refers to 'by force nor by strength' this is a word to remind Zerubbabel that even though Solomon had enormous resources to build the Temple, Zerubbabel would also have all that he needed to rebuild it. Rather than relying on worldly wealth like that of Solomon, Zerubbabel should depend on the help of the Spirit of God who was instrumental in the creation of the world! Gen. 1:2. Which would you choose? Of course we can be too simplistic at times and not give enough thought to the provision we need to complete God's work. However we usually tend to be too much the other way assuming that only if the means are available may the project proceed! Many a project has been done with worldly provision and has failed to fulfil what God wanted. On the other hand I don't know of anything that has been completed by the Spirit of God and failed to be what God wanted!

Flying Scrolls And Mighty Chariots!

The Big Picture

The visions of Zechariah continue unabated but can be very difficult to understand. It's no surprise that Zechariah regularly asks what all this means and scholars have echoed his cry ever since! There is a vision of a giant scroll of judgement for all who disobey some of God's laws. Then a basket filled with sins which is quickly transported to Babylonia. The vision of four chariots with horses of different colours continues to mystify many. It could signify God's actions against Israel's enemy nations from the four corners of the earth. However as we are only given details of three chariots this poses problems! We conclude with further glimpses of the coming Messiah referred to as 'branch.'

Thinking Step

6:2-3 – The horse colours, three of which are repeated from 1:8 may have some significance. The dappled or mixed is linked by some to the pale horse of Rev. 6:8.

1. Red – bloodshed, war and judgement.
2. Black – mourning, scarcity, famine and death.
3. White – triumph and peace.
4. Dappled – mixed colours, therefore able to undertake any function.

Action Step

5:7-9 – 'Then the heavy lead cover was lifted off the basket and there was a woman sitting inside it. The angel said "The woman's name is Wickedness" and he pushed her back into the basket and closed the heavy lid again. Then I looked up and saw two women flying toward us gliding on the wind. They had wings like a stork and they picked up the basket and flew into the sky.'
When reading a vision like this it can be useful to ask God for an interpretation for yourself. That's what I did and immediately found that here we have a graphic picture of each of us with our old selves constantly popping up and having to be suppressed. Zechariah's vision has a lady called wickedness being taken away into the sky and away to Babylonia. A beautiful picture of our sins being removed and taken far away. I don't know about you but no matter how well I 'put the lid on my sins' they always escape! Of course when we do the right thing and confess our sins they are in a real sense, taken away. The major problem that follows is when the devil reminds us about them. Remember when God forgives He also forgets – Jer. 31:34b. As God says that our sins are forgotten I intend to live in the comfort of knowing that!

The Exile Is Over – Expansion Is Beginning

The Big Picture

Men from Bethel come to Zechariah asking if they should be continuing to commemorate every year the destruction of the Temple. He asks them why they have been keeping this annual remembrance anyway – what were their motives as they seemed less than genuine Under God's guidance Zechariah tells them to get on with life and live it better by treating others more fairly. In other words, learn from your forefather's mistakes which resulted in the exile. God reassures the people once again that things will get better very soon. More immigrants will be welcomed and Jerusalem will be thronged with happy smiling faces once again. They must not forget however that the Temple still needs to be completed.

Thinking Step

By Zechariah's time the northern tribes have not existed as tribes for about 200 years. The belief that many faithful Jews migrated south and joined the faithful of Judah is enforced in 8:12 – '...Once more I will cause the remnant in Judah and Israel to inherit these blessings.' Judah had indeed become Israel!

Action Step

8:23 – 'This is what the Lord of Heaven's Armies says: In those days ten men from different nations and languages of the world will clutch at the sleeve of one Jew and they will say "Please let us walk with you for we have heard that God is with you."' What a wonderful picture Zechariah paints here. People will actually come looking for God rather than having to be chased! When I was employed as a technical rep. for a large building supplies company I was sent to many conferences and training courses. We used to dream of a perfect product that would not have to be sold but that people would just buy! A quick look at the early Church suggests that witnessing was only a small part of spreading the Gospel. Lifestyle and attitude and their love for one another was far more effective. Zechariah is telling the people of his day that they should be shining lights for their religion. How much more should we be beacons for our living faith. How is it done? Not by putting on an act and certainly not by brashly proclaiming it to strangers. Just being yourself should do it! If it doesn't then you need to change! Here's a challenge for you – name one thing that would improve your image as a witness for God in your society. Now ask God to help you change.

God's Judgement And
God's Messiah Are Both Coming

The Big Picture

Zechariah speaks words of doom for Damascus, Tyre and Sidon and the land of the Philistines. These enemies of Israel will be defeated and at the same time Jerusalem will know real abundance. Just keep a lookout – the King will come riding on a donkey. A very clear foretelling of what was to happen many centuries later when Jesus enters the city riding on the colt of a donkey. Ultimately Jerusalem will be re-populated and re-established and then thrive under the guidance of God Himself. The people must stop consulting fortune tellers and the like and look to God who has always been so faithful.

Thinking Step

When Jacob gathers his sons together he has a particular word for Judah – Gen. 49:11 – 'He ties his foal to a grapevine, the colt of his donkey to a choice vine...' This seems the inspiration for Zechariah's proclamation about the coming King – 9:9. Looking back at the patriarchs gives a clear hint about the coming Lion of Judah.

Action Step

10:2 – 'Household gods give worthless advice, fortune-tellers predict only lies and interpreters of dreams pronounce falsehoods that give no comfort. So my people are wandering like lost sheep; they are attacked because they have no shepherd.' This word from the Lord for the Children of Israel after the exile period could just as easily be for today in the 21st century. In these days of crystals, fortune tellers, horoscopes and lots of other 'new age' mumbo jumbo too few people rely on the living God for guidance. It seems little has changed! I realise that this is the Old Testament and many folk would have you believe that the Old Testament is out of date and the New Testament is the only one to follow. I believe our God is out of time and therefore when He inspired the writers of the Old Testament He was the same God who fulfilled it through Jesus and inspired the New Testament writers. Some folk today are like the little girl who came home from Church to tell her parents about the story she had been told which included hundreds of people being massacred and thousands of animals being slaughtered. Her parents couldn't resist asking if this was the same God who wants everyone to love each other. "Of course it's the same God" the little girl said "However these things happened in the Old Testament before God was a Christian!"

381

A Glimpse Of The Good Shepherd

The Big Picture

Words of coming judgement are given to Lebanon and Bashan (Syria). Zechariah is told by God to care for a flock of sheep being prepared for slaughter. Then he declares that just as there is no remorse over their demise so God Himself will not regret what is to happen to Judah's inhabitants. Zechariah cares for his sheep and dismisses the existing bad shepherds. The sheep, God's people, turn against Zechariah so he resigns and demands his wages – 30 pieces of silver! God told him to return to the flock but to act as a worthless shepherd – a sign of what's to come. God promises that He will protect Jerusalem and that the family of David will know much blessing.

Thinking Step

11:13b – '...So they counted out for my wages, thirty pieces of silver.' This was the same compensation for a slave gored by a bull – Ex. 21:32. It's interesting that when a slave is pierced the payment is the same as when Jesus is betrayed and pierced! There are other parallels in this passage too with Matt 27:3-10.

Action Step

Chapter 11 is a clear picture of the rejection of the Good Shepherd, namely Jesus Christ. Even the amount of money and what happened to it in the end are details that coincide with the gospel account. Rejection is a costly thing. For both the one who makes the gesture and for the one who rejects it. We can see from the Gospels that the payment made by Jesus was immense. It cost so much more than His life. It cost Him rejection by God an experience He had never previously known. It also cost Him the pain of bearing the sin of the whole world, which is unimaginable. All of this only to have it thrown back in His face by so many of the very people it was offered to. Of course for most of us reading this we can say that we have not rejected Him but have accepted His sacrifice for us and are eternally grateful. What about daily rejection though? What about those times when we reject what He offers and take our own direction and fulfil our own dreams? Care to think again about some of the selfish decisions you have recently made? When you reject what Jesus offers throughout your life, you reject the best in favour of the mediocre! That doesn't make sense so why not remake a previously foolish decision – today!

The Ultimate Victory

The Big Picture

Zechariah is told by God to anticipate that great day when Messiah comes and will become a cleansing fountain available to all Jerusalem and ultimately the whole world as they acknowledge Him. God also warned that there must be vigilance because some amazing things are certain to happen in the future. Even the prophet himself concedes that 'only the Lord knows how this will happen' – 14:6. The Mount of Olives will split in two and waters will run south from Jerusalem to the Dead Sea and also run west to the Mediterranean Sea! Judgement will come to all who have opposed Jerusalem but finally the city will enjoy total security from God – and it will last forever!

Thinking Step

If you have experienced difficulty understanding the prophecy of Zechariah especially the later chapters, take heart! Martin Luther wrote two commentaries on this book. In the first one he passed over the whole of chapter 14 without a mention! In the second he said "In chapter fourteen I surrender for I am not certain of what the prophet speaks!"

Action Step

14:20 – ' On that day even the harness bells of the horses will be inscribed with these words: Holy to the Lord and the cooking pots in the Temple of the Lord will be as sacred as the basins used beside the altar.' This is another reference from Zechariah that takes us all the way back to the garments of the priests and in particular the gold plate that was at the front of the turban and bore the inscription 'Holy to the Lord' – Exodus 28:36. If you ask most people to define 'holy' they usually come out with 'pious' or 'religious' or other similar 'churchy-type' words. However, how can such a word be used to describe harness bells on horses? Well holy really means set apart for God. Like the ground in Exodus 3:5 this had been set apart for God's purposes. It was ordinary ground before and reverted back to ordinary ground after Moses had his encounter with God. It's the same for the bells – and you and me! 1 Peter 1:15-16 – '... now you must be holy in everything you do, just as God, who chose you, is holy.' For the Scriptures say "You must be holy because I am holy." It is clear that we are to be set apart for God. Remember that you are the nearest to Jesus that many people will see! We are holy people so let's live like it!

Malachi

Malachi

So we arrive at the very last prophet in the Old Testament, Malachi. He was about 100 years after Haggai and Zechariah and supported the work of Nehemiah as the walls of Jerusalem are rebuilt. He brings the curtain down on the prophetic period and the whole Old Testament. The land had been resettled after the exile but it didn't take the people long to slip away from God. Malachi addresses the leaders about their corrupt practices. Dishonest priests and unacceptable sacrifices as well as intermarriage with pagan wives was once again a big problem for God's people. Malachi looks forward to all that God has for His people if only they will listen – but they won't! With sadness in His heart God refuses to give up on His people but He stops talking to them for 400 years! Then along comes John the Baptiser and the silence is broken.

Below is an acrostic which summarises each chapter of the book.

1. **L**esson of polluted sacrifice
2. **O**ffences of the priests
3. **R**obbing God is cursed
4. **D**awning of new day

Some Sacrifices Are Better Than Others

The Big Picture

God makes it clear to Malachi that despite their constant rejection and disobedience God still loves His people. Even though they offer dishonouring sacrifices, God still loves them but He hates their sacrifices! Malachi condemns the leaders too and tells them that the covenant they have with God is for their benefit and enjoyment but they insist on choosing the bits they like and rejecting the other bits that are not convenient! The people are told that God won't accept their sacrifices until they start living like covenant people again. A good start would be being faithful to each other especially for the men to be faithful to their wives.

Thinking Step

The name Malachi means 'My messenger' and is probably a shortened version of the name Mal'ak-ya which means 'Messenger of Yahweh.' How significant and appropriate a name for this last prophet of the Old Testament who proclaims that Elijah will be Yahweh's messenger who declares the coming Messiah, Jesus Christ the Lamb of God.

Action Step

1:12 – ' ...you dishonour My Name with your actions. By bringing contemptible food, you are saying it's all right to defile the Lord's table.' It's rather significant that this Old Testament verse sounds as though it could have come from the New Testament! Instead of the anticipated 'Lord's altar' which you would perhaps expect we have 'Lord's table' which takes us immediately to the Lord's Supper or Communion or Eucharist. We are taught clearly in 1 Cor. 11:27 – 'So anyone who eats this bread or drinks this cup of the Lord unworthily is guilty of sinning against the body and blood of the Lord.' Of course some folk take this act so seriously that they stop reading the Bible at this point and feel it's right to leave the table if they feel unworthy. I suggest they read on to the next verse – 'That is why you should examine yourself before eating the bread and drinking the cup.' The ancients were not worthy to come to the table but when they offered the right sacrifice in the right way God accepted it. We are not worthy either, otherwise there was no need for Jesus to go to Calvary. However God accepts us because of the perfect sacrifice of Jesus and when we examine ourselves and resolve to put right any of the issues revealed to us by the Holy Spirit – then we may take communion, according to the Scriptures.

3 - God Has Kept His Side Of The Covenant
4 - Be Patient - Messiah Will Come!

Day 273
Malachi 3-4
30th September

God Is Faithful To The End

The Big Picture

God tells the people that it won't be long before the forerunner comes to declare the arrival of Messiah. There will be a delay of 400 years but God keeps His side of the agreement that He made with Abraham, Isaac, Jacob, Joseph and their descendants. The people don't deserve what God has for them but God is a loving trustworthy God all the way through. Right at the end the faithful followers of Yahweh listen to Him and prepare a scroll bearing all their names. However it's all a bit too late and God's prophetic voice is silent for the next four hundred years but He does keep His promise – as we always knew He would!

Thinking Step

Are you glad you are reading the Old Testament instead of the Jewish Tanakh? The books are the same but the order is different. If you were reading the Tanakh you would have finished the Torah and the Prophets with just the Writings next. That is Psalms, Proverbs, Job, Song of Solomon, Ruth, Lamentations, Esther, Daniel, Ezra, Nehemiah and 1 & 2 Chronicles!

Action Step

3:10 – "Bring all the tithes into the storehouse so there will be enough food in my Temple. If you do" says the Lord of Heaven's Armies "I will open the windows of heaven for you. I will pour out a blessing so great you won't have enough room to take it in! Try it! Put me to the test!" Wow! What a way to finish the Old Testament. If we give all we have and are to the Lord then He will give us so much that we won't be able to contain it. I don't for a second think that this is a verse about material wealth. I am convinced that God is saying if we sell out to Him He will more than compensate us – with real living! Do you know anyone who on their death bed says that they wish they had been less committed to God? No I don't either! However I can imagine the opposite and I don't want that to happen to me – or you. As we complete the Old Testament, well done by the way, we now have its fulfilment to enjoy – the New Testament. I hope you are looking forward to it as much as I am. When we give God our all we will lack nothing. If we hold some back it will, like the manna of old, rot away and be of no use. Just let it go!

NEW TESTAMENT

New Testament Structure

PAUL'S LETTERS TO PASTORS

1 Timothy	2 Timothy	Titus	Philemon

PAUL'S LETTERS TO CHURCHES

2 Thessalonians		Hebrews
1 Thessalonians		James
Colossians		1 Peter
Philippians		2 Peter
Ephesians		1 John
Galatians		2 John
2 Corinthians		3 John
1 Corinthians		Jude
Romans		Revelation

GENERAL LETTERS

Matthew	Mark	Luke	John	Acts

HISTORICAL BOOKS

390

Four Distinct Views Of Christ

	MATTHEW	MARK	LUKE	JOHN
OCCUPATION	Tax Collector	Missionary	Doctor	Fisherman
ORIGINAL AUDIENCE	Jews	Romans	Greeks	All People
KEY VERSE	4:17	10:45	19:10	20:31
OUTSTANDING FEATURE	Sermons	Miracles	Parables	Teachings
ARRANGEMENT	Topical	Chronological	Chronological	Topical
TONE	Prophetic	Practical	Historical	Spiritual
GENEALOGY	To Abraham	None	To Adam	None
SPOKEN BY CHRIST	60%	42%	50%	50%
QUOTATIONS FROM OLD TESTAMENT	53	36	25	20
ALLUSIONS TO THE OLD TESTAMENT	76	27	42	105
UNIQUE MATERIAL	42%	7%	59%	93%
BROAD DIVISION	Synoptic Gospels (Humanity of Christ)			Supplemental Gospel (Deity of Christ)
CHRIST PORTRAYED AS	King	Servant	Perfect Man	Son of God

Matthew

Matthew

This Gospel is primarily written for Jews by a Jew called Matthew Levi and is the first of the synoptic (similar viewpoint) Gospels. It is full of the language of fulfilled prophecy that would attract Jewish readers. It is the first book in the New Testament and bridges the gap between the old covenant and the new one seamlessly as it begins with a genealogy full of Old Testament names. Matthew's aim is to declare that Jesus is 'King of the Jews.' It is thought that Matthew kept notes in his daily language of Aramaic when he was with Jesus and then wrote the full account in Greek for a worldwide audience. It seems probable that it was written before the destruction of Jerusalem and the Temple in AD70 as he makes no reference to this catastrophe for all Jews. He uses parables extensively and is essentially in topical order.

Below is an acrostic which summarises each chapter of the book.

1. **G**enealogy of Jesus Christ
2. **O**pposition of King Herod
3. **S**pirit's descent upon Jesus
4. **P**ower over Satan's temptations
5. **E**stablishment of kingdom principles
6. **L**essons on proper priorities

7. **O**utline for personal relationships
8. **F**aith of the Centurion

9. **M**atthew's call from Jesus
10. **A**postles sent to preach
11. **T**estimony about John's message
12. **T**rue Messiah called demonic
13. **H**idden message of parables
14. **E**xecution of the Baptist
15. **W**isdom of Jesus' message

16. **K**eys of the Kingdom
17. **I**mpact of Jesus' transfiguration
18. **N**eed for true forgiveness
19. **G**rounds for divorced clarified

20. **O**pportunities in the vineyard
21. **F**ig tree is cursed

22. **T**axes paid to Caesar
23. **H**ypocrisy denounced by "woes"
24. **E**vents of second coming

25. **J**udgement of the nations
26. **E**vents of Calvary's eve
27. **W**ay of the cross
28. **S**aviour's resurrection & commission

Day 274
Matthew 1-4
1st October

1 - Genealogy Of Jesus The King
2 - Magi Visit Jesus The King
3 - John Baptises Jesus The King
4 - Satan Tempts Jesus The King

Credentials Of The King

The Big Picture

We begin with the genealogy of Jesus which is of primary importance to this Jewish writer and indeed to his Jewish readers. Now we have established that Jesus fulfils Old Testament prophecy and is Son of David the stage is set for His amazing life-story. A visit by magi confirms that Jesus is King of the Jews and more prophecy is fulfilled as King Herod massacres all boys in and around Bethlehem who are under two years of age. After a stay in Egypt Jesus and His parents settle in Nazareth and when He is a mature man He is baptised by John the baptiser and subsequently tempted by Satan as His ministry begins.

Thinking Step

2:2 – '...We saw His star as it rose and we have come to worship Him.' Despite the message of many nativity plays and Christmas cards it is clear that the magi did not follow the star for the whole journey but only from Jerusalem to Bethlehem 2:9 – '...the star they had seen in the east guided them to Bethlehem.'

Action Step

Today we have read the most amazing narrative. Immortal God becoming a human being and living on earth like us! Of course this is an account that has been blurred considerably by Dickensian Christmas festivities and lots of misleading slogans like 'Christmas is all about children' or 'M & S Food – that's what it's all about.' Don't get me wrong I love the secular side of Christmas and still have fond memories of my Mum telling me to "Go to sleep otherwise he may not come!" For a five year old being told to go to sleep is on a par with being told to sit down and be good! It's impossible. You must also have heard about the lady who went shopping for Christmas cards and came home complaining "They have even put religion into Christmas now!" So what is the essence of Christmas, what is it all about? God coming down to mankind. All other religions that have a god depend on mankind getting up to him. He stays put and waits for his adherents and worshippers to reach the standard required. Uniquely God came down to mankind and that's what it's all about. It may not be Christmas when you read this but it's still a great time to express your gratitude to God for doing everything necessary and all we have to do is receive the benefit. More information may be found on Day 21 in this book.

5 - Beautiful Beatitudes
6 - Private Prayer Works Best
7 - Build On A Sure Foundation

Day 275
Matthew 5-7
2nd October

Sermon On The Mount

The Big Picture

These chapters probably contain a compilation of several teachings from Jesus. In three short chapters He gives us the immortal beatitudes and a challenge not to use others as our model. The denouncing of hypocrisy is covered and is a theme that runs through the whole life and ministry of Jesus. Living to please God rather than impress other people is something He did every day and we need to follow that example. Stop judging others because in reality we need to attend to our own faults first before trying to help others with theirs! It's a narrow gate that leads to eternal life and a narrow road that will take you to it – and sadly very few find it!

Thinking Step

One of the things Matthew notices here is that Jesus is speaking on the mountainside. The parallel passage in Luke 6:20-26 doesn't mention this. Luke was writing to Greeks whereas Matthew was writing to Jews and their authority had always come down from the mount ever since Moses came down from Mount Sinai. So Matthew remarks on it!

Action Step

Have you ever had a debate with someone who does not believe the Bible but insists on telling you that they live by the sermon on the mount? The beatitudes, the Lord's prayer and all that! It can be impressive if you don't know another vital ingredient in this famous teaching. It's found at the end of chapter 5 – '...you are to be perfect, even as your Father in heaven is perfect.' Jesus is quoting Lev. 19:2. So if God's standard is perfection what hope do we have? The only answer is the perfect Son of God acting as our intermediary. It is very hard to grasp the concept of not being good enough. That's one of the attractions of other religions which teach that if you do the right things regularly, then you are okay. I believe that this is one of the biggest stumbling blocks for men in particular. It's summed up in a line from that great old hymn 'There is a green hill far away' by the prolific hymn writer Cecil Frances Humphreys. The line is – 'There was no other good enough to pay the price of sin. He only could unlock the gate of heaven and let us in.' Please bear this hurdle in mind when you next witness. Admitting our need and inability to meet it by ourselves, is something that can only be understood with the help of the Holy Spirit.

Day 276
Matthew 8-10
3rd October

8 - Many Gentiles Are Welcomed Into The Kingdom
9 - Many Jews Are Welcomed Into The Kingdom
10 - Many Are Ministered To By The Apostles

The Kingdom Of God Is For Everyone

The Big Picture

A leper is healed and then told to fulfil Lev 14:2. Peter's mother-in-law is healed and many other needy people are ministered to, with Isaiah 53:4 being quoted. Jesus takes one of His regular sailings across the Sea of Galilee which takes Him to the Gentile side – but not before a storm teaches the disciples a lesson. On the Gentile lakeside we learn of a man who has his demons cast out and put into pigs who all commit suicide! Jesus and His followers return to the Jewish side where Jews and Romans alike are healed by Jesus. The twelve apostles are chosen by Jesus before they are sent out to minister in His Name.

Thinking Step

10:1-2 – 'Jesus called his twelve disciples together and gave them authority to cast out evil spirits and to heal every kind of disease and illness. Here are the names of the twelve apostles: ...' Disciples are those who follow Jesus. Apostles are those who are sent out by Jesus. All Apostles are disciples – not all disciples are Apostles!

Action Step

8:15 – '...when Jesus touched her hand, the fever left her. Then she got up and prepared a meal for Him.' I have often been to the site of Capernaum on the north shore of the lake of Galilee. The site which is believed to be Peter's house is just a short walk from the remains of a synagogue which is built on the foundations of a 1st century one. This older one could very well be the one where Jairus was a leader. When you visit Capernaum there is a sense in which you do feel you are walking where Jesus walked and spent lots of His adult life. It's easy to be sidetracked into concentrating on Peter, the first 'pope' – and the fact that he was married! A more fruitful avenue for contemplation however, is pondering exactly what happened in this house so many years ago. The family house where additions would have been made as the family grew and would have been very similar to some Asian and African homes today. When Peter's mother-in-law was healed it was for a purpose. When God chooses and equips us it's for a purpose too. Why not resolve now that as you grow older you will never become 'pew fodder' but will always be a spiritually active member of Christ's Church. Plenty of time to rest when there are no souls to save!

11 - Despite Evidence Some Don't Believe   Day 277
12 - Working On The Sabbath!   Matthew 11-13
13 - Faith Requires Some Thinking Too!   4th October

Rejection Of King Jesus Begins To Show

The Big Picture

Disciples of John the Baptist come to Jesus to ask if He is Messiah. Jesus tells them to look around at what He has done. Jesus denounces cities that have witnessed much of His ministry but have failed to repent. His disciples are criticised for breaking the law but Jesus reminds them that King David broke the law too! A man with a deformed hand is healed in the synagogue – on the Sabbath! Matthew justifies this from Isaiah 42. When He is asked for a sign, Jesus tells his listeners He will be like Jonah! It's around this time that Jesus shares one of His best known parables, the parable of the sower.

Thinking Step

12:13 – 'Then He said to the man "Hold out your hand." So the man held out his hand and it was restored just like the other one!' This man was now cleansed. He would be able to eat with his clean right hand and attend to his toilet with his left hand. Before the miracle he was permanently unclean.

Action Step

11:25 – 'At that time Jesus prayed this prayer "O Father, Lord of heaven and earth, thank you for hiding these things from those who think themselves wise and clever and for revealing them to the childlike."'
This reminds me that we are saved by faith and not by intellect. This means God is open to all no matter what their ability or academic status may be. How different to the movement of so called intellectuals many of whom promote themselves as Darwinians and are hard insensitive atheists and agnostics. They describe themselves as 'the brights' because they think they are particularly clever. They are fanatically anti-God and one of their declared aims is to 'promote a world view that is free of supernatural and mystical elements.' In other words they believe only stupid people believe in God and if they were all as clever as the brights all the Churches would be empty! It seems from what Jesus is saying in today's reading that there must have been people just like 'the brights' in His day too. The early Church had its gnostics, literally the 'know-alls' and there has been a stream of these folk within Christianity ever since. Today some secularists appear to be banding together against all believers in God. Let's remind ourselves that if cleverness was sufficient, some of us wouldn't have made it. Thankfully our salvation depends on Jesus!

Day 278
Matthew 14-17
5th October

14 - John The Baptist Is Killed
15 - Jesus Denounces Hypocrites
16 - Peter Declares "You Are The Messiah!"
17 - Transfiguration Confirms Jesus Is Messiah!

Feeding With Food And Spiritual Insights

The Big Picture

John the Baptist is cruelly killed by Herod the tetrarch who then suspects Jesus is John come back from the dead. It's amazing what a guilty conscience can do! A crowd of 5,000 is fed. Religious leaders from Jerusalem travel north to denounce Jesus and His followers for not keeping the law correctly. Jesus tells them to look at themselves first as they don't keep the law properly and are hypocrites to denounce Him. Matthew confirms what Jesus says with Isaiah 29. A further 4,000 are fed. Peter declares Jesus is Messiah when questioned at Caesarea Philippi. As they continue north the transfiguration takes place, probably at Mount Hermon.

Thinking Step

Counting hasn't changed! Numbers 1:2-3 '...List all the men twenty years old or older...'
14:20-21 – 5,000 Jewish men fed, producing twelve small baskets of fragments. One for each tribe.
15:37-38 – 4,000 Gentile men fed, producing seven large baskets of fragments. Seven, the Jewish perfect number is only achieved when the Gentiles are included!

Action Step

16:19 – '...I will give you the keys of the Kingdom of Heaven. Whatever you forbid on earth will be forbidden in heaven and whatever you permit on earth will be permitted in heaven.' Firstly the forgiveness comes from Father in Heaven. Secondly Peter is so in tune with his Father in Heaven that he is able to confirm what has already taken place in Heaven. The 'will be' that occurs twice could easily have been translated 'has already been.' When Jesus forgave sins He was accused of blasphemy – Matt. 9:3 – "That's blasphemy! Does He think He's God?" This is a different situation with Peter, he is a representative of God and not God Himself. This reading reminds us that forgiveness is an essential part of God's gift of salvation. We are also reminded that we should readily forgive others when they sin against us. If you have already repented, no matter how long ago, then your sins are forgiven but what about your account with others? Is there a need to forgive someone who recently wasn't all they could have been to you? Or is there a need for you to ask for forgiveness when you have been less than you should have been? Why not take this opportunity to get your accounts in balance.

The King Discusses The Kingdom

The Big Picture

The disciples are keen to know who will be the greatest in the Kingdom. Jesus tells them that they are all equally precious to God and they must never cause others to sin and must always be ready to forgive, no matter how many times. From the disciples attitude as Jesus' ministry enters its final stages, it seems unlikely that they are ever going to grasp what they need to learn! The itinerary of Jesus takes them south and then east of the Jordan river into the region of Perea (today called Jordan). Healings and essential teaching to prepare the disciples continues apace. The final days of Jesus' ministry are approaching fast and the disciples seem far from ready!

Thinking Step

19:1 – 'When Jesus had finished saying these things He left Galilee and went down to the region of Judea east of the Jordan River.' This includes the area where Jesus was baptised, Bethany beyond the Jordan and was a region dominated by Gentiles. The Jews always referred to it as 'beyond the Jordan' rather than use its proper name – Perea!

Action Step

19:17-21 – "...if you want to receive eternal life keep the commandments." "Which ones?" the man asked.
Jesus replied "You must not murder. You must not commit adultery. You must not steal. You must not testify falsely. Honour your father and mother. Love your neighbour as yourself." All of these commandments are found in Exodus 20 – except the last one which is not included in the ten and is in Lev. 19:18. Why did Jesus add that one? The young man may possibly have been close to keeping all of those mentioned up to that point but he was most certainly not keeping this one! If he was loving his neighbour as himself he would not have been so reticent to give his wealth away. What can we learn from this? Why not check the ten commandments now and see if there is one that causes you a real problem. Then ask God to help you get to grips with it. You will probably have a choice to make! This is a great practice whenever you read the Bible. Don't be like that foolish young man about whom we know very little. He is remembered as someone not willing to pay the price to follow Jesus. He got so close but refused to be totally committed. May that never be true of you or me.

Day 280
Matthew 21-23
7th October

21 - Triumphal Entry On A Donkey's Colt
22 - Leaders Look For Faults In Jesus
23 - Leaders Condemned By Jesus

Dismal Failure To Find Fault In Jesus

The Big Picture

The prophecy of Zech. 9:9 is fulfilled as Jesus enters Jerusalem on a young donkey. He cleanses the Temple telling the people it should be a house of prayer as Isaiah and Jeremiah described it. Lots of pressure is exerted by the religious leaders of the day as they seek to find a weakness in the life and claims of Jesus. Once again failing with the usual subjects of taxation and keeping the law. Jesus is simply too true, honest and eloquent and they have no answers to His arguments. Jesus condemns the leaders with a number of statements. Some Bible translations repeat these evocative words several times in this passage 'Woe to you Scribes and Pharisees, hypocrites!'

Thinking Step

Only Matthew recalls there were two donkeys – 21:7. He also remembers that the crowd shouted "Hosanna" literally "Set us Free." This was the freedom fighters' cry of the Maccabees two hundred years earlier. The shouts as Jesus made His triumphal entry were made between the Roman Antonia Fortress and the Jewish Temple. Little wonder they were advised to keep quiet!

Action Step

At a recent exhibition I was talking to a Christian priest who had served the Lord faithfully in the UK for the past twenty years. I asked him about the Bible and challenged him to discuss the books of 1 Thessalonians and 2 Thessalonians using Walk Through the Bible Keywords Cards (you can get more info. on our website www.Bible.org.uk). I mentioned that Paul wrote his first letter urging his readers to stay on target and not be deflected from what God had for them. He stopped me and said that obviously my Bible knowledge was exceptional! Actually everything I said was included in the Keyword Cards I was showing him. It's simple basic information. What does he preach and teach from his pulpit each week? I hope this doesn't sound judgemental, it's not meant to be but surely a trained priest should know at least a little about Paul's two letters to the Church in Thessalonica. In our reading today I see real significance in Jesus criticising the leaders of His day for their lack of Bible knowledge – 21:42 and 22:29. Sadly we don't seem to have made much progress. You are obviously not included because you are not far from completing a reading through the whole Bible but remember that's just the start. Basing your life and all you believe on Biblical principles is, I believe, the major quest for all believers.

Jesus Promises That He'll Be Back!

The Big Picture

Jesus foretells the destruction of the Temple which is fulfilled in every detail even though, like some of our cathedrals today, some historians believe it wasn't quite finished when the Romans attacked! Two chapters are dedicated by Matthew to the second coming and some of the details are graphically revealed in parables – the last ones in this Gospel. Passover is only a couple of days away and Jesus knows He will be the ultimate sacrifice on this unique Passover Festival. His disciples are still unclear and despite hearing much teaching about Jesus' death and resurrection they still seem to be acting as though it's avoidable! Jesus is betrayed by Judas and denied by Peter and the end is in sight.

Thinking Step

24:2 – '...they (Temple walls) will be completely demolished. Not one stone will be left on top of another!' This was fulfilled by the Romans in AD 70. The Temple sacrifices had outlived their usefulness, Heb. 10:10 – 'For God's will was for us to be made holy by the sacrifice of the body of Jesus Christ, once for all time.'

Action Step

24:13 – " ...the one who endures to the end will be saved." These are the definitive words of Jesus Himself. When I first became a Christian I have to admit that when the Bible words I was reading were by Paul or another apostle I didn't sense the same authority about them as I did when they were the actual words of Jesus as in our verse today! What we are reading today is very clear. We have to endure to the end and these are words for a world that rarely endures to the end. I have lost count of the number of people leaving a football match before the final whistle. I despair of those who watch the news headlines but don't listen to the whole bulletin. I could go on! We have to endure to the end! The Bible is talking here of life and death not just a football match or TV programme. How many folk do you know from your fellowship who were once firm in their faith and have now drifted away? I challenge you to get in touch with just one of them. Have a coffee and a chat but DON'T mention Church! Let them know that you are interested in them as people and with the help of the Holy Spirit we could win them back and see them continuing their walk with Christ – and enduring to the end.

Day 282
Matthew 27-28
9th October

27 - Mankind Does It's Worst - Jesus Is Killed!
28 - God Does His Best - Jesus Is Raised!

Crucified And Buried
Then Raised From The Dead!

The Big Picture

As his account draws to a close Matthew continues to remind his readers of the many prophecies that are being fulfilled. He tells us of Judas' demise, as prophesied. Then Jesus is crucified with two others, again as prophesied. Towards the end of the crucifixion the earth grows dark, just like it did at the very first Passover during the ninth plague. The tomb is sealed to stop the disciples stealing the body, thereby confirming that it really is a miracle when He is raised from the tomb! The early witnesses are some of Jesus' women followers who then tell the disciples. A final meeting at Galilee culminates in the 'Great Commission' which has inspired missionary zeal throughout history.

Thinking Step

27:37 – 'A sign was fastened to the cross above Jesus' head, announcing the charge against him.' It read: "This is Jesus, the King of the Jews." Each of the crosses would have had a similar plaque stating the reasons for each crucifixion. Pilate could find none for the sinless Lamb of God so he simply states who Jesus was!

Action Step

The 'Great Commission' is a great way to conclude a Gospel. It confirms that the work has just started and that the best is yet to come. In the early days of Walk Through the Bible, at the end of our events which are designed to whet appetites to read the Bible, we regularly used the phrase 'the adventure is just beginning.' In other words, in the words of Winston Churchill "Now this is not the end. It is not even the beginning of the end. It is perhaps, the end of the beginning." This is most definitely the situation that Matthew creates at the end of his Gospel. I am sure most of us reading this will have decided to follow Christ some time ago. If not then that's the starting place and you can get further help on day 21 of this book. Are you building on the foundation of a sound conversion or are you still a 'babe in Christ.' In the final few verses Matthew quotes Jesus who tells us that we are to make disciples and sadly too many of us are happy to make converts. The 'Great Commission' is a constant spur to action and a reminder that we still have much to do. What's the next step you need to take towards maturity in Christ, to make you a better disciple? Take it today and then be ready for another one tomorrow.

Mark

Mark

Mark is the shortest of the Gospels and is commonly believed to have been the first one written. It has no birth narrative or genealogy and very few allusions to the Old Testament – which supports the idea that it was written for a Gentile readership, possibly specifically a Roman one. His emphasis is to show Jesus as a servant, a leader willing to serve – an unusual trait in Roman leaders! Many believe much of Mark's information was obtained from Peter, his spiritual father 1 Peter 5:13. Mark himself was probably the young man in 14:51 and the same one who deserted Paul Acts 15:38. The first 10 chapters deal with the majority of the ministry of Jesus and Mark uses 'immediately' many times in his haste to tell the story. The pace of the final 6 chapters slows considerably as we consider Jesus' last week on earth.

Below is an acrostic which summarises each chapter of the book.

1. **C**hrist the working Servant
2. **H**ealing of the paralytic
3. **R**esults of divided house
4. **I**llustration of the soils
5. **S**ervant's power over Gerasene
6. **T**eaching the five thousand

7. **T**raditions of Pharisees attacked
8. **H**ealing the blind man
9. **E**lijah at the transfiguration

10. **S**ervant attitude is mandatory
11. **E**ntry into Jerusalem triumphant
12. **R**esurrection questions are answered
13. **V**iolent destruction of temple
14. **A**gony experienced at Gethsemane
15. **N**arrative of Jesus' death
16. **T**omb is found empty

Jesus' Established Galilean Ministry

The Big Picture

We hit the road running with Mark and before we know where we are Jesus has been baptised, tempted, attracted followers and healed lots of sick and needy people – all in chapter one! In the town of Capernaum on the shore of the lake, Jesus experiences some men breaking into His meeting by lowering their friend down on his bed – at the feet of Jesus – to be healed! One of the things that dogged Jesus throughout His ministry was criticism about the way He acted on the Sabbath which was so different to the norm. The Apostles are chosen and many parables are taught before they all set sail for the other side of the lake – only to encounter a storm!

Thinking Step

1:17 – 'Jesus called out to them "Come, be my disciples and I will show you how to fish for people"'. Fisherman remove anonymous fish out of their everyday routine to kill them. Now they would transform individual people to revolutionise their routine so they could live life to the full. They had many new skills to learn!

Action Step

4:38 – 'Jesus was sleeping at the back of the boat with His head on a cushion. Frantically they woke Him up, shouting "Teacher, don't you even care that we are going to drown."' I always detect a strand of humour in this account. Don't you think it's amusing that fishermen panic in a storm and ask a carpenter to save them? Of course they had seen this carpenter do amazing things and they were already suspecting He was more than a carpenter. Having said that they did panic didn't they! All this after they had seen a man's deformed hand healed and a large crowd filled with food that miraculously seemed to come from nowhere! Then a perfectly normal occurrence, a storm on a lake where there were storms every week – and they panic. These storms happen in modern times too – I have witnessed them – but they are usually short lived. Most sailors simply adjust their proposed activities for the day. Storms are part of everyday life. I think that's the point. We shouldn't panic over things that deep down we know God can deal with as He has before . We have to learn to trust Him. Do you think this group of fair-weather sailors would have reached the other side okay? Yes, I do too. So next time you are in a fix try changing your default setting to TRUST rather than PANIC.

Day 284
Mark 5-7
11th October

5 - Miracles On Both Sides Of The Lake
6 - Nazareth Doesn't Believe In Jesus
7 - Challenges From The Authorities About Keeping The Law

Religious Authorities Worried By Jesus!

The Big Picture

On the other side of the lake Jesus sets a man free from many demons. When He returns to the Jewish side Jairus's daughter is healed as well as a woman who has suffered from a haemorrhage for many years. Jesus sends out the twelve to minister in twos. Meanwhile John the Baptist is murdered. Jesus teaches by the lake but the crowd won't go home until He feeds all 5,000 of them! Later Jesus sees the disciples in trouble on the lake – so He walks out to them! Religious leaders come from the south to challenge Jesus on His cleansing rituals. He tells them it's what is in the mind that defiles rather than what goes in the mouth.

Thinking Step

There were many pig farms in the land of the Gerasenes. Further south is Perea where the story of the prodigal son was probably told. In Luke 15:13 when Jesus talked of 'a distant land' He would have meant non Jewish rather than a long way away – probably pointing north to the area we're thinking about today.

Action Step

5:18-20 – 'As Jesus was getting into the boat, the man who had been demon possessed begged to go with Him but Jesus said "No, go home to your family and tell them everything the Lord has done for you and how merciful He has been." So the man started off to visit the Ten Towns of that region and began to proclaim the great things Jesus had done for him and everyone was amazed at what he told them.' There is something about crossing water, no matter how little, that makes mission more attractive. Try to raise a group of volunteers to witness for a weekend in Hartlepool on the north east coast of the UK where I was born and then try for a similar project in Hawaii and you will see what I mean! Go on to explain it will be to work amongst Brits in the English language but it will probably make little difference. So imagine the disappointment of this man who has a life changing experience on the east side of Galilee and he is told to stay home and witness rather than join the group of followers who are travelling with Jesus! For the vast majority of us our mission field is where we live. Why not thank God for the opportunities where you live and do what this man did – go out and tell about the great things Jesus has done for you.

8 - Disciples Continue To Be Confused

9 - Miracle On Mount Of Transfiguration

10 - Divorce Was A Concession From God

Day 285

Mark 8-10

12th October

Doubting Disciples Need Repeated Teaching!

The Big Picture

The Pharisees continue to pester Jesus trying to prove He is a fraud rather than the Messiah everyone is waiting for. A declaration by God on the Mount of Transfiguration is very clear but the disciples are still having trouble grasping the fact that Jesus is to die but is really God! Questions come from religious leaders who seem determined to show that Jesus is rejecting the law of Moses rather than the reality which is that He is fulfilling the law and all that the prophets said. Jesus tells the disciples that they must be as trusting as a child rather than squabbling over who will be the most important in the coming Kingdom. Bartimaeus is healed in Jericho.

Thinking Step

A traditional route for north south journeys was to travel on the east side of the Jordan River and cross the river where Joshua crossed, so avoiding unclean Samaritans. 10:1 – 'Then Jesus left Capernaum and went down to the region of Judea and into the area east of the Jordan River...' 10:46 – 'Then they reached Jericho...'

Action Step

In these days of 'instant everything' it's refreshing to read that even the miracles of Jesus were not all immediately effective. 8:24 – 'Jesus took the blind man by the hand and led him out of the village. Then, spitting on the man's eyes, He laid His hands on him and asked "Can you see anything now?" The man looked around. "Yes" he said "I see people, but I can't see them very clearly. They look like trees walking around." Then Jesus placed His hands on the man's eyes again, and his eyes were opened. His sight was completely restored, and he could see everything clearly.' We can theorise – as many have previously done – but the answer is that we don't know why it took two actions from the Lord to complete this miracle. However there is an important lesson to learn. There is infinite variety in the ways God deals with us. If you are struggling with an issue in your life that has changed but not completely – take heart, sometimes it just takes more than one action to resolve an issue. Don't resign yourself to it but ask God if He will complete His work in you. Whatever the issue don't leave open wounds for Satan to infect, ask God to complete the healing of any issue He has brought to your mind as you read this today.

Day 286
Mark 11-13
13th October

11 - Jesus' Triumphal Entry And Temple Cleansing
12 - Misunderstandings About Heaven
13 - 'End Of Time' Warnings

Only One Week Left!

The Big Picture

Today we see Jesus and His disciples on the Mount of Olives. He enters the city riding on the colt of a donkey, as prophesied by Zechariah in Zech. 9:9. Due to the ever increasing burden of taxes from the occupying Roman authorities the Jews are constantly looking for relief. They ask Jesus, as a trap but also probably secretly hoping for a solution – but He tells them to pay what they are due to pay. Comments are made by the disciples about the magnificent Temple built for the Jews by Herod the Great. They are really amazed by the whole building but Jesus moves on to teach about the end of the world.

Thinking Step

11:17 – 'He said to them ...but you have turned it into a den of thieves.' Who were these Temple thieves?
Priests who rejected an unblemished animal for sacrifice so a replacement was required – from them!
Money-changers who used inflated exchange rates when Roman coins were exchanged for Temple currency to make these unnecessary purchases.

Action Step

12:38-39 – 'Jesus also taught "Beware of these teachers of religious law! For they like to parade around in flowing robes and receive respectful greetings as they walk in the marketplaces... how they love the seats of honour in the synagogues and the head table at banquets."' Do you remember the old Biblical epics from the 1950s and 1960s. Remember how Jesus was always dressed in white and was the only one who spoke in 'King James English' while the other actors playing the parts of disciples etc. all spoke normally? I hope there is nothing false or 'put on' about your daily witness. I hope what people see when they look at you is what you are! In His teaching here Jesus is referring to the false front many of us wear to stop others seeing the real you and me. An image that we project in order to impress others and inflate our importance. Of course we are all different in public compared to when we are at home but we need to be sure that what others see is an accurate reflection of the real you and me. Is there something that you do which might mislead others? Stop it today! Be as genuine as you can otherwise your witness may be marred into ineffectiveness. God loves you just as you are and so will others if you let God have His way in your life.

Jesus Seems Defeated But Is Victorious!

The Big Picture

Mark records that Jesus is visited by a woman who washes His feet in expensive perfume. Meanwhile preparations are made for Passover, which will be the last one Jesus celebrates with His disciples. After this 'last supper' they leave, singing. This is the only instance when we hear of Jesus actually singing! (Probably from Psalms 113-118). Betrayal is completed in Gethsemane and Jesus is taken away. Despite strenuous efforts by Pilate to free Jesus, He is flogged and led away to be crucified. On the way Simon of Cyrene carries the cross for Him. On that first 'Good Friday' Jesus is crucified and buried. His resurrection is witnessed by women and many others before He ascends back to Heaven.

Thinking Step

14:13 – 'So Jesus sent two of them into Jerusalem with these instructions "As you go into the city, a man carrying a pitcher of water will meet you. Follow him."' Only Essenes would carry water in the city as they were monastic with no wives to carry it! They are best known as writers of the Dead Sea scrolls.

Action Step

Have you ever let Jesus down? If you are anything like me you are spoilt for choice with the many examples that spring to mind now. Bear in mind that this Gospel, though written by Mark, was probably based on the thoughts and memories of Peter. It must have been with mixed emotions that Peter shared these details with Mark. He will have recalled the sheer desperate emptiness of denying Jesus and fearing that there would probably be no opportunity to put things right as Jesus is taken away and passes just a few feet away from Peter as he shelters by the fire. There are two thoughts that I would like to share with you. If you have denied Jesus in the past but have repented and therefore been forgiven – please enjoy your membership of the 'Peter Club' because that's exactly what happened to him. On the other hand if you have denied Jesus in something you have said, thought or done, then you need to turn to Him now and repent. Unlike Peter who thought he might have missed the opportunity – you haven't. However please don't assume you have an endless quantity of tomorrows. None of us have. Take the chance today, while it is available to do what Peter did – repent and be reconciled with Jesus – then really enjoy the rest of your life, to its fullest.

Luke

Luke

Luke is the longest Gospel and when added to his other book Acts of the Apostles results in Luke being the largest contributor to the New Testament; slightly longer than all of Paul's Epistles added together. It is a masterly work and makes the claim to be in consecutive order which makes it an authority when determining the chronology of the life of Jesus in the other Gospels too. Luke was not one of the twelve and probably never met Jesus. He was a Gentile doctor who wrote his Gospel specifically for Greeks and other non Jews. Despite or maybe because of not being an eyewitness Luke makes special efforts to research and clarify before writing about the 'Perfect Man.' He also includes secular references to help date the events he records. Luke covers the whole of Christ's life from just before His birth right through to His Ascension.

Below is an acrostic which summarises each chapter of the book.

1. John named by Zacharias
2. Events during Jesus' childhood
3. Spirit descends on Jesus
4. Undergoing the tempter's test
5. Simon Peter follows Jesus

6. Choosing the twelve disciples
7. Healing the centurion's servant
8. Rejection by the Gerasenes
9. Instruction given on discipleship
10. Seventy preach and report
11. Tragic woes against Pharisees

12. Treasure of the parables
13. Healing on the Sabbath
14. Emphasis on true discipleship

15. Prodigal son comes back
16. Entrance into Abraham's bosom
17. Response of ten lepers
18. Faith must be persistent
19. Entry into Jerusalem triumphant
20. Christ repeatedly outwits Pharisees
21. Temple destruction is predicted

22. Mockery of the trial
23. Acceptance of penitent thief
24. News of Jesus' resurrection

Messiah Comes At Last – Exactly As Promised!

The Big Picture

Luke relates the birth of the prophesied forerunner John the Baptist, before declaring the miraculous arrival of Messiah. He exclusively includes two beautiful passages – Mary's song, often called the Magnificat – and Zechariah's prophecy. Luke names Caesar Augustus and Governor Quirinius in his account and both are mentioned in other historical records. These are details that his Gentile readers would have appreciated and they also substantiate this gospel's historical accuracy. Luke tells us of Jesus being visited by shepherds and uniquely relates the time when Jesus stayed behind in the Temple resulting in His parents fearing they'd lost Him. This event, which took place when Jesus was twelve is the only recorded incident of Jesus as a youth/teenager.

Thinking Step

Luke 2:7 – '...She ... laid Him in a manger because there was no lodging available...' Luke uses two different words that are translated 'inn or lodging.' 'Pandocheion' is the 'Good Samaritan inn' – 10:34. 'Kataluma' is a 'guest room' or the 'upper room' of 22:11. 'Kataluma' is the word used in 2:7 – so no innkeeper is required!

Action Step

2:40 – '...He was filled with wisdom, and God's favour was on him.' 2:52 – 'Jesus grew in wisdom and in stature and in favour with God and all the people.' If we are to be followers and imitators of Jesus then we need to take these two verses very seriously. Like Jesus we need to grow in wisdom. Notice that the Bible does not say that we have to grow in knowledge but in wisdom. Only with the help of the Holy Spirit can we be best use the knowledge that we gather as we progress through life. In both verses there is a sense of continuation. We don't grow to maturity and stop but we continue to grow more mature with Christ's help and guidance. If you are anything like me you will be aware of your personal failings more than ever as you grow older. Does this mean we are getting worse? Not necessarily – we should become spiritually more sensitive as we walk with Jesus. One of our housegroup members commented recently that bad language was irritating them more now than it had ever done previously. A perfect example of becoming more sensitive to the Holy Spirit. Don't ever get discouraged if you feel you are growing worse, you could be getting more sensitive! Ask God to confirm it!

3 - Jesus Is Messiah And Has Genealogy To Prove It!
4 - Jesus Counteracts Temptations With Deuteronomy!
5 - Jesus Teaches Those Who Criticise Him

Day 289
Luke 3-5
16th October

Jesus Teaches And Heals In Galilee

The Big Picture

Luke moves on and tells us that Tiberius is now Roman Emperor. Pilate is governor of Judea. John the Baptist is arrested and will be punished by being beheaded! After His baptism Jesus is tempted by Satan and He responds by quoting from Deuteronomy and Psalms! Next He visits Nazareth where He is invited to read at Synagogue. His comments result in being driven out of town. Much of this early ministry of Jesus takes place in the north around Galilee where He is safe from heavy persecution from the authorities in Jerusalem in the south. As time goes by the Jewish religious leaders criticise Him more and more. He teaches His critics the truth whenever He can.

Thinking Step

Two different genealogies because Joseph had two fathers! In Luke, Joseph's father is Eli – 3:23. In Matthew he is Jacob – 1:16. In Judaism if a man died childless then his brother would endeavour to have a child for him – Deut 25:5. Eli could have been the biological father whilst Jacob was his brother who died.

Action Step

Tradition indicates that Joseph, father of Jesus, died young leaving Mary a single parent. It seems Jesus takes His role as eldest son and stays with them until they could be left to care for themselves. It's only when this calling is completed that He then responds to God's call to ministry. Of course we don't know this for certain but we do know that Jesus had been an adult man for 17 years at least by the time He left home to be an itinerant preacher. That's assuming a bar mitzvah at 13 years old. I think it is very significant that family is an important part of the life of Jesus. They are high on His priority list. He even designates John to care for Mary as if she was His own mother – John 19:27. Look at your future commitments and answer the question "How well am I following the call of God to be the best spouse and parent that I can be?" Of course your Christian life and witness are very important but we must never forget that our partners and children are gifts from God and we have a responsibility towards them. So many families have been torn apart by following a call to 'ministry' rather than 'family.' In reality, family is ministry! So what does your diary show? Does it need some re-adjusting? Now is a great time to do it!

Apostles Called And Jesus Teaches Crowds

The Big Picture

Criticism is levelled at Jesus for not keeping to the letter of the law. He responds by reminding His critics that the great King David sometimes failed to keep the law. Sabbath healing by Jesus disturbs religious leaders and to make matters even more interesting, Jesus forgives sins! The twelve Apostles are selected and then Jesus proceeds to teach them and others what we recognise as the sermon on the mount from Matthew 5-7. Healing 'by remote control' astounds people in Capernaum as a Roman official's slave is healed without Jesus seeing him! An anonymous widow from Nain sees her son raised from the dead. Meanwhile John the Baptist is defended. Forgiveness plays a large part in Jesus' teaching.

Thinking Step

6:14-16 – Jesus chooses His twelve Apostles during His northern ministry in Galilee. That's probably why eleven of them have Galilean roots with only one coming from Judea in the south. My sympathy goes to any southern readers but the southern apostle was Judas Iscariot. At least he was clever enough to be the treasurer – John 12:6.

Action Step

6:27 – "...to you who are willing to listen, I say, love your enemies! Do good to those who hate you. Bless those who curse you. Pray for those who hurt you. If someone slaps you on one cheek, offer the other cheek also. If someone demands your coat, offer your shirt also." On first reading these seem to the actions of a weak person but on reflection they are the marks of a truly good and strong individual. Of course every one of us needs the help of God to be like this. Almost all of us would naturally fall into a revengeful response rather than the approach that Jesus suggests. In New Testament days if you were hit across the face it was usually with the palm of the hand so some dignity could be maintained. However if you were slapped like this and then a second time, the second one was almost inevitably with the back of the hand. This was a real 'slap in the face' and an insult usually reserved for slaves and servants only. Jesus is telling His hearers and that includes you and me, don't be afraid to take second place, to be the first to apologise or admit blame. Don't insist on your rights but rather teach others that humility is a strength!

Busy Spreading The Good News
But The End Is In Sight!

The Big Picture

Jesus travels extensively with His disciples and several lady supporters. After a sudden storm on the lake a man has multi-demons cast out into a nearby herd of unsuspecting pigs. Capernaum is by now a well established replacement for Nazareth as Jesus' ministry base for Galilee. It is the place where Jairus's daughter is healed and where the woman suffering from a haemorrhage finds healing power as she touches the fringe of Jesus' robe. Apostles live up to their names and are 'sent out' by Jesus to minister in other localities. 5,000 are also fed and the transfiguration takes place. The disciples are still slow catching on but when they travel through Samaria they have lots to say!

Thinking Step

9:52-54 – '...Samaritan village...did not welcome Jesus...James and John...said ..."Lord, should we call down fire from heaven to burn them up?"' Jews who made purchases had to drop money into a bucket of water before the Samaritans would pick it up. Any footprints would be filled with straw and set alight to remove every Jewish trace.

Action Step

I remember being on a sales training course many years ago but recall only some of its teaching. We were all from different companies and one of the participants was from the Automobile Association. No matter what the question was, no matter what the topic being discussed, he always included his mantra "Are you a member of the AA?" He was laughed at and ridiculed because he really over did it but I bet everyone else, like me, still remembers him! One of my favourite tracks from an old Don Francisco album is "I gotta tell somebody what Jesus did for me." In the song he recalls how Jairus must have felt when his daughter was healed – and those unexpected words in 8:56 – 'Her parents were overwhelmed but Jesus insisted that they not tell anyone what had happened.' I understand the reason for this prohibition as the Bible makes it clear particularly in John 7:6 NIV 'Therefore Jesus told them "The right time for me has not yet come; for you any time is right."' This is a perfect example of needing to read a verse in context. The Bible does not tell us to keep the 'Good News' to ourselves but you could be excused for thinking that in some Churches! No, we are to spread it everywhere, anytime. If someone could get so enthusiastic about the AA surely we can get excited about Jesus – can't we?

Please Tell Us What We Need To Know!

The Big Picture

Door to door evangelism continues as Jesus sends out 72 disciples, two by two. They return rejoicing at all the things that God did and that they had experienced. A question from an expert in the Jewish law prompts Jesus to tell the story of the Good Samaritan. I am so glad that this question was asked otherwise we may have never heard this magnificent story which only Luke records. Whilst in the south Jesus visits His friends Mary and Martha. The disciples ask for a crash course on prayer! Jesus gives them a brief outline and then teaches how important prayer is. Jesus must have been so sad as He implored the Pharisees to stop spreading their dead legalism.

Thinking Step

To insult a Jew you could question his standing before God or even better call him a Samaritan! John 8:48-49 – 'The people retorted "You Samaritan devil! Didn't we say all along that you were possessed by a demon?" "No" Jesus said "I have no demon in me. For I honour My Father – and you dishonour Me."'

Action Step

Sending out a team of doorstep evangelists is a great way to train to witness for Christ. In fact I think it's the best. Too few do it today because they have never been taught how to. So few have been taught how to because so few have been taught how to! I still remember introducing myself to a young man at his front door who told me "Sorry but I am Jewish." "So was Jesus" I replied. He laughed and said that this usually got rid of folk like me! Then he spent the next 30 minutes or so listening to what we had to share about our faith in Jesus. We had an extensive programme of door knocking at a Church in the north east of England where I was an elder. I remember talking about 'old times' with the pastor when we recently met. He said there had been occasional evenings when he just didn't fancy going out but he did because he couldn't let the rest of the team down, never mind disappoint God. I told him there were similar evenings when I felt the same! The Apostle Paul wrote specific words for just a situation as this – 1 Thes. 5:11 – "So encourage each other and build each other up ..." Do what you are doing to glorify God but never forget how encouraging your faithfulness can be to others who may be experiencing difficult times.

Parables From The Master Storyteller

The Big Picture

Crowds are growing and Jesus responds to questions by teaching them about the folly of collecting treasure on earth that will not last compared to eternal treasure in Heaven. Pilate's murderous ruthlessness gives Jesus the opportunity to remind His hearers that ultimately all of them will die. However if they repent they will not perish! He doesn't panic when told that He would be safer if He fled from Herod Antipas because He knows for certain He will die in God's good time. Dining with Pharisees, Jesus notices that they all want the best seats. He tells them that it is better to go for the least and be 'upgraded' rather than to go for the best and be 'downgraded.'

Thinking Step

13:15 – '...don't you untie your ox or your donkey from its stall on the Sabbath and lead it out for water?' Knots could not be untied using two hands on Sabbath but one hand was okay! If you were not able to master this then you could use an item of womens' clothing when two hands were permitted!

Action Step

12:6 – "What is the price of five sparrows – two copper coins? Yet God does not forget a single one of them." It's interesting to compare this with Matt. 10:29 – "What is the price of two sparrows – one copper coin? Not a single sparrow can fall to the ground without your Father knowing it." Sparrows were of such low value that the traders offered discount – 'buy four get one free!' Yet Jesus reminds us that God doesn't forget a single one of them. In the light of this we should not worry about our welfare. Of course telling someone not to worry is like telling my grandson not to play with his new model truck! Assurance is only as good as the assurer. Does it get any better than God giving the assurance? I think the biggest insult we can give to God is to worry about things that He has taken care of on previous occasions. He honours us in a particular situation only to be doubted when those same circumstances re-occur. It doesn't make sense does it? Challenge yourself today. What are you worrying about that God proved was well within His control only a few days ago or a month ago or even several years ago? Whatever it is let's honour God by believing that He means what He says and is totally able to live up to His promises.

Day 294
Luke 15-18
21st October

15 - 'Losing And Finding' Parables
16 - Parables About Godly Justice
17 - Second Coming Explained
18 - More Parables And A Blind Man Healed

Jesus In Parable Teaching Mode

The Big Picture

We begin today with three parables about losing things culminating in one of the greatest parables ever – 'The Prodigal Son.' Jesus continues teaching parables which would be a real challenge to Luke's readers as they are about ethics and life after death. After more parables Jesus begins some teaching about His return. Jesus has much to say about prayer and how easy it is to become legalistic rather than passionate and relevant. He has more dealings with Samaritans when one of them responds in a beautiful way which Jesus commends. Journeying south will take Him to Jerusalem in a matter of days and His final sacrifice is about to be offered for you and for me – at Calvary.

Thinking Step

The roots of the Prodigal Son are in Deut. 21:18-21 – 'Suppose a man has a stubborn and rebellious son who will not obey his father or mother ...then all the men of his town must stone him to death.' Jesus the master story-teller changed the end to emphasise how much our Heavenly Father loves each of us!

Action Step

Lazarus is the only named character in any of the parables of Jesus and his name is the Latin version of the Hebrew name Eleazar which means 'God is my helper.' The last verse of this story cannot go without comment. It reminds us that even someone rising from the dead is not enough evidence for some people to believe! Wow! This was a prophetic word that was to be proved so true. However something else caught my eye too as I read this evocative story which is unique to Luke's Gospel. We usually think of sin and disobedience as being a result of actions either foolish or deliberate but this time punishment is as a result of inactivity. The rich man simply does nothing! Philosopher Edmund Burke said 'The only thing necessary for the triumph of evil is for good men to do nothing.' In other words 'when good men do nothing, they get nothing good done.' Is your Church one of the 20:80 fellowships? With 20% of the fellowship doing 80% of the work! Do you hide behind being an ideas person rather than a worker? Ideas that result in no action are pretty worthless. We all need to be children of God – and you know what kids are like – they are on the go all the time! Go on and try being a bit 'childlike' and see how much you achieve for the Lord!

19 - Zacchaeus Praised, Then On To The Temple   Day 295
20 - A Full Day Of Questions For Jesus   Luke 19-21
21 - More Teaching About The 'End Times'   22nd October

Sinners And Questions Galore As The End Nears

The Big Picture

As Jesus travels to Jerusalem for the climax of His whole life which is His crucifixion, He comes across an infamous tax collector called Zacchaeus who repents of his evil deeds. Luke records Jesus' triumphal entry into Jerusalem as prophesied by the prophet Zechariah. Many of the closing events in the life of Jesus include questioning sessions. He is asked where He stands regarding His own authority, John the Baptist, taxes and Heaven. So it seems the people want to know but their reactions confirm that they don't particularly want to change! The crowds continue to grow and Jesus explains many things to them including His imminent death and return to Heaven.

Thinking Step

19:8 – Zacchaeus said '...if I have cheated people on their taxes ...' Having previously purchased his 'tax collectors' franchise' from the Romans, Zacchaeus had 'a license to print money!' I doubt if there was anyone who had not been cheated by him! A queue would form quickly as he offered well in excess of the legal recompense – Lev 6:5.

Action Step

As an itinerant preacher it is often thought easier for me to teach about giving than for the resident preachers in local churches. I disagree. It is far better for the local leadership to teach that giving is an act of worship and a great privilege as well as a most satisfying part of being a Christian. Doing your part to support what God is doing is terrific! It is a vital part of our Christian life and should be encouraged for it's own sake. In our reading today Jesus witnesses offerings being given in the Temple. The offering bowls were trumpet shaped and could produce a unique sound when coins were spun in by expert donors! The coins specifically mentioned in our reading today are often called 'the widow's mites.' Their proper name was lepta. One coin, a lepton, was the smallest coin of all and its name means 'the thin one.' Each coin was probably worth around 75p in the 21st century purchasing power. So she gave £1.50. I think that's more than some put into the offering bowl! If you put in a £1 coin you are giving less than the widow's mites – in real terms! So do you give meaningfully or simply out of your loose change? It needs to be proportional to your income to be Biblical! The starting point is 10%. Surely you're not going to be out-given by this poor widow!

There Is No Going Back Now!

The Big Picture

The dark deeds of betrayal by Judas open up this very long chapter. Then we have preparation for the Last Supper when the Apostles and Jesus will celebrate Passover together. The city of Jerusalem would have been totally overcrowded as Jews and God fearers from all over the world gathered for this most important festival. Josephus estimated that 2.5 million people could have been there to make 250,000 sacrifices! During this most special meal Jesus 'drops the bombshell' that He is going to betrayed – by someone present! It's hard to imagine the atmosphere. They leave for Gethsemane and their last prayer meeting. It is interrupted by Judas the betrayer and Jesus is taken away for trial, then denial by Peter.

Thinking Step

You could always tell a Galilean by his rough northern accent. Verses 57-60 even sound northern to me. I'm sure I'm not imagining it!!
Peter denied it. "<u>Woman</u>" he said "<u>I don't even know him!</u>"
"You must be one of them!" "<u>No, man, I'm not!</u>" Peter retorted."
Peter said "<u>Man, I don't know what you are talking about.</u>"

Action Step

Have you noticed when someone believes in you it's so much easier to believe in yourself? We have a wonderful example of such belief in the words of Jesus in our reading today. Verses 31-32 – "Simon, Simon, Satan has asked to sift each of you like wheat but I have pleaded in prayer for you Simon, that your faith should not fail. So when you have repented and turned to me again, strengthen your brothers." Jesus is initially referring to all the Apostles when He says that Satan has asked to sift all of them. Doesn't this remind you of the opening to the book of Job? Later in our reading we see that Satan has homed in on Peter (probably more confident after his success with Judas Iscariot) but the Lord assures Peter that He has personally prayed for him. Isn't it an amazing thought that this assurance is available to each of us every day too! An even more encouraging portion however is left to the end when Jesus confirms that Peter will know victory – "So <u>when</u> you have repented and turned to me again, strengthen your brothers." Jesus NEVER gives up on us – Rom. 8:34 – '...He is sitting in the place of honour at God's right hand, pleading for us.' Are you being tempted to give up on a Godly dream or a needy individual? Follow the example of Jesus and never give up.

Plan Of Salvation Completed

The Big Picture

Trial follows trial, all of them either illegal or a mockery of justice. The religious leaders are determined to eliminate Jesus, even expressing a preference for Barabbas and getting the crowd to support the idea of his release rather than Jesus. Despite desperate final efforts by Pilate, Jesus is finally taken away for crucifixion. He is buried in a borrowed tomb. The following day Sunday, women go to the tomb but realise Jesus has risen from the dead! They tell the disciples who are less than convinced! Two disciples are on the road to Emmaus when they meet the risen Jesus. Later the disciples witness Jesus appearing amongst them before He finally ascends back to Heaven.

Thinking Step

Simon of Cyrene the cross carrier, probably came from Libya. His two sons Alexander and Rufus are named by Mark in Mk. 15:21. Paul refers to Rufus in Rom. 16:13 – 'Greet Rufus, whom the Lord picked out to be His very own and also his dear mother, who has been a mother to me.' The cross produces another great family!

Action Step

23:43 – 'Then he said "Jesus, remember me when you come into your Kingdom." Jesus replied "I assure you, today you will be with Me in paradise."' Wow – that was close! Almost too late but just in time.

As William Camden's poem about a man falling from his horse puts it – "Betwixt the stirrup and the ground...Mercy I asked, mercy I found." This is not a reason to leave everything until the last minute but a reminder that it is never too late. There are debates about paradise – is it the same as Heaven? The important thing is what Jesus said – that He would be there too. I believe Heaven is where Jesus is and I want to be there. Hell is where Jesus isn't and I don't want to be there. Just think someone getting to Heaven without ever having been baptised or confirmed or attending preparation classes or even Church! This is a very clear reminder that we are saved by grace but we can be tempted to add something – don't! Remember this when you are next tempted to be critical because someone at Church isn't doing something the way you always do – or dressing the way you always do – or worshipping the way you always do. Remember the thief on the cross got to be with Jesus for eternity by faith – and that's the only way we can do it too! More information on Day 21 reading.

John

John

This is often described as the supplementary Gospel written by the disciple who outlived all the others – which was probably why Jesus asked him to look after Mary. John's approach is totally different to the previous three synoptic Gospels as he emphasises the fact that Jesus is the Son of God and more than 90% of his narrative is unique. Sadly by the end of the first century whilst John was still alive, there were some who doubted the deity of Jesus whilst others questioned that He was ever a man of flesh and blood. John takes his opportunity as the last living link with the earthly Jesus to make things very clear. John takes seven of Jesus' miracles or signs and expands each with the appropriate teaching of Jesus. There is no birth narrative but the upper room details are significantly more than all the other three Gospels put together.

Below is an acrostic which summarises each chapter of the book.

1. Jesus is the Word
2. Opening of Jesus miracles
3. Hope offered to Nicodemus
4. Need of Samaritan woman

5. Testimony to Jesus' deity
6. Hidden meaning of bread
7. Encounter with the Pharisees

8. Grace for adulteress defended
9. Opposition to removing blindness
10. Shepherd and His sheep
11. Power to raise Lazarus
12. Entry into Jerusalem triumphant
13. Last supper and discourse

14. Offer of Holy Spirit
15. Fruit of the Vine

16. Believer's comfort and joy
17. Extended prayer of Christ
18. Lord's betrayal and denial
19. Illegal trials and crucifixion
20. Eyewitnesses to the resurrection
21. Final commandment of Jesus

Day 298
John 1-3
25th October

1 - John The Baptist Prepares The Way
2 - Jesus Performs His First Miracle
3 - Nicodemus Acknowledges Jesus As Messiah

North And South Believe In Jesus

The Big Picture

John begins with the prophesied forerunner John the Baptiser and tells how he proclaims Jesus as the Lamb of God only to see his own disciples deserting him to follow Jesus. It says a lot for John that he continued to declare that Jesus was the one to follow. The wedding in Cana of Galilee is recorded as the first sign performed by Jesus. We then hear of one of Jesus' visits to Jerusalem to celebrate Passover. He cleanses the Temple after seeing the cheating and sharp practices of those who should have known better. Nicodemus visits Jesus and is taken aback to hear "You must be born again." He debates with Jesus and finally comes through believing – 19:39.

Thinking Step

This Gospel opens with 'In the beginning' just the same as Genesis. This arrests the attention of all Jews for whom words have enormous power. Genesis reminds us that God spoke and it was so. John also incorporates 'logos' meaning word or reason which would attract all the Greeks. Then he declares Jesus to everyone! Introductions are so important.

Action Step

1:50 – 'Jesus asked him "Do you believe this just because I told you I had seen you under the fig tree? You will see greater things than this."' How many meetings have you attended when at the end the question is asked "Any other business or questions?" – and the deafening response is a short silence before everyone departs! It never ceases to amaze me how unquestioning many Christians are. They take as truth everything said from their pulpits and everything read in books by authors who have sound reputations. We really need to question more and thereby work out our own salvation rather than living in the shadow of someone else's. In our reading today Jesus is amazed by the seeming naivety of Nathanael who seems full of questions when he learns that Messiah has come but who simply accepts the first answer he receives. Some people think asking questions is showing doubt. I think it can be the exact opposite. Questions are often asked by people who simply want to go a little deeper and understand more. Of course asking questions is only part of the equation. We have to really listen to the answers too. As I read my Bible I make a note of anything that puzzles me and take that deeper at a later time. Continue to read and study so that you are always ready to explain why you believe what you believe.

Samaritans And Sabbath Working

The Big Picture

They set off for Galilee but on their way travel through Samaria rather than the more traditional route which would have taken them east of the Jordan river and north through Perea. The classic encounter of Jesus and the woman at the well dominates this chapter. Without John we would know nothing of this meeting or for that matter Jesus' previous one with Nicodemus. On their arrival at Cana in Galilee Jesus is asked to heal the son of a government official who is ill in Capernaum. Jesus does this without leaving Cana! Back in Judea Jesus heals a man who has waited 38 years by the Pool of Bethesda! Many questions from the religious leaders of the day follow.

Thinking Step

As long as the water from the well was not touched by anything 'Samaritan' it was okay for Jews. However many of the Essenes took purity levels to an extreme in the days of Jesus. They believed that when the water flowed into the Jewish bucket it would have taken Samaritan impurity with it and so was eternally impure.

Action Step

4:35 – 'You know the saying 'Four months between planting and harvest' but I say, wake up and look around. The fields are already ripe (or white) for harvest.' In other words get on with it! The Samaritan woman did. 4:39 – 'Many Samaritans from the village believed in Jesus because the woman had said "He told me everything I ever did!"' She didn't wait for training or until she knew more, she just shared what had happened to her and with the help of the Holy Spirit it was enough. This is not to say that training and learning more are not important – they are. However if we wait until we know enough or feel adequate then we will get very little done. I remember visiting a man as part of an evangelistic programme I was running in my Church and taking someone with me as a trainee. The person we were visiting was particularly argumentative and despite my best efforts we seemed to make little headway. When we made contact again to arrange another visit I was staggered when my trainee's presence was insisted upon. When I pressed a little more I was told that our contact was so impressed by him and his genuine unprofessionalism that his authenticity was never in doubt! Eloquence isn't the most powerful tool after all – but the Holy Spirit can use our sincerity to help overcome obvious deficiencies!

Many Signs Of Opposition To Jesus

The Big Picture

Jesus and His followers cross the Sea of Galilee and He feeds a crowd of 5,000 men plus women and children. Very similar basic details to Elisha in 2 Kings 4:42-44. Shortly after this Jesus is asked for a miraculous sign – 6:30! It seems there are none so blind as those who will not see. Jesus declares He is the Bread of Life as He makes the first of His seven 'I am' claims. Jesus delays His journey south to Jerusalem to celebrate the Feast of Shelters. When He does arrive the Temple authorities are amazed by His teaching. Despite all this evidence of His Messiahship, many of His followers desert Him.

Thinking Step

John's Gospel indicates that the '5,000 feeding' took place on the 'other side' of the lake and that it was a Jewish crowd who followed from the west – 6:1-2. Lack of Kosher food was now a real problem as Jesus asks "<u>Where</u> can we buy?" – 6:5. The disciples misunderstood and thought it was simply about money – 6:7.

Action Step

Just one anonymous young lad's lunch and it made the world of difference! I wonder if he was with his parents or had simply followed the crowd in those days when children could manage to survive without being protected by legislation and risk assessments! It's only the old man John as he writes his Gospel who remembers the food belonged to a young boy. He's not even mentioned in the other three Gospels. Children are so happy to share what they have – unlike many adults. Before our second son was born his brother spent hours playing with his substitute sibling, our pet shih tzu. When he began to crawl we used to often put him in a play pen so we knew where he was. I still remember him sharing his ice cream with his best friend. The child on the inside of the play pen and the dog on the outside with his head through the rails, licking for all he was worth! Sharing is a true mark of the Christian Church. Acts 2:45 tells us – 'They sold their property and possessions and shared the money with those in need.' I believe there will be many questions asked of a Church rich in property and goods which have not been used to benefit the Kingdom. Before you think this is a comment on any particular denomination remember that the Church simply consists of many people like you and me!

8 - I Am The Light Of The World
9 - Unique Healing Miracle With Mud!
10 - I Am The Gate And The Good Shepherd

Day 301
John 8-10
28th October

Jesus Clearly Declares His Deity

The Big Picture

Jesus shows great wisdom towards a woman presented to Him having been caught in the act of adultery. The death penalty seems inevitable until Jesus challenges the crowd. Jesus is also asked who is to blame if a couple have a child who is blind. He responds with a unique healing using mud smeared onto the man's eyes. However this is done on the Sabbath which brings more criticism from the religious leaders who are always looking for faults in Jesus and His teaching. In a rural society Jesus claims to be the gate for the sheep and the Good Shepherd are very clearly challenges to the religious leaders who are proving to be very poor shepherds for the people.

Thinking Step

"I am the Good Shepherd" is one of the most famous statements of Jesus but is more respectable today than in His day. Shepherds 2000 years ago were near the bottom of the social ladder and often Gentiles who were only young children or teenagers. They were rarely religious Jews as they could not keep all the laws whilst shepherding sheep.

Action Step

Some time ago I was called out to a family who lived next door to members of our local Church. They were a young couple who had just discovered that their baby had died overnight. The husband asked me with white knuckles and ghostly white face, why this had happened to them. I told him that I was very sad about their loss but I had no idea why it had happened. He immediately relaxed and sat down. Then he told me that if I had quoted the Bible or given him some trite advice he would have 'put me through the window.' Our reading today takes me back to that day – 8:4-5 – '"Teacher" they said to Jesus "this woman was caught in the act of adultery. The law of Moses says to stone her. What do you say?"' This woman was told what the Scriptures said and then informed what the consequences were. This almost certainly helped the Pharisees more than it helped the woman. The religious leaders had done their duty but had not helped the situation! Glib unthoughtful comments may help you to know you have 'said the right thing' but if they don't help it would be better if they weren't uttered. Ask God for wisdom first. Take time to think as Jesus did. Use what you say to help the situation rather that simply clear your own conscience.

Day 302
John 11-13
29th October

11 - I Am The Resurrection
12 - Triumphal Entry And Death Threat
13 - Last Supper Feet Washing And Betrayal

Master Of Life Is Now To Die

The Big Picture

Thanks to John we have a whole chapter dedicated to Lazarus. Amazingly he is not mentioned in the other three Gospels. Despite Jesus' timetable being different to that of the sisters of Lazarus there is a miraculous resurrection that attracts many to Jesus. Ironically having proved He has power over death, the religious leaders now declare that He must die! The Triumphal Entry is recorded by John with the prophesy of Isaiah being quoted to confirm that Jesus is Messiah. Amazingly most people still refuse to believe! The Passover Meal begins with Jesus washing the feet of the disciples and witnesses the early departure of Judas as he leaves to betray his Master.

Thinking Step

The Last Supper table was three sided. Peter was at the 'lowest end' opposite Jesus and probably the last to have his feet washed – 13:6. He also had to lean forward to speak to Jesus – 13:25. At the 'VIP end' John leans back touching Jesus' chest and Judas is close enough to receive the special guest's dipped bread morsel.

Action Step

What a great chapter we have here that is dominated by Lazarus and teaches us so much. I love to observe the way Jesus and His Father in Heaven work together. 11:39 – 'Roll the stone aside" Jesus told them.' Of course Jesus could have done that but He left it to mankind to do it. 11:43 'Then Jesus shouted "Lazarus, come out!"' – this was something only God could do! Then 11:44b – 'Unwrap him and let him go!' Another job that people could do for themselves. Do you see the pattern here? God only does things for us when we can't do them for ourselves! Be sure not to ask God to do everything. Be ready to do your part and then allow God to do His. Have you ever heard prayers or sung hymns which ask God to make us do good and stop doing wrong? I think that is probably why God rarely answers prayers like these. Let's not be like the little boy who arrived home after school to be confronted by his Mum and Dad who had just heard that he had broken a window in the gym. Solemnly he told them "I thought it might be wrong so I prayed to God and asked him to stop me but when He didn't I thought it must be okay to do it!" Do the good that you can and trust God to do the rest.

14 - I Am The Way, The Truth And The Life   Day 303
15 - I Am The One True Vine   John 14-17
16 - Jesus Prepares The Disciples   30th October
17 - Jesus Prays For The Disciples

Final Preparations For The Disciples

The Big Picture

Jesus teaches the disciples so much more and sadly Judas has left so misses it all. They are full of questions and doubts and Jesus assures them that even when He returns to Heaven they will not be alone as the Holy Spirit will come to be with them. Jesus tells them that they are like branches of a vine and He is that vine. He aches to tell them so much more but knows that they are unable to cope with it now. Thankfully John recorded all of this otherwise we would know nothing of the detailed teaching in these last hours of Jesus' earthly life. Finally Jesus prays for His disciples and all believers.

Thinking Step

15:2 refers to 'cutting off' branches. 'Cutting off' seems rather brutal and permanent but the word may also be rendered 'lifting up' – as in Matt 14:20 when baskets are 'lifted up' after the 5000 are fed. Branches that trail on the ground getting dirty and unproductive are lifted up and cleaned by the vinedresser to become productive again.

Action Step

When I have invigilated at examinations in colleges and schools I have sometimes had problems making sure students don't copy. I remember clearly invigilating an all day bricklayers practical test when each student was given a drawing and a labourer who would prepare bricks and mortar for them as they built the item from the drawing supplied. One student appeared better than the others and started well whilst the others stood around waiting to see developments! When he was well on the way the other students followed his design. Was I to stop them for cheating or not? In an open workshop it was impossible so I allowed everything to proceed. After several hours the 'inspired bricky' stopped, lit a cigarette and looked at his drawing very carefully. Then he folded the drawing, extinguished his cigarette and – kicked the project down! You could have heard a pin drop! They all needed help now but none was forthcoming and they all failed! It's a good job life isn't like that. We are not left to our own devices with only our fellow humans as inspiration – but we have God Himself, in the Person of the Holy Spirit to guide us. When you feel desperate and alone just try asking the Holy Spirit to guide you. He is longing to do it because that's His job – and He's very good at it too! I commend Him to you.

Day 304
John 18-21
31st October

18 - Betrayed, Tried And Denied
19 - Crucified Instead Of Barabbas
20 - Resurrected And Appears To Disciples
21 - Jesus' Final Appearances At Galilee

The Wicked Deeds Are Completed But Fail!

The Big Picture

Jesus is arrested in Gethsemane and twice declares "I am He" – a clear statement of His deity. He is taken to be questioned by Annas and Caiaphas and then on to other trials finishing with Pilate who has Him flogged and led away for crucifixion. None of His disciples speak up for Him, in fact most of them run for their lives whilst Peter remains but denies Him three times! At the cross Jesus arranges for John to take care of His mother before He surrenders His life and is buried in a borrowed tomb. His resurrection is witnessed first by women who immediately tell the disciples. Jesus meets the disciples by Galilee where Peter is reconciled to Him.

Thinking Step

Annas was the power behind the role of High Priest. He held the position himself as did his four sons and Caiaphas his son in law. His influential family gained their wealth from the 'Bazaars of Annas' where sacrificial animals were sold at extortionate prices. It was Annas's business which was hit when Jesus cleansed the Temple!

Action Step

When your neighbours have a barbecue I suspect you can smell it for miles around. It's that sort of smell isn't it? A charcoal fire is where Peter huddles for warmth in the Courtyard of Caiaphas. The pungent smell of charcoal will have been in his nostrils as he denied Jesus three times. Peter smells that same evocative odour when he meets Jesus at Galilee where the Lord has prepared a charcoal fire on the beach. I am sure Peter would have been transported back to his shameful denying behaviour when he declared he had never heard of Jesus. Ever since that dreadful night Peter had said nothing to Jesus. John reminds us that Jesus appeared to all of the disciples except Thomas, so Peter was there but said nothing. Then Jesus appears again when Thomas is present and once again Peter stays silent. Now he is given another chance to put things straight with the man he acknowledges is the Son of God. In 21:12 Jesus invites him to 'come and have breakfast.' A very Jewish way of being reconciled. Peter responds but doesn't find it easy – nevertheless he knows he has to do it otherwise he fears he could lose his last chance. I believe many of us have invitations to come and be reconciled but prefer to leave it for another time. Today is the day to come back no matter why you slid away.

Acts

Acts

This book should be called 'some of the acts of some of the Apostles' as it concentrates on Peter and then Paul and almost totally ignores all the other Apostles. Written by Luke, it has a similar introduction of historical authenticity as Luke's Gospel. Both writings are dedicated to an unknown person called Theophilus (Lover of God). It is a very clearly structured book and falls into three sections. The first seven chapters are based in Jerusalem and dominated by Peter and his ministry to the Jews. The centre section of five chapters reflects the interim between Jews and Gentiles and gives an outline of the early Samaritan Church. The largest section tells us about Paul and his outreach to the Gentiles. These sixteen chapters cover his missionary journeys and concludes with his house arrest in Rome. The Church continues it's expansion as the Great Commission is being fulfilled worldwide.

Below is an acrostic which summarises each chapter of the book.

1. **H**eavenly ascension of Christ
2. **O**utpouring of Holy Spirit
3. **L**ame man is healed
4. **Y**ield from public preaching

5. **S**apphira and Ananias judged
6. **P**icking of the deacons
7. **I**njury inflicted upon Stephen
8. **R**ising persecution scatters believers
9. **I**ntensity of Paul's conversion
10. **T**aking Cornelius the gospel

11. **W**orship with Gentiles defended
12. **O**utbreak from the prison
13. **R**elaying gospel to Antioch
14. **K**eep preaching the gospel
15. **I**nvestigation by Jerusalem Council
16. **N**eed for missionary vision
17. **G**ospel presented in Athens

18. **I**nterview with Aquila, Priscilla
19. **N**ew believers in Ephesus

20. **T**estimony of Paul's work
21. **H**oly Spirit warns Paul
22. **E**ffect of Paul's testimony

23. **C**ouncil of the Sanhedrin
24. **H**earing held by Felix
25. **U**rgent appeal to Caesar
26. **R**easoning with King Agrippa
27. **C**alamity on the sea
28. **H**ope of every missionary

Jesus Ascends – Holy Spirit Descends
Church Is Established

The Big Picture

Luke repeats the ascension of Jesus with which he concluded his Gospel, using an overlap of the story like all good TV dramas! Matthias is appointed as Judas's replacement by the drawing of lots. Of course this method was BEFORE the Holy Spirit came down. When the Spirit comes it is with power and impact. Peter is inspired to preach his first sermon and sees 3,000 converted and baptised. Later Peter and John are on their way to the afternoon prayer meeting in the Temple when they are asked for money by a lame man. In the immortal language of the KJV, he asks for alms and gets legs!! Peter takes this opportunity to preach his second sermon to the onlookers.

Thinking Step

At the south wall of the Temple Mount near the Huldah Gates are the remains of a mikvah. This is adjacent to the Rabbinic Steps and would have been the site of Peter's first sermon. It was a short distance from the steps to the mikvah for baptism in its waters which were previously reserved for cleansing of visiting pilgrims.

Action Step

We read today of a great miracle that takes place as the Holy Spirit comes down to continue the ministry of Jesus through His disciples and amongst the people. We have to go all the way back to Genesis for the roots of what happened. At the Tower of Babel languages were confused to encourage the people to spread and populate the earth – Gen. 10:7. I believe this is a different type of 'tongues' to that practised in the early Church and by many believers today. In my experience tongues today tends to be used in worship and may be described as heavenly language which needs an interpretation for others present. The tongues on the Day of Pentecost needed no interpreting and was indeed a translation of what Peter was saying. Consequently everyone heard what God was saying through Peter in their own language. Such a wonderful gift and a timely reminder that our God really is in control. Of course that doesn't mean we don't have to do our best to do God's will and just leave it all to Him. However it is consoling to know, in the words of an old hymn – 'God is working His purpose out as year succeeds to year' We have a God who despite having to resort to what may appear to be 'plan B' is big enough to work through us and with us and still get things done!

Day 306
Acts 4-6
2nd November

4 - Apostles Are Warned To Keep Quiet
5 - Ananias And Sapphira Make Fatal Mistake
6 - First Deacons Are Appointed

Church Grows – Despite Persecution And Sin

The Big Picture

Peter and John preach about life after death and are arrested. After severe warnings they are released but decide they must obey God rather than the religious leaders of the day. Barnabas shows great generosity but the efforts of Ananias and Sapphira to follow his example end in disaster. The Apostles are jailed again but following the sound advice from a Pharisee called Gamaliel they are released. The first deacons are appointed to ease problems within the early Church but it isn't long before persecution shows itself again and Stephen, one of the Church's most promising leaders, is arrested. This arrest proves to be a major step in the conversion of one of the world's greatest missionaries – the Apostle Paul.

Thinking Step

Due to Greek influences that began with Alexander the Great, some Jews spoke Greek whilst others stayed loyal to Hebrew. The early Church was probably dominated by Hebrew speakers. In 6:1 the Greek speakers complain about the Hebrew speakers. This was resolved by appointing the first deacons who all appear to be Greek speakers as they have Greek names!

Action Step

4:13 – 'The members of the council were amazed when they saw the boldness of Peter and John, for they could see that they were ordinary men with no special training in the Scriptures. They also recognised them as men who had been with Jesus.' This should never be used as an alibi for not learning and studying but it is worth noting that despite all the knowledge of the religious leaders of the day, the people were impressed most by ordinary untrained men. Or as Dave Bilbrough wrote when describing the Church of Jesus – 'An army of ordinary people. A kingdom where love is the key.' A friend of mine took up his first leadership role in a Church situated in a typically straight talking working class area of the north east not far from where I grew up and found Christ as a teenager. He was staggered to learn that his congregation was not impressed by his knowledge of Hebrew grammar or the niceties of Greek words! Personally I have found the childrens' address in many services is often the only bit of the service that everyone understands – but that may say more about my preaching than I care to think about! May we continue to be ordinary people empowered by an extra ordinary God and used in a multitude of ordinary ways.

Jews Look Back And Samaritans Leap Forward

The Big Picture

Stephen is challenged to explain himself and he does, in great detail! Starting at Genesis he proceeds to tell the whole story that led up to Jesus. This is very significant bearing in mind the people he was speaking to knew the 'Old Testament' very well indeed. Stephen's long accurate answer is very uncomfortable for the hearers and they stone him to death. This started a wave of persecution led by Saul of Tarsus who witnessed the stoning. As a result believers were spread in all directions and Philip finds himself preaching in Samaria. Things are going well but he is called away to witness to a lone Ethiopian who is converted and baptised before going on his way rejoicing.

Thinking Step

The eunuch was reading Isaiah 53. Then along comes Philip to show him the answer is just a couple of chapters further on – 56:3-4 – '...Don't let the eunuchs say "I'm a dried-up tree with no children and no future." For this is what the Lord says "I will bless those eunuchs who ...commit their lives to me."'

Action Step

Some time ago I was promoting Walk Through the Bible in a large Church in London and reading from Acts 7 to show them one of the earliest 'Walk Throughs' in the New Testament. I stopped near the end and pointed out a salutary couple of verses that are a warning to all preachers – 7:57 – "'Then they put their hands over their ears and began shouting. They rushed at him and dragged him out of the city and began to stone him...'" "Hopefully you won't be doing that to me" I said. This was greeted with total silence! Assuming they had not fully understood my northern humour I asked them "Would you like some time to think about it?" This brought another silent response so I proceeded quickly making sure I left at the end whilst most of the congregation were still in Church! It seems they were having difficulty taking on board the concept of reading the whole Bible. I believe the religious leaders of Jesus' day knew what they believed but only concentrated on those passages of Scripture that confirmed it. Stephen really rattled their cages as he showed them the 'Big Picture.' When you read the whole Bible you will discover sections that 'throw you' for a while, until you have thought them through. Anything you hold dear must be able to withstand the test of Scripture. If it can't, then it has to change!

The Gospel Spreads To The Gentiles

The Big Picture

Saul travels to Damascus vowing to eradicate the early Church. On his way he is confronted by the risen Jesus and is blinded and taken into Damascus to recover. God sends a believer, Ananias by name, who greets Saul as a brother and sees him recover and be baptised. God's Apostle for the Gentiles has been selected. Meanwhile Peter raises Tabitha from the dead during a stay in Joppa. Later, men come from Caesarea and as they travel to see Peter, God prepares his heart with a triple vision. Peter travels north to see Cornelius, a Gentile from Caesarea and is in the process of explaining all about Jesus when the Holy Spirit falls for a Pentecostal experience for the Gentiles.

Thinking Step

9:25 – The basket which carries Saul to safety is the same type that is used to collect the fragments left after the feeding of the 4,000 – Matt. 15:37. This is a different and much larger basket to the one used to collect the leftovers following the feeding of the 5,000 – Matt. 14:20.

Action Step

Just imagine the headlines 'Head of Militant Terrorists converted to Christ' – Of course we wouldn't be cynical or doubting would we!! Of course we would and the press would be too, only 100 times more. This is a good parallel of what happened when the arch enemy of Christianity, Saul of Tarsus, is confronted by the risen Christ and thereafter follows Him. This is a reminder, if we needed one that Christ can reach anyone and I mean anyone! Years ago I remember challenging a congregation that anybody could be converted. Did they agree? There was a general murmuring of agreement which for British Christians is enthusiastic wholehearted support! I continued by suggesting to them "Just imagine when we get to Heaven who we might see." I raised my finger and placed it on my top lip and put my other hand on my brow indicating a deep diagonal fringe. Everyone knew who I meant, especially those who had lived through the second world war. On their way out I was bombarded for my suggestion that Adolf Hitler could be in Heaven – surely not! However I believe any repentant sinner could get there and who can say he couldn't have repented at the very end. Pray for your most unlikely prospect with renewed faith now as no one is beyond the reach of the Gospel of Christ and that includes your least favourite relative or work colleague!

1st Missionary Journey

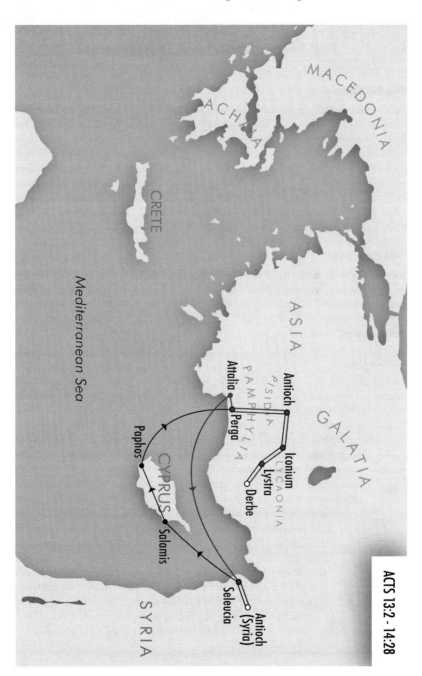

Day 309
Acts 11-13
5th November

11 - If God Says Something Is Acceptable Don't Say It Isn't!
12 - Peter Is Imprisoned And Unbelievably Released!
13 - Barnabas And Saul Set Aside To Spread The Gospel

Full Steam Ahead For The Gentiles

The Big Picture

Some of the Church were not happy with Gentiles being accepted and Peter tells them about his vision and God telling him that Gentiles were acceptable. He goes on to describe what happened with Cornelius in Caesarea. Persecution increases as James is killed and Peter is imprisoned. Miraculously Peter is set free by an angel. Then he goes to the home of Mary, mother of John Mark, where they are praying for him. For all their praying they don't believe it when Peter turns up! In Antioch where believers are first called Christians, Barnabas and Saul are set aside with the laying on of hands for their specific ministry. Barnabas and Saul become Paul and Barnabas as Paul's leadership blossoms.

Thinking Step

Joseph becomes Barnabas meaning 'son of encouragement.' What a name to be given by your friends and colleagues! Saul on the other hand swaps a name meaning 'chosen by God' for one that means 'small' – (least of the Apostles?). The other benefit of 'Paul' is that it is a Latin name for the Roman world rather than a Jewish name.

Action Step

I am sure most of us have been in prayer meetings when unusual things have happened. I doubt if many of us have been praying for a miracle and when that miracle happens during the prayer meeting, we deny it and try to explain it away! Today's reading includes such an event – 12:14-15 – 'When she recognized Peter's voice, she was so overjoyed that instead of opening the door she ran back inside and told everyone, "Peter is standing at the door!" "You're out of your mind!" they said. When she insisted they decided "It must be his angel."' There is a sense in which we must pray believing God will answer otherwise what is the point. In one sense it's encouraging to know that we are no worse than people in the early Church but they had little history of answered prayers in such a new Church whereas we have 2,000 years to look back on. When you pray are you surprised when a clear answer is produced? We shouldn't be should we? It's almost as if we pray but only because it's the right thing to do rather than because it can be a source of real power. There are few atheists on a sinking ship, they all try a prayer! Why not pray for a specific person or event right now – and promise God faithfully that you will not be surprised when He clearly answers you!

1st Missionary Journey To Galatia

The Big Picture

Paul and Barnabas travel on into cities in southern Turkey which was then called Galatia. Their impact was such that the locals in Lystra insist Barnabas and Paul are gods. Despite vehement denials the situation was in danger of getting out of control and Paul is stoned following the arrival of some Jewish antagonists. He survives and travels on to Derbe with Barnabas before returning to Antioch knowing that the circumcision controversy has to be resolved. A decision is made at the Jerusalem Council that circumcision is not necessary and Paul and Barnabas then plan to return to the infant Churches to help them mature in Christ. Barnabas and John Mark go to Cyprus and Paul takes Silas to Galatia.

Thinking Step

The Jerusalem Council's resolution on circumcision is a declaration of independence from Judaism and confirmed that Christianity is not simply a sect within Judaism. This meant persecution by the Jews would ultimately be replaced with Roman intolerance as Rome only allowed one official religion per country. However it also produced a worldwide faith available to all – Jew and Gentile alike.

Action Step

14:11-12 – 'When the crowd saw what Paul had done, they shouted in their local dialect "These men are gods in human form!" They decided that Barnabas was the Greek god Zeus and that Paul was Hermes, since he was the chief speaker.' I am sure none of us have adulation like this even when our preaching has been exceptionally good! However sometimes things are said that can deflect some of God's glory onto us if we are not careful. It begins very simply when we overuse the 'I' word. We start talking about 'I did this' or 'I did that' rather than God did it. I resolved long ago that I would always try to use 'We.' This can mean 'a colleague and me' or 'the Holy Spirit and me' or even both. When we first began teaching Walk Through the Bible events in the UK in 1984 they made a big impact. So much so that our Instructors were constantly complimented on their presentations. We resolved that each of us would be known as the second best Instructor. None of us was the best! It was a harmless bit of humour but helped keep our feet on the ground and firmly rooted in Christ and His Word. If we stop talking as though we are lone rangers we will stop misleading others and more importantly, we will stop fooling ourselves! Give it a try, please!

2nd Missionary Journey

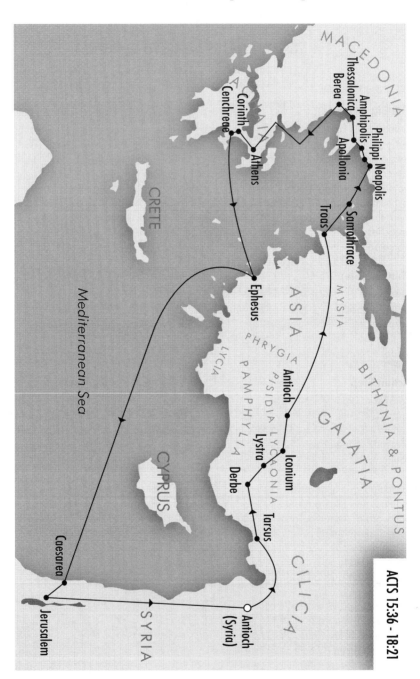

MACEDONIA

Thessalonica
Berea
Amphipolis
Philippi Neapolis
Apollonia
ACHAIA
Corinth
Cenchreae
Athens
Samothrace
Troas

CRETE

Mediterranean Sea

Ephesus

ASIA

MYSIA

PHRYGIA

LYCIA

PISIDIA

Antioch

PAMPHYLIA

LYCAONIA

Lystra

Iconium

Derbe

Tarsus

BITHYNIA & PONTUS

GALATIA

CYPRUS

Caesarea

Jerusalem

SYRIA

Antioch
(Syria)

CILICIA

ACTS 15:36 - 18:21

16 - Call From A Man From Macedonia   Day 311
17 - Thessalonica, Berea And South To Athens   Acts 16-17
7th November

2nd Missionary Journey
To Macedonia And Achaia

The Big Picture

Timothy joins Paul and Silas after his circumcision. They travel west through Galatia but are unable to enter the province of Asia so proceed to Troas in Mysia. Paul sees a vision there and responds to the call of 'a man from Macedonia' in northern Greece. Ironically when they travel to Macedonia they initially encounter only women rather than men. This is the first step into Europe. Many are converted in Philippi including Paul and Silas's jailer. Pursued by Jews who disagree with them they travel to Thessalonica then Berea and south to Athens. In Athens Paul preaches at Mars Hill and explains that he has found the unknown God who is worshipped by the Greeks.

Thinking Step

Timothy had a Jewish mother and a Greek father. When Paul was a Pharisee he would probably have counted a Jewish girl as dead if she married a Gentile. By acknowledging Timothy as Jewish and circumcising him, Paul shows just how much he has changed. Timothy proved to be a perfect replacement trainee missionary for John Mark.

Action Step

16:37a – '...Paul replied "They have publicly beaten us without a trial and put us in prison – and we are Roman citizens ...' To be a Roman citizen had many privileges, not the least being that you could not be tortured or whipped. Citizenship was only available to men and even if they were found guilty of serious crimes they could not be crucified. This was a punishment reserved for non citizens. Of course the jailer was unaware of the full facts of the situation when he jailed Paul and Silas otherwise he would have taken other actions. So how did Paul and Silas prove they were Roman citizens? Was there a secret password or were they tattooed? No! The only way you could prove your citizenship was by referring to someone else who was a fellow citizen and would vouch for your status. I wonder how we would fair if we had to do something similar to prove we were Christians? I don't mean a fellow Church member but someone who simply knew you as a citizen of your country. Would there be enough evidence to prove you are a believer? Re-appraise your life now and look at the evidence. The accusation is that you are a follower of Jesus Christ. Would you be found guilty or not guilty? How sad it would be if there was not enough evidence!

3rd Missionary Journey

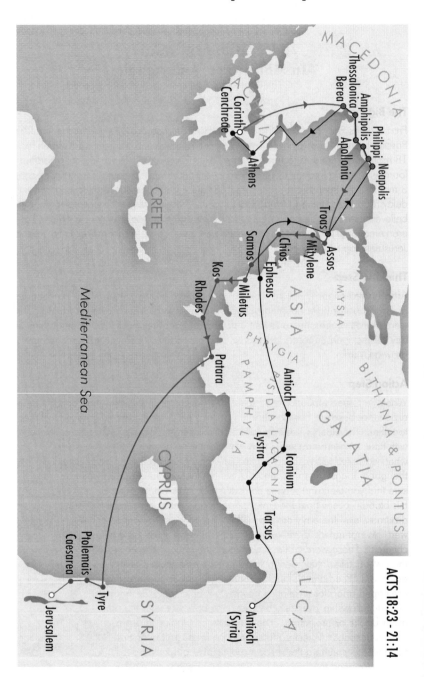

ACTS 18:23 - 21:14

Second Journey Ends
And Third One Is Completed

The Big Picture

From Athens Paul travels west to Corinth. Here he meets fellow Jews and tentmakers Priscilla and Aquila who have recently arrived from Italy. Paul remains in Corinth for 18 months then returns to Antioch before setting off on his third and final missionary journey travelling through the Province of Asia and on to Ephesus where he stayed for 3 months. He spends a further 2 years in Asia. Problems with Demetrius in Ephesus delay his planned return to Macedonia. Paul finally leaves for Greece to encourage believers there, then starts his last journey to Jerusalem as a free man. On his way there is an emotional meeting at Miletus with the elders of Ephesus before Paul continues his Jerusalem journey.

Thinking Step

After his rejection by the Ephesian Synagogue – 19:9 Paul taught in the 'School of Tyrannus' for 2 years. Such schools were well known in the Greek world. They were places where open and free teaching and debate could take place on almost any subject. Open to enquirers and committed alike they were an ideal place to grow a Church.

Action Step

When Paul meets the elders of Ephesus at Miletus it must have been an emotional experience because they all knew that this was probably the last time they would meet together. The elders willingly travelled 30 miles from Ephesus to Miletus to fellowship with Paul. While he waited for them he must have been mulling over exactly what he wanted to say. His words are recorded in 20:18-35. One practical thought amongst the many that he mentions may be found in 20:28 – 'Be sure that you feed and shepherd God's flock – His Church, purchased with His blood – over whom the Holy Spirit has appointed you as elders.' On a human level the early congregations were as dear to Paul as if they were his natural children. In fact many of them were his spiritual children. These words reflect much of what Jesus said to Peter on the last occasion they meet at Galilee before His ascension. The essence is "Feed and shepherd God's flock." So many fellowships are ripped apart for unspiritual things. Perhaps there are decisions in your fellowship over things of no eternal consequence – like hymn books or projector. Printed notices or announcements. Hymns or songs. Music group or organ. Need I go on? Jesus told Peter to shepherd His sheep. Paul tells the elders to do the same. We need to shepherd the Church rather than let it be ripped apart over irrelevancies.

Day 313
Acts 21-23
9th November

21 - Paul Ignores Warnings
22 - Paul Shares Testimony With Jews
23 - Paul Survives Death Threat

Paul Is Determined To Explain All

The Big Picture

Paul continues his journey to Jerusalem with more tearful farewells as he says "Farewell" to believers in Tyre and Caesarea. Despite prophecies and pleas from his fellow believers Paul is determined to follow what he is convinced God has told him to do. He is rescued by Roman soldiers after trying to share his testimony with a crowd of Jews who have dragged him out of the Temple. The soldiers' commander takes Paul to the Jewish High Council in an effort to get justice for him. The council is split between the Pharisees who support Paul and the Sadducees who don't! Paul later survives a death threat and is taken under armed guard to Governor Felix in Caesarea.

Thinking Step

Felix was a truly remarkable man. Totally unscrupulous, he was the only slave who ever became the governor of a Roman province. He married three princesses, one after another. No one knows the name of his first wife but his second was a granddaughter of Antony and Cleopatra. His third wife was Drusilla, daughter of Herod Agrippa the first.

Action Step

22:1-21 – Of all the things Paul could have said, he simply shared his testimony and used the language of the Jewish people rather than the more sophisticated language of Greek. In my experience there are few people who are persuaded of the claims of Christ by argument and clever debate. In order to communicate you need to be 'one of them' rather than 'one above them.' When a speaker seems to be 'on your wavelength' most folk are willing to listen. In our reading today when Paul is talking to the commander of the soldiers he uses Greek which has an immediate effect and bonds them both as brothers and fellow citizens. When he speaks to the Jews he comes over as one of them which gives him the best chance to influence. When Paul shares his testimony he is in effect telling his hearers that what happened to him is real and could just as easily happen to them. As believers we are constantly on view as representatives of Christ. Just like Paul we should always be ourselves but try everything we know to communicate with others for the sake of the Gospel. Of course we should do this even when we are not 'witnessing' but simply living our daily lives. Why not try today to be as natural as you can and listen for opportunities to commend Christ for all He has done for you.

24 - Felix Holds Paul Prisoner For Two Years   Day 314
25 - Festus Suggests Jerusalem For The Trial   Acts 24-26
26 - Agrippa Can Find No Charge Against Paul   10th November

Felix, Festus, Agrippa – Caesar Next!

The Big Picture

Jewish leaders come to see Paul in Caesarea but cannot persuade Governor Felix to take action. He is like a cat (very appropriate with a name like Felix). All he does is walk the fence without coming down on either side! Festus suddenly replaces Felix. More pressure follows from the Jewish leaders but Festus was not able to do much after Paul appealed to Caesar. King Agrippa offers to 'get to grips with it' but fails to resolve the situation. By this time Paul seems resigned to travelling to Rome for trial but at least he will be able to tell more about his Messiah Jesus. It's not the way Paul imagined going to Rome but at least it was free!

Thinking Step

Festus was a man of integrity and untainted reputation. Sadly he didn't live long after this episode. King Agrippa's character was totally corrupt. He was a puppet King of Galilee and Perea and willing to do anything to retain his comfortable position of luxury. His wife Bernice was sister to Felix's wife Drusilla but she was also his own half sister!

Action Step

26:28 – 'Agrippa interrupted him. "Do you think you can persuade me to become a Christian so quickly?"' Bearing in mind it only took a brief encounter with Jesus for Paul to become a Christian this is an ironic question from Agrippa. In a Church where we were members some years ago we had a programme of visiting contacts in order to explain the Gospel in a friendly personal way. We had arranged to visit someone else one particular evening with another name pencilled in just in case there was time. Both visits fell through so we decided to call it a day and were just about to leave for home when another name came into our minds. We decided 'on the off chance' to go that way home and see if he was free. We rang his door bell and he answered with a warm greeting and commented that he wasn't sure if we were coming but he was very glad we had! It was very obvious the Holy Spirit had been busy! Leading our new brother to the Lord was such a joy and so quick! It was a truly God arranged meeting. In personal evangelism one of the dangers is that we pick blossom instead of fruit. This time it was beautifully ripened fruit. I am convinced there is regularly fruit like this to pick. Anyone spring to mind? Why not travel in their direction today?

God's Protection At Sea And In Rome

The Big Picture

Paul's 'prison-ship' sets sail but soon encounters problems off the coast of present day Turkey and Paul continues his journey in another ship as they set sail from the port of Myra. Later in the journey conditions worsen and they finish up ashore on Malta after the ship is totally wrecked. All 276 passengers and crew survive just as God promised Paul in a vision. Paul survives a snake bite and also ministers to local people during his stay on Malta. Taking another ship he later proceeds to Sicily and on to Italy. Greeted by some believers who had heard of his coming Paul settles in Rome ministering and witnessing from his rented home for the next two years.

Thinking Step

Most of Acts is written in third person plural but occasionally Luke changes to first person plural. This is when 'they' becomes 'we.' These 'we' passages are obviously eye witness accounts when Luke was actually part of the group whose 'acts' we are reading about in 'Acts.' 16:10-17 ; 20:5-15 ; 21:1-18 ; 27:1-28

Action Step

28:3 – 'As Paul gathered an armful of sticks and was laying them on the fire, a poisonous snake, driven out by the heat, bit him on the hand.' Paul had a real servant's heart and didn't think gathering firewood was beneath him. The greatest missionary and Church planter the world had ever seen and he was doing the work usually reserved for slaves. Isn't that what Jesus would have suggested and indeed done Himself if He had been there? In your Church can you determine who everyone is by the things they do on Sunday? I hope not! If we are not able to do the most menial of tasks then we need to check on our willingness to serve. Jesus was willing to wash dusty feet. Paul was willing to gather rough bits of wood (snakes as well!). What about you? I believe that door keepers in any Church are the most important people every Sunday. What visitors think of your fellowship is often determined by the 10 seconds they spend with the person who welcomes them in. If you ever see someone 'sneaking in' without being welcomed then you go and welcome them. The same goes for the end of the service. Don't let people slip out without at the very least acknowledging that you have seen them. Have fun 'people watching' on Sunday.

Romans

Romans

Considered by many to be Paul's greatest work Romans is appropriately placed no.1 in his list of epistles. Paul does not actually write his own letters but dictates to a scribe who in this instance was Tertius who adds his own greeting in 16:22. From the beginning it has been assumed Romans was written primarily to the Church in Rome which was a fellowship Paul had very little personal knowledge about. Of course it would have been copied to others Churches. The letter was probably written by Paul near the end of his third missionary journey during his stay in Corinth – Acts 20:3-6. Paul's major emphasis is that the price for our salvation has been paid in full and that we are to live a life of righteousness. He describes God's righteousness and then goes on to explain how it may be applied to our daily lives.

Below is an acrostic which summarises each chapter of the book.

1. **T**heology of man's sin
2. **H**uman judgement of sin
3. **E**vidence of God's justification

4. **G**od counts Abraham righteous
5. **O**btaining righteousness by grace
6. **S**in's power is broken
7. **P**roblem of two natures
8. **E**mbracing the Spirit life
9. **L**ove shown for Israel

10. **O**utcome of open confession
11. **F**orgiveness offered to gentiles

12. **J**oy in using gifts
13. **E**levation of higher authority
14. **S**trong and weak brethren
15. **U**nity within the church
16. **S**ummary of Paul's ministry

1 - Gentiles Have Sinned Since The Beginning   Day 316
2 - Jews Have The Law But Are No Better   Romans 1-3
3 - Jesus' Sacrifice Is Essential For <u>All</u>   12th November

Jew And Gentile Both Need Sacrifice Of Jesus

The Big Picture

Paul writes declaring he has been chosen by God just as his readers in Rome have. He tells them that he longs to visit them someday. Little did he know that he would – but not as a free man! Acts 28:16. In the meantime he assures them of his constant prayer support. He reminds them that people are made in God's image and with a knowledge of Him but they have turned away from the creator and now worship the creation instead. Before the Jews can puff out their chests Paul tells them that they are no better than the Gentiles! Keeping the law and being circumcised are insufficient. Jesus' sacrifice is essential for both Jew and Gentile.

Thinking Step

1st century – 'Yes they knew God, but they wouldn't worship Him as God or even give Him thanks. They began to think up foolish ideas of what God was like... their minds became dark and confused.' – 1:21

21st century's 'enlightened atheist' – "It's not that I don't believe in God, I don't want there to be a God!"

Action Step

1:28 – 'Since they thought it foolish to acknowledge God, He abandoned them to their foolish thinking and let them do things that should never be done.' True love is allowing those we love to make mistakes but to be there to pick up the pieces when they fail. Of course God could have simply knocked mankind into shape by stopping them doing anything wrong and always doing what He wants. Some people foolishly think the world would be a better place if God did that now. They protest "Why does God allow that?" 'Of course that must not affect my life in any way but it's the others who are causing problems anyway!' So the argument goes. As long as we have freewill there will be the possibility of tragic circumstances – but if God removes our freewill then relationships with Him are impossible. We all become robots. Everyone is part of the problem and God is the only solution. More than that, God made mankind in His image so every single one of us has a knowledge of God from our birth. This helps me with the age old question "What happens to those who haven't heard?" So next time God is blamed for 'an act of God' – as insurers call it, remember that God could enforce total inflexible equality onto us – but He loves us too much for that.

Day 317
Romans 4-6
13th November

4 - Abraham Is A Great Example To Follow
5 - Troubles Can Be Blessings!
6 - To Live We Must Die To Sin

Salvation By Faith Not Works

The Big Picture

Paul uses Abraham as an example for Gentiles as well as Jews. He was accepted by God through faith long before the law of Moses was given by God. Abraham is the father of all – Jew and Gentile alike. God didn't wait until we were good enough. Jesus came and died for us while we were still sinners. People have sinned since Adam. Adam brought death but Jesus has brought us life. Should we continue to sin or should we refuse to be controlled by sin which has been defeated through the death of Jesus. Choose to do good and live rather than drift back into sin and death.

Thinking Step

In response to Paul the Rabbis insisted that Abraham kept the law hundreds of years before Moses brought it! They could never concede that faith was enough so they insisted that Abraham kept the law by anticipation. Keeping it without knowing that he was doing so! There are truly none so blind as those who will not see!

Action Step

5:3-4 – 'We can rejoice, too, when we run into problems and trials, for we know that they are good for us – they help us learn to endure and endurance develops strength of character in us ...'

When we imply that coming to Christ will help us avoid all future problems we are teaching a travesty of the real truth. Paul knew what it meant to encounter problems and these two verses really sum up the reality available to all Christians when life doesn't go as smoothly as they hope. Rejoicing when we come into difficult times is easier said than done! It can only be done when we fully trust the Lord. If you are not having troubles at the moment then you cannot imagine how the Holy Spirit will undertake when you need Him and His comfort. The reality only comes when there is a need. We are not given a 'free sample fix' ahead of time. God doesn't deal with us like that. Learning to endure is something that we have to experience to know how good God can be. It's seeing over the situation and trusting God now, knowing that He sees the end and the beginning and will guide us through it. If you are 'going through the mill' these verses are for you now. Be encouraged and you will become a stronger character for God. Then you are equipped to encourage others.

The Spirit Is Superior To The Law

The Big Picture

The law only applies to the living so when you die with Christ you die to the law. Now you are free to live in the spirit of the law not just to the letter of the law. The law serves its purpose by showing us we are sinners but the only effective remedy for our sin is Christ Himself. Just trying to do the right thing is impossible. Paul knows because he has tried many times. Only with the spirit of Jesus can we know true victory. We are children of God, sharing Christ's glory and suffering. Even in sufferings remember that everything works for good for all believers doing God's will. God and us are inseparable because of Jesus!

Thinking Step

Paul refers to the children of Abraham, the Jews, by recalling that God is like Abraham – only better! Abraham was willing to offer his only son Isaac and through him all Jews descend – Gen. 22:16. God was willing to offer His only Son Jesus and through Him all mankind can be blessed and be children of God – 8:32.

Action Step

When writing to the Church in Rome and dealing with the subject of difficulties in daily life Paul gives us one of his best known quotes – 8:28 – 'We know that God causes everything to work together for the good of those who love God and are called according to His purpose for them.' Sadly there are believers who only read the first part of this verse and wonder what is going wrong. It does not simply say that 'God causes everything to work together for good.' It is not a guarantee that problems will not come our way and even if they do, God will brush them aside for His children. The verse goes on to indicate who will qualify for this Godly promise. It clearly tells us it is for 'those who love God and are called according to His purpose for them.' When problems come into your life be sure that you don't simply lean on this promise no matter what. God sometimes uses difficulties to attract our attention to things in our lives that are not what He wants and we must act to deal with them. If you are going through a bad time at the moment be sure to check that you are currently working out His purposes for you. With that 'green light' you can then cling to this wonderful promise that so many saints have clung to over the centuries.

451

The Jews Need To Move On From The Law

The Big Picture

Paul is grief stricken for his people the Jews. He even goes so far as to say he would sacrifice his relationship with Christ if that was the only way the Jews could be saved! He repeats that being a child of Abraham is insufficient. We have to be a child of the promise between God and Abraham – available to all who believe. Paul refers to several giants in the Old Testament to prove his point that works are not enough. Paul muses "If only Jews could believe rather than depend on their ability to keep the law." If only they would believe in their heart and confess with their mouth then they would be saved – and so can we!

Thinking Step

9:5 – '...and Christ Himself was an Israelite...' I remember telling a congregation this and adding that Jesus never said "Verily verily I saith unto thee." A lady interrupted "Yes He did!" I pointed out that He didn't because he didn't speak English. She had to admit that it had never occurred to her. She always thought of Him as British!

Action Step

Paul longs that those he loves will turn to Christ. He wants this so much that he says he is willing to forfeit his own salvation if his beloved Jews could be saved. That is very Christ-like and reveals something of Paul's love for people who he didn't know personally! It can be totally frustrating when you ponder just how hopeless the task of evangelism can be if we simply rely on our eloquence and ability to argue our case. The Holy Spirit is essential if salvation is to be given and received but there also has to be a willingness from the repenting sinner, to receive what God offers. I worked with a man whose whole life revolved around supporting his 'beloved football team' – Sunderland AFC. As a life long supporter of this same team I am able to be empathetic. When his first child was born he registered him as a supporter before he registered his birth! Now that's dedication or maybe madness! I had to remind him that the child would have to make up their own mind when they grew up. He couldn't simply transplant his own beliefs and convictions into another. His response was an empty gaze as he realised I was right. Do you have friends or relatives who are still unbelievers as far as you know? Offer a prayer for them now, that the Holy Spirit might shake them from their apathy today.

Live Your Life In The Power Of The Spirit

The Big Picture

Paul reminds his readers that all Jews are not lost. Sadly however there are many who have turned away from the God of their Fathers. The Jews are still God's chosen people but He loves the Gentiles too. Submit yourselves to God and be transformed into new people. Do the things that God enables you to do but above all live lives full of genuine love. Never just pretend to love. Don't seek to 'get even' when you are wronged. Trust God and He will get justice for you. Be a good citizen and pay your dues. Pray for those over you and love your neighbour as yourself. If you live like this, everything else will slot into place.

Thinking Step

When Paul refers to Jews and Gentiles he is of course thinking of large groups of people. Salvation is not for large groups of mankind it is for individuals. In a large Church in Texas I remember seeing a placard proclaiming "Saving the World for Jesus" and I gulped – until I read the next line "One person at a time!"

Action Step

During Church services I know that many congregations try to vary the order of things to retain freshness and spontaneity. One Sunday morning when I was preaching I had left the offering until after the sermon, just before the final hymn. I have never seen such animated stewards waiving to me as my sermon came to a close, thinking I had forgotten it! Another time we had the offering after the first hymn and I was confronted by an elderly man at the end of the service who said to me "The first thing you asked for today was our money!" Money can be such a touchy subject! I find it interesting that Paul is quite specific about using money in chapter thirteen when he urges believers to 'pay their taxes, pay their bills, pay their import duties and all of their other debts.' Then interestingly, he sums up everything by telling his readers that they should 'Love their neighbour as themselves and so satisfy all of God's requirements.' It seems if we love as Christ loved then money will not be a issue. We used the same local garage for many years and one time I rang them and began explaining who I was, the receptionist interrupted me saying that she knew exactly who I was – I was the man who always paid his account on time! People are always watching – be careful what your actions say about Jesus!

Day 321
Romans 14-16
17th November

14 - Show Compassion To Those Whose Faith Is Weak
15 - Accept Others As Christ Accepts You
16 - Personal Greetings And Commendations

Show Weak Brethren That They Are Accepted

The Big Picture

This letter comes to a close as Paul advises believers not to reject believers who are not as 'sound' or 'respectable' as them. Honour others in the way you live. If you have habits or customs that cause difficulties for some try not to do them in front of them. Paul tells the Romans that it is his intention to first take gifts to Jerusalem from the Churches in Greece and then leave for a long trip to Spain – and on his journey he planned to visit Rome. As it happened he was taken to Rome as a prisoner several years after this and we are unsure if he ever made the journey to Spain.

Thinking Step

Archaeologists have uncovered a block of marble in Corinth which bears an inscription in Latin. It declares – 'Erastus, commissioner of public works, laid this pavement at his own expense.' This is almost certainly the same Erastus mentioned by Paul in his greetings at the end of Romans – 16:23 – '...Erastus, the city treasurer, sends you his greetings ...'

Action Step

Years ago we had a lady attending our Church who had just moved into the area. She seemed very nice and respectable and I arranged to visit her. She told me she was a widow and had lost her husband a long time ago. When I arrived at her home there was a man in the garden who I assumed was her gardener. She told me his name and explained that they lived together but purely as friends. In those days I was shocked! I have to say I wouldn't be today! I gently told her that her situation was something that needed to change if she was to become a member of our Church. We never saw her again. I believe my action was not what Paul would have done in the light of what he tells us in his letter today. 14:1 – 'Accept other believers who are weak in faith and don't argue with them about what they think is right or wrong.' Keeping a good standard of witness and at the same time welcoming weaker brethren into fellowship is becoming increasingly difficult in the 21st century. Remember this verse when you are next tempted to get on your 'moral high horse!' Of course we have our witness to consider but don't forget that Christ accepts all of us just as we are – and then works on us!

1 Corinthians

1 Corinthians

Corinth was the most important city in Greece in Paul's day and had a population of 700,000 of whom two thirds were slaves. It was a city of rampant immorality and the last place most of us would have chosen to plant a Church! The location of Corinth made it a vital centre as it linked mainland Greece with the Peloponnese and had the Adriatic Sea on the west and the Aegean Sea on the east. These two seas were connected by a canal towards the end of the 19th century but before that ships were dragged overland by teams of slaves to reduce the length of voyages. In this disciplinary letter Paul tries to correct wrong teaching and practice. The Corinthian Church was founded during Paul's second missionary journey – Acts 18:1-7. The letter was probably written by Paul from Ephesus during his third missionary journey – Acts 19.

Below is an acrostic which summarises each chapter of the book.

1. Exhortation to Christian unity
2. Response of natural man
3. Reasons for Christian carnality
4. Observations of Paul's ministry
5. Rebuking immorality in Church
6. Sins against the body

7. Importance of Christian marriage
8. Nature of Christian liberty

9. Believers must yield rights
10. Eating the Lord's supper
11. How to approach communion
12. Abilities within Christ's body
13. Virtues of true love
14. Instructions of using tongues
15. Outcome of the resurrection
16. Recognition of Paul's friends

1 - Stop Splitting Into Unhelpful Factions

2 - Preach Jesus - That's Enough!

3 - You Don't Seem To Be Growing

4 - Do What God Commands - As I Do

Day 322

1 Corinthians 1-4

18th November

You Need To Grow Up In Christ

The Big Picture

After his usual greetings Paul tells the Corinthians to stop arguing amongst themselves. They may be surrounded by people who think what they are doing is foolishness but the cross is only foolish to those who are not saved. Preaching Jesus will create scope for the Spirit to do the rest. No one will ever work God out for themselves without the Spirit's help. Paul challenges them by saying that if they resent him treating them like immature believers they need to act more like spiritually mature grown ups! He acknowledges that we all need to get on with the tasks God has entrusted to us. He pleads with them to follow his faithful example and disregard worldly ridicule.

Thinking Step

I regret that Paul's letters were ever called epistles! 'Epistle' has come to mean an unnecessarily long letter of a rather boring nature. That's despite a young child thinking that epistles were simply the wives of Apostles! Nearly all of Paul's letters are vital responses to real people's issues and are a rich treasure house for all believers and enquirers.

Action Step

Of course we don't align to individuals in the same way as the Corinthians did with Paul, Apollos and Peter but we still tend to 'pigeon hole' people by the the way they dress or worship or even speak. I recall speaking to a lecturer in a very respectable theological college where I was teaching a Walk Through the Bible event on the New Testament for his students. He had a broad Australian accent and played up to it as much as many think I do with my north of England one! I asked him how he coped with the image of a raucous loud Aussie. He said he loved it especially when folk realised who he was and what he did for a living! I still remember a traditional baptist friend of mine who, when things happened in Church that he was not happy with would retort "If you want that sort of thing go to another Church. We don't do that here!" Any splits in a Church dilutes its impact to the world. Why don't all of us resolve today that we will not criticise other denominations; Not negatively remark on the way others worship? Try not to be distracted by the way others dress. Wouldn't the Church be a much better place and more effective witness. What I have just written will be a bigger task for me than many of you reading it!

457

Day 323
1 Corinthians 5-7
19th November

5 - Church Discipline is Not an Option but a Necessity
6 - Law Courts are Not the Answer for Believers' Disputes
7 - One Man and One Woman is the Ideal

No Place In The Church For Sexual Immorality

The Big Picture

Paul is amazed by the way the Corinthian Church accepts open sinfulness amongst its congregation. Serial sinners should be confronted and ejected otherwise their bad behaviour will spread. He tells them very clearly that they are to resolve their own internal disputes rather than taking their grievances through the civil law courts. There are so many immoral sexual practices taking place that Paul feels he has to underline that individual bodies are temples for the Holy Spirit and therefore must be treated with respect. Paul condones celibacy but recommends one man/one woman marriages are the best. The fundamental basics of activities within a marriage are then outlined for a Church that seems to have lost its moral compass.

Thinking Step

After the flood – the visual reminder of a rainbow. At the Last Supper – bread and wine are visual reminders. It's the same with circumcision – Gen. 17:10-11. This was the very sign that was designed to remove the sinful sexual behaviour that was rampant in Corinth. Every time sexual sins were committed they could see it was wrong!

Action Step

I have seen so many couples divided by one of them being converted! In the excitement of conversion one of them forgets that they have a covenant already with their partner and God does not want them to break it. There is an unholy rush to get the other one converted rather than resting in this lovely profound promise that Paul reveals to the Church in Corinth. 7:12-14 – 'If a Christian man has a wife who is not a believer and she is willing to continue living with him, he must not leave her. If a Christian woman has a husband who is not a believer and he is willing to continue living with her, she must not leave him. For the Christian wife brings holiness to her marriage, and the Christian husband brings holiness to his marriage...' If you are half a couple, one committed and one not yet, please read this carefully and rely on God to work through you on the human being you have already promised yourself to. Unless both partners are converted at the same time and most aren't, then this tension is inevitable. A specific word for this sex crazed Church in Corinth – please be patient and God will work His purposes out. What He said to Corinth holds good for anywhere else on the earth today. Trust Him and be the 'holiness influence' you are meant to be.

8 - Be Careful What You Eat For The Sake Of Others   Day 324
9 - Adapt Your Behaviour To Where You Are   1 Corinthians 8-11
10 - Temptation Will Be Present But Never Overpowering   20th November
11 - This Is How To Celebrate The Lord's Supper

Advice On Food, Behaviour, Temptation And Communion

The Big Picture

Now Paul turns to the subject of food and more specifically meat from pagan temples. He argues that pagan gods are nothing more than useless idols but as long as it is not a problem for others it is permissible to eat meat from their temples. Paul touches on a real sore point of his acceptance as a real Apostle as he never met the Lord Jesus other than in a vision on the road to Damascus. On a broader subject he encourages the Corinthians that temptations are just part of life. However God will never allow temptation to be so strong that it cannot be withstood. Our final chapter includes the well known words of institution for the Lord's Supper.

Thinking Step

Paul's training under Gamaliel in Jerusalem and Jesus' public ministry could easily have overlapped. It's an intriguing thought that they could easily have met! The fact that they didn't could be because Paul just felt he had better things to do! Perhaps he never gave Jesus a second thought until it was too late and He'd been crucified!

Action Step

11:24-25 – '...and gave thanks to God for it. Then he broke it in pieces and said "This is my body, which is given for you. Do this to remember Me." In the same way, He took the cup of wine after supper, saying, "This cup is the new covenant between God and his people – an agreement confirmed with My blood. Do this to remember Me as often as you drink it."' As this letter was probably written before any of the Gospels were in written form, we have here the very first words of Jesus in writing. Twice Jesus asks us to remember what He has done for us. In those days bread and wine were part of the staple diet for everyone. So in a way Jesus was asking us to remember Him daily. Do you remember Him and His goodness in your life whenever you eat or drink? The art of 'saying grace' seems to be almost dead now so why don't we revive it? Whenever we have visited Israel or any of the lands of the Bible we have always 'given thanks' before our meal in the hotel and you would be amazed how many "Amens" we have had from folk at other tables. Try saying a simple grace next time you eat. It will be a beautiful reminder of all Jesus has done for you and you never know who's watching and listening!

Day 325
1 Corinthians 12-14
21st November

12 - All You Always Wanted to Know about Spiritual Gifts
13 - All You Always Wanted to Know about Real Love
14 - All You Always Wanted to Know about Balanced Worship

Instruction Manual For The Early Church

The Big Picture

Paul tackles spiritual gifts head on. It is obvious that the Corinthian Church was in total disarray as they grappled with gifts and their exercising. All of this takes place in a city where excess and chaos were the norm. Having talked about gifts Paul then shows them something far superior – love! He encourages them to pursue love and then desire the gifts. He wants them to get their priorities right rather than simply running after the spectacular experiences of worship. Towards the end of this passage Paul implores the Corinthians to do everything to the glory of God and in a good, proper and orderly fashion.

Thinking Step

Worship of Dionysus and Cybele in Corinth was very loud and exciting. Priests were stirred by clashing cymbals, loud drums, and screeching flutes and would at times dance themselves into a frenzy of excitement. Paul points out that sadly there was no love included. The vital ingredient was missing. It was all clash and bang but no life changing love.

Action Step

1 Cor. 14:12 – 'Since you are so eager to have the special abilities the Spirit gives, seek those that will strengthen the whole church.' It seems that while the Corinthian Church had many faults, simply being a sedentary member of the congregation wasn't one of them! I used to be an elder in a Baptist Church where the minister's elder son, who had Down's Syndrome, was soundly converted as a teenager and then baptised. He immediately pestered his Dad for a job in the Church as he knew everyone should be doing something. His Dad commented that at least someone was listening to his sermons! In the end he was asked to take care of refreshments at elders' meetings. We were graciously asked what we wanted, with milk and/or sugar, in a cup or a mug – and the service was prompt. However, what we asked for and what we received rarely coincided but it was wonderful to know that he understood the concept of the Body of Christ better than many others in that Church! Just imagine if everyone in your Church was as keen as a Corinthian to discover their gift and then exercise it. Why not concentrate on you and your gifting and determine or confirm it today? God really wants you to know so get ready to act. Then it's away with passive Church membership and on into vibrant participation in the Body of Christ.

Jesus Really Did Rise From The Dead!

The Big Picture

Paul reminds the Romans of those great days when he had the privilege of sharing the Gospel with them. The same Gospel that transformed so many of them. He can't believe that there is a faction in the same Church doubting the resurrection. If Jesus was not raised from the dead then we are all lost! He pleads with them not to be confused by clever ideas. Death has been defeated and Jesus lives! Paul can't resist giving a piece of advice about finances! He tells them to systematically put money to one side every Sunday. He closes by confirming that he plans to return. Sadly the situation doesn't improve and Paul has to write again.

Thinking Step

The New Testament provides the primary historical source for information on the resurrection. Written by eye witnesses and those influenced by them they have been a major factor in transforming millions of lives. Little wonder that many critics, especially since the 19th century, have attacked the reliability of Biblical records and thereby tried to throw doubt on the resurrection itself.

Action Step

A man was teaching in a school and asked the children what would they do if they saw him die but later come back to life again in a miraculous way. Having been certified dead he comes back to life! "Would you believe it?" "Would you tell your parents when you went home?" he asked. All the kids confirmed of course they would believe it and would tell their parents. "Do you think your parents would tell other people?" was the next question. They were sure they would. Then he asked them if they would tell their children when they were parents in 10/20 years time. They couldn't believe he thought they wouldn't – of course they would. He finally asked them if there would come a time when people would doubt if this resurrection was true. After some thought they had to concede some might doubt if they weren't there at the time. "Can't you see?" he went on "That's what happened in the early Church. Going from certainty to some questions – to some doubt – to denial that it happened at all. Even though it had been written down. That's what happened in Corinth but Paul, with the help of the Holy Spirit, refreshes their memories with the amazing news that Jesus lives. May your memory be refreshed and your heart encouraged as you hear and re-consider the certainty of Christ's resurrection.

2 Corinthians

2 Corinthians

After Paul's first letter to Corinth the situation seems to have deteriorated causing Paul to have to make another visit – 12:13 – before writing to them again from Macedonia, possibly Philippi. There are some scholars who theorise that 2 Corinthians is made up of more than one letter from Paul stitched together to make one almost as long as 1 Corinthians. There is little doubt that this Church in Corinth had a special place in Paul's heart. He visited it at least a couple of times and wrote at least two letters to it. He saw it as strategically important. An important thrust of this letter is Paul's attempt to persuade the Corinthians to accept him as a legitimate Apostle. He wanted to be accepted, not for his ego's sake but so that his words would have more influence over the trouble makers and doubters in the Church at Corinth.

Below is an acrostic which summarises each chapter of the book.

1. **T**estimony to Paul's sincerity
2. **H**eaviness of Paul's heart
3. **E**xcellence of new covenant

4. **T**reasures in earthen vessels
5. **R**econciliation offered to all
6. **U**nion with unbelievers forbidden
7. **E**xhortation to perfect holiness

8. **G**enerosity of the Macedonians
9. **O**pportunity for cheerful giving
10. **S**piritual authority of Paul
11. **P**aul's boastings in Christ
12. **E**xperience of Paul's thorn
13. **L**iving the Christian life

Day 327
2 Corinthians 1-4
23rd November

1 - A God of Real Comfort Produces Comforters
2 - Forgive the Corinthian Troublemaker
3 - The New Covenant of Christ by the Spirit
4 - Despite Troubles We Will Continue to Preach the Truth

Paul Begins To Explain His Ministry

The Big Picture

Greetings from Paul and Timothy who continue to thank God for His timely comforting. He was particularly faithful to us during our recent suffering in Asia Minor. Paul apologises for any distress that his letters and visiting plans may have caused. The man who caused the original problems in Corinth must now be forgiven and everyone must move on. We continue to preach Christ freely and God is honouring that wherever we go. What has happened in Corinth is proof of that. Remember the old covenant was written in stone but the veil covering it has been removed by Jesus Christ. We have a new covenant in the Spirit. Despite our many falls we constantly rise and continue God's work.

Thinking Step

How many letters in 2 Corinthians?
6:14 – 7:1 could be the previous letter of 1 Cor. 5:9.
6:13 – 7:2 flows well without these verses.
2 Cor. 10-13 could be the letter of rebuke sent with Titus – 2 Cor. 8:17-18.
2 Cor. 1-9 then becomes Paul's reconciling letter ending with 9:15.

Action Step

The concept of comfort is mentioned 29 times in this letter with 10 of them coming in the first 7 verses. It is obviously something that Paul senses is important if his relationship with the Corinthians is to survive the stresses and strains of his letters and visits. A God who comforts must have seemed like a cooling balm to Corinth in the hustle and bustle of such a wicked and chaotic city. However the main thrust that Paul is giving here is not so much that they need the comfort of God but that they must then become comforters for others who are hurting or are in distress. 1:4 – 'He comforts us in all our troubles so that we can comfort others. When they are troubled, we will be able to give them the same comfort God has given us.' In other words we are to be channels for the comfort of God rather than containers. I realise that being a giver of comfort is not for our benefit but nevertheless there is real benefit in it for the giver as well as the receiver. Isn't God good? I have found tremendous satisfaction in doing God's work. Of course there are frustrations too but when we pass on the comfort of God we can get a real benefit too. Sometimes it's obvious who needs comforting but other times it can be a surprise. Keep your antennae up today.

5 - Totally New Bodies For All Believers
6 - Make The Most Of Today And Stay Pure
7 - Great Progress With Corinthian Church
8 - Donations For Jerusalem Believers Are Excellent

Day 328
2 Corinthians 5-8
24th November

Discipline Brings Positive Results In Corinth

The Big Picture

Paul tells the Corinthians that God has planned new bodies for all believers in Heaven. Not 'upgrades' but totally new ones! He encourages them to keep going and reminds them that today is the day of salvation. Paul's shares his sadness that many criticise his efforts and those of all Christians but he tells them all to stay pure and effective for God. Keep all relationships 'pagan-free' including marriage. Always stay away from close relationships with unbelievers. Paul is thrilled by the news of the progress in Corinth that he hears from Titus. He tells them to stay faithful in their giving to the Jerusalem Church just as the Macedonians Churches have. They are all such an encouragement.

Thinking Step

6:14 – 'Don't team up with those who are unbelievers. How can righteousness be a partner with wickedness?' We usually associate this with marriage but the story is told of the heir to a brewery empire witnessing drunken violence outside a public house. He was so distressed that he withdrew from the family business. He could no longer partner with wickedness!

Action Step

I had an interesting talk with an elderly neighbour of ours about Heaven. She told me the last place she wanted to go was Heaven! Now that's unusual as most people secretly hope they will get there even if they lived as though they didn't care. I enquired further to see what had put her off Heaven. "I have had enough of my life already and the thought of it going on and on for ever depresses me. I just want it to end!" she said. When Paul writes to the Church in Corinth he stresses that what they will be in Heaven will not simply be an improvement on what we all have here! It will be eternal life not just everlasting life. Eternal life is a life of real quality, a life of fullness. Everlasting life is simply something that goes on and on and lasts for ever. 5:2-3 tells us '...we long for the day when we will put on our new Heavenly bodies ...we will not be spirits without bodies but we will put on new Heavenly bodies.' In other words everything will be new not reconditioned! I believe that is true as soon as eternal life begins at our conversion. It is a case of new lives for old and not a haunting ghostly promise when you die! Make sure you don't miss out! You can find more information on Day 21 in this book.

465

Day 329
2 Corinthians 9-11
25th November

9 - Be Ready To Give Your Gifts On Time
10 - Stop Behaving Like Fleshly Human Beings
11 - Don't Be Fooled By All Who Say They're Apostles

Suffering For The Gospel Is Real For Paul

The Big Picture

After a final reminder to have their gift ready to be collected, Paul then changes tone altogether. Some believe from chapter ten to the end of chapter thirteen is a separate letter which has been added. See Day 327. Paul acknowledges that his writing can be more severe than his speaking. In fact his speaking is not as good as his writing and some describe him as a poor preacher! He warns the Corinthians not to simply believe everyone who says that they are an Apostle! So many others are keen to brag about who they are but Paul will rest on his background which is impeccably Jewish – and all he has done and suffered for the Gospel's sake.

Thinking Step

9:7 – '...don't give reluctantly or in response to pressure. "For God loves a person who gives cheerfully."'
The Greek translation of Proverbs includes an extra one at 22:8 – 'God blesses a man who gives cheerfully.' Seneca, a Roman philosopher and contemporary of Paul said "If you give with doubt and delay it's almost worse than not giving at all!"

Action Step

11:5-6 – '...I don't consider myself inferior in any way to these "super apostles" who teach such things. I may be unskilled as a speaker but I'm not lacking in knowledge. We have made this clear to you in every possible way.' In desperation Paul speaks up for himself to defend his ministry against those who are seeking to undermine him. In my experience when someone has to tell me how effective their ministry is or how powerful their witness has been it is usually because no one else would! When I was a technical representative in the construction industry we used to have regular meetings for training and team building. At my first one I was introduced to Barry who was obviously the best in the company. He knew every architect on his patch and was on excellent terms with every major building contractor. After a chat with him I felt totally inadequate. The following day I was talking to some of my other colleagues and something I said prompted one of them to ask if I had been speaking to Barry! When I said that I had they advised me not to believe more than 10% of what he said! What about you in the more important field of ministry? If you are tempted to exaggerate your effectiveness – don't! Instead, praise others and build them up. Enjoy personal encouragements but don't crave them or rely on them.

12 - Paul's Amazing Experience And His Thorn In The Flesh   Day 330
13 - Get Ready For Paul's Visit By Examining Your Faith   2 Corinthians 12-13
26th November

Final Thoughts Before Paul Re-Visits

Big Picture

Paul seems to get a little carried away as he describes his amazing experience in the Spirit. He does this with the best of intentions rather than to boost his own ego. He also tells the Corinthians about his thorn in the flesh which God refused to remove despite three requests. It's interesting that Paul is willing to accept God's will when it has been made very clear. Paul warns those who are still doing the same sinful things that they were doing when he was last with them. He tells them that they will have to pay the price for this disobedience. Finally he advises them to examine their lives to check that their faith is genuine.

Thinking Step

12:7 – Paul's 'Thorn in the flesh.'
Tertullian and Jerome wondered if it was severe debilitating headaches.
Luther thought it was the constant animosity and undermining from others.
Calvin suspected it was the spiritual temptations and doubts of Paul. It's significant that Paul doesn't tell us what it was but simply extols the positive influence it has in his life.

Action Step

12:7-8 – ' ...So to keep me from getting puffed up, I was given a thorn in my flesh, a messenger from Satan to torment me and keep me from becoming proud. Three different times I begged the Lord to take it away. Each time He said "My grace is all you need. My power works best in weakness." So now I am glad to boast about my weaknesses, so that the power of Christ can work through me.' Here we have a profound fundamental of the Christian faith. Rather than remove a problem from Paul's life God gives him the strength to withstand it. He actually makes it positive rather than negative. I have a friend who is a recovering alcoholic and has been for many years. Rather than try to forget his past and be all negative and defensive about it he is using it as a positive to help others who are in similar difficulties to those he encountered many years ago. It could be that you have had particular experiences in your life that you have always considered negative. Why not use your unique experience to help others? Make your negatives into positives! Next time you are tempted to be negative about any part of your life ask God to help you see the hidden positive potential! It could help others and it could help you. Don't delay, do something NOW!

Galatians

Galatians

Many believe this letter is amongst Paul's earliest writings. It addresses the increasing pressure from Jews who wanted the Law's requirements to be part of the initiation to becoming a Christian. One of the main issues being circumcision. This was resolved at the Jerusalem Council around AD49 – Acts 15. As Paul makes no reference to the council in his letter it seems probable that it was written before the Council was held. Freedom from the shackles of the Law is Paul's liberating emphasis as he writes to the Galatian Churches. Unlike his other letters which are written to one Church this one is specifically written to a group of Churches. Probably written from Antioch, where believers were first called Christians, as Paul travelled to Jerusalem for the Council meeting. Something else worthy of note is that 6:11 implies Paul wrote it personally rather than through a scribe.

Below is an acrostic which summarises each chapter of the book.

1. **T**urning from the Gospel
2. **H**allmark of Paul's ministry
3. **E**scape from the law

4. **L**aw versus true liberty
5. **A**mazing Grace through faith
6. **W**hatsoever a man soweth

Day 331
Galatians 1-3
27th November

1 - The Gospel Is God's Gift To You And Me
2 - We Are All Saved By Faith - Jew And Gentile Alike
3 - The Law Points Us To Christ

We Are Saved By Faith Alone

The Big Picture

Paul's greetings begin this letter. He tells the Galatians he is disappointed that they are slipping away from the straight clear path of Christ. He confirms that the Gospel is given by God to those who believe. Mankind cannot work it out alone! He tells them God revealed it to him and it was three years before he met any of the other Apostles and in the meantime God had taught him much. Paul confirms that he and the leadership in Jerusalem agreed that Gentiles must be included. He challenges the Galatians to question whether they received the Holy Spirit by keeping the Law. They didn't! Like Abraham we are all accepted by faith and not by keeping the Law.

Thinking Step

The Galatian people came originally from Gaul in western Europe. They migrated east into the land which is now called Turkey. This was as a result of the Gallic wars when Julius Caesar conquered Gaul which was an area comprising today's France, Belgium and Luxembourg. They retained their traditional name and therefore Paul's letter is addressed to the Galatians.

Action Step

3:24 – 'So that the Law served [to us Jews] as our trainer [our guardian, our guide to Christ, to lead us] until Christ [came], that we might be justified (declared righteous, put in right standing with God) by and through faith.' [Amplified Bible translation] This is such an important verse that I have used the Amplified Bible in order to get as many strands as possible from the original Greek text. Of course it refers to the Jewish people but by implication it is for the Gentiles too as Paul is writing to Gentiles to explain that they are now seen as equal to Jews as far as the Gospel is concerned. Ask most people how they can get a place in Heaven and they will without exception opt for works rather than faith. After hearing the Gospel from Paul the Galatians reverted back to works even though they knew they received Jesus by faith. That's what we all do! That's why we need to constantly check on who our faith is in. As soon as you say "In Jesus and...attending Church/reading my Bible/saying my prayers/preaching/singing in the choir/living a good life etc. etc. etc..." you are getting to be like a Galatian. Do a quick checkup now and see what other things seem essential for salvation and then jettison them and rest in your faith in Jesus alone.

4 - At Just The Right Time Jesus Came Into The World   Day 332
5 - Live In The Spirit And Produce Fruit Of The Spirit   Galatians 4-6
6 - Help And Support One Another   28th November

Only The Spirit Can Produce Spiritual Fruit

The Big Picture

God timed it perfectly concludes Paul. Jesus came at just the right time to free Jews from the Law and Gentiles from pagan slavery. When Paul first brought the Gospel to Galatia his hearers rejoiced. He cannot figure out why they have changed so much. He can't understand why they believe his enemies. Relying on the Law or circumcision will result in failure and disappointment. The only way to live life to the full is in the Spirit. Live under the Spirit's control and He will produce beautiful sweet Spiritual fruit in your life. In closing Paul pleads with the Galatians to stay faithful to the Gospel and care for each other. Never getting fed up of doing good.

Thinking Step

4:4 – 'But when the right time came, God sent his Son...'
Three final key events happened after the Old Testament – then Jesus came.

1. Greece brought the world its first international language.
2. Israel's century of 'independence' increased Messianic expectations.
3. Rome brought crucifixion and also peace with a safe road system for the spread of the Gospel.

Action Step

5:22-23 – ' ...the Holy Spirit produces this kind of fruit in our lives: love, joy, peace, patience, kindness, goodness, faithfulness, gentleness and self-control. There is no law against these things!' Many people equate the fruit of the Spirit with the gifts of the Spirit but they are very different in many ways, not least of which is that the fruit is singular and the gifts are plural. We are encouraged by Scripture to seek and exercise our own Spiritual gift – 1Cor.14. However in the case of the fruit we are to show all these aspects or segments in our lives! The Bible clearly tells us that 'the Holy Spirit produces this kind of fruit in our lives' and this is followed by a comprehensive list. There is a temptation to concentrate on our weaknesses rather than our strengths but when you think about it there is far more logic in improving what we are naturally suited to rather than spending lots of effort on something that we will never excel in. Take a moment now to consider the list. Which best describes you? Thank God for it and ask Him to help you progress further. Then look again to discover which is your weakest and thank God for the challenge and ask for wisdom to work it through. Never mind eating 'five fruits a day' we need to produce 'nine segments of Spiritual fruit.'

Ephesians

Ephesians

It is possible that this letter was sent for a number of Churches but was originally directed specifically to Laodicea. Col. 4:16 could be referring to this very letter. It seems that the Ephesian copy is the only one that survived and that this resulted in the letter being associated with Ephesus and their name added. Paul visited Ephesus at the end of his second missionary journey. It was a strategically important city and was a centre of worship of Diana (or Artemis) at the magnificent temple which was one of the seven wonders of the ancient world. This letter is one of Paul's 'prison epistles' written during his Roman imprisonment. Acts 28:16-31. Paul's main emphasis is one of maturing the Body of Christ and remaining 'in Christ.' The first three chapters tell us of our privileges and the second three remind us of our responsibilities in Christ.

Below is an acrostic which summarises each chapter of the book.

1. **C**alling of the church
2. **H**eaven by faith alone
3. **U**nity shown by love
4. **R**easons for spiritual gifts
5. **C**haracteristics of the believer
6. **H**elp in spiritual warfare

Day 333
Ephesians 1-3
29th November

1 - We Have So Much Power In Christ
2 - Both Jews And Gentiles Are One In Christ
3 - Paul, In Prison, Rejoices In Christ

All Believers Are Truly One In Christ

The Big Picture

Greetings from Paul with a resounding affirmation that God is so good! He said that he wanted believers everywhere to discover true fullness and how powerful they can all be in Christ. He reminds them that all of them, like him had been dead in their sins then God stepped in. This was true for both Jews and then Gentiles. Both are now brothers in Christ because God blessed them with a salvation that they could neither afford nor deserved. Paul mentioned that he was in prison in 3:13 but despite his circumstances he encouraged them all to experience Christ even if they can't understand how this wonderful free salvation works.

Thinking Step

This letter to Laodicea was later assigned to Ephesus.
In 1539 Thomas Cromwell declared every parish church should have a copy of the Great English Bible. The village of Trumpington didn't get one so borrowed one from nearby Ely. When they read 'Eli, Eli, lama sabachthani' in Matt 27:46 they dutifully amended the text to read 'Trumpington' instead of Eli!

Action Step

Paul overflows as he describes what it is like to be in Christ in these first three chapters. I have sympathy for his scribe because it seems he hardly takes a breath! It seems quite certain that Paul was a prisoner in Rome at the time of writing but he is far from downhearted because he knew God had everything under control. Of course it would have made more sense if Paul had been free to travel and preach – or would it? If he had never been in that Roman prison we are unlikely to have such letters as this one, along with Colossians, Philemon and Philippians. We can also thank prison for Paul's second letter to Timothy which was probably written during a later period of incarceration shortly before his death and after the historic period covered by the twenty eight chapters of Acts. Of his thirteen letters five of them were written in prison so if he had always been free our New Testament would have been much the poorer. Do you get frustrated sometimes at being 'in the wrong place' and think "If only I was somewhere else I could be so much more productive for God!" When people ask me about missionary service I always ask them what they are doing for God where they live now. Inactivity locally rarely produces activity anywhere else! Be a star where you are and twinkle no matter what.

Work Hard To Be All God Wants You To Be

The Big Picture

Paul encourages his readers to work well together and be united in Christ. He reminds them that Jesus came down from Heaven and then returned as He ascended back to His Father. Having left earth He then equipped His believers with the Holy Spirit who gives gifts and abilities to the Church so that the work of Christ may continue. Paul implores them to remain sexually clean and pure and to steer clear of unwholesome language and ungodly living. He gives some practical advice to families and encourages them to live Christian lives as befits their Saviour. Lastly He tells them to put on the armour of God and so be equipped to do the work of God on earth.

Thinking Step

As you walk towards the library in Ephesus you pass many statues. One of them is nothing special but all the guides point her out! Her name reminds you of the way many people lived in that city – and today. Her influence is encapsulated in a simple tick. Her name is Nike and the advice is, "Just do it!"

Action Step

I remember hearing one of my favourite preachers as I was growing up in Christ. Dr Alan Redpath said that when he first came to Christ he didn't see any reason why he couldn't carry on living as he had done before he was converted – so he did. "Don't believe people when they say you have to change when you become a believer!" My ears perked up because I was struggling with things like smoking and wondering if I had to give up! He continued "I didn't change and I was the most miserable man in Northumberland!" It's such a basic thing but vital if we are to mature in Christ. Life change is hard work even with the help of the Holy Spirit. Be suspicious of anyone who tells you different! However it is vital if we are to truly live a full life that satisfies us – and God Himself. It seems that Paul is telling his readers that simply accepting Jesus as Lord and Saviour is only the beginning! It's a great start that will propel you off on a life that is worth living but there is effort involved! These last three chapters are filled with practical advice. Are you holding on to something or some activity that you are hoping God will overlook? Don't waste your time! Give it up, move on and see how God will fill that void in your life with good things.

Philippians

Philippians

Philippians is another of Paul's prison letters written from Rome where Acts 28 records his detention. He wrote his letters to the Ephesians, Colossians and Philemon there too. The Church he was addressing was planted during his second missionary journey when he responded to the Macedonian call – Acts 16:10. Philippi was the place where Paul was imprisoned and beaten only to see the jailer converted. Despite it being written in prison this is one of Paul's most positive and encouraging letters. His resounding cry is "For me to live is Christ, to die is gain" – 1:21. He also urges his readers to rejoice and just in case they missed it he tells them twice – 4:4. The letter breaks into four sections with the first one describing Paul's personal situation. The other three cover the Mind of Christ, the Knowledge of Christ and the Peace of Christ.

Below is an acrostic which summarises each chapter of the book.

1. **J**oy of Christian fellowship
2. **O**utward evidences of humility
3. **Y**our focus is Christ
4. **S**ecret of God's peace

Happily Humble In Prison

The Big Picture

This letter comes from Paul and Timothy. They are planning to visit the Philippian Church but in the meantime Epaphroditus will be going. Paul tells them that despite being in prison, or maybe because of it, the Gospel continues to spread. He pleads with the Church to remain faithful no matter what happens to him. He encourages them to remember that they are to be as humble as Jesus was. Recalling that Christ became as nothing for each one of them – so they must be humble and willing to serve each other. Paul tells them that when they see Epaphroditus they will realise how good God was in answering their prayers when Epaphroditus was so close to death.

Thinking Step

Philippi was established by Philip of Macedonia, the father of Alexander the Great, in 356 BC and named after him which was the norm in those days. As a military centre rather than a city it didn't have a need for its own synagogue – Acts 16:12-13. This is why Paul goes down to the river on the Sabbath.

Action Step

1:14-18 – '...because of my imprisonment, most of the believers here have gained confidence and boldly speak God's message without fear. It's true that some are preaching out of jealousy and rivalry but others preach about Christ with pure motives... but that doesn't matter. Whether their motives are false or genuine, the message about Christ is being preached either way, so I rejoice and I will continue to rejoice.'

I have long been convinced that most of us, if not all, turn to Christ for selfish reasons. Escaping judgement, getting a better life etc. etc. This goes a step further in Philippi where some preachers were even evangelising for the wrong reasons! Isn't God gracious? He can still work out His purposes despite us! I know a minister of the Gospel who was seeing many folk soundly converted in his Church when it was discovered he was having an affair with a member of his congregation! I don't know about you but I am so glad that God doesn't need perfect servants – and so was he! However we do not have a mandate to be impure even if we are being outwardly effective! We have a reminder here to repent of any known sin in our lives – today. Then recommit ourselves to God's service and gratefully receive God's forgiveness once again. If you need to – take action and repent now! Be a clean vessel!

The Bottom Line Is,
"Being In Christ Is Sufficient"

The Big Picture

From his prison cell Paul encourages the Church in Philippi with the fact that the Lord's joy will always be with them – no matter what. He warns them to resist those who are still insisting on circumcision. He reminds them that if adherence to the Law was all that was necessary then He, Paul, would qualify ahead of all of his critics! He tells them that he still strives daily and that they should be doing the same! There must have been a big problem with two named ladies in the fellowship and they are urged to come back and be effective workers once again. Paul also mentions how much he appreciated the generosity of the Philippian Christians.

Thinking Step

2:30 – 'For he (Epaphroditus) risked his life for the work of Christ ...the Greek word used here is paraboleuesthai' – meaning bravery bordering on foolhardy or irresponsible. In the early Church there was a brotherhood who undertook the care of the sick and the burial of the dead and consequently exposed themselves to contagious diseases. They were called the 'parabolani.'

Action Step

4:2 – 'Now I appeal to Euodia and Syntyche. Please, because you belong to the Lord, settle your disagreement... Help these two women, for they worked hard with me in telling others the Good News.'

Very few of us can choose how we will be remembered by the generations who follow us. Of course the majority of us will soon be forgotten by the world but not by Jesus. Some anonymous characters about whom we know almost nothing are given 'immortality' by being included in the Bible. The two ladies mentioned in this verse are typical examples. They have obviously fallen out 'big time' with the fellowship in Philippi but we don't know why. It could be that they have fallen out with each other, we just don't know! We do know however that they were deeply committed to the cause of Christ before their disagreement. What a tragedy that they are remembered for all the wrong reasons! All the good that they did will be for ever in the shadow of what they did that was so unhelpful. So how will you be remembered? You cannot undo what has already been said and done but you can resolve to try, with the help of the Holy Spirit to live the days you have left so that people will smile when they remember you rather than frown or shed a tear.

Colossians

Colossians

This letter from Paul and Timothy is addressed to the Church in Colossae but is also meant for Laodicea – 4:16. Both of these Churches are in Asia Minor where the seven Churches of Revelation were established. In fact Laodicea was one of them in Rev. 3:14. This is another of Paul's letters written during his imprisonment in Rome – Acts 28. The emphasis of the whole letter is the supremacy of Christ. The first two chapters describe Jesus as our Head with us as the body. The second two chapters help us apply what we have learned as they continue the great overview of glorious Jesus. It seems from 1:4 and 2:1 that the Church in Colossae was as a result of the ministry of Epaphras rather than Paul – 1:7. It is possible that Epaphras was himself a convert from Paul's faithful teaching in Acts 19:10.

Below is an acrostic which summarises each chapter of the book.

1. **H**eresies exposed by Paul
2. **O**bjections to false teachers
3. **P**rinciples for Christian living
4. **E**nding prayer of Paul

For Real Freedom We Have The Real Christ

The Big Picture

Paul tells the Church at Colossae all the great things he has heard about them and thanks God for their faithfulness. He reminds them what they are doing is thanks to Christ who is the visible image of the invisible God. This same Jesus died for both Jew and Gentile and now unites them. Paul links Colossae with Laodicea even though he has met none of the Laodicean believers. It seems from 2:8 that heresy is already creeping into the early Church. Paul pleads with the Colossians to stay pure and trust in Christ alone. He confirms that false teachers are not part of Christ's body. He emphasises that living in Christ is the best and only way forward.

Thinking Step

The Church in Colossae seems to have been predominantly Gentile but there was a considerable number of Jews in the region too. In 62 BC the local Roman governor seized about twenty pounds of gold destined for Jerusalem to pay Temple taxes. This represented taxes from 11,000 men representing a sizeable population of up to 50,000 devoted Jews.

Action Step

2:9 – 'For in Christ lives all the fullness of God in a human body.' This is an incredible claim that many unbelievers don't think Jesus ever made for Himself. They claim that it was the early Church and men like Paul who 'invented' Christ's deity in order to establish their new religion. This isn't credible when you consider how many times Jesus declared Himself to be 'I Am' in the Gospels. 'I Am' being the name of God in Ex.3:14. However there is another instance that may be the real clincher for this argument. In Matt 18:20 we read "For where two or three gather together as my followers, I am there among them." The Jews had a similar saying in the days of Paul when they had no access to the Temple and particularly after the Temple was destroyed in AD70. The Jewish version went something like this 'Where two sit together studying Torah there is God in between them.' So what Jesus said was a very clear claim to be God! The great religions of the world have been established by remarkable men but none of them claimed to be God. Christianity has at it's heart a man who claimed to be equal with God. We ignore this remarkable claim from this remarkable man at our peril! See Day 21 for more information about receiving Jesus as Lord and Saviour.

A Holy Life Is The Way Forward

The Big Picture

As he approaches the end of his letter Paul urges believers to think on a heavenly plane rather than an earthly one. He lets them know very clearly that many of the things that were part of their earlier life are not good for Christians. He continues to advise replacing them with wholesome and pure things befitting Christ. Remember to forgive others as you have been forgiven. Wise instruction is also given to wives, husbands, children and slaves. Wives submitting and husbands loving. Together they create the perfect balance for a great relationship. He pleads with slave masters to be just and fair remembering that they have a master too, their heavenly Father. Final personal greetings close this letter.

Thinking Step

The lifetime of Demas in three verses.
4:14 – 'Luke, the beloved doctor, sends his greetings and so does Demas.'
Philemon 24 – 'So do Mark, Aristarchus, Demas and Luke, my co-workers.'
2 Tim 4:10 – 'Demas has deserted me because he loves the things of this life ...'
First he's with Paul then he's a co-worker then he slides away!

Action Step

3:21 – 'Fathers, do not aggravate your children, or they will become discouraged.' This is a very significant suggestion in a day when fathers were generally very remote and dictatorial but it was relevant then and is equally relevant today in the 21st century. In Paul's time a child was little more than a slave and could be sold or even executed. I found it helpful to refer to the Amplified Bible to get a broader understanding of this verse – 'Fathers, do not provoke or irritate or fret your children [do not be hard on them or harass them], lest they become discouraged and sullen and morose and feel inferior and frustrated. [Do not break their spirit.]' In other words do all you can to be positive and affirming with your children. Of course there are times for correction but not every time you speak! I recently heard a well known opera singer being interviewed and she was telling how negative her father had been for the whole of her life. When she was first being acclaimed as a new opera superstar she invited her parents to an opening night. After the performance she excitedly ran to them. Her father looked at her and said "At least you didn't bump into any of the scenery!" Paul's advice today is equally appropriate for parents and grandparents. Be positively positive today and that is what children will learn to be!

1 Thessalonians

1 Thessalonians

The Church of Thessalonica was planted by Paul during his second missionary journey – Acts 17. After visiting Philippi Paul travelled south to Athens with stops at Thessalonica and nearby Berea both of which showed great interest in the Gospel but also raised much hostility from enemies of the Gospel. In those days Thessalonica was the capital of Macedonia (today's northern Greece) and situated on the main road that linked the east and west extremes of the Roman Empire. This road still exists today and is part of the main shopping centre of modern day Thessaloniki. In ancient times it was a centre where many Jews lived and their ethical monotheism was found attractive by disillusioned Greeks who didn't like the empty Greek pantheism of the day. Acts 18:5 – records one of Paul's stays in Corinth and was probably the time and place when Paul wrote this letter.

Below is an acrostic which summarises each chapter of the book.

1. **F**oundation of the church
2. **A**chievements of the church
3. **I**mportance of God's love
4. **T**ruth of Christ's return
5. **H**elp for the battle

Thessalonian Partnership Works Well

The Big Picture

This letter is sent from Paul, Silas and Timothy. It is full of praise for the terrific witness of the Thessalonian Church as they anticipate the return of Jesus Christ. They remember with fondness their visit to Thessalonica after their troublesome stay in Philippi. The refreshingly positive response in Thessalonica as the local people listened, accepted and acted upon all that was shared with them. Paul reminds them that financial support was never an issue for Paul and his team as he worked hard to earn money rather than being a drain on the Thessalonian believers' resources. There is a genuine pride and respect that comes over from Paul, Silas and Timothy in this letter.

Thinking Step

When King Philip of Macedonia defeated the Thessalians he learned that his wife had given birth to a daughter. He named her Thessalonica meaning 'Victory over the Thessalians.' She went on to marry Cassander who succeeded Alexander the Great in Macedonia. When he founded a new port city he named it after his wife Thessalonica, half sister of Alexander the Great.

Action Step

1:5 – 'For when we brought you the Good News, it was not only with words but also with power, for the Holy Spirit gave you full assurance that what we said was true. You know of our concern for you from the way we lived when we were with you.'
This is a great reminder from Paul that witnessing is so much more than speaking. Many believers freeze at the thought of sharing their faith. They think that the only way to do it is by using words but Paul gives us some remarkable insights as he writes to the Thessalonian Church. I have broadened this text to provide a workable framework for personal evangelism and witnessing. I have deliberately made it personal so that they are not for someone else but are for you and me individually.

1. I must be daily in fellowship with God through prayer and His Word.
2. I must depend on the Holy Spirit at all times. No one was ever argued into the Kingdom of God.
3. I must be able to clearly give the simple facts of the Gospel that I believe and which saved me.
4. I must base all I say on the Bible. Memorising some verses can be helpful with this.
5. I must not be side-tracked into fruitless arguments no matter how tempting or interesting.

I find reviewing the basics of my faith helps strengthen my beliefs.

3 - Paul Longs To Visit Thessalonica
4 - Continue To Grow And Be Ready
5 - Stay Alert And Faithful For The Lord's Return

Day 340
1 Thessalonians 3-5
6th December

Stay Faithful For The Surprising Return Of Jesus

The Big Picture

Paul reminds the believers in Thessalonica about when Timothy came and visited them. How he was so excited when he heard such a glowing report from Timothy of all that was happening to glorify God. He tells them that he is really looking forward to visiting them soon. He rejoices with them that they are living Godly lives and urges them to keep going. Paul slots in some teaching here, confirming that when Jesus returns those who have died will rise first and then be joined by those who are still alive. He tells them to encourage each other with this news. Paul tells them we don't know the date of this return. Finally, remain faithful and honour your leaders.

Thinking Step

I used to have a job where I was responsible for hiring out school rooms. We had an enquiry for a room to celebrate the end of the world but they needed extra chairs from another school! I confirmed the room was available but asked how they would return the chairs. The response was "We'll take them back the following morning!"

Action Step

Paul is anxious that the Thessalonians may be distracted by concentrating on the Lord's return so he makes the point very clearly at the end of his letter. Rejoice in the Lord's return but live for today. Stay on target! 5:13-22 – 'Show them great respect and wholehearted love because of their work and live peacefully with each other. Brothers and sisters, we urge you to warn those who are lazy. Encourage those who are timid. Take tender care of those who are weak. Be patient with everyone. See that no one pays back evil for evil but always try to do good to each other and to all people. Always be joyful. Never stop praying. Be thankful in all circumstances, for this is God's will for you who belong to Christ Jesus. Do not stifle the Holy Spirit. Do not scoff at prophecies but test everything that is said. Hold on to what is good. Stay away from every kind of evil.' Wow! How impossible all this would be without the Holy Spirit! Distraction is one of the tools the evil one loves. If he can get believers doing good but peripheral things then he is winning. Are you doing something that, in itself is fine but which is taking time that could be spent doing something more fruit bearing? Consider your work load now. You may need to make adjustments to stay on target.

2 Thessalonians

2 Thessalonians

Paul's second letter follows on from the first one very quickly. He was almost certainly still in Corinth when he wrote it. There was still an imbalance regarding the second coming and Paul addresses this as well as the associated problem of inactivity as many sat around waiting for the Lord to return! Paul details the events that will lead up to the second coming but above it all would have been the reminder of what Jesus said about it. Matt. 24:42 – "So you, too, must keep watch! For you don't know what day your Lord is coming." Of course at that time the Gospels were probably not yet available in written form but the oral tradition was very reliable. Paul urges the Thessalonians to work each day to extend the Kingdom. It was unhelpful and wrong to sit back and wait for things to happen around you.

Below is an acrostic which summarises each chapter of the book.

1. **D**escription of their faith
2. **A**postasy in last days
3. **Y**ardstick for Christian living

Day 341
2 Thessalonians 1-3
7th December

1 - Stand Firm In This Time Of Persecution
2 - Stand Firm In Paul's Teaching About The Second Coming
3 - Stand Firm And Rebuke Those Who Will Not Work

Stand Firm And Work While You Wait

The Big Picture

Another letter from Paul, Silas and Timothy in which they praise God for the Thessalonians and their resilience in the face of all the difficulties they are experiencing. He reminds them that God will take care of those who are persecuting His Church. Paul warns them to disregard some of the fanciful ideas about the second coming of Christ. They are wrong and very unhelpful. He tells them to remember what they were taught by him in writing as well as in person. He has already assured them of his continued prayer and closes by asking them to pray for him and the rest of his workers. A final word for all those sitting around 'No work = No food!'

Thinking Step

Have you noticed that Paul's letters seem to be getting shorter and shorter? Beginning with Romans which is the longest, each letter gets slightly shorter until we reach 2 Thessalonians which is the shortest of Paul's nine letters to fellowships in the early Church. There seems no other explanation for the order of these epistles other than their length!

Action Step

When we launched Walk Through the Bible in the UK in 1984 we had no funds or even promise of funds. It surprises me how little we doubted and how much we simply had faith in a God who would work things out! We taught events and sold books and the accounts balanced. As we grew we attracted financial supporters, some of whom have been with us since the very beginning and they have enabled us to extend our work into schools and colleges. We continue to thank God for them. We always believed that individuals who benefited from our ministry should wherever possible play their part by paying towards our costs. It was an approach that was not without its critics but we were then and we are now convinced that it was the right path for us to tread. In our reading today Paul takes a very hard line – 3:10 – "...Those unwilling to work will not get to eat." His work ethic was very firm and typical of rabbis of his day who always had money earning skills as well as ministry gifting. Am I playing my full part in the ministry of the Church? Should I be giving more time or just being a wiser steward of what God has entrusted to me in my gifting and finances? What is God saying to each of us today?

1 Timothy

1 Timothy

After his invaluable writing to the early Church Paul focuses his later efforts encouraging the leadership that will continue the work he has laboured hard to establish. These next four letters have become known as the 'Pastoral Epistles'. There are some questions about their author being Paul himself but he remains the best option by far. The first letter is addressed to Timothy and was probably written after the imprisonment recorded in Acts 28. Paul had probably been freed for further ministry and may even have visited Spain – Rom. 15:24. It was during a period in Macedonia when he acknowledged that the next generation needed preparation to 'carry the baton' so he wrote to Timothy who he regarded as 'a true child in the faith' – 1:2. Paul shares his visions and concerns with Timothy and clearly trusted him to 'carry on the good work.'

Below is an acrostic which summarises each chapter of the book.

1. **A**dvice concerning false teachings
2. **D**irections for Godly women
3. **V**irtues of Christian elders
4. **I**nstructions for Godly living
5. **C**ounsel concerning the widows
6. **E**ffects of worldly living

Get The Foundation Right Timothy

The Big Picture

This is probably the earliest example we have of Paul writing a personal letter to a Pastor. He shares something of his testimony and urges Timothy to confront those who are teaching heretical distortions of the Gospel. People who were constantly looking back to Judaism or deliberately misunderstanding the teaching they heard regularly would be a headache for young Timothy. God was gracious with Paul so Timothy can be secure that He will be gracious with him too. 'Don't forget to pray for those in civic authority' is a timely reminder to Timothy who has so much to learn. The roles and qualifications of elders and deacons are clearly described and have been a 'Leadership Manual' or Biblical blueprint ever since.

Thinking Step

The simple Gospel was being confused by some who 'thought they knew better! – (gnostics).' Paul warns Timothy in chapter one about...

v3 – Teachers of wrong doctrines   v6 – Teachers talking foolishly
v4 – Myths and endless genealogies   v7 – Teachers ignorant of the Scriptures

Paul gave Timothy simple advice – v19 – 'Cling tightly to your faith in Christ and keep your conscience clear.'

Action Step

Paul is very honest with Timothy right from the beginning of this personal letter. He describes the problems in the Church and how important it was to combat them. Paul is also very candid about his own imperfections. In 1:2 he describes himself as once being a blasphemer and persecutor of the early Church. He also confirms that he was a violent man against the same people whom he now loves as his brothers and sisters in Christ. He had so much in his past to drag him back if he had been so minded but he wasn't! In Phil. 3:13 Paul urges believers to be – '...forgetting the past and looking forward to what lies ahead.' In this brief concept I believe we have a very important quality that should be in our lives day by day. All of us have things that can stunt our growth if we persist in looking back at them. Like the Apostle Paul I urge you to keep pressing on in the knowledge that we have all done wrong things in the past but we have the assurance that God has forgiven us. Are there things right now that the devil constantly uses as breaks to slow your progress down? Ask God to strengthen you to put these things away once and for all and go on from strength to strength in your ministry for Jesus Christ today.

Day 343
1 Timothy 4-6
9th December

4 - Always Put The Scriptures First
5 - Pastor The Flock Faithfully
6 - Live Lives Worthy Of Jesus

Live Lives Founded On Christ And The Bible

The Big Picture

Paul warns that when the last days approach some will fall away because of the false teaching by false teachers who are serving their own needs rather than being called of God to minister to His people. He especially encourages Timothy to continue his faithful ministry week by week despite being young! He tells him to stay true and exercise the gifting that God has given him – respecting everyone, caring for the needy and paying the Church leadership where appropriate. On a personal note Paul suggests that Timothy looks after himself by drinking wine medicinally. Paul tells him to urge all to live Godly caring lives and then reminds the wealthy that 'they can't take it with them' when they die!

Thinking Step

Some years ago a leading clergyman was interviewed on TV and asked about his teetotal convictions. In particular he was asked about Paul's advice to Timothy to take a little wine for his stomach's sake – 5:23. Undisturbed he answered "He didn't say to drink it! I believe it was meant to be rubbed into the skin of his tummy!"

Action Step

4:13 – '...focus on reading the Scriptures to the Church, encouraging the believers and teaching them.' The order of priorities used by Paul is rather interesting. Scripture first, then encouragement and then teaching. I remember attending a Church with some relatives and feeling really 'beaten down' by the preacher. I asked one of my relatives how she was getting on with her minister she gave an interesting reply. "I do feel like a tent peg sometimes as Sunday by Sunday I am hammered a little lower into the ground!" Her minister got the order wrong didn't he? He was faithful to reading and teaching the Scriptures then but he was missing out encouragement altogether. We must encourage one another. If we don't encourage our congregations there is a danger of them feeling worse when they leave Church than they did when they arrived. Actually when you look at the average congregations coming out of Church on a Sunday morning it makes you suspect my experience wasn't unique! In my view disregarding encouragement is an ideal way to dissuade your Church from doing anything positive! They certainly won't have the time or inclination to encourage each other or reach out to their neighbours if they have not been encouraged and prepared for it! When unsure – encourage – but remember to teach the Bible faithfully first!

2 Timothy

2 Timothy

It appears Paul is back in prison when he writes to Timothy for a second time. This letter was probably the last one that Paul wrote which has survived. 4:13 indicates that he was in a cold prison now rather than under 'house arrest' as described in Acts 28. Christianity was under growing persecution from Rome which was led by Emperor Nero who blamed them for the fire in Rome which destroyed half of the city in 64 AD. By now Timothy was leading the Church in Ephesus. Paul urges Timothy to use the Word of God to combat the persecution and faithfully proclaim the Gospel even if it results in more persecution. He has already given him a 'Leadership Manual' but now he delivers a 'Combat Manual' with his personal encouragement to stand up for all he believes even if the going seems to be getting tougher.

Below is an acrostic which summarises each chapter of the book.

1. **H**onour the true Gospel
2. **O**bedience to God's Word
3. **L**essons of last days
4. **D**iligently preach God's Word

1 - You Must Never Be Ashamed
2 - You Must Always Be Ready For Action
3 - You Can Always Rely On God's Word
4 - Your God Is Faithful To The End

Day 344
2 Timothy 1-4
10th December

Be Encouraged – Never Be Downhearted

The Big Picture

Paul begins by telling Timothy that he is longing to see him again soon. He tells him not to be ashamed of the God he serves nor the fact that Paul is in prison again. He sounds rather isolated as he confirms all his friends from Asia who he used to see, now no longer come near. Paul encourages Timothy to be always vigilant and ready to be a clean instrument for God. He describes his society and it sounds very like ours in the 21st century! He reminds him that the Scriptures remain reliable and very effective. In this emotional and personal letter Paul is convinced his end is near but he rejoices in the glory that awaits him.

Thinking Step

Chapter two. The essential daily reading for every Christian...
1. A multiplying ministry – v 1-2, Teach others what you've learned.
2. An enduring ministry – v 3-13, Endure suffering as a soldier of Christ.
3. A studying ministry – v 14-18, Work hard and stick to the right path.
4. A Holy ministry – v 19-26, Keep yourself pure and available to work.

Action Step

Never a century passes without someone somewhere declaring a 'new truth' or the discovery of a new bit of information that disproves the Bible that has underpinned our faith since the very beginning. These theories come and go but rarely stick around for long. It seems they were already around back in the days of Timothy when Paul simply advises him to stick with the Word of God never mind all the negativity bombarding him about all he has been taught. It seems to me that most new discoveries are only news if they are negative to the Christian faith. If they substantiate the Bible or some element of our teaching then they're not deemed worthy of reporting! The Church I currently attend has been described as that place where they worship Father, Son and Holy Bible! Not accurate at all but a firm reminder that the Bible really is important even though it can't compete with the Trinity! The Apostle Paul declares in 4:2 – 'Preach the Word of God. Be persistent whether the time is favourable or not. Patiently correct, rebuke and encourage your people with good teaching.' This is great advice. Of course it doesn't mean burying your head in the sand rather than investigating false teaching. Our faith will stand any amount of criticism because it is based on the truth and the risen Son of the Living God. Be ready to stand today.

Titus & Philemon

Titus & Philemon

Titus is the leader of the Church in Crete when Paul writes to him in a similar vein to his letters to Timothy. By doing this he was playing his part in preparing the next generation of leaders. Some believe Titus could even have been the brother of Luke. Paul refers to him as his 'true child in the faith ...' – 1:4. Crete was notorious for its deceit and immorality. If you were an immoral liar you were often referred to as a 'cretan.' The letter to Titus was probably written by Paul about the same time as 1 Timothy. Philemon has a different 'flavour' altogether as it was written to accompany a runaway slave called Onesimus when he returned to his master Philemon – verse 10. It was one of the 'prison epistles' written by Paul during his imprisonment in Acts 28. His pleads for Christian compassion for brother Onesimus.

Below is an acrostic which summarises each chapter of the book.

Titus

1. **S**ermon for qualified elders
2. **O**bject of sound doctrine
3. **N**eed for good works

Philemon

1-7   **L**ove of brother Philemon
8-14   **O**nesimus becomes a Christian
15-20 **V**indication requested for Onesimus
21-25 **E**xpectation expressed by Paul

Day 345
Titus & Philemon
11th December

1 - Appoint Elders and Dismiss False Teachers
2 - Encourage Sound Teaching
3 - Promote Good Works
Philemon - Treat Him Like a Brother

Leaders Must Teach Well And Live Like Christ

The Big Picture

Titus is not mentioned in Acts but is obviously a trusted co-worker of Paul – 2 Cor. 7 and 2 Tim. 4. Having been left in Crete by Paul – 1:5 Titus then receives this letter to further help him in his important task of keeping the Church sound and Biblical. Paul reminds him of the sort of people he is dealing with and how important it is to have sound reliable leaders to work alongside him. Paul goes into some detail about relationships and the importance of sound teaching producing Godly living. The earlier letter to Philemon is a very practical one and is probably the primary reason that escaped slave Onesimus felt safe returning to his old master.

Thinking Step

Paul is not renowned for his humour! In his short letter to Philemon we have a rare example. Verse 11 – 'Onesimus hasn't been of much use to you in the past but now is very useful to both of us.' As the name Onesimus means 'useful' you can almost hear Paul adding 'Boom Boom!' to this feeble attempt at humour!

Action Step

2:2-8 – Paul declares that there is an obligation for Titus to do all he can to equip believers to live Holy and God honouring lives. He is to teach...

1. Older men to exercise self control and have a strong faith filled with love and patience.
2. Older women not to speak evil of others but set a good example.
3. Young women to each look after their husband and children and also their home.
4. Young men to live wisely in all they do.

Remember that discipling and mentoring can never be just the responsibility of the leaders in our Churches. Titus appointed elders to work with him and I am sure other believers supported them in their work. The question is "Are you playing your part in discipling and maturing believers in your congregation?" It's not just youngsters who need your best 'role model example' and kindest words but older folk too. In our country which has turned its back on God for many decades we are now seeing people of all ages turning to Christ with little or no knowledge of the Bible or Christian lifestyle. Why not consider taking a positive step this Sunday by doing a little more than just saying 'Good morning." You may be the very one who will help your leaders do the work that Paul is urging Titus to do.

Hebrews

Hebrews

This letter to the Hebrews is unique in several ways. It is specifically addressed to those Jews who have recognised Jesus as Messiah and have turned to Him. However they soon find themselves under pressure to return to mainstream Judaism where life would be much safer. We know little of when it was written or who wrote it but it seems likely that it was written before the Temple destruction in 70 AD as no reference is made to this disaster for the Jews. Having said that some would date it much later in the first century as persecution is a real threat. Ironically its writer appears to have a poor knowledge of the Hebrew language as references are always from the Greek Septuagint. Its overall message is of the supremacy of Christ. He is greater than all who went before Him and offers the supreme sacrifice, priesthood and covenant.

Below is an acrostic which summarises each chapter of the book.

1. **N**ature of God's Son
2. **E**ffect of Christ's sacrifice
3. **W**rath reserved for unbelief

4. **P**romise of God's rest
5. **R**emembering the High Priest
6. **I**dentity of the Priest
7. **E**xamination of Melchizedek Priesthood
8. **S**uperiority of new covenant
9. **T**estimony of Christ's blood
10. **H**oliness through Christ's sacrifice
11. **O**ld Testament examples of faith
12. **O**bject of Christian living
13. **D**uties of the Christians

Christ Is Supreme And Deserves Our Devotion

The Big Picture

The writer shares their amazing revelation that over the years God sent prophets but now He has sent His only Son who is superior to the angels in Heaven. There is a warning for believers that they must listen carefully to what is being said now. Along with many other Jews the writer is aware that messages already received from angels were really from God and were therefore totally trustworthy and true. However what God has done now is so much better than this and must not be ignored. The astounding truth is that Jesus became lower than the Angels and became a man and then the ultimate sacrifice to reconcile Abraham's descendants with their God.

Thinking Step

We nearly didn't have Hebrews in the Bible! Not until the 4th century was it generally accepted as authoritative thanks to the support of Jerome and Augustine who recognised its undoubted inspirational qualities. The early Church loosely attached it to Paul's writings as his 14th epistle. Many candidates to be its writer have been suggested but 'Anon' seems the most likely!

Action Step

I don't know about you but I don't want second best when the best is available. These first two chapters of Hebrews make it abundantly clear that angels are second best and Jesus is the best. Isn't it remarkable that there are still lots of people who believe in angels rather than believing in Jesus who is their superior. I have heard people state their belief in angels as though it's something new. Belief in angels is as old as the Bible itself with many examples and encounters recorded in both the Old and New Testaments. However the writer to the Hebrews is simply declaring that we now have something or more accurately someone who is better! I think in the 21st century deep down everyone is looking for spiritual reality in their lives. Turning to angels is far less demanding than turning to Jesus and you don't even have to go to Church! I know that many of our new Church attenders who come from a Biblically illiterate world don't really know what they are looking for. We have a duty and a privilege to make sure, with the Holy Spirit's help, to guide folk to Jesus rather than a 'second class' spiritual experience. I believe the devil is more than happy when we worship angels or anything else that will keep us away from the 'real thing.' Be sure to keep Jesus at the centre of your life today.

Day 347
Hebrews 3-5
13th December

3 - Jesus Is Superior To Moses
4 - Ultimate Rest Is Being Offered By God
5 - Jesus Is Our High Priest

Jesus Is Supreme And He's Our High Priest

The Big Picture

The writer of Hebrews urges Jewish believers to consider Jesus as superior to Moses. Moses was a faithful servant for God but Jesus is God's only Son! Many were hard hearted and refused what was offered in Moses' time. Don't miss out on God's gracious offer today. The position of High Priest could not be earned but had to be offered by God as it was to Aaron. Today God has appointed Jesus to be the ultimate High Priest for all who believe. In frustration the writer asks the readers if this is too hard for them to understand and accept! They are challenged to move on from milk for babies to meat which is for all maturing believers.

Thinking Step

4:13 – '...Everything is naked and exposed before His eyes ...' Wrestlers fought naked in those days and this is the vivid imagery here. Naked so that nothing can be hidden. Exposed as if gripped by the throat and unable to move with your powerful opponent staring into your face and you can look nowhere else but into his eyes.

Action Step

3:15 – 'Remember what it says "Today when you hear his voice, don't harden your hearts as Israel did when they rebelled."' The Hebrews are being told that their fathers have already missed a golden opportunity once when Moses was leading them. They must not miss this even richer chance when God has sent His only Son to redeem His people. This is too good a chance to fritter away. I remember my Dad telling me that he had often heard the Gospel when he was growing up but I could never get him to admit that he had either rejected or accepted Jesus. He never told me! I hold on to the hope that in his last days in hospital the Holy Spirit would have brought these thoughts back into his mind. What about you? I am sure like me you have heard preachers talk about this possibly being your last chance to receive Jesus. By definition one of them has to be your last. The harsh reality is that we all will have a last chance but we don't know when that will be. I don't believe this is a time for drama and emotionalism but for sheer reality. A decision cannot be nearly made any more than you can be nearly pregnant! It's one thing or another. No middle ground. Don't waste what could be your last chance – turn to Day 21 and accept Christ.

6 - Grow Up And Become Mature
7 - Jesus Is Superior To Melchizedek
8 - The New Covenant Is Superior To The Old One

Day 348
Hebrews 6-8
14th December

Jesus And His New Covenant Are Supreme

The Big Picture

Our reading today begins with a plea to "Grow Up!" To get away from the beginnings of faith and get to grips with the more mature aspects of it. The writer is convinced that back sliders are almost impossible to win back so don't go there. When Abraham took God at His word he showed us all that God can be trusted. This was confirmed as God rewarded Abraham for believing. Jesus is our new High Priest. The argument continues, Melchizedek was revered by Abraham with tithes as the tribe of Levi has been for many years. However in Christ we have a complete sacrifice which is superior and needs never to be repeated.

Thinking Step

Melchizedek. His name is made up from two Hebrew words. Melek meaning King and tsedeq meaning righteousness. He is mentioned twice in the Old Testament – Gen. 14:18 and Psalm 110:4 but several times in Hebrews where we find he has no ancestral record. Many have concluded that as King of righteousness and without parentage Melchizedek must have been Jesus Christ Himself.

Action Step

I preached at a Church many years ago but was never invited back! My sin was that I didn't preach a Gospel message to an elderly congregation that I later learned hadn't changed for decades! If I ever get another chance to preach there my text would be Heb. 6:1 – 'So let us stop going over the basic teachings about Christ again and again. Let us go on instead and become mature in our understanding...' Immature Churches are often as a direct result of shallow or incomplete teaching and inadequate 'self-discipling.' I have talked to folk many times who have faithfully attended Church for many years and yet have a faith as thin as tissue paper despite being 'under the Word' every week. What's the solution to being a baby? Growing up! Unlike physical growing over which we have little control, spiritual growing is something that will not happen unless each person puts some effort into it! Of course we need the work of the Holy Spirit in our lives for any maturing to take place but an essential ingredient will always be some effort on our part. So when was the last time you made a real effort to grow up a little more? Has something immature in your life popped into your mind just now? Why not ask God to help you bring that aspect of your life out of the infantile into maturity?

Many Sacrifices Were Inadequate
One Sacrifice Is Enough

The Big Picture

The first covenant involved a tent which was divided into two areas by a curtain. This was then common knowledge to all Jews. They were aware that only the High Priest could enter the Holy of Holies. Don't forget however that the Temple was destroyed in 70 AD. God removed it because the unique sacrifice of Jesus was enough for all people and for all time. Until Jesus came the repetition of sacrifices seemed destined to go on forever. All of this was abolished and replaced by the unique sacrifice of Jesus Christ. Depending on the date when Hebrews was written the Temple's destruction had just happened or would happen very soon. God's replacement plan then became a physical reality!

Thinking Step

10:4 – 'For it is not possible for the blood of bulls and goats to take away sins.' Link this with John 14:6 – 'I am the way, the truth and the life. No one can come to the Father except through me.' There may be things to admire in other religions but never lose sight of Jesus' unique saving power.

Action Step

10:25 – '...let us not neglect our meeting together, as some people do, but encourage one another, especially now that the day of His return is drawing near.' Of course simply attending Church only makes us Church attenders! In itself it does not make us Christians any more than me spending years queueing and paying to see Sunderland AFC play at Roker Park made me a footballer! Why do you attend Church? Of course in the early Church they did not 'go to Church' as there were no buildings to meet in. They gathered together in homes or other suitable meeting places. Proper Church buildings were unknown until Christianity became the state religion under Emperor Constantine in the 4th century. Then the rot set in but that's another story! I know there are loads of Churches that have well structured home groups but I don't know of any congregation where more than 50% of them regularly attend them! In our home group we have some great times of learning and fun – especially at our open question evenings. There is an atmosphere of growing and maturing. This is the place where true discipling takes place. Simply preaching from the front doesn't do it. If you are not a member of a home group – you should be! If there isn't one nearby then why not consider talking to your leadership about you having one? This could help others as well as you.

11 - The Faithful Believers Of The Past
12 - Endure Difficulties As Positive Things
13 - Live Holy Lives That Honour God

Day 350
Hebrews 11-13
16th December

Be Faithful And Live Godly Lives

The Big Picture

Chapter eleven is full of faithful men and women of the Old Testament. Some well known by name and reputation whilst others are anonymous but nevertheless all are commended for their faith. The writer of Hebrews then challenges believers, in the light of all their faithful ancestors. We need to remember that we are inheriting a Kingdom that cannot be destroyed. Accept today's persecution as discipline from your Heavenly Father. After all, a good Father disciplines his children as an act of love. The final challenges of this letter are to live lives loving each other. Honouring marriage and shunning the love of money. In these difficult times remember Jesus never changes and is always totally reliable.

Thinking Step

Stanley Baldwin, three times Prime Minister of the UK said "If I did not believe that our work was done in the faith and hope that some day, it may be a million years hence, the Kingdom of God will spread over the whole world, I would have no hope, I could do no work, and I would resign from office..."

Action Step

11:1 – 'Faith is the confidence that what we hope for will actually happen, it gives us assurance about things we cannot see.' Today we have read about many examples of faith from men and women throughout history. They stimulate me but they intimidate me too! It is so easy for faith to begin well and to slip into pride and then arrogance before you know where you are! Or even worse it may collapse altogether! I recall attending a thanksgiving service for a friend who was a stalwart of the faith and a very active and effective man of God. Several folk spoke about him and recalled stories of his great faith in the God he served all of his adult life. The man leading the service who had a similar reputation for being a giant of the faith closed the service with a beautiful bit of honesty which made a bigger impression on me than all the other dynamic comments. He said "Let me address those of us who have doubts and fears and may be 'blown away' by all that has been said so far. I have to say that my faith is so weak compared to that of our friend. However it's not how much faith but who the faith is in. Mine is in Christ and if yours is too then we are on the winning side and we can rejoice in that truth today."

James

James

A likely candidate as author of this letter is a brother of Jesus Christ – Matt. 13:55. More accurately of course he was a half brother with Mary as his mother and Joseph as his father. He is very likely to be the same James who was a prominent leader in the early Church in Jerusalem – Acts 12:17 and a leader in the Jerusalem Council – Acts 15:13. According to Josephus, James was martyred in 62 AD. This letter could easily be the earliest part of the New Testament with a date as early as 45 AD being suggested due to the distinct lack of Gentile converts referred to in 1:1. There is little theology but many practical suggestions in James. He challenges those who say they have faith to show it in their daily lives. In short he declares that faith without works is dead!

Below is an acrostic which summarises each chapter of the book.

1. **W**isdom of following Christ
2. **O**utline for good works
3. **R**ules for avoiding worldliness
4. **K**nowledge that corrects worldliness
5. **S**igns of His coming

Day 351   1 - Faithfully Listen And Then Act Accordingly
James 1-3   2 - Faithfully Treat Everyone As Equals
17th December   3 - Faithfully Keep Your Tongue Under Control

Real Faith Transforms Lives

The Big Picture

James begins on a positive note by urging his readers to make opposition into opportunities. He tells them that they must have faith that results in actions. They must also treat others equally and stop giving special treatment to the influential and wealthy in their meetings. He shares the serious thought that breaking a single law means you have broken the whole Law. Teaching is a very important role within the Church so prospective teachers need to consider everything very carefully before becoming a teacher. Overall James warns of the power of the tongue. Like a ship's rudder can steer an enormous vessel so the tongue can guide or manipulate a whole person for good or bad.

Thinking Step

Matt 13:55 '...we know Mary his mother and his brothers – James, Joseph, Simon and Judas.' Some prefer to take the KJV translation which talks of brethren rather than brothers. This means James and the others could be close relatives of Jesus but not sons of Mary. The word 'adelphos' can mean brother or close relative but brother suits the context best.

Action Step

James presents a simple and yet profound fundamental of the Christian faith. Faith changes people if it's real faith. Many religions in the world simply demand compliance to certain acts or methods of worship. Christianity goes further and insists on internal faith changing outward behaviour. It is so much easier for faith to be in one pocket and available to use when appropriate but Christian faith is so much bigger than that. A well known British politician was asked about his faith and he said it was real and a substantial aid and comfort to him. When asked if it was helpful in making decisions in government his response was interesting. He said that his faith was personal and had little to do with detailed policy decisions. His faith was a very personal part of his life. I wonder what James would say about that? I would give the benefit of the doubt to the politician but conclude that if he only makes decisions from a political stance then his spiritual life will be seriously restricted. With real faith I believe there is no choice about it influencing daily thought. All convictions do that. The only question is whether you will allow your faith to influence actions in your life! When a decision is called for today give the Holy Spirit's opinion top slot rather than just relying on your own judgement! You'll be amazed by the difference.

Trust God Daily And Minister To One Another

The Big Picture

There is no need to be jealous of what others have. Ask God and He will supply all your needs when your motives are right. Resist the devil and draw close to God. Don't plan your future in too much detail because none of us knows what is going to happen tomorrow. Look around at the wealthy among you and witness that riches don't satisfy completely and are nothing but a burden after death! Just be patient as you await the Lord's return. Regarding taking oaths, keep them simple. A simple 'Yes' or 'No' is ideal. Pray for the sick amongst you and you will be pleasantly surprised what the simple prayers of believers can achieve.

Thinking Step

5:2b – '...your fine clothes are moth-eaten rags.' In Bible times clothes were so much more than things to wear, they were an alternative currency. Gen. 45:22 – ...Joseph gave...Benjamin...five changes of clothes...' – Judges 14:12 – 'Samson said "...If you solve my riddle... I will give you thirty fine linen robes and thirty sets of festive clothing."'

Action Step

4:11b – '...your job is to obey the law, not to judge whether it applies to you.' If ever there was a pithy statement that the 21st century would benefit from hearing this is it! Try chastising a litter dropper in the UK and in amongst the likely blasphemy strewn reply you will hear something like "If it wasn't for people like me there would be more unemployment. I am creating work for folk!" Some years ago one of my sons witnessed a litter dropper in a restaurant car park and was so incensed that he followed him home in his car! Not a wise thing to do when he had time to consider later. On stopping outside his home it turned out that the litterer was a member of a nearby local fellowship and recognised my son. The offender was suitably repentant and embarrassed and promised not to transgress again! When James is referring to the law in our reading today he was probably referring to the Jewish Law rather than civil law but in those days the two merged in most people's minds. In any case I believe the principle is the same today. As believers we are to honour the law even when we don't agree with it. Please bear this in mind as you go about your daily tasks today as a law abiding citizen.

1 Peter

1 Peter

Traditionally attributed to Peter and despite some recent doubts there are still no better candidates than Simon Peter himself. This letter is addressed to believers scattered throughout the nearby Roman dominated Asia Minor. The first half of the letter concentrates on what Christians should believe and how they should live. The second half has a lot to say about the practicalities of withstanding the persecution that the early Church was experiencing. There is no reference to early Church leadership such as deacons or bishops which indicates it was written quite early. Many believe it was written in Rome around 67 AD immediately after the persecution by Nero. The city where traditionally Peter was crucified. This was at a time when there was still growing suspicions of this new religion which spoke of a new Kingdom to come and which was still distrusted by many after the fire of Rome incident.

Below is an acrostic which summarises each chapter of the book.

1. **T**eaching about Christian trials
2. **R**esults of following Christ
3. **I**nsights into God's love
4. **A**dvice for unjust suffering
5. **L**essons for the elders

Stand Firm And Grow In Your Faith

The Big Picture

Peter writes to a Church which has been scattered as far as nearby Asia Minor. Despite current problems Peter encouraged them that there is so much better for believers to look forward to. He confirms that they have total security in Christ because the ransom has been paid through Jesus' death and resurrection. He warns them not to slide back into their old ways of living. He begs them to love one another and support those civic leaders who are in authority over them. He reminds them that just as Jesus suffered for them they should not be surprised if they have to suffer too when they live as His followers.

Thinking Step

In 2:24 Peter describes the cross with the word 'xulon' which is a piece of tree. It seems to be a favourite word of his as he uses it when preaching in Acts – 5:30 and when he speaks to Cornelius in Acts 10:39. It is unused by other Gospel writers and is rarely used by Paul.

Action Step

Just recently I saw a young man who seemed familiar but I couldn't place him. This seems to be happening more and more but that's another subject! You know how it is, your brain keeps on exploring your hard drive memory and out of nowhere you suddenly recall where you have seen him before. He used to be one of our young people at Church. He must have slipped away and now no longer attended our Church. Maybe he was attending another? I don't know. The following day I read this portion of 1 Peter and the words in 2:3 really hit me 'Like newborn babies, you must crave pure spiritual milk so that you will grow into a full experience of salvation.' So why didn't he? Why didn't we enthuse him with the excitement of the Gospel? All unanswered questions! More to the point, how can we make sure there are less casualties? It's a fine line between being aware of someone who shows an interest in spiritual things compared to frightening them off like an inadequate rabid salesman! I think very few of us 'overdo' it when we meet this situation. Most of us 'underdo' it just in case we cause offence. Just be sure to do something next time an opportunity presents itself and if enough of us are like minded then the number of casualties should drop considerably. Just be sensitively aware!

3 - Godly Witness Between Wives And Husbands

4 - Godly Witness For Friends And Neighbours

5 - Godly Respect To Leaders And Each Other

Day 354

1 Peter 3-5

20th December

Shine Out Even In Difficult Times

The Big Picture

Wives are to be patient with unbelieving husbands and that way they will be persuaded by their Godly witness. Husbands should honour their wives at all times. The whole congregation should live together in harmony and everyone should be willing and able to explain their faith. Don't be saddened when you are rejected by former friends who don't understand what has happened to you. Keep living Godly lives and your friends will be influenced greatly. Finally, elders must keep shepherding the flock of believers. Remember all leaders are answerable to God Himself. This letter came from Peter with the help of Silas. Some believe the help was with his Greek as Galilean fishermen were not often natural linguists!

Thinking Step

3:19 – 'So He went and preached to the spirits in prison...' This preaching (kerussein) was a proclamation by Jesus of His victory over evil. The Greek word translated preached is not the one used for preaching the Good News (which is euangelizein) so must not be taken to mean there is a chance to repent and believe after death.

Action Step

4:4 – 'Of course, your former friends are surprised when you no longer plunge into the flood of wild and destructive things they do. So they slander you.' The longer you have been a Christian the harder it is to empathise with this. By now everyone you know knows you are a believer and accepts you as such. For those who have recently found Christ it is more difficult. Friends who thought they knew you now see a different you and wonder how genuine you are now. No matter how far down the Christian road you are there are regular temptations to lean a little more towards the world in order to be able to create more witnessing opportunities. In my experience this rarely works well because as soon as you do something that unbelievers think a Christian shouldn't be doing you have probably compromised too much. When I left my secular employment to enter the ministry I took everyone out to the pub for a lunchtime snack as was the tradition in my old office. One of the senior secretaries said to me "I am surprised that you did this with alcohol being involved. I thought your standards would have been higher now you are in the Church!" I didn't feel I compromised my faith and after a chat she didn't either but it was a warning that it is a very thin line and very easy to cross. Be warned!

2 Peter

2 Peter

Peter's second letter addresses problems inside the Church. These are far more difficult to deal with than the external problem of persecution which dominated his first letter. There are considerable difficulties regarding the authorship of this letter and it was not until the 4th century that it was accepted as being genuinely written by Simon Peter. Part of its difficulties could have been its brevity. Having said that 3:1 clearly claims it as Peter's second letter and the fact that this is half way through makes it more acceptable than if it had simply been added to the beginning. He was probably in Rome when he wrote it shortly before his martyrdom in 64-66 AD. He begins by encouraging all believers to grow in Christ and mature as believers. The central section warns of false teachers and he concludes with the eternal hope of the second coming of Christ.

Below is an acrostic which summarises each chapter of the book.

1. **A**doption of Godly virtues
2. **D**anger of false teachers
3. **D**octrine of Christ's return

Day 355
2 Peter
21st December

1 - Remember That Faith In God Really Works
2 - False Teachers Are Doomed To Failure
3 - God Is Patient Not Inactive

Rejoice In The Truth And Reject The False

The Big Picture

Peter urges believers to mature in Christ and constantly be aware of God's promises being fulfilled in their daily lives. He tells everyone that he probably has little time left before he will die but exhorts them to remember what they have been taught and cling tightly to the truth he taught them. He warns them of false teachers who have always been a problem since the beginning. They will be judged by God and will be total failures. He adds that as the end time approaches there will be scoffers who want to knock down all that has been built up. He tells them to endure the ridicule because believers will have the victory on judgement day!

Thinking Step

2:22 – 'They prove the truth of this proverb "A dog returns to its vomit" and another says "A washed pig returns to the mud."' Dogs and pigs are unclean to Jews and are often used to describe unbelievers and Gentiles. Peter's disgust of these false teachers brings out such a vitriolic condemnation that we are left in no doubt about his feelings.

Action Step

3:3 – 'Most importantly, I want to remind you that in the last days scoffers will come, mocking the truth and following their own desires.'
People do laugh at believers sometimes don't they? Sometimes we deserve it but sometimes it's just that people don't understand us and simply build up their own picture of us from things they have heard. Visiting door to door a few years ago we finally got a glimmer of interest from a lady in one of the houses we were visiting. She asked if the Church we were representing was the one that baptised people in a big pool. We confirmed that it was. "Oh!" she said "I could never go there." When I pressed her for more details she added "I couldn't be bothered with all that fuss. Just imagine being dipped in water every Sunday and always having to take a change of clothing to Church!" Of course we put her right but isn't it amazing what some people think we do? Of course I can live with this scoffing but it does upset me when people are so inaccurate about things that matter. Why not make it your habit to listen to what people actually say about Church and then seek a way of gently correcting them. If they spot that you are doing this you are too heavy handed! Be gentle!

1 John

1 John

As with most books of the Bible there are questions about who wrote this first of three epistles attributed to the Apostle John. Nevertheless scholars agree that there are many similarities with this letter and the Gospel of John. There are also several Johns to be encountered but to keep it as simple as possible and also to stick to the majority opinion amongst scholars, it is perfectly reasonable to accept that the Apostle John wrote the Gospel, all three epistles and Revelation. I always imagine John as an old man who is aware that time is limited as he is writing to his children in Christ. One of the principle points John emphasises in this letter is the importance of fellowship. By this time there are heresies creeping into the Church and John is at pains to get things back on an even keel for the next generation.

Below is an acrostic which summarises each chapter of the book.

1.   Lessons on the Light
2.   Instructions about God's love
3.   God's goals for Christians
4.   Help for young believers
5.   Three principles for faith

1 - Jesus Really Was Man And God Together   Day 356
2 - Love One Another - That's The Key   1 John 1-3
3 - Children Of God Will Fellowship Together   22nd December

Real Fellowship Produces Purity In Life

The Big Picture

John begins by clearly stating that Jesus was definitely a man and definitely God too. God is light and hates darkness so we must be children of light as forgiven sinners if we are to enjoy His fellowship. A basic principle which is laid down by John is that you must love one another as Christ loves us. Stick with the teaching you heard in the beginning and don't be influenced by these falsehoods that are being taught by those who deny the basic truths of what we believe about Jesus. We have the privilege of being called the children of God and our lives must reflect that as we fellowship together.

Thinking Step

In John's lifetime there was a widespread idea that Jesus was only a spirit and only seemed to be a man. This was Docetism. John clearly refutes this heresy in 1:1 – '...we saw Him... and touched Him with our own hands.' It is John's Gospel that records the breakfast at Galilee when Jesus ate with His disciples after His resurrection.

Action Step

3:8 – '...when people keep on sinning, it shows that they belong to the devil, who has been sinning since the beginning but the Son of God came to destroy the works of the devil.' This is a verse that the devil regularly hits me over the head with! The world does the same with comments like "Call yourself a Christian and you're doing that..." I remember disciplining one of our sons for deliberately disobeying me and continuing to throw stones down a drain that I had just spent an hour clearing. Of course at that very moment our next door neighbour happened to be passing by! It gave him yet another alibi not to attend Church! I believe John means repeated calculated sinning rather that slipping back into the old habits and needing to repent yet again. Remember that Paul had a real problem with doing the wrong things when he wanted so much to do the right things and vice versa – Rom. 7:19. When the devil tells you that you have sinned once too many times to still be a real believer – don't believe him. However this does not give you an alibi to keep sinning but it should give you a spur to resist a little more and ask God for victory over any long-standing defects in your character. Today would be a great day to begin.

Love Provides Real Fellowship

The Big Picture

John urges his readers to test everything and everyone. As God's children we have the Spirit of God who will enable us to discern who is false and needs to be rejected. The same is true of what is said and taught. God has shown His love for us by sending Jesus and providing His Spirit to believers. Working with God's Spirit will enable us to love like Him. If we are truly children of God we should act like them! God proved His love for us by sending Jesus so we must prove our love for each other by the way we love and live in genuine fellowship. Be sure to pray for others if you see them sinning.

Thinking Step

The heresy of gnosticism taught that only a select knowledgeable few were able to be true believers. John emphasises in this letter that God loves all men and that we are to reflect that love by loving everyone not just those who are specially knowledgeable or gifted. As he had previously written 'For God so loved the world...' – John 3:16.

Action Step

If you were giving your last words of advice I wonder what they would be. If you had lived a long faithful life and actually ministered alongside Jesus Himself what would you say towards the end of your life? Which words would you choose to influence the next generation? The Apostle John chose a beautifully simple piece of advice. His last words in this letter were – 5:21 – 'Dear children, keep away from anything that might take God's place in your hearts.' Literally 'Keep yourselves from idols.' In chapter four John refers to love almost thirty times! We are to love as God loves in Jesus and the only way to do that is for Him to be central. Are there things in your life that 'might' take God's place? Then they need to be moved or sometimes removed altogether in order to give God His necessary central place. Remember that things which have replaced God's central place in your life are not necessarily bad. There may be some that are simply taking too much time already and we need to prune or remove them. There may be some new ventures that seem very attractive but we haven't found time for them yet. It could be that we shouldn't find time for them! Check it out with God first and be careful to keep away from anything that might take God's place in your hearts.

2 John, 3 John & Jude

2 John, 3 John & Jude

Both of these short letters of John state that they are from 'the elder.' The Apostle John is the likely writer. They were written after the letter of 1 John, probably from Ephesus and for the Asia Minor Churches. They are very brief and address the issue of supporting visiting preachers who are commended by John. The issue of heretical teaching is growing and obviously John who was the last living link with the historical Jesus is very concerned that the true Gospel should not be distorted. There are close links between the letters of Jude and 2 Peter in combating heresy in the early Church. In fact as the New Testament letters come to a close the warnings of heresy get louder! Jude brother of James, was possibly a brother of Jesus – Matt. 13:55. He attacks heresy and its promoters and closes with the greatest doxology in the Bible.

Below is an acrostic which summarises each chapter of the book.

2 John

1-3   Lady and her children
4-6   Admonition to love others
7-11   Detection of the Antichrist
12-13 Yearning to see again

3 John

1-4   Greetings to brother Gaius
5-6   Actions toward ministering brethren
7-8   Invest in God's work
9-10   Unjust words of Diotrephes
11-14 Special thanks to Demetrius

Jude

1-4   Jude's warnings against apostasy
5-7   Urgent warning against unbelief
8-19   Description of false teachers
20-25 Encouragement to stay faithful

Resist False Teaching And Cling To The Truth

The Big Picture

2 John is addressed to 'chosen lady' and her 'children' – probably analogies for the Church. We all need to love one another and remain a unified fellowship despite ridiculous untruths being taught about Jesus not having been a real man. Bolt the door on these preachers. 3 John is more personal and is addressed to faithful Gaius. It contains criticism against Diotrephes who is being very antagonistic. John pleads with the local leadership to listen to sound preaching from itinerant preachers who are commended by him. Jude's letter reflects a change of heart. He had planned to write about their common salvation but instead writes a warning about heresies which are encouraging immorality and which must be condemned.

Thinking Step

Jude is a shortened version of Judas which is the Greek form of the Hebrew name Judah. He was a son of Jacob – Gen. 29 and became founder of the tribe of Judah. The name was very popular until Judas Iscariot brought shame on it. Even today in the 21st century it's a name few parents choose!

Action Step

Having implored believers to love one another John continues his theme in these two short letters but with a sharper cutting edge aimed at heretics. It must have been heart breaking for the last of the twelve disciples to see their clean precise pure Gospel being distorted by those who professed to be followers of Jesus. I think we all know how he felt when we hear criticism from within our Churches today from men and women who are part of the Church rather than genuine critics from outside. John and Jude both tell us that we need to combat error but in a loving positive way. Simply denouncing heresy is not enough. We need to promote the truth and trust the Holy Spirit to do His sovereign work. I am convinced that a lot of the criticism aimed at Christianity is actually against the Church – you and me! One of the 'evangelical' rampant antagonistic atheists of the 21st century said this "I have nothing against God. It's His followers that I can't stand!" Check your lifestyle today to see if there are things there that don't project a true pure image of Jesus. These are the things we need to change rather than simply throwing proof texts around. We must denounce untruth but even more we must love as Jesus loved in every aspect of our daily lives.

Revelation

Revelation

This book was written by the Apostle John when he was exiled on the Island of Patmos. As John's authorship was readily acknowledged it very quickly became accepted in the early Church. It was written at a time when Roman persecution under the Emperor Domitian, (81 – 96 AD) was becoming harder to bear. Revelation begins with messages to the seven main Churches in Asia Minor where John had spent much of his time as a missionary and Church planter. John's writing plan is best described in the words of Jesus 1:19 – 'Write down what you have seen – both the things that are now happening and the things that will happen.' He does this faithfully. He fills the first three chapters with the things he has seen and which are now happening. The final nineteen chapters look into what is yet to happen using amazing imagery and apocalyptic language.

Below is an acrostic which summarises each chapter of the book.

1. **P**icture of coming events
2. **R**evelation to seven churches
3. **O**utcome of falling away
4. **P**raise before the throne
5. **H**oly Lamb is worshipped
6. **E**vents of the seals
7. **C**ries from the tribulation
8. **Y**oke of the trumpets

9. **A**nnouncement of the woes
10. **B**enefit of the book
11. **O**utcome of two witnesses
12. **U**pset of Satan's plan
13. **T**error of the beast

14. **T**orment for the unbelievers
15. **H**orror of the vials
16. **E**mptying of the bowls

17. **F**ormation of ten horns
18. **U**ltimate judgement of Babylon
19. **T**heme of Second Coming
20. **U**nion of death and hell
21. **R**adiance of New Jerusalem
22. **E**ternal reward of obedience

The Seven Churches

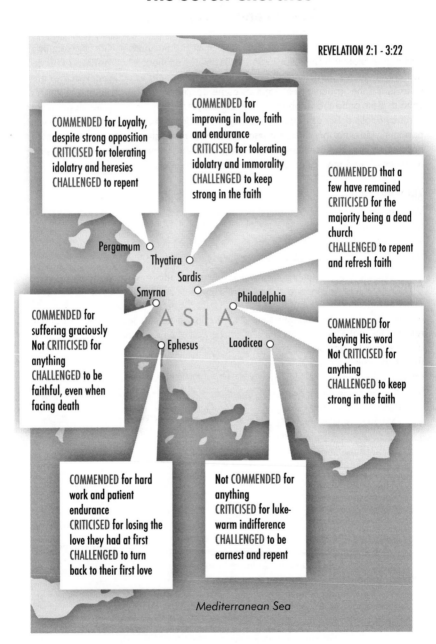

1 - Revelation From Jesus To John For All Of Us   Day 359
2 - Messages For Ephesus, Smyrna, Pergamum And Thyatira   Revelation 1-3
3 - Messages For Sardis, Philadelphia And Laodicea   25th December

Seven Letters From Jesus

The Big Picture

This is a revelation from Jesus to John. John tells us that he is in exile on Patmos as punishment for preaching about Jesus – 1:9. We need to be very clear that this book is not the revelations of John as some describe it but a single revelation for John to pass on to the Churches of Asia Minor. He receives them personally from Jesus and falls down as dead when he sees Him in all His glory. John knew Jesus personally so what happened underlines that the Jesus in Heaven is vastly more impressive than the earthly Jesus. John also knew these Churches well and the messages would have affected him as much as they would each Church.

Thinking Step

What a great day to begin the last book of the Bible! Revelation is a book which talks of the future and the second coming of Jesus Christ. Christmas day is when we remember the first coming of Jesus as a baby and is such an appropriate day to remember the second coming when Jesus will come as King!

Action Step

These seven Churches are nothing but memories today. In fact for some all physical remains have disappeared completely. However what Jesus says to them is equally relevant for many today. Why not read the precis of all seven that is laid out below and then ask God to pinpoint one of the comments for your own life today? On this Christmas day when we remember the perfect gift of His Son let's make a special effort to act positively to remedy our personal weaknesses which are shown to us from the messages to the seven Churches.

Ephesus – Very vigilant but your first love has gone. *Is this true for you?*

Smyrna – More troubles are coming but you will survive. *Remember God is in control!*

Pergamum – Steadfast but you are overlooking wickedness in your fellowship. *Repent and stay pure.*

Thyatira – Great hard working Church but some have been led astray into compromising. *Keep focused.*

Sardis – You look good but only on the outside. *Repent and be cleansed from within.*

Philadelphia – Even though you're weak, you are faithful and will succeed. *God is strong in our weakness.*

Laodicea – There is nothing positive here. You are neither hot nor cold. *Repent and start afresh.*

Day 360
Revelation 4-6
26th December

4 - God Is Worshipped On His Throne
5 - Jesus Is Uniquely Able To Open The Scroll
6 - Jesus Breaks The First Six Seals

Seals Are Broken Before The Throne

The Big Picture

John is called to see God on His throne and also witnesses four creatures and twenty four elders. A scroll is brought which has writing on both sides and which bears seven seals. Only Jesus, described as a Lamb and also the Lion of Judah, is declared able to open the seals. The first seal results in a white horse of victory which appears to be Jesus Himself. The second produces a red horse which reminds us of the many wars that will take place before the second coming. The third seal shows a black horse – of justice. This is followed by the fourth seal and a pale horse reminiscent of our ultimate enemies death. The fifth seal reveals martyrs from history and the sixth seal produces an earthquake reminding us of coming judgement.

Thinking Step

Twelve is a special number for Jews. It is reflected in 12 tribes and 12 disciples as well as many other times in the Bible. The number 2 is one of strength and certainty as reflected in 2 tablets of stone bearing the commandments and two covenants, old and new. So we have 12 x 2 = 24 elders around the Throne.

Action Step

The major point that is clear in these chapters about God on His Throne and the scroll sealed with seven seals is the total supremacy of Jesus. He is described as the Lamb which reminds us of His sacrifice and He is also given the title of 'Lion of Judah' reminding us that He was victorious at Calvary and reigns victorious even as we read about Him. In this world of superlatives we have difficulty sometimes being honest and accurate. I remember when we had some publicity printed in the early days of Walk Through the Bible and someone said that we weren't 'selling' our events enough! He said we needed to make outlandish claims to catch attention. I suggested telling the truth was enough and anyway I want people to come away from one of our presentations totally empowered rather than wondering why we had felt it necessary to exaggerate when the real thing was so good. I have often had people tell me that our Walk Through events are so much better than they thought they would be. I have then informed them that I had told them that beforehand. They responded without the hint of a blush "Oh, I didn't really believe you, I thought it was all hype!" Well there is no hype here. Jesus really is the only one who is able to break the seals. He is the only one who can provide salvation too.

7 - 144,000 Jews And Countless Gentiles
8 - Seventh Seal And Four Trumpets
9 - Fifth And Sixth Trumpets

Day 361
Revelation 7-9
27th December

Jews, Gentiles, Seals And Trumpets

The Big Picture

12,000 Jews from each of twelve tribes of Israel are sealed by God. Then a multitude of Gentiles from the great tribulation gathered and worshipped God. The seventh seal is broken and produces a silence for half an hour before a group of seven Angels are each given a trumpet. Meanwhile a sacrifice of incense and prayer is offered. Four of the seven Angels blow their trumpets. This evokes four worldwide plagues upon the land, sea, water and heavenly bodies. Then from the bottomless pit came giant locusts which attacked those who do not have God's seal. As the first terror ends the sixth trumpet is blown and four Angels are released to reek havoc on earth but there is still no repenting.

Thinking Step

7:5-8 – Lists those who are sealed – 12,000 per tribe. There are often variations with lists of tribes like this but these usually involve Joseph's sons Manasseh and Ephraim. This time however there is the notable omission of Dan. Irenaeus, an early church father solved the problem! He declared the Antichrist would come from Dan! Not a popular theory!

Action Step

7:14 – 'Then he said to me "These are the ones who died in the great tribulation. They have washed their robes in the blood of the Lamb and made them white."' This can be a description of all who have accepted Jesus as Lord and Saviour. Notice it says that they washed their robes in the blood of the Lamb. Sometimes people have problems with conversion because they are waiting for God to do everything. Of course He has already done everything at Calvary but there is something that you must do too. It is not an act of emotion but an act of will. When people tell me that they have intellectual problems it is not always a matter of knowledge or even wisdom but often stubbornness! The blood made them white as a sign of the cleansing that takes place when the Holy Spirit comes into our lives. Too many wait until they are cleansed before they come to Jesus for cleansing! The order is vital. First you come and then you are cleansed. The other way round would render the cross redundant. As we approach the end of our reading marathon some of these chapters are hard to follow but this verse is clear. We need to wash our robes in the blood of the Lamb and we will then be made white. Have you done that yet? Turn to Day 21 and do it today!

Day 362
Revelation 10-12
28th December

10 - A Little Scroll For Heaven
11 - Two Witnesses Prophesy
12 - The Red Dragon Is Defeated

Months Of Prophesy
Then War Is Declared On All Believers

The Big Picture

The amazing account continues. Another mighty Angel descends from Heaven shouting. John is told not to write down what is said in reply but all will be revealed at the seventh trumpet. John eats the scroll he is given and is told to continue prophesying. John's next task is to measure the Temple where two witnesses will prophesy for forty two months. They will be killed but will rise again. An earthquake concludes this second terror. The seventh trumpet is blown and the Ark of the Covenant is opened. John sees a pregnant woman in Heaven with a red dragon waiting to consume her baby. The plot is foiled and the dragon is thrown to earth where he declares war on all believers.

Thinking Step

10:3 – '...he (mighty Angel) gave a great shout like the roar of a lion and when he shouted, the seven thunders answered.' The seven thunders were probably the voice of God as described in Psalm 29 where the words 'The voice of the Lord' are repeated seven times as David describes the sheer power of God's voice.

Action Step

This passage is written in a language that is very difficult to understand. There is a tension between just reading it literally as some do and alternatively reading everything allegorically and trying to see meanings behind the text. Or a mixture of the two. These last three chapters seem filled with one side opposing the other. They are dominated by good versus bad. Very much like life really! In these days of situational ethics we are creating a culture where good and bad are being merged. All things seem permissible sometimes and I don't believe that is true. Living in a democracy means that ultimately anything is okay if the majority of people want it. In Christ's family this is not true. Many would say that the easiest way to live is just to stick to the rule book. Some Christians live like that and become very legalistic which is very unattractive to the world and in my opinion not Christ like at all. When given the opportunity to stick to the letter of the law with the woman caught in adultery Jesus chose to show compassion – John 8. I find I feel a lot better when I forgive others who do wrong to me! I suspect it's a fringe benefit that God put in us as a reward for doing the right thing! Next time someone needs to be forgiven try forgiving them and you'll feel good too! Just try it...

13 - The Mark Of The Beast - 666
14 - Jesus Reaps His Harvest On Earth
15 - Plagues And Seven Bowls Of Wrath
16 - Armageddon But Still No Repentance!

Day 363
Revelation 13-16
29th December

Despite God's Judgements
There Is No Repentance

The Big Picture

Next John sees the beast coming out of the sea and it's empowered by the dragon and worshipped by the world. Everyone present receives the mark of the beast – 666. Then John saw the Lamb with 144,000 bearing His name. Angels pass over and declare that judgement is coming soon and John sees the 'Son of Man' reaping His harvest on earth with help from His Angels. Next there were seven Angels each with a plague to end God's wrath and each was given a bowl of God's wrath. The plagues and bowls of wrath caused havoc on earth. All is prepared for Armageddon then the 7th bowl of wrath is emptied and God cries "It's finished!" Still no repentance.

Thinking Step

13:17-18 – '...no one could buy or sell anything without that mark... His number is 666.' Most scholars believe that 666 refers to Roman Emperor Nero whose name, written in Aramaic, can be valued at 666. This was a way of speaking in code about contemporary figures whom it would have been politically dangerous to criticise openly.

Action Step

From our reading today we can see that God's judgement is inevitable. We can be encouraged that Jesus' harvest is guaranteed too. 14:15-16 – "Then another angel came from the Temple and shouted to the one sitting on the cloud 'Swing the sickle, for the time of harvest has come; the crop on earth is ripe.' So the one sitting on the cloud swung His sickle over the earth and the whole earth was harvested." Looking back at Acts 1:9 we read that Jesus ascended back to Heaven on a cloud – 'After saying this, He was taken up into a cloud while they were watching and they could no longer see Him.' This is exactly how John sees the ultimate day of harvest. This must have reminded him so much of that amazing day when Jesus ascended back to the Father. This glorious vision is such a great reminder that one day all who follow Jesus will be gathered up to be with Him. Remember however that before that we need to recall Matt. 28:19-20 – 'Therefore, go and make disciples of all the nations, baptising them in the name of the Father and the Son and the Holy Spirit. Teach these new disciples to obey all the commands I have given you ...' What practical steps can you take to contribute to this harvest? What a great event we have to look forward to!

Day 364
Revelation 17-19
30th December

17 - Judgement On Babylon
18 - Weeping For Babylon
19 - Wedding Feast Is Announced

We're Almost There As God's Enemies Fall

The Big Picture

One of the seven Angels spoke to John and took him to see the judgement of the Prostitute Babylon. Her ultimate defeat is anticipated. Then an Angel came declaring Babylon had now fallen! God warns His people to come away from her otherwise they will share in her punishment. There is weeping and wailing from the world when they realise that they have lost the woman who bought their goods and kept them in business! A voice comes from heaven declaring that it was now time for the wedding feast of the Lamb. Then John saw a rider on a white horse – obviously Jesus. The beast summons an army to fight him but he and his false prophet are defeated.

Thinking Step

19:7b – '... For the time has come for the wedding feast of the Lamb and His bride has prepared herself.' This is what Jesus must have been anticipating in Mark 14:25 when He said "I tell you the truth, I will not drink wine again until the day I drink it new in the Kingdom of God."

Action Step

18:19 – '...they will weep and throw dust on their heads to show their grief and they will cry out "How terrible, how terrible for that great city! The shipowners became wealthy by transporting her great wealth on the seas. In a single moment it is all gone."'

In the first decade of the 21st century the world saw the worst financial crisis in history which will continue to be a salutary warning for most of this century. The world wobbled, as the banks and financial institutions struggled to stay afloat. This is remarkably similar to our verse here. What a reminder we have of our dependency on material things that can crumble away in the blink of an eye. Jesus warns of having the right foundation in His 'sermon on the mount' – Matt. 7:24-25 – 'Anyone who listens to my teaching and follows it is wise, like a person who builds a house on solid rock. Though the rain comes in torrents and the flood waters rise and the winds beat against that house, it won't collapse because it is built on bedrock.' We deceive ourselves if we think there is anything as reliable as Jesus. I was talking to our financial adviser very recently and as believers, we both agreed that investments and projections are not solid. Only Jesus is solid and only those who build their lives on Him will stand all the stresses of life.

20 - 1000 Years Imprisonment And Then Total Defeat   Day 365
21 - All Things New - Heaven, Earth And Jerusalem   Revelation 20-22
22 - Eternal Healing Water Of Life   31st December

History Concludes With A Perfect Ending

The Big Picture

Another Angel came down from Heaven and threw the dragon and Satan into the bottomless pit for 1000 years. Meanwhile believers reign with Christ. On his release the Devil will make one final doomed attempt at overcoming the Lamb. John sees a preview of Judgement Day with God on the White Judgement Throne. God shows John the New Heaven, New Earth and New Jerusalem and promises a joyful pain free future. One of the seven Angels shows John Christ's bride i.e. the New Jerusalem which is a jewel encrusted spectacular sight. Lastly he sees a river flowing with the water of life. All is perfect now and John concludes with the last words of Jesus "Yes, I am coming soon!"

Thinking Step

The Bible was originally written using three languages – Hebrew, Aramaic and Greek but you read it in English! You completed 66 books containing 1189 chapters which were made up of 31,101 verses or almost 4 million letters and spaces. It gets easier each time, so look forward to next time with a smile on your face!

Action Step

Our last reading still includes many struggles and problems but finally Jesus triumphs and John has the privilege of seeing this in a vision and then sharing it with you and me. Of course some of what we have read is still a mystery to us! It is to me anyway! However there have been specific shafts of certainty all the way through this concluding book. Today we have several more. Here are a few more promises from God to His people...

    20:10 - Satan disappears for ever.
      21:3 - God's home is now among His people!
          He will live with them and they will be His people.
      21:4 - There will be no more death or sorrow or crying or pain.
      22:4 - They will see His face.

What a wonderful future we have but what is even better is to know that we don't have to die to experience it! Remember God gives us eternal life which is a quality of life that money cannot buy but Christ supplies free of charge to you and me because He has already paid the full price. Be sure all you have read over the past year doesn't stop in your brain! Shake it down a cubit or 18 inches or 50 cm into your heart. Finally, if you need more help please turn to Day 21 or get in touch with us via our web site www.Bible.org.uk

Index Of Tables, Maps & Charts

What's the **big idea?**

**Piecing together the
BIG PICTURE of the Bible**

Bringing the Bible to Life

**Book a live event at your church
contact 01255 871000**

www.Bible.org.uk/events_what.html

Isn't R.E. boring?

Want to prove it isn't?
Support us teaching the Bible in schools

So far we have taught over
half a million children
Help us reach a new generation

www.Bible.org.uk/Children_Bible_Events.html

What's the **fun idea?**

Laugh and learn your way through the Bible

memora**BIBLE**.org.uk
the Big Picture in Little Pictures

the best **audio Bible?**

Our top three reasons why

Each day
contains
a practical
devotional

The whole Bible
in 365 sections
(18 mins a day)

British
narration

Step by Step mp3

Listen to an extract at www.Bible.org.uk/Bible_Resources.html

Little by Little

The Big Picture Through Key Verses

365 daily sections take you through the Big Picture of the Bible using key verses

The 'Little Brother' of Step by Step

Buy at www.Bible.org.uk